CREATING

COMPOSITIONS

CREATING
COMPOSITIONS

Fourth Edition

HARVEY S. WIENER

The City University of New York
LaGuardia Community College

McGRAW-HILL BOOK COMPANY

New York   St. Louis
San Francisco   Auckland
Bogotá   Hamburg
Johannesburg   London
Madrid   Mexico
Montreal   New Delhi
Panama   Paris
São Paulo   Singapore
Sydney   Tokyo
Toronto

CREATING COMPOSITIONS

1 2 3 4 5 6 7 8 9 0   DOCDOC   8 9 8 7 6 5 4

ISBN 0-07-070162-8

This book was set in Baskerville by Black Dot, Inc.
The editors were Jim Dodd and David Dunham;
the designer was Charles A. Carson;
the production supervisor was Diane Renda.
The cover illustration was done by Thomas Charles Fleetwood.
R. R. Donnelley & Sons Company was printer and binder.

See Acknowledgments on pages 525-526.
Copyrights included on this page by reference.

Chapter-Opening Photo Credits

1 Ginger Chih, © Peter Arnold, Inc.
2 © 1979 Maureen Fennelli, Photo Researchers, Inc.
3 Charles Harbutt, © 1969 Archive Pictures, Inc.
4 © 1980 by Jim Kalett, Photo Researchers, Inc.
5 © Ed Lettau, Photo Researchers, Inc.
6 Jacqueline Gill, Art Resource
7 © Eleaner Beckwith, Rapho/Photo Researchers, Inc.
8 © 1975 by Arthur Sirdofsky, Art Resource
9 © Bonnie Freer, Photo Researchers, Inc.
10 © Chester Higgins, Jr., Photo Researchers, Inc.

Library of Congress Cataloging in Publication Data

Wiener, Harvey S.
     Creating compositions.

     Includes index.
     1. English language—Rhetoric. I. Title.
PE1408.W5819   1984   808'.042   83-18760
ISBN 0-07-070162-8

TO THE MEMORY OF DON MARION WOLFE
whose ideas take on new power with each generation
of young writers

AND TO MY STUDENTS
who illustrate with every theme they write the eternal
freshness of those ideas

CONTENTS

Preface   xv

PART I   PARAGRAPHS

Chapter 1   DESCRIPTION: Rooms That Linger, Rooms That Breathe   3

Vocabulary   4
Building Composition Skills   5
  Sensory Language   5
  Topic Sentences   7
  Transitions   14
  A Sentence Review   15
  Coordination   19
Solving Problems in Writing   22
  Mirror Words I   22
  Run-on Sentences   27
Writing the Descriptive Paragraph   35
  Prewriting   38
  Manuscript Form   41
  Proofreading   42
The Professionals Speak   45
Reaching Higher   48

Chapter 2   NARRATION: The Body in Action   51

Vocabulary   52
Building Composition Skills   54
  Expanding the Topic Sentence   55
  Chronology   58
  Expanding Sentences   60
Solving Problems in Writing   60
  Quotations   60
  Sentence Fragments: Part I   63
Writing the Narrative Paragraph   72
The Professionals Speak   79
Reaching Higher   83

Chapter 3   ILLUSTRATION: Street Scenes and Sandlots,
            Memories of Youth   87

Vocabulary   88
Building Composition Skills   90
  Paragraph Unity: Subtopic Sentences   91
  Arrangement of Details by Importance   94

Transitions	96
Subordination	100
Titles	109
Solving Problems in Writing	110
Sentence Fragments: Part II	110
Plurals	118
Writing the Paragraph of Illustration	121
The Professionals Speak	128
Reaching Higher	129

Chapter 4   COMPARISON AND CONTRAST: People You Know, Side by Side

	131
Vocabulary	132
Building Composition Skills	133
Figures of Speech	134
Transitions	137
Expanding Quotation Sentences	139
Comparison and Contrast: Three Paragraph Patterns	141
Solving Problems in Writing	151
Mirror Words II	151
Agreement of Subject and Verb	157
Writing the Comparison-Contrast Paragraph	172
The Professionals Speak	177
Reaching Higher	180

Chapter 5   USING EXPERT TESTIMONY: Spotlight on Jobs

	185
Vocabulary	187
Building Composition Skills	190
Statistics and Cases	190
Quotations and Paraphrase as Details	200
Ending a Paragraph	205
Expanding Sentences: Verb-Part Openers	208
Solving Problems in Writing	215
Capital Letters	215
Formal and Informal Language	217
Abbreviations and Numbers	222
Writing the Paragraph from Data	225
The Professionals Speak	239
Reaching Higher	244

PART II   THE LONGER THEME

Chapter 6   WRITING ESSAYS: A Place of Spirit

	247
Vocabulary	248
Building Composition Skills	249
Hints for Strong Descriptions	250
Essay Form	253
Paragraph to Essay	256

    Proposal (Thesis) Sentences 258
    Introductions 261
    Combining Sentences 266
Solving Problems in Writing 269
    Punctuation Guidelines 269
    Commas 280
Writing the Descriptive Essay 290
The Professionals Speak 300
Reaching Higher 302

Chapter 7   AN ESSAY ON PROCESS: You the Expert   305

Vocabulary 306
Building Composition Skills 307
    Including and Arranging Details 308
    Audience 313
    Essay Transitions 316
    Expanding Sentences and Changing Word Order 320
Solving Problems in Writing 322
    Showing Possession 322
Writing the Process Essay 329
The Professionals Speak 335
Reaching Higher 340

Chapter 8   A SHORT RESEARCH ESSAY: The World of the Child   342

Vocabulary 343
Building Composition Skills 344
    Starting Research: Browsing 346
    Limiting the Topic 348
    Bibliography Cards 349
    Note Cards 351
    Developing a Proposal 353
    Organizing Notes 354
Solving Problems in Writing 357
    Degrees of Comparison 357
    Parallelism 360
    Misplaced Modifiers 363
Writing the Brief Research Essay 365
The Professionals Speak 371
Reaching Higher 374

Chapter 9   ARGUMENTATION: Women in the World of Men   375

Vocabulary 377
Building Composition Skills 378
    Interview Techniques 380
    Logical Arguments 381
    Using Opposing Arguments 385
Solving Problems in Writing 390
    Verb Tense 390
Writing the Essay of Argument 401

The Professionals Speak   413
Reaching Higher   419

Chapter 10   AN EXTENDED DEFINITION: Life's Moments for Meanings   421

Vocabulary   422
Building Composition Skills   429
    A One-Sentence Definition   430
    A Paragraph Definition   432
    Writing Conclusions   433
    Imitating Sentence Patterns   437
Solving Problems in Writing: Pronoun Practice   440
    Pronouns as Subjects   440
    Pronouns as Objects   443
    Pronoun Agreement   449
    Pronouns That Point Out Demonstrative Pronouns   451
Writing the Definition Essay   455
The Professionals Speak   461
Reaching Higher   463

PART III   A MINIBOOK OF EIGHTEEN SPECIAL SKILLS

  1. Improving Spelling   469
    Spelling Demons: Group A   469
    Spelling Demons: Group B   471
    Spelling Demons: Group C   473
    Some Spelling Rules for Difficult Problems   475
    Your Own Demon List: Words You Mistake   480
  2. Learning Vocabulary   480
  3. Reading a Dictionary Entry   482
  4. Using a Thesaurus   483
  5. Confusing Words: A Glossary   484
  6. Using the *Reader's Guide to Periodical Literature*   491
  7. Using the Card Catalog   493
    Title Card   493
    Author Card   494
    Two Subject Cards   494
  8. Preparing a Bibliography   495
  9. Writing Simple Footnotes   497
 10. Quoting from Books and Articles   499
 11. Format of a Business Letter   500
 12. Applying for a Job You Want   502
    Preparing a Résumé   502
    A Letter of Application   505
 13. Filling Out Applications   505
 14. Taking Notes   506
 15. Writing a Summary   509

16. Writing about Literature: Some Approaches to Consider   510
    Approaches to Writing about Literature   511
    An Essay on a Book Character   512
17. Answering Essay Examination Questions   513
18. Making a Formal Outline   515

Appendixes

A Vocabulary Exercises: Definitions by Chapter   517
B Theme Progress Sheet   522
C Record of Teacher-Student Conferences on Compositions   524

Acknowledgments

Acknowledgments   525

Index

Index   527

CONTENTS
SKILLS IN GRAMMAR AND MECHANICS

Basic Sentence Errors

Sentence Review	15
The Run-on Error	27
Sentence Fragments	63,110

Common Problems on the Run

Words That Look and Sound Alike	22
Plurals	118
Possession	322
Capital Letters	215
Abbreviations and Numbers	222
Glossary of Confusing Words	284
Parallel Structure	360
Spelling Demons	469
Spelling Rules	475

Agreement of Subject and Verb

What Is Agreement?	157
Subject Pronouns and Verb Agreement	160
Four Troublesome Verbs: *to Be, to Have, to Go, to Do*	163
Agreement with More than One Subject	166
There Is, There Are	167
Words between the Subject and Verb	168
Special Subjects and Agreement	169
Agreement with *Who, That, Which*	170

Reviewing Agreement Problems — 170

Verbs: The Time Tellers

Tense of Verbs	390
Troublesome Verb Parts	392
Shifting Tenses	396
Some Confusing Verbs (*Lie-Lay; Sit-Set; Rise-Raise; Leave-Let; Can-May*)	397
Using the Active Voice	355

Pronouns

Pronouns as Subjects	440
Pronouns in Other Places	443
Agreement of Pronouns	449
The Pronoun *You*	452

Punctuation Pointers

Period, Question Mark, Exclamation Point	269
Commas	280
Quotation Marks	60,270
Underlining and Italics	271
Semicolons and Colons	272
Parentheses, Brackets, Hyphens, Dashes	274
Apostrophes	278,322

Modifiers: Avoiding Errors

Misused Verb Openers	213
Degrees of Comparison	357
Misplaced Modifiers	363

Combining, Expanding, and Transforming Sentences

Coordination	19
-*ly* Openers	60
Subordination	100
Building Quotation Sentences	139
-*ing* Openers	208
Infinitives to Open Sentences	212
Other Verb Parts as Sentence Starters	212
Tightening Sentences	266
Expanding Sentences and Changing Word Order	320
Changing Verb Forms to Expand Sentences	387
Active Voice Verbs	355
Sentence Imitation	437

Manuscript Preparation

Manuscript Form	41
Proofreading	42
Follow-Up	44

PREFACE

Although this fourth edition of *Creating Compositions* maintains its established approach to learning how to write well, it continues to offer you new elements that meet the needs of today's students and that address current theory and practice in composition.

In order to stress the value for writers of receiving feedback on drafts, for example, I have added Reader Response Guides to each chapter so that students now can look over each other's papers and, using these Guides, can offer concrete suggestions about how the writer can make revisions for the next draft. Also, I have improved and expanded the Progress Reminder Checklists to help you understand the steps in creating a piece of writing. A completely revised Chapter 5, with a new focus on jobs and careers, will help you to practice the important skills of summarizing, paraphrasing, quoting, and citing material from expert testimony. Data Clusters provide an array of statistics, cases, other factual data, and informed opinion from which you can draw to develop substantive paragraphs. A section on integrating testimony into your own writing will teach you how to use other people's words and ideas in your essay. Building upon those skills, a new Chapter 9 will help you produce a short research essay, from your own data that you've gathered at the library and from other sources of information. A new Chapter 10 highlights the writing of a definition essay, for which you can draw upon many of the skills you learned in earlier parts of the text. Throughout this fourth edition I have again stressed prewriting (including brainstorming, free association, timed writing, and subject trees, just to name a few) and stylistic variety by means of activities in sentence combining, expanding, and embedding. Several new student compositions provide updated models for paragraph and essay assignments, and many new exercise questions will help you practice important writing skills.

Despite all these changes, the basic philosophy of *Creating Compositions* remains unaltered. The text continues to affirm that if you live by feeling and looking and hearing and responding, then you can write. The individual's life is the most important source for writing; your experiences—the countless moments of pleasure and sorrow and surprise that fill each day—make the best compositions. After you learn, through this book, to recreate your experiences in written words, then you can move easily into the world of abstract ideas where details other than those based upon experience are often needed to support a written assignment. Moving gradually into the formal college "essay", the text examines first the well-developed paragraph. As in previous editions, each chapter of this book explores a topic whose meaning your own life can dramatize: moments with friends, a room or a street alive in your memory, the role in your life of the liberated woman, to name a few. Most chapters urge class discussions about the quality of your own experience so that well before actual writing begins you can share ideas and can listen to other people's thoughts about a topic.

The basic format of *Creating Compositions* remains the same. In each chapter, vocabulary exercises present words helpful for the writing assignment at hand, words you might want to use in your own composition. These words are clearly and easily presented, and you will have the chance to figure out definitions without always having to look first in a dictionary. Further, correct definitions appear for your convenience in Appendix A.

A section in each chapter called Building Composition Skills explains different techniques in the construction of paragraphs and essays. You will also learn about and practice writing the different kinds of details required to support a topic idea—from details alive with sensory experience to details built upon statistics and quotations from reliable sources.

The section called Solving Problems in Writing looks at typical problems in written communication: the run-on error, the sentence fragment, problems with subject and verb agreement, punctuation skills, and a number of others. In all the explanations the stress is on clear presentation. Clearly marked model sentences illustrate principles by example more often than by rule and without the often confusing language of grammatical terminology. Exercises often require that you apply each skill in the language of your own sentences. You probably will not need to do all the exercises and you can omit those activities that deal with skills that you and your instructor agree you already know. Perforated pages make it possible for your instructor to collect the work you do directly in the book.

In each chapter a section called Writing the Paragraph offers specific goals for the writing exercise. Before you have to write your own composition, you will read some examples of what other students wrote in response to the same assignment. The questions that appear after these student models suggest directions for your own writing; so does the checklist of goals that remind you of the specific skills you are trying to build. Suggested topics will give you additional ideas for your own themes.

The section called The Professionals Speak gives you writing samples to illustrate how professionals deal with the same kinds of materials you treat in your writing. And to provide a special challenge either through review or through more practice in composition, there is at the end of each chapter a section called Reaching Higher for students who want to advance their skills in writing even further. Part III at the end of the text contains "A Minibook of Special Skills" that presents briefly a number of important areas of communication for successful college work, including how to write a business letter, how to prepare a résumé, how to answer essay exam questions, and several other skills.

As in the past, I have many debts to friends and colleagues who helped me with *Creating Compositions*. From Don Marion Wolfe come the philosophy of sensory language in writing and the need for exploring individual moments in order to write with meaning. His too are the ideas for using model paragraphs as the heart of any composition program and for using activities in language that require students to call upon their own resources in communication. His death in April 1976 took from those who knew him a brilliant teacher and a warm, faithful friend. Andrea Lunsford of the University of British Columbia first suggested providing clusters of data as sources for writing from expert testimony, and I want to acknowledge her good idea with thanks. To my wife Barbara Koster Wiener go thanks for her patience during the preparation of the materials and for her skills as a teacher of reading, which made her assistance invaluable. Don Linder assisted me ably in producing the manuscript. To my colleagues at LaGuardia Community College who used *Creating Compositions* and who made valuable suggestions for improvement I am deeply indebted, as I am to those colleagues in colleges across the country who wrote to me with new ideas. Robert Esch at the University of Texas at El Paso read the manuscript with his usual thoroughness and attention, and I thank him. Karen Greenberg of Hunter College, Heloise Ruskin of Bergen Community College, Ruth Falk Redel of Elizabethtown Community College of the University of Kentucky, and John Trimbur of Rhode Island College, offered sound and useful advice for this fourth edition. Finally, it is to the students in my composition courses who prove each term anew the infinite resources of their own lives and their ability to commit those vital elements into words—it is to them I owe special thanks.

Harvey S. Wiener

PART I
PARAGRAPHS

CHAPTER 1

DESCRIPTION:
Rooms That Linger, Rooms That Breathe

INTRODUCTION TO DESCRIPTION

A kitchen in a warm apartment, a hospital room that smells of alcohol and ether, an attic in a lonely house—each of us knows some indoor place that has fixed itself clearly in our minds. To reproduce such a place in words is to describe for others the details that make it come alive. Because many writing tasks demand the reproduction of details, description is a basic element in the writer's craft. As a writer, you have to observe a scene around you with great care; and you have to present it faithfully so readers know exactly what you see.

This first paragraph assignment in description requires that you make a room come to life through your writing. Selecting some place filled with colors, noises, and people in the midst of actions, you will present a scene that is clear and vivid for any reader to appreciate. You will call upon your sense impressions of sound, color, smell, touch, and action to illustrate your major reaction to this room. Before you write your paragraph, you will read what students before you have written in response to the same assignment.

VOCABULARY

Step 1. Words to Describe Situations. These words specify reactions you may have to the room you want to describe. For any words you do not know, check a dictionary or Appendix A of this book. Write definitions on the blank lines below.

1. boisterous _____

2. amiable _____

3. awesome _____

4. malevolent _____

5. dismal _____

6. spacious _____

7. elegant _____

8. tranquil _____

9. cluttered _____

10. musty _____

Step 2. Applying Vocabulary. After you are sure of the meanings of the above words, write:

1. a word to describe a friendly place _____

2. a word that means peaceful _____

3. a word to describe a graceful place _____

4. a word to indicate a very roomy place _____

5. a word to describe a gloomy place _____

6. a word to describe a place that inspires respect _____

7. a word that means showing bad will _____

8. a word that would describe a damp place _____

9. a word to describe a place of great excitement _____

10. a word to show things heaped in a disorderly way _____

Step 3.   Words that Name Sounds. For the writer of description, words that indicate sounds are very important. For each word in italics below write a definition that explains the word accurately. Use a dictionary when you need one; check Appendix A for more help.

Example

1. He *guffawed* at the jokes, his whole body shaking with delight.

   laughed in a loud burst _____

   _____

2. The senator tried to speak over the *din* of the reporters.

   _____

   _____

3. She spoke so low that her words were *inaudible.*

   _____

   _____

4. The baby *squealed* with delight whenever she was tickled.

   _____

   _____

5. Wild applause *resonated* throughout the theater.

   _____

   _____

BUILDING COMPOSITION SKILLS

Sensory Language

Step 1.   Listening Well. Listen a moment to the sound of the room in which you are now sitting. Write three sentences that tell sounds you hear. Use a color in each sentence.

Examples
I hear the thump of a guitar from behind the green wall.
Pink gum cracks as Paul blows a bubble at his seat.

1. _____

   _____

2. _____

   _____

3. _____

   _____

Step 2.   Action and Color. Look around. Write three sentences that show some action in the room. Use a specific color in each sentence.

Examples
In front of me Marina munches on yellow corn chips.
Jeff's orange pen darts back and forth across the clean white page.

1. _____

   _____

2. _____

   _____

3. _____

   _____

Step 3.   What You Feel. Touch your desk, your shirt or sweater, your pen, or your wristwatch. Move around and touch the walls, the doors, the windows, and other objects in your room. Write a sentence that includes a word to show what you feel. Use a color or a sound as well.

Examples
The blue walls feel damp with mildew.
I hear the squeak of my chair as I touch its smooth wooden sides.

1. _____

   _____

2. _____

   _____

3. _____

   _____

The practices above demonstrate an important technique in writing: *concrete sensory detail. Concrete* means specific, solid; *sensory* means relating to any of the senses. The highly specific pictures that result are call *images*. Notice in the two following columns how the images in Column I are general and have little sensory appeal, while the examples in Column II are concrete because they appeal strongly to the senses.

I	II
Examples	
1. a tie	*a red silk tie painted with bright yellow daisies*
2. a chair	*a mahogany rocking chair that clacks and groans*
3. the window	_____
4. an old book	_____
5. the chalkboard	_____

Step 4. Concrete Details. In the blank spaces under Column II, above, write concrete sensory details for the general pictures in Column I.

Step 5. Naming Specifically. One way to create pictures is to use the exact word you want rather than a general term that needs too many descriptive words to make the picture specific. Readers prefer the word *elm* or *oak* to *tree* because they get an added identification for the object through the exactness of the name.

For each general term in Column I, write in Column II three different *specific* terms to replace it.

I	II
Example	
1. tool	*hammer, pliers, screwdriver*
2. car	_____
3. book	_____
4. animal	_____
5. game	_____
6. metal	_____

Topic Sentences

The key to a good paragraph is its topic sentence. For your purposes at this point, the topic sentence should always come as the first sentence of the paragraph.

Look at these three sentences and try to judge which you think most effective as the opening topic sentence in a paragraph:

1. It all happened last night.
2. My room is on the second floor of our house.
3. My room is the messiest room on the second floor of our house.

If you selected 3, you rejected 1 and 2 for good reason. Sentence 1, though typical of many papers by beginning writers, lacks a clear statement of topic. What is the *it*? The element of suspense the writer tries to achieve can be lost in a drift away from the topic. Not having stated the topic clearly at the beginning, the writer can easily lose control. Besides, the "It all happened. . ." opening is so familiar and overused by now that it pays to avoid it.

Sentences 2 and 3 are superior because they both state the topic immediately: it's clear to readers that they will be reading descriptions of rooms. Sentence 2, however, is merely a statement of fact. It gives the writer too little control over the topic. What details can be included? What details can be left out? Sentence 3, on the other hand, by introducing the word *messiest*, states an opinion about the room and helps the writer determine which details to use in the description. Any image not contributing to the overall effect of *messiness* would be omitted.

The best topic sentences are those that state both the topic and the writer's opinion of or attitude toward that topic. The box below highlights the qualities of strong topic sentences.

A TOPIC SENTENCE REMINDER

Good Topic Sentences:	**Why:**
1. Introduce the topic immediately.	So that your reader knows what you will write about. So that you know what you will write about. *Hint:* Do not surprise your readers. Tell them immediately what you want to write about.
2. Limit the topic.	So that you will not have too much to write about. So that you will have enough to write about. So that you will focus on only one major feature or point.
3. Give an opinion or an attitude or a reaction or an impression that the writer has about the topic.	You get readers interested in the topic: they will want to find out why you feel the way you do about your subject. You can introduce a key word that will help you relate all your supporting ideas to one dominant impression.

Here are two more topic sentences, which are successful because they introduce a limited topic clearly *and* give the writer's opinion about that topic.

1. Everyone in my writing class this Monday morning looks restless and uncomfortable.   *Topic:* people in the writing class Monday morning
Opinion: restlessness
2. Last Friday night I realized the bitterness in my husband's character.   *Topic:* my husband last Friday night
Opinion: bitterness

The writer of sentence 1 above would need to show in the sentences that follow it just why everyone appears to be restless.

The writer of sentence 2 would need to show specific details of her husband's bitterness.

Step 1. Determining Topics and Opinions. In the following topic sentences, underline the topic and circle the word(s) that tell the opinion or attitude.

Example
1. Most new students are (shocked) at college registration procedures.

2. My twentieth birthday was the saddest day of my life.
3. My hometown has every convenience I will ever need.
4. My family always loved Uncle Yee's sense of humor and wit.
5. On this chilly October morning I am sitting in the students' cafeteria, watching the commotion around me.

Step 2. Improving Topic Sentences. The following topic sentences need words of opinion or attitude, words which will help limit and specify the topic. Rewrite the sentences in the space provided. You may wish to change the idea of some of the sentences as you introduce opinions. Try to avoid overused words like *good, nice, pleasant, enjoyable* by using some of the vocabulary in Appendix A.

Example
1. I have a collection of old coins. *My collection of old coins is the envy of my Uncle Dave.*

2. This car is more than fifty years old. _____

3. Beth drinks tea with honey every morning. _____

4. My father called me from Florida late last night. _____

5. I send Sonia a postcard every week. _____

6. I spent many summer afternoons in my grandmother's attic. _____

_____

7. Letters of the alphabet sponsor commercials on the children's television program *Sesame Street*. _____

_____

8. My uncle taught me carpentry. _____

_____

9. Ernest Hemingway was a writer. _____

_____

10. In the past two years the unemployment rate has risen. _____

_____

Step 3. Clearing Up Topics. The topic sentences below fail to specify the topic to be developed in the paragraph. Many lack key words to express opinions. Others give important details but fail to clarify exactly what the topic will be. On separate paper rewrite the sentences to make them clearer and more effective paragraph openings.

Example

1. I will never forget what happened last winter. *One evening last winter I watched in amazement as a calf was born.*

_____

2. On the train I saw several people arguing. _____

_____

3. I will drive to Phoenix next Saturday. _____

_____

4. Our dog barks whenever a stranger appears. _____

_____

5. Light streams through the window and leaves spots of yellow on the living room floor. _____

_____

Step 4. Details and Topic Sentences. The most effective way to construct your sentence is to decide beforehand those details you wish to discuss. Suppose you wanted to write a paragraph on pollution and you wanted to discuss these two issues.

1. machines, such as cars and trains and lawn mowers, as major pollutants
2. humans as careless destroyers of our air and water

Here is a topic sentence that would permit the writer to discuss those two issues:

Both machines and human beings share the awful guilt of polluting our air and water.

The topic is clearly stated. Which words give the opinion or attitude?
    Suppose the topic sentence were

Pollution is a terrible problem.

The writer would then have presented too broad a topic for treatment in a composition of limited length. There are just too many possibilities to consider with such a topic sentence, and the writer would tend to treat too quickly many points without examining closely two or three that are especially important.
    For each group of three details in Column I, write a topic sentence (including opinion and limited topic) in Column II.

I Details in Paragraph	*II Topic Sentence*
1. On our vacation in San Francisco it rained for three days. The cable car operators went on strike. My wife had the flu.	1. _____ _____ _____
2. The smell of varnish filled the room. Power saws buzzed. The pounding of hammers echoed through the halls.	2. _____ _____ _____
3. Inflation hurts old people who are living on fixed incomes. Inflation affects the poor who are struggling to pay their bills. Inflation hurts young people raising a family.	3. _____ _____ _____
4. Late night television programs fill time for people who cannot sleep. Late night programs offer lively talk on key world problems. Late night programs are fun in an adult way.	4. _____ _____ _____

5. Marie trembled as she opened David's letter.

Marie cried all night after she read David's letter.

In the morning Marie ripped David's letters to shreds.

5. _____

_____

_____

Step 5.   Predicting Topics. A good topic sentence suggests for the reader some of the details to be found in the paragraph. For each topic sentence below, write two kinds of information you might expect to find in the paragraph.

Topic Sentence   *Details in Paragraph*

Example

1. In this complex society there are many vital reasons to explain why teenagers drop out of school.

1. a. *pressure by friends to cut classes* ___

_____

b. *personal problems at home* ___

_____

2. The Fourth of July is a day of special pleasure for me.

2. a. _____

_____

_____

b. _____

_____

_____

3. Leaving home was not as difficult as Debbie thought it would be.

3. a. _____

_____

_____

b. _____

_____

_____

4. Owning a car often presents many problems.

4. a. _____

_____

_____

b. _____

_____

_____

5. Housing conditions in today's urban centers are disgraceful.

5. *a.* _____
_____
_____

b. _____
_____
_____

Step 6. More Topic Sentence Practice. For each general topic, note in Column II details that you might develop in a paragraph. Then write a topic sentence in Column III.

I *General Topic*	*II* *Details for Paragraph*	*III* *Topic Sentence*
Example 1. diets	A crash diet I went on to lose weight always left me hungry. It made me very sick. I gained back all the weight I lost anyhow.	I learned from a crash diet I foolishly followed to lose weight that serious problems may result from an unwise eating program.
2. a college diploma		
3. cooking		
4. a first date		

_____   _____

_____   _____

_____   _____

_____   _____

5. a walk in the country   _____   _____

_____   _____

_____   _____

_____   _____

_____   _____

_____   _____

Transitions

In a descriptive composition, the writer can move smoothly from one feature of the description to another by using *transitional expressions*. A transitional expression is a connector; it is a bridge between statements and ideas in paragraphs. Here are some transition words, which can relate ideas in a paragraph that describes a place; they will be valuable as you write your theme because they help move your reader through space from one part of the room to another.

there	alongside
behind	next to
up above	in the rear
to the left	in front of
to the right	up front
nearby	over
below	around
against	surrounding
on	beyond
at the . . .	near the back
beside	forward
far off	through the . . .
inside	from the

Step 1. Seeing Transitions at Work. Examine the sentences in Column I below. The ideas seem unrelated and unclear. By adding transitional expressions in the blank spaces in the same sentences under Column II, make the relationship between ideas clearer. You may want to add a word or two after the transition as well.

I

As I cleaned Paul's bedroom, I realized what a sad and lonely place it had become since my brother had joined the army last November. I saw his dusty football trophies, which he had polished so carefully. I passed his blue and gold football jacket, which hung proudly. I picked up one of several detective novels Paul loved to read; the tattered bookmark indicated that he had never finished the story. I suddenly heard my mother call me. Taking one last look, I slowly closed the door.

II

As I cleaned Paul's bedroom, I realized what a sad and lonely place it had become since my brother had joined the army last November. _____ I saw his dusty football trophies, which he had polished so carefully. _____ I passed his blue and gold football jacket, which hung proudly _____. _____ I picked up one of several detective novels Paul loved to read; the tattered bookmark indicated that he had never finished the story. _____ I suddenly heard my mother call me. Taking one last look, I slowly closed the door _____.

A Sentence Review

Writers need to know how to build and to analyze sentences. The review chart below will help you write strong, complete sentences.

WRITING COMPLETE THOUGHTS: A SENTENCE REVIEW CHART

1. To be a sentence, a word group must contain a subject and a verb and must express a complete thought. In the following sentences, the verb is underlined twice, and the subject once.

Our teacher gave us an assignment.

The men work hard.

Hint: To find a verb, try these tests:

A. Put *yesterday, today,* or *tomorrow* in front of the sentence. The word that changes is the verb because only verbs show tense—time change.

The children *laugh* while playing hide-and-seek.
Yesterday the children *laughed* while playing hide-and-seek.

Laugh changed to *laughed* with the word *yesterday*. Only verbs change in this way. *Laugh* is the verb.

Tomorrow the children *will laugh* while playing hide-and-seek.

Laugh changed to *will laugh* with the word *tomorrow*. Only verbs change this way. *Laugh* is the verb.

B. When you have the word you think is a verb, put *he, she, we, it, you, I,* or *they* in front of the word. If you've created a word group that makes sense with one of these subject pronouns (see page 440), you have a verb.

(continued on next page)

WRITING COMPLETE THOUGHTS: A SENTENCE REVIEW CHART (CONTINUED)

Word	Test	
work	I work, they work	Verb
sings	he sings, it sings	Verb
laughter	I laughter, they laughter	No verb
is	she is, he is	Verb
seldom	I seldom, you seldom	No verb

C. Some words are *always* verbs, no matter how they are used in a sentence. Often working along with other verbs, these *auxiliaries*—helping verbs—are worth memorizing. When you see them, you know that they are verbs; and you know also that they may be signaling other verbs soon to follow in a sentence. Here are some of the most important helping verbs:

have	has	will	might	had	am	was
may	does	can	do	should	is	were
could	did	shall	would	must	are	been

2. Some sentences have verbs made up of more than one word. Notice how *had*, *should have*, and *were* are helping other verbs in these sentences:

Our teacher had given us an assignment.

Those men should have worked hard.

They were laughing aloud.

3. Some sentences have more than one verb for the same subject.

Those men worked and laughed.

4. Some sentences have several sets of subjects and verbs joined together.

Those men worked, but because they laughed, the job was finished late.

5. Some word groups, although very brief, are grammatically correct and are considered complete sentences because they express complete thoughts.

He ran.

It fell.

You might logically say, "We do not know who *he* is nor what *it* is. Aren't those sentences incomplete?" However, from a grammatical point of view, these word groups, because they contain subjects and verbs and express complete thoughts, *are* sentences. You might need more information to understand fully the correct meaning of the sentence, but often that information appears in sentences that come earlier or later on.

(continued on next page)

WRITING COMPLETE THOUGHTS: A SENTENCE REVIEW CHART (CONTINUED)

6. Some sentences have more than one subject for the same verb or verbs.

My brother and sister attended the concert.

Mr. Holmes and his son went to Boston but returned today.

7. Some sentences express complete thoughts, although the subject does not actually appear in the sentence.

Walk!

Go down the steps quickly!

In both these sentences, the subject is understood to be the word *you*.

8. Some words can be either a subject or a verb, depending upon how they are used in a sentence. However, the guidelines above will help you to decide if the word is a verb. If you are still uncertain, check a dictionary.

Cats cry outside my window at night.   (Here *cry* is the verb: yesterday, cats *cried*.)

A cry awoke me.   (Here *awoke* is the verb; tomorrow the cry *will awake* me. *Cry* is the subject: What awoke me? The cry.)

9. Some describing words often separate parts of a verb when the verb is more than one word. Don't be confused into thinking that words like *only, not, never* and others are verbs simply because they appear near or because they break up verbs. Look at the word in italics in the examples below:

The crow could *not* flap its wing.

They had *never* seen so strange a sight.

In the first sentence *could flap* is the verb. (*Could* is one of the helpers; and both *could* and *flap* work in the test with subject pronouns: *I could, I flap*.) The word *not*, though it appears between the two words that serve as verbs in the sentence, is not a verb: *I not? They not?* Similarly, in the second sentence *had seen* is the verb; *never*, despite its position in the sentence, is not a verb. Both *not* and *never* describe the verb and are called *adverbs*.

Step 1. Sentence or Nonsentence? Only some of the word groups below are complete sentences. Read each item aloud; then, using the principles suggested in the Sentence Review Chart, pages 15–17, write *S* before each word group that makes a complete sentence and *NS* before each word group that is not a complete sentence. For each *NS* you write, explain how you would make the word group complete so that it qualifies as a sentence.

1. Across an empty field.
2. Raking the yard before dusk last Saturday.
3. Jeffrey fed the chickens before dawn.
4. Singing and laughing in loud voices from across the yard on Cameo Drive.
5. The judge carefully reviewed the case and decided in our favor.
6. Based on important facts.
7. We screamed.
8. Wait!
9. Leave these premises immediately.
10. A very intelligent child.

Step 2.   Verbs and Subjects. Among the words below, only eight may serve as verbs. Circle them. From the words remaining, select subjects that make sense with the verbs. Then write six sentences of your own, including in each a correct subject-verb combination. Use separate paper.

Example
Sparrows fly swiftly.

faucet	draw	vanish
dim	leaks	light bulbs
lion	listen	roars
children	sparrows	airplanes
(fly)	artists	engine
crowd	noises	audiences

Step 3.   Finding Subjects and Verbs in Sentences. Using the pointers in the Sentence Review Chart, find the subjects and verbs in each sentence below. Underline the subjects once and the verbs twice.

Example
After <u>I</u> <u>had fallen</u>, an old <u>man</u> <u>helped</u> me to my feet.

1. Because of the heavy rain, Roger lost control of his car and swerved into a truck.
2. Because my sister had ridden the subways only in the United States before this, she was amazed at how spotless the Toronto stations and trains are kept.
3. Always revise your writing, or your paper may contain several grammatical errors.
4. The odor of fresh lilacs filled the tiny bedroom as the sun streamed through the venetian blinds.
5. Arlene put her son Ramon at a window seat on the bus so that he could see the desert cactus in bloom along Route 10.
6. Before Mary had finished her song, the director clapped his hands and another girl came on stage, ready for singing.
7. The children screamed so loudly outside that Elizabeth and Ray could not study for their final exams.

8. Never forget your homework when you leave for class.
9. Hanging on the line, the red sweater flapped lazily in the summer breeze as Pedro put out the rest of the clothes.
10. The day Gil rented the apartment, he stripped the old paint off the refrigerator, cleaned the grime off the windows, and mopped the mud off the floors.

Coordination

Read the sentences below. Then write on the blank line your first reaction to the way the sentences sound.

The Nursery

(1) My baby's room is the happiest room in our home. (2) I love to spend time there. (3) The walls are painted a sunny yellow. (4) Above the crib hangs a musical mobile. (5) It plays Brahms' Lullaby. (6) Stuffed dogs and cats rest on the floor. (7) The sweet smell of talcum powder is in the air. (8) A brown rocking horse sits in the corner. (9) My baby sucks his little pink thumb. (10) He suddenly awakens. (11) He doesn't see me in the corner. (12) He rests his head on the pillow. (13) I tiptoe quietly to the door.

Did you write *choppy* or *childish*? If you did, you probably sensed that some of the sentences needed to be joined in some way. Although very brief statements as sentences are often effective in writing, there are several other ways of structuring sentences for a clear development of ideas.

One way is to use *coordination*. The words *and, but, or, for, nor* (called *conjunctions*), and the semicolon (;) are called coordinators. Coordinators help ideas flow smoothly in a paragraph by joining two complete thoughts together so that they both are equal in importance and strength. When you use *and, but, or, for,* or *nor* to join complete sentences, always use a comma before the coordinators.

	What They Mean	*How to Use Them*	
and	The information that follows in the second complete thought is true along with, in addition to, the related information in the first complete thought.	The boys sat in the schoolyard with their shirts off, **and** they enjoyed sunning themselves.	[comma] [This part of the sentence tells what the boys do in addition to sitting in the schoolyard with their shirts off.]
but	The information that follows in the second complete thought is something you would not expect to happen, according to the information in the first complete thought. Idea two tells an *exception* to idea one.	I wanted to see that Japanese film on television, **but** I had too much homework.	[comma] [You wouldn't expect someone who wanted to watch the program (as stated in the first part of the sentence) to miss it.]

for	The information in the second complete thought tells why the events in the first complete thought happened or should happen.	We were not permitted to visit the baby, **for** we both had colds. [comma]	[This tells why the visit (stated in the first thought) could not occur.]
or	The information in the second complete thought is an alternative—another possibility—to the information in the first. *Or* suggests that only one of the two ideas will be possible.	[comma] You must arrive on time, **or** you will miss the first part of the examination.	[This will occur only if what is told in the first part of the sentence does not occur.]
nor	*Nor* continues into the second complete thought some negative idea begun in the first.	[This word begins the negative idea.] [comma] He never ate candy, **nor** did he miss the taste of sweetness.	[This continues the negative idea.]
;	The semicolon indicates close relationship between both complete thoughts.	[semicolon] It was time for a new car; even his father agreed to that.	[This thought depends for its sense on the thought before the semicolon.]

Hint

Remember to use a comma whenever you use a conjunction to connect two complete thoughts.

Notice how well sentences 1 and 2 in the paragraph called "The Nursery" may be coordinated.

My baby's room is the happiest room in our home, *and* I love to spend time there.

Similarly, sentences 10 and 11 may be united.

He suddenly awakens, *but* he doesn't see me in the corner.

What other sentences might be coordinated effectively?

Three Important Hints

1. Too many coordinated sentences can weaken prose style. Use coordination sparingly.

2. Don't coordinate a whole string of complete sentences with conjunctions. Your paragraph will be just as dull as if you had not used any coordinators. Sometimes semicolons or a combination of semicolon and conjunction may be used effectively to coordinate *three* complete thoughts.

Example

  We drove carefully through the strange neighborhood; all of us watched the street signs, but nothing looked familiar.

3. Make sure that the two complete thoughts you coordinate make sense together.

Step 1.   You Pick the Coordinator. Here are five coordinated sentences written by professional writers. The coordinator in each case is left out. Write in the blank space the best coordinator from the choices given on the right.

peNAME _____ CLASS _____ DATE _____ 21

1. The big patch of shadow might be a hut certainly, _____ it might be a cave leading down into the very depths of the earth.
—Leo Tolstoy

for	;	but

2. A breeze must have blown outside, _____ the net on the basket moved . . . .
—Philip Roth

or	for	nor

3. The sand was hot as fire, _____ I could have sworn it was glowing red.
—Albert Camus

for	and	but

4. . . . the last corn went flying into the silo with a clackety roar and a smell as sweet as honey _____ the beans were harvested in a half day, like an afterthought _____ on the porch and out by the roadside stood mountains of pumpkins.
—John Gardner

but	;	for
but	;	nor

5. At my father's funeral I had nothing black to wear, _____ this posed a nagging problem all day long.
—James Baldwin

for	but	and

Step 2.   Completing Sentences. Basing your choice upon the coordinator used in each statement below, add a complete thought to the beginning word group that appears. Make sure that your final sentence makes sense. Look at the example.

Example
1. Jimmy found five dollars, but *he tried not to spend it.*

2. We stopped for lunch at a cheap hamburger stand, for _____

_____

3. The radiator hissed as we strode into the room; _____

_____

4. A husband should never take his wife's love for granted, nor _____

_____

5. We ran out of gas halfway to Jacksonville, but _____

_____

6. You can hand your paper in on time, or _____

_____

NAME _____ CLASS _____ DATE _____

Step 3.   Coordinators in Your Sentences. Using any of the methods of coordination, write a sentence about the topics listed below. Use each type of coordinator at least once. Be sure a complete thought (containing subject and verb) follows each coordinator.

1. autumn _____

_____

2. the supermarket _____

_____

3. your kitchen _____

_____

4. television _____

_____

5. running _____

_____

6. nuclear energy _____

_____

7. college instructors _____

_____

8. working mothers _____

_____

9. your childhood _____

_____

10. inflation _____

_____

SOLVING PROBLEMS IN WRITING

Mirror Words I

The following exercises focus upon words that are especially difficult to spell because they look and sound so much like other words with different meanings. Words that look and sound alike but have different spellings and different meanings are called *homophones*.

IT'S   ITS

it's: it is	*It's* too quiet.
it has	Tell us if *it's* true.
	It's been a week since I saw her.
	Hint: You must be able to use the words *it is* or *it has* whenever you want to use *it's*.
its: possession or ownership by some nonhuman thing	The Raggedy-Ann doll lost *its* stuffing.
	As winter approached, the tree lost *its* leaves.
	Hint: If you can use *his* or *her* and the sentence gives a sense of ownership, you can use *its*.
	The tree lost *his* leaves.
	His gives the sense of ownership; since trees have no male or female qualities, *its* should be used.
~~its'~~	This form does not exist!
	Do not use it.

Step 1. *It's* or *Its?* Write the correct word, *it's* or *its,* in the blank spaces below.

1. _____ freezing now, but _____ supposed to warm up this afternoon.
2. Although _____ easy to read a poem, _____ meaning is often difficult to understand.
3. _____ been a few years since the end of the Vietnamese war, but _____ disastrous effects still linger in the minds of _____ veterans.
4. _____ clear that the cat is freezing; notice how it rubs _____ fur against the bark of the old maple tree.
5. _____ never too late to plan a study schedule for your school work.

TWO   TOO   TO

two: the number 2

too: **1.** One meaning is *very, more than enough, excessively,* or *in a great degree.*

    The color is *too* dull.
    My cousin is *too* tall.

    2. *Too* means *also* as well.

    Let me go *too.*
    Will the mayor, *too,* speak at the luncheon:

    Hint: When you use *too* [meaning *also*] at the end of a sentence, you must use a comma before it to indicate a pause and to give emphasis to your statement.

    I shook Senator Carter's hand, too.

to: **1.** *To* is used to show direction. It means *toward, for,* or *at.*

    Carry the milk *to* the refrigerator.
    To me he is always fair.

    2. *To* is used as part of the infinitive. An infinitive is the starting point of any verb used in a sentence. In the sentence "He likes food," *likes* is the verb whose infinitive is *to like.* All infinitives are preceded by the word *to.* These two sentences use infinitives correctly: notice the word *to.*
    [infinitive]
    They like to fish in a stream.

    To run in track meets, you must begin to train your legs.
    [infinitive]   [infinitive]

Step 2.   *To, Two, Too.* Fill in the blanks below with the correct form: *too, two,* or *to.*

Listening _____ the _____ men arguing outside about a parking

space was _____ much _____ put up with. It was hard enough

having _____ finish this essay in just _____ more hours, but

listening _____ these _____ men cursing each other was starting

_____ drive me crazy, _____. I guess it's my fault; after all, I should have listened _____ my father when he told me _____ start the assignment _____ weeks ago. Instead, as usual, I got _____ involved with other things and waited until _____ in the morning _____ begin writing.

Step 3.   Using *To, Two, Too* Correctly. Follow directions.

1. Write a sentence that uses *too* to mean *very*. _____

_____

2. Write a sentence that uses *to* as an infinitive. _____

_____

3. Write a sentence using the word *two*. _____

_____

4. Write a sentence using *too* to mean *also*. _____

_____

5. Write a sentence that uses *to* as a direction word. _____

_____

THERE   THEIR   THEY'RE

there: a place   Was it *there?*

Hint: *There* often starts a sentence. It is sometimes followed by *are, were, is,* or some other verb.

   There are three birds.
   There was a good movie at the Rialto.
   There sat two children playing.

their: ownership (possession) by a group   It's *their* car.
                                              Was it *their* house that burned?

they're: they are

Hint: If you can say *they are,* you can use *they're.*

   They're late again!
   If *they're* tired, they should sleep.

Step 4.   Listening for *Their, They're, and There*. Read the brief paragraph below, noting the use of *their, they're,* and *there.* Then on separate paper write the paragraph as your instructor dictates it.

In the past my mother and father loved their apartment, but they're just not happy there anymore. There is no longer room for all Dad's trophies, and Mom's plants lie cluttered over the entire living room. My folks are starting to look for a new place that they're both going to enjoy as much as their old apartment. There must be an apartment building in their area that has large rooms to hold many precious belongings. I'm going to look in today's paper. An apartment must be listed there that my parents will find right for their needs.

YOUR   YOU'RE

your: ownership. It means *belonging to you.*

　　Is that *your* car?
　　Give *your* theme a lively title.
you're: you are

Hint: If you can say *you are,* you can use *you're.*

　You're late.
　When *you're* out of town, call.

Step 5.   *Your* and *You're*. Circle the correct words in the parentheses.

1. (Your, You're) not the actor who can play the flute.
2. (Your, You're) farm is larger than I expected.
3. If (your, you're) uncertain of the date, check (your, you're) calendar.
4. (Your, You're) driving is as bad as (your, you're) cooking.
5. (Your, You're) bill can be mailed if (your, you're) in a hurry.

WHO'S   WHOSE

who's: the contraction for *who is* or *who has*

   Who's at the door?

   Tell him *who's* on the phone.

   Who's been to El Paso?

Hint: If you can say *who is* or *who has,* you can use *who's.*

whose: possession. It asks a question (*Belonging to whom?*) or it refers to some person or thing named earlier in the sentence.

   Whose dime is that?

   The man *whose* briefcase was lost offered a reward.

Step 6.   Sentences with *Who's* and *Whose*. Complete the following sentences so that they make sense.

1. I will predict whose _____.

2. I will predict who's _____.

3. My sister, whose _____, will meet us for dinner.

4. Whose _____?

5. Who's _____?

Run-on Sentences

As you remember from the review chart, pages 15–17, every sentence must have a subject and a verb to be complete. Run-on sentences are word groups that mistakenly push two or more sentences together as one. Find the "sentence collisions" in the following example:

I ran to the door my sister stormed in suddenly she burst into tears.

HOW TO FIX THE RUN-ON ERROR

1. The easiest way to fix the run-on is to use a correct end mark between sentences: a period, a question mark, or an exclamation mark. *A comma is not an end mark. It does not separate complete sentences.* If you read aloud the run-on sentence above, listen to the sound of your own voice. Where your voice stops and drops, use a period.

                [capital letter]   [capital letter]

I ran to the door. My sister stormed in. Suddenly she burst into tears.

                         [period]

Of course, you need to use a capital letter to start each new sentence. If you had used a comma after *door* or *in* in the sentences above, you would have incorrectly separated two sentences (the subjects and verbs are underlined for you to help you see how the standards for completeness are met). A comma is too weak a punctuation mark to separate complete thoughts. Some instructors like to call the run-on error that uses a comma to separate complete thoughts *a comma splice*. A *comma splice* is merely two or more sentences run together with a comma between them.

2. When two run-on word groups, each complete with subject and verb, are very closely related in meaning, these word groups may be separated by a semicolon. A semicolon, which includes both a period and a comma in its structure, indicates a stronger pause than a comma. The semicolon can separate complete thoughts. If you choose to use a semicolon, always begin the word group after the semicolon with a small letter.

                        [small letter]

I ran to the door. My sister stormed in; suddenly she burst into tears.

                    [semicolon]

Hint: A subject and a verb must come both before and after the semicolon. The structure of the sentence looks like this: *Complete thought; complete thought.*

3. Instead of keeping complete word groups apart, you may join them together with suitable joining words (*conjunctions*) and proper punctuation.
   a. When the two sentences have equal importance in your mind, use one of these joining words: *and, but, or, for, nor.* Use a comma before the conjunction. (You learned about combining sentences in this way—called *coordination*—on pages 19–20.)

                [conjunction]

I ran to the door, and my sister stormed in. Suddenly she burst into tears.

            [comma]

(continued on next page)

HOW TO FIX THE RUN-ON ERROR (CONTINUED)

[conjunction]

I ran to the door. My sister stormed in, and suddenly she burst into tears.

[comma]

b. You may also join the run-on sentences by making one complete word group less important than the other (see pages 100–109). Many different conjunctions perform that function. Here are a few: *because, while, although, since, when, if, as.* Use a comma after you complete the word group that begins with one of these joining words. Sometimes you need to add a new word or two, to take away words, or to change the position of words when you correct the run-on with one of these conjunctions.

[less important word group]

As I ran to the door, my sister stormed in. Suddenly she burst into tears.

[comma]

[word *suddenly* left out]

[less important word group]

I ran to the door. When my sister stormed in, she burst into tears.

[comma]

Step 1. One Error, Five Corrections. Here are two complete sentences run on as one:

The room was much too small Lisa and I felt as if we were trapped in a cage.

Fix the run-on error on the blank lines below. The words and punctuation will tell you which methods to use.

1. The room was much too small; _____

_____

2. Since _____ , _____

_____

3. The room was much too small. _____

_____

4. The room was much too small, _____

_____

5. Lisa and I felt as if we were trapped inside a cage _____

_____

Step 2.   One Error, Five Corrections. Here are two complete thoughts joined by a comma. On separate paper correct the comma splice in five different ways.

The train was about to leave, Juan darted toward the closing doors.

How to Find Run-on Errors

Repairing the run-on mistake is easy, once your instructor points out the error by writing in the margin of your paragraph "RO" for run-on or "CS" for comma splice. The trick is, of course, to find the run-on errors yourself.

1. Here are some simple hints to help you find run-on sentences:
   a. Read your paragraph aloud. When your voice stops and drops, use a period.
   b. Read your paragraph from the last sentence to the first sentence. That will help you keep apart complete thoughts.
   c. Count your sentences. In this way, you will be looking for end marks, and you will be aware that a small number of sentences probably means run-ons in your paragraph.
2. The best way to recognize the run-on is to learn carefully two groups of *run-on stop signs*. These words, used at the start of complete-thought word

---

RUN-ON STOP SIGNS: GROUP I

then	there	consequently
now		moreover
finally		therefore
suddenly		however

Hint: These words are not conjunctions. They do *not* join sentences correctly. If they open complete-thought word groups, they must be preceded by a period or a semicolon. At times, a conjunction and a comma work as well.

In this word group, the run-on stop sign starts a complete-thought word group and must have either a semicolon or a period before it:

                                        [run-on
                                        stop sign]
                                             ↓
We drove for a long time. However, we rested afterward.
We drove for a long time; however, we rested afterward.

In the word group below, the run-on stop sign is used correctly in the middle of the sentence; *however* does not start a complete-thought word group here:

We drove, however, for a long time

---

groups, mean trouble to you because they, more than any other words, frequently cause run-on errors. Each time you use one of the words in either group, you must stop to think of the possibility that you may be writing a run-on sentence.

Step 1.   Correct Punctuation for Run-ons. Correct the run-on errors below by inserting correct punctuation or by changing incorrect punctuation. Two sentences are already correct.

> *Hint*
> If you have doubts about where your voice stops and drops, check for subjects and verbs to test sentence completeness.

1. I ran to the beach, finally the sun came out.
2. I love to wander through rows of corn there is a peacefulness that I enjoy.
3. By the time the Ramos family arrived, the food was cold, consequently no one wanted to eat.
4. The plumbers finished their work, now we can wash again.
5. The water was a clear blue color, however, the sand was filled with pebbles and litter.
6. Alyson is a textbook editor, however, she has always wanted to be a pilot.
7. We should try, therefore, to find a restaurant that serves food without preservatives.
8. The doorbell rang mysteriously; suddenly, the lights dimmed as well.
9. Always wipe food preparation counters dry, there is less chance of having roaches.
10. The experiment was a failure, therefore, we must start over again.

RUN-ON STOP SIGNS: GROUP II		
it	we	**Hint:** Although these words are frequently used in the middle of
she	he	sentences, they are also used as sentence openers. If one of these
you	they	words opens a complete-thought word group, the word must be
I		preceded by a period or a semicolon.

Step 2.   Rewriting the Run-on. Fix the run-on errors below by rewriting the word groups correctly on the blank lines. Use any of the methods explained on pages 28–29. All the run-on mistakes are caused by Group II *stop signs*. Write the letter *C* if the sentence is correct.

1. Despite the dinginess of the room, they managed to brighten up the place

   with a few posters and plants. _____

   _____

2. Lenny spent all winter bundled up in sweaters it sometimes reached below
   zero in his bedroom. _____

   _____

3. Professor Kent entered the classroom frowning he held the final exams in his
   hand. _____

   _____

4. Although the weather in Juarez looked fine, rain began right after noon.

   _____

   _____

5. Rosa told us the news we could not believe it. _____

   _____

   Use the two brief run-on review charts below to help you complete Steps 3 to
5 correctly.

RUN-ON REVIEW CHARTS

Run-on Finder

1. Read word groups aloud. At stop and drop of voice, use a period.
2. Read word groups from the last complete thought to the first complete thought. Look for subject and verb to test completeness.
3. Count sentences.
   Recognize run-on stop signs:
   a. Group I: *then, now, however, finally, there, consequently, moreover, therefore.*
   b. Group II: *it, she, you, I, we, he, they.*

Run-on Fixer

1. Use end marks between complete sentences. Use capital letter for next word after period.
2. Use a semicolon. Start next word with small letter.
3. Use a conjunction
   a. With one of these, use a comma directly before: *and, or, nor, but, for.*
   b. With one of these, use the comma after the whole word group is completed and when the word group opens a sentence: *because, since, while, although, as, when.*
4. Never use only a comma to separate complete sentences.

Step 3.   Avoiding the Run-on Mistake. Follow directions given in each statement below.

1. Write two sentences about jogging in the park. Start the second sentence with
   the word *it.* _____

   _____

   _____

2. Write two complete thoughts about your best friend, separating them with a semicolon. Open the second thought with the word *however*._____

_____

_____

3. Write two sentences about the last book you enjoyed reading. Begin the second sentence with the word *I*. _____

_____

_____

_____

4. Write a pair of sentences about pollution, opening the second sentence with the word *there* or *now*. _____

_____

_____

_____

5. Write two complete-thought word groups about your third-grade classroom. Join the two thoughts with the word *but*. _____

_____

_____

6. Write three sentences about television violence. Use the word *it* to start the second sentence. Use the word *moreover* to start the third sentence. _____

_____

_____

_____

_____

Step 4. Stop-sign Words in Sentences. Use correctly in the blank space the *stop sign* that appears in parentheses before each set of word groups. Use correct punctuation and capitals when needed.

(however)   1. The lawyer _____ tried to influence the jury unfairly.
(then)   2. Hans hailed a taxi _____ the bus came.

(they) 3. Remember to care for those horses _____ must be wiped down after you ride them.

(there) 4. The living room felt like an icebox _____ were no heating ducts in that part of the house.

(however) 5. I love to cook _____ I hate to wash the dishes afterwards.

(finally) 6. We spoke to the landlord five times last week _____ she fixed the front door.

(there) 7. Cutting wheat properly is not easy _____ are several steps to follow.

(consequently) 8. I watched soap operas instead of studying for the final exam _____ I failed the course.

(I) 9. As I turned the corner, I saw the ambulance in front of my house _____ was so scared!

(therefore) 10. The theater had only one projector _____ we had a five-minute wait between reels.

Step 5. Correcting Sentence Errors. In the blank lines after these run-on errors, rewrite the sentences correctly in any way you wish. Write *C* if the sentence is already correct.

1. I watch the stars from my bedroom window it's such a peaceful sight.____

_____

2. Try to drink less coffee you will feel less nervous._____

_____

3. Skiing is an exciting, stimulating sport however, on an icy slope skiing can be dangerous. _____

_____

4. The floors, moreover, are solid oak under all that linoleum._____

_____

5. My sister spent her junior year traveling then she returned to Boston to finish her degree. _____

_____

6. I stood there in the hospital waiting room, my mind went blank for a second then details of the wreck started coming back to me. _____

_____

7. Since he was my cousin, I trusted him however I found out that he had lied to me. _____

_____

8. Because there is less humidity, the heat in Tucson is not as unbearable as it is in Arkansas. _____

   _____

9. What did Lucy say when her son disappeared she was afraid he had run away? _____

   _____

10. It was no longer a feeling of friendship that was inside me, it was a feeling of love, I adored Ellen. _____

   _____

WRITING THE DESCRIPTIVE PARAGRAPH

ASSIGNMENT:

Write a paragraph of at least ten sentences in which you describe a room. To *describe* means to use concrete sensory detail to create images that make it possible for the reader to experience what you did. For other specific elements to consider as you write, see the checklist on pages 44–45.

Student Samples

Your first assignment is to write a paragraph of at least ten sentences that bring a room to life. You are going to have the chance to develop your ideas about this topic before you actually begin writing your paragraph (see pages 38–40). You should plan to write several drafts of your paper. A *draft* is an attempt that you work over and recreate until your writing fully expresses what you want to say. Each draft will also help you discover exactly what your focus is.

Read the paragraph below, written by a student in response to the same assignment. When you finish reading, write the answers to the questions about the topic sentence and about concrete sensory detail.

The Gloom Room

On this dreary October afternoon in my writing class here on the second floor of Boylan Hall at Brooklyn College, a shadow of gloom hangs over the people and things that surround me. The atmosphere is depressing. There is an old brown chair beside the teacher's desk, a mahogany bookcase with a missing shelf, and this ugly desk of mine filled with holes and scratches. As I rub my hand across its surface, there is a feeling of coldness. Even the grey walls and the rumble of thunder outside reflect the atmosphere of seriousness as we write our first theme of the semester. When some air sails through an open window beside me, there is the annoying smell of coffee grounds from a garbage pail not far off. My classmates, too, show this mood of tension. Mary, a slim blonde at my right, chews frantically the inside of her lower lip. Only one or two words in blue ink stand upon her clean white page. David Harris, slouched in his seat in the third row, nibbles each finger of each hand. Then he plays inaudibly with a black collar button that stands open on the top of his red plaid shirt. There is a thump as he uncrosses his legs and his scuffed shoe hits the floor. A painful cough slices the air from behind me. I hear a woman's heels click from the hall beyond the closed door and a car engine whine annoyingly from Bedford Avenue. If a college classroom should be a place of delight and pleasure, that could never be proved by the tension in this room.

—*Harry Golden*

Step 1.   Understanding the Selection

1. Underline the topic sentence.
2. What key word (or words) shows Harry Golden's opinion of the subject he is writing about?
3. There are two things in particular that Harry Golden will discuss about his writing class, and he announces them both in the topic sentence. What are they?
4. Pick out three groups of words that describe sounds.
5. Pick out three word groups that use color to paint a picture.
6. Tell in your own words two specific actions you see in Harry Golden's theme.
7. Which sentence appeals to the sense of smell?
8. Which words include an appeal to the sense of touch?
9. Which word picture, in your opinion, is most vivid?
10. Why does Harry Golden mention the time of year and time of day in the first sentence?

Step 1.   More Sample Themes. As you read the themes below, make note of the vivid pictures the writer paints of the room she is describing. Underline the topic sentence. Circle words that show color, sound, smell, or touch. Put a check in the margin next to the line that you think contains the best word picture in the paragraph. Afterwards, answer the questions.

SOME WORDS TO KNOW BEFORE YOU READ

sulky: gloomy
stark: harsh, stiff, rigid
loom: to come into sight with an appearance of great size
menacing: threatening to cause evil or harm
anesthetist: a physician who administers the drug that lets a patient lose the sensation of
    pain during an operation
reel: to sway or rock from dizziness

A Birth Room

At General Hospital there I lay on stark white sheets in a stark white room, only a large clock with black hands, a worm-eaten chair, and a window in my view, as I waited with fear for the arrival of my first born. While the sulky, snowy January dawn rolled lazily through the window, I could see the wind making snow drifts outside and could feel it blow crystals through the rotting window sill. Overhead loomed a menacing light pressed to a vast white ceiling. In front of me an orderly in a green nylon gown cheerily imprisoned my ankles in metal stirrups. "Don't fret none honey," she said. "You ain't the first to have a baby." I forced a smile, but then a sharp pain in my back made me twitch. It passed in a moment although I swore I saw black spots growing on the empty walls. I looked to my left as I ran my fingers over the worn leather straps that held my wrists. The thin second hand moved swiftly on the clock near the door. It was five after seven. Behind me the anesthetist, all in white with mask in hand, fussed with some metal tools, and I saw his intense black eyes darting swiftly. The sudden smell of alcohol nauseated me. In the distance I heard moans reverberating down the corridors—moans of women in labor. I felt reassured about this, for I was one step higher. I was in the delivery room; they still suffered in the labor rooms. To my right Dr. Kassop paced inaudibly, his rubber shoes sliding on the polished green tiles. Then he moved close and with warm fingers touched my brow. How such a small thing can be so comforting! Near my feet Nurse Day bustled about adjusting the tubes from a bottle hanging upside down on a metal stand. No sympathy for a frightened person from her, I thought. To her it was just another birth. Then as I stared at those erupting black spots on the walls I heard a liquid splashing. Suddenly I felt the icy coldness of antiseptic between my thighs as a cry of "Oye!" from a Spanish woman far off rang in my ears. A great pain made me scream and the stark white room reeled. Was that my new baby's cry? That's all I remember. The anesthetist covered my nose with the sharp, welcome smell of his medicine as everything went blank, my fears and the white birth room lost in sleep.
—*Gwendolyn Wellington*

My Bedroom

My tranquil bedroom is my favorite room in the house. As I stand at the door looking in, the first thing I see on the far side of the room is a yellow wall, its soft color framing a computer printout picture of my boyfriend Clyde and me. Underneath it is a bed covered with a flowered bedspread and, to the left, my night table, holding a beige telephone, a small lamp, and a radio alarm clock. Behind the night table fresh air from my window gently rustles the yellow and green curtains back and forth. A toy red snake lying on top of the curtain rod smiles down at me. When I pull the door behind me, it squeaks. I feel a burst of air sailing through, carrying with it the scent of lemon soap from the bathroom down the hall. As I turn to examine the wall where the door is, I see my twelve-drawer bureau. The polished mahogany glistens, showing me my reflection. To protect the wood from scratches, a white dresser scarf sits on top in a neat square. On top of it are a black and white television set, a wooden jewelry box, three bottles of perfume, and a baby picture of me in a silver frame. Hanging on the wall beside my dresser is a calendar with large black numbers. For October there is a picture of a brown and white kitten playing gently with a ball of wool. When I hear a hissing sound, I realize that the steam is coming up; in the corner below the calendar my lavender-painted radiator clamors for attention. Above it on the adjacent wall are three bookshelves. The top shelf holds some dusty hardcover novels and my history books on the Civil War; the middle shelf holds the paperback novels, plays, and biographies I've collected over the years; and the bottom shelf supports stacks of disco record albums, copies of *Ebony, People,* and *TV Guide,* loose papers, and all my samples of lipstick and nail polish. After I select a book from one of the shelves, pull off my socks and shoes, and run my toes through the soft shag carpet, I lie down on the bed to enjoy my peaceful room.

—*Tanya M. Fitzgerald*

1. What words in each closing sentence go back to the topic and attitude expressed in the topic sentence?
2. What are some transitions the writers use? Make a list of at least ten.
3. Why does Gwendolyn Wellington call the room *stark*? Why does she say "Overhead *loomed* a *menacing* light" instead of "Overhead *was* a light"?
4. What words in Tanya Fitzgerald's theme best name sounds? smells? actions?

Some Topics for Your Paragraph on a Room

Select some indoor place you know well and plan to write a paragraph that describes the place clearly. You might want to choose one of these topics:

1. a concert auditorium
2. a college classroom
3. a locker room
4. your kitchen
5. a favorite restaurant
6. a hotel or motel room
7. your place of worship
8. the library
9. the place where you work
10. a hospital room
11. an art gallery
12. a bus terminal
13. a hardware store
14. your secret hiding place
15. the waiting room at your doctor's office
16. a health-food store
17. a movie house
18. a disco
19. a biology or chemistry lab
20. a hairstyling shop

Prewriting

Handing in a paper written for someone else to read is the last in a series of steps writers take to produce their work. Writing begins long before writers put pens to paper. A convenient word to describe many of the steps that lead up to the actual writing of a first draft is *prewriting.*

WHAT IS PREWRITING?

Prewriting is a set of activities writers use to shake loose ideas and details before writing begins. In order to limit a topic and to uncover possible ideas about it, you have to let your thoughts take shape informally. It is very helpful to get opinions and advice about your drafts from other people you trust. Plan on showing your drafts to other students in your class, your friends, or relatives. When you actually begin writing a paragraph, then you can develop and refine ideas you have already had a chance to examine.

Some prewriting techniques many writers use include:

1. making lists
2. brainstorming
3. making subject trees
4. preparing scratch outlines or other kinds of groupings for ideas
5. looking at what other writers have written on the same topic
6. doing timed writing
7. limiting broad topics
8. doing free association
9. doing research
10. conducting interviews

Various chapters in this book define and explain these techniques so that you will have a chance to practice them for different writing tasks.

Making Lists

Since good descriptive writing requires a number of strong sensory images, recording those images in lists is a valuable prewriting technique. With a list of many images before you, you can build a description alive in detail.

PREWRITING: MAKING LISTS OF SENSORY IMAGES

Topic: Gino's Pizza Parlor

Sight

fingers kneading white dough

bubbling mozzarella cheese

red tomato paste

crisp brown crust

Sound

ring of a cash register

quarters and dimes clinking on the blue counter

cries of "One slice and a coke"

rumble of the juke box

Smell

tangy smell of garlic and pepper

cigarette smoke

hot dough

sweet orange drink

Touch

wave of heat from the oven
hot olive oil on my fingers
cool ceramic counter
icy cup of Coke
greasy dollar

Taste

spicy sauce
fiery sausage
hot, bland cheese

— Lisa Roth

Step 1.   Exploring Lists of Images. Look at Lisa Roth's lists of sensory images. Answer these questions about them.

1. Which image do you find most original? Where does the writer combine senses to create especially clear pictures?
2. Using any one or a combination of images on her list, write a complete sentence alive in sensory language.
3. What single dominant impression could you suggest to help the writer organize her details? How would you incorporate that impression in a topic sentence?

Step 2.   Listing Ideas in Groups. Once you have selected the place you want to describe, develop images (see pages 5–7) under various sense headings. Write *sight, sound, smell, touch,* and *taste* above five columns on a blank sheet of paper. Under each heading develop images about the place you are describing. (Remember, images of action and color go under *sight*. And you may not be able to come up with images under *taste*, the most difficult of the senses to convey in language.)

  Practice making lists of this kind with one of the topics suggested below if you are not yet sure about your own topic. Study Lisa Roth's example above.

1. your kitchen at breakfast
2. a local bar
3. the college library
4. a video-game arcade
5. a fast-food restaurant

GETTING READER RESPONSE

After you have done your prewriting, write a first draft of this paragraph of description and bring it to class. In groups of three, read each other's papers and make either written or spoken comments to help the writer move on to the next draft. As discussion guidelines, answer the questions listed below for each paper you read and refer to the checklist on pages 44–45, especially items 7–10 and 13–14.

1. Which sensory images are sharp and concrete? Which images need more vivid details?
2. Which senses are not adequately represented? Where in the paragraph could the writer develop those senses?
3. Which transitions help you to follow the writer's movement around the room or area as he or she moves from one section to another?
4. What dominant impression of the place has the writer given you?
5. What general suggestions can you make for improving the paper?

Manuscript Form

A manuscript is the final copy of an author's created work. It should be carefully prepared before it is submitted. Mess up your first and later copies all you like. Draw arrows. Cross out words. Draw pictures. Use purple ink or crayon or pencil. Use scissors to cut out words and sentences. Paste or tape the words in new positions where they make more sense. Rip up pages you don't like and start again. Your first effort, called a *draft,* is a worksheet for you, the writer. But as soon as you submit your paragraph or essay for evaluation by your instructor, you have to prepare your work so that it follows correct manuscript form. Your instructor will insist that your paper be clean and easy to read and that you follow procedures most professional writers follow before they submit their manuscripts.

1. Leave wide margins (1 to 1½ inches) on all four sides.
2. Write in ink on one side of each page only. Use regulation theme paper if you write by hand. If you type, use sturdy bond, 8½- by 11-inch typing paper. Do not use onionskin. Use blue or black ink: nothing fancy.
3. Make sure your name, your class, and the date appear where your instructor asks for them.

4. If you write by hand, *print* all your capital letters (this makes them easier to read). Leave a large space after each end mark. Make periods firm and clear. They remind you that you are starting a new idea in a new sentence.
5. Check your theme by proofreading (see below) for any careless errors.
6. Occasional errors may be corrected with correction fluid or with a good ink or typewriter eraser.

IF YOU WRITE THE COMPOSITION IN CLASS

1. Do not plan on rewriting: you will not have time.
2. Think for several minutes about the topic. Spend a minute or two examining the topic sentence you write.
3. Jot down some ideas on scrap paper. If an outline helps you, draw one up quickly (see pages 173–175).
4. You are still responsible for errors. Check your theme by proofreading (see below) for careless mistakes. Save at least five minutes at the end of the session to proofread.
5. Most instructors encourage you to use a dictionary and thesaurus even when you write your composition in class. Check with your teacher, and if it is all right, look up words to check spelling errors. See pages 482–484 for reminders on using the dictionary and thesaurus.

Proofreading

Proofreading is a convenient term to name what writers do when they look over their work for errors.

As a writer you should not expect to proofread your writing at all stages of creation. There's not much point in worrying about being correct when you are trying to develop ideas in a rough draft. In fact, the *last* thing you want to think about as your ideas first take shape on paper is correctness. Drafts are for putting thoughts down clearly and logically.

When you revise each draft, you look especially for ways of improving your language and the structure of your sentences. Part of that process will involve correcting major sentence errors of the kinds explained in this chapter and in other parts of the book.

Productive proofreading takes place at two critical stages in the writing of any paper. First, you need to check for errors in the draft that you will turn into a final manuscript. Next, you need to check over your final manuscript itself to make sure that no errors have slipped by.

The suggestions below will help you locate careless mistakes that may appear in your writing.

TIPS FOR EFFECTIVE PROOFREADING

1. Read *slowly*. This is not a job done by skimming. Look at—and read aloud, if necessary—every word. Don't let your eyes move too swiftly from one word to the next.
2. Use a ruler or a blank sheet of paper below each line; this will help you locate spelling errors by cutting off later words from your line of vision. Block any words that may distract you on the line you are checking. The fewer words you examine at a time, the easier it is to find spelling errors.
3. Examine each syllable of each word. Try pointing at each word as you pronounce it to see if it is correct.
4. Be aware of your own usual errors. A glance at your Progress Sheet (page 523) before you do any written work puts you on your guard. If you're a chronic run-on writer, know the run-on Stop Signs. If you write fragments, know the fragment Stop Signs. (See pages 68 and 115). If you usually confuse *its* and *it's* and you have used one of those words in your paragraph, stop for a second to analyze the spelling you've chosen.
5. If you are writing in class, cross out errors neatly or erase them neatly. Some students like to skip lines in order to insert any words or ideas left out through carelessness. If you've left out a word or words, draw a caret (ʌ) below the line and insert what was omitted. Do it this way:

So we awakened early and ʌ *went to the beach*

6. You can't look up every word to check spelling, but you do know which words you are unsure of. *Look them up in the dictionary.* And keep a record of the words you usually spell wrong (see Your Own Demon List, page 481).
7. You can make minor corrections on your final manuscript, but if too many errors require corrections there, you should consider it as a draft and should write another manuscript to submit.

Step 1. Practice with Proofreading. Correct these errors by following the suggestions above.

The nicist think about raining dayes in our old house was the oportunite to play in in the attic. Are attic was with old stage costums witch are grandparents wore many years a go. There collection of wiggs an beeded dresses kept us busie for hours, for instance, i was always pretended that I was a beatiful princes who would be rescud by a hansome Prince. I whish I could relieve those child hood days.

FOLLOW-UP: AFTER YOUR INSTRUCTOR RETURNS YOUR GRADED THEME

1. Check your paper to make sure that you understand your instructor's writing and any correction symbols used in the margin.
2. Correct all errors in mechanics—grammar, spelling, and punctuation.
3. Rewrite your entire paper if your instructor suggests that you do so. Correct problems in content and thought development, using the comments in the margin to guide you.
4. Enter on page 481 all the words you misspelled.
5. Enter on the Theme Progress Sheet (Appendix B) the total number of errors you made in each category listed on top of the page. In that way you can see before you write the next theme just what kinds of mistakes you usually make.

Progress Reminders: A Checklist

Make your theme lively, vivid, and well organized by following carefully the directions given in the checklist below. Check off each item as you evaluate your own writing. When you hand in your paragraph, submit the checklist along with it.

1. Think carefully about the topic. Select for description some _____ place that is especially clear in your mind, a place you can make alive with concrete sensory detail. If you select a place that you can visit again before you write, so much the better. In that way you can gather fresh sensory responses.

2. Do prewriting (see page 39) that works best for you. You _____ might want to try listing sensory images in groups. Read on pages 35–38 the student themes as models for your own writing.

3. From your prewriting activities prepare a rough draft in _____ which you write consecutive sentences that describe as best you can the place that you have selected.

4. Write as many other drafts as you need to show your ideas _____ clearly. When you prepare your final draft, be sure to follow the guidelines on pages 41–42.

5. Make sure that you share your draft with someone else in _____ the class, either in the activity listed on page 41 or in some other way your instructor suggests. Use your reader's response to write another draft.

6. Don't jump too quickly from one feature of your subject to _____ another. As you describe some person or thing, take two or three sentences to show clearly what you see before you move on to another aspect of your subject.

7. Mention time and place as early as possible in the para- _____ graph.

8. Use at least three words that appeal to the sense of *sound*. _____
   See page 5 for some new "sound" vocabulary.

9. Use at least three *colors* in different places throughout the _____
   theme.

10. Use at least one group of words to appeal to the sense of _____
    touch and one group of words to appeal to the sense of *smell*.

11. *a.* Write one sentence that uses the semicolon correctly. See _____
    page 20.
    b. Use at least one of the *run-on stop signs* to open a _____
    complete-thought word group. See pages 30–31.
    c. Try to use one or two words from the vocabulary _____
    introduced at the beginning of the chapter.

12. If you can, mention the names of people you see. Show _____
    people as they perform some action: Harry Golden says that
    Mary chews the inside of her lip. Gwendolyn Wellington
    shows Dr. Kassop pacing the floor.

13. Give the reader an idea of your surroundings by describing _____
    parts of the room. Try to make the details support the
    opinion word you state in the topic sentence.

14. Use words like *up front, to my left, nearby, across the room, far* _____
    away, above, beside, in the corner to help you move from one
    thing you wish to describe to another.

15. Write a topic sentence that includes an opinion and states _____
    clearly what your topic will be. Make sure that the topic is
    properly limited.

16. Give your paragraph a title. *A title is not a topic sentence. If you* _____
    can use part of the topic in your title, you must still repeat the topic
    in the topic sentence (see pages 7–14).

17. Proofread your paper twice: once *before* you prepare your _____
    final manuscript and once *after* you prepare it. (See pages
    42–43.)

18. Check your theme for errors, especially for run-ons and for _____
    the spelling problems noted in this chapter.

19. In the last sentence of your paper, be sure to let your reader _____
    know that your paragraph is coming to an end (see pages
    205–208).

THE PROFESSIONALS SPEAK

Concrete details are essential parts of a good description of a room. Writers
know that to make a firm impression on the reader's mind, they must give lively
sensory images so that the scene may be easily visualized.

Step 1.   A Vivid Kitchen. Read the selection below and answer the questions on sensory language.

SOME WORDS TO KNOW BEFORE YOU READ

contend: to struggle in opposition
recessed: set back
mantelpiece: the shelf above a fireplace
hearthstone: a stone forming the place where fire can be made
partition: something that divides
rubbly: rough
inflexibly: in a way that is rigid
welt: a swelling on the surface of the body
perpetual: happening all the time

The Kitchen

The kitchen was living room, dining room, and cooking room. There were two long narrow windows in one wall. An iron coalrange was recessed in another wall. Above the stove the recess was made of coral-colored bricks and creamy white plaster. It had a stone mantelpiece and a slate hearthstone on which Francie could draw pictures with chalk. Next to the stove was a water boiler which got hot when the fire was going. Often on a cold day, Francie came in chilled and put her arms around the boiler and pressed her frosty cheek gratefully against its warm silveriness. Next to the boiler was a pair of soapstone washtubs with a hinged wooden cover. The partition could be removed and the two thrown into one for a bath tub. It didn't make a very good bath tub. Sometimes when Francie sat in it, the cover banged down on her head. The bottom was rubbly and she came out of what should have been a refreshing bath, all sore from sitting on that wet roughness. Then there were four faucets to contend with. No matter how the child tried to remember that they were inflexibly there and wouldn't give way, she would jump up suddenly out of the soapy water and get her back whacked good on a faucet. Francie had a perpetual angry welt on her back.

—*Betty Smith*
A Tree Grows in Brooklyn

1. Which two word groups identify colors?
2. Name two verbs that tell sounds.
3. Underline the one sentence that you think shows the liveliest action.
4. Lines 7 and 8 contain four words that appeal to touch. What are they? What other sentences use touch words?
5. Circle any words that show transition.

Step 2. A Room in a Boarding House. In the selection below, the writer creates a mood in the place he describes by mixing his own thoughts with specific images of the room. How would you say the writer's inner feelings compare with the physical environment he describes? When you finish reading, answer the questions that follow.

My Room at the Lilac Inn

As I look around this room in this third-rate boarding house, my eyes are greeted first by the entrance to its gloomy interior. The door is painted a dirty cream color. There is a crack in one panel. The ceiling is the same dingy color with pieces of adhesive tape holding some of the plaster in place. The walls are streaked and cracked here and there. Also on the walls are pieces of Scotch tape that once held, I presume, some sexy girls, pictures of *Esquire Magazine* origin. Across the room runs a line; upon it hang a shirt, a grimy towel, and washed stump socks belonging to my roommate, Jack Nager. By the door near the top sash juts a piece of wood on which is hung—it looks like an old spread. It is calico, dirty, and a sickly green color.

Behind that is a space which serves as our closet; next to that is the radiator, painted the same ghastly color. The landlady must have got the paint for nothing. On top is Jack's black suitcase, his green soap dish, and a brightly colored box containing his hair tonic. Over by the cracked window are a poorly made table and chair. On top of the table, a pencil, shaving talcum, a glass, a nail file; one of my socks hangs over the side. Above the table is our window, the curtains of cheese cloth held back by a string. There is also a black, fairly whole paper shade to dim such little sunlight as might enter.

This window is my only promise of a better future. Through it, I can see the well-lit and nicely furnished living room of a modern apartment house across the street. Someday I'll live like that.

There, next to the window, leaning against an aged bureau, as if resting, are my faithful crutches. On the oilcloth covering the top of the bureau lie some seventeen odd books. These I used at the _____ University here in Washington, D.C. I am attending a six-month course, getting the fundamentals needed to be a Service Officer for veterans. There are enough books on that bureau to take at least a year's reading for absorption. Beard's *American Government and Policy, Anatomy, How to Interview, Soldier to Civilian,* government laws, manuals, textbooks, a public speaking guide and what-have-you are all reflected in the cloudy mirror. On the bureau stands a picture of my love, my faithful wife. I think of her. I wish I were with her tonight.

Standing alongside this bureau is this *thing*. A leather cup, straps and buckles dropping from it. Below this cup, the flesh-colored *thing* and calf, and on its foot a brown sock and oxblood shoe. This is a prosthesis. I've called this wooden leg a lot of other things. This is the replacement for the real one that was shot off in France. O, what the hell! A leg isn't everything. You've got to keep living. There are a lot worse things in this world to reckon with than an artificial leg.

On the parlor chair, here probably because there's no other place for it, my brown pants are thrown, together with my old khaki shirt. On the floor my recently painted foot locker that was in many an army camp with me is still doing service.

Jack Nager grunts alongside me in the double bed as he turns over; he is getting a good sleep tonight. His below-the-knee stump quivers as he touches some close-to-the-skin nerve on the bed. His foot was also a donation for democracy. I reach to turn out the twenty-five watt bulb on the shadeless lamp; I find the light switch. The room is in darkness. From the street three stories below comes the sound of a motor car; it fades away. Occasionally a click, click of heels hitting the pavement as someone passes by. Within the house the sound of muffled voices, the flushing of a toilet, someone blowing his nose.

I forget everything and concentrate on sleep.

—*John J. Regan*
The Purple Testament
ed. Don M. Wolfe

1. What key word or words in the first sentence show the writer's attitude toward the place he is describing? In the first paragraph and a half, there are several words that repeat this attitude.
2. Which images best appeal to your senses of sight and sound?
3. Where do the writer's thoughts take over from the actual description of the place?
4. What is a prosthesis? Notice how John Regan gives you the definition of the word in the sentence after he uses it.
5. In the first two paragraphs what hints do you find that suggest who and what the writer is? Where do you actually learn that he is a veteran and that he is wounded?
6. How does the physical setting of the room compare with the writer's inner thoughts and feelings?

REACHING HIGHER

Step 1.   Photo into Words. Look at the photograph on page 3. Decide what kind of room it shows; then, decide on your own attitude toward the room as it is represented. Write a topic sentence. In a paragraph of about fifteen sentences, support the opinion in your topic sentence with lively sensory details. Use a variety of words to show color and action. Imagine the sounds you might hear and some of the touch sensations you would experience: include these as well in the paragraph. Identify people you might see by using clear images.

Step 2.   Run-ons in a Paragraph. Correct the run-on errors and comma faults by changing some of the punctuation in the paragraph below. Capitalize the first letter of any word that starts a sentence. You may add words if you wish. Study the charts on pages 27–29 for review.

The View from My Window

Shivering, I look out my window and view the fury of the wind and snow on this blustery January day, as the storm-darkened sky approaches, I see the blue spruces and the dreary leafless maples cringe with fear. The aggressive wind races across the icy roads and creates a precarious moment for the jogger all bundled up in her green-and-blue sweat suit, her leather mittens, and her red, knitted cap, however she doesn't get very far today. Persistent, smoke-ejecting chimneys fight the wind that encircles them, similarly, the intense snow shoveller battles to dig a foot-wide tunnel through the white mountains. Gentle, peace-loving homes stand guard nearby their heavily snow-covered roofs sit silently below the hills, waiting for the next display of wrath, the crackling, crusted snow groans as if to inquire as to the rage of this stormy winter day. I take one last look outside thankful for the coziness of my kitchen, I turn from my window to let the storm conduct its business without me.

Step 3. Describing a Person. For further practice in description focus a paragraph on a person you observe. Ask one of the people in the class to stand in front of the room as a model. As you watch the person up front, decide on one single impression that the person creates: is the man or woman *handsome, nervous, playful, cheerful, charming, serious, strange, relaxed, confident?* After you state the impression in the topic sentence, describe the details that you feel contribute to that impression. Use images (see pages 5–7) to discuss the person's face, clothing, stance, gestures, and way of speaking to the class. Read your brief paragraphs aloud, as your instructor directs. But before you write, study the following sample and the chart of hints.

Richard

Richie Fries sits confidently atop the brown desk before us on this English theme day in late November. He speaks immediately, brown eyes sparkling at his audience of fellow classmates. His pressed blue shirt stresses his tall straight posture as his hand motions express words. He scratches his neat black hair as if in thought. "Next question!" he says. "Gotta wake you up. Ya look like you're falling asleep." The class watches his every expression, but there is no sign of nervousness in Richard, not a drop of sweat falling from his brow. "Look at me," his apple cheeks shout. "Look at me," his smile says. "Look," his position at the edge of the table screams. "Look at me. This is my moment of glory." His actual words race by at record pace. "My father tells me I should think in seventy-eight and talk in thirty-three," Rich speedily adds. Susan asks him to smile and change his position. Propping himself upon his elbow, he leans back on the desk. "Hey, why isn't this guy in Hollywood?" I think to myself. His eyes dance. They illuminate when he talks and glow softly when he is silent. His exciting brown eyes hold the class in a strong grip. They are only brown, same as so many other eyes, but they twinkle and they bubble and they look squarely at their audience without so much as a nervous blink. His eyes smile even when his lips fall. The girls like him: he is lively, has a good physique—I suppose it is understandable.

Michelle asks where he goes to meet girls and the class giggles squeamishly. After a long, funny answer, Richie leans back, the edges of his lips pushing his cheeks up. His brown eyes now stare at no one. Everybody is writing. He takes a deep breath. Then, in a sudden leap from the table Richie returns to his seat like a conqueror.

—*Debbie Osher*

HINTS FOR SUCCESSFUL PARAGRAPHS ABOUT A CLASSMATE

1. Mention in the first sentence the time, the place, and the single impression you have of the student.
2. Use some details of setting. Debbie Osher says "brown desk."
3. Use only those details in the rest of the paragraph that contribute to the single impression. *Leave out any details that do not help create the impression.*
4. Mention the person's size, color of hair and eyes, clothing. Use images of sound, color, and touch.
5. Write a sentence that tells what the model says. Richard says, "My father tells me I should think in seventy-eight and talk in thirty-three."
6. Toward the end of the paragraph, describe the one feature of the person's face that gives you the impression you have. Notice how in "Richard" the writer concentrates on the eyes of her subject.

Step 4. Your Own Photo Essay. With an Instamatic camera or a Polaroid, take several pictures of some room. Try to take pictures that will convey *one* dominant impression you have about the room. You may want to show that the room is a *lively* place or one that is *tense, happy, dull, hectic,* or *somber.* When you get the photos back, mount them and present them to the class. Ask other students to determine from your pictures the impression you are trying to create.

CHAPTER 2

NARRATION:
The Body in Action

INTRODUCTION: WRITING A NARRATIVE PAPER

If you have ever screamed yourself hoarse at a football game, if you have ever run miles along a river bank, or if you have ever slid into home plate to break a tie, you know the delight of sports and exercise and their hold on our lives. Both as spectator and participant you can, no doubt, recall many experiences, some joyful, others bitter. Maybe you remember the fear you felt at learning to ride a bicycle, or the spirit of teamwork that allowed you to win the freestyle relay at the town pool. Perhaps you still hear your coach's shrill voice yelling at you, or recall your father's consoling words, "Well, you did your best." Perhaps some moments in sports gave you a better understanding of your character, such as the time you tried to hurt your opponent while playing soccer or the time you let a friend score a basket when you yourself might just as easily have made the points. Maybe you are one of those enthusiasts of lifetime sports, running or swimming or biking to keep your body healthy. For you it is not simply competition that excites your blood: you enjoy the thrill of your limbs in action and the joy of mental release that accompanies vigorous exercise.

These moments that stand out vividly in your lives are the subjects for your next theme. The paragraph you write will narrate (tell a story about) a brief, meaningful event that you experienced with sports or exercise.

VOCABULARY

Step 1. Words for Actions. These words are useful in describing people's actions and help create specific pictures. Check a dictionary and write in the definitions in the blank spaces. See Appendix A for more help.

1. grimace _____
2. stagger _____
3. hurl _____
4. swagger _____
5. saunter _____
6. plunge _____
7. careen _____
8. bellow _____
9. collapse _____
10. lunge _____

Step 2.   Using New Vocabulary. Fill in each blank with a word from the list in Step 1 so that the sentences make sense.

1. When the workmen tested the microphones, the announcer's voice _____ through the vast, empty arena.

2. Grunting as he spun around to gather momentum, Ricardo _____ the shot put for a new county record.

3. Balancing herself carefully on the high diving board, Mary suddenly _____ into the icy water.

4. Hurt, exhausted, and dirty, the defeated football players _____ into the dressing room.

5. The wrestler _____ across the room, boasting that no one could match his strength.

6. Enjoying his slow, relaxed walk, the old man _____ around the block.

7. Because the driver was tired, his Pontiac _____ from one side of the road to the other.

8. As Sarah _____ her fencing foil at her opponent, she shouted, "Touché!"

9. After two overtimes, the team _____ on the bench with exhaustion.

Step 3.   How People Do or Say Things. The following words, all ending in -*ly*, are helpful in showing how people do or say things. Check them in a dictionary and write definitions. For more help, see Appendix A.

1. irresponsibly _____

2. contemptuously _____

3. sullenly _____

4. spontaneously _____

5. benevolently _____

6. brazenly _____

7. precariously _____

8. painstakingly _____

9. infrequently _____

10. vehemently _____

Step 4. Seeing the Words at Work.

1. When would you do something *vehemently?* _____

   _____

2. If a team played *infrequently,* how well would you expect them to play?

   _____

3. How could you tell if something was being done *spontaneously?* _____

   _____

4. Why might a teenager behave *sullenly?* _____

   _____

5. What types of workers would perform their jobs *precariously?* _____

   _____

6. If someone spoke *contemptuously,* how would you expect him to sound?

   _____

7. What kind of job would you do *painstakingly?* _____

   _____

8. How could you tell if someone acted *brazenly?* _____

   _____

9. How could someone tell if you were acting *benevolently* toward others?

   _____

10. How would a group of demonstrators have to act for you to say that they
    were *acting* irresponsibly? _____

    _____

BUILDING COMPOSITION SKILLS

Finding the Topic

One of the best ways to get ideas on any topic is to talk about and listen to the
ideas of the people around you. Thus you can air out your own thoughts and can
see how they sound before you begin to put them on paper. You also can recall
ideas about your own experiences when you hear the ideas your friends may
have.

Step 1.   Talking about the Topic. Pick any word group below and read it aloud, adding your own ending. Then, in a few more sentences, explain what you said. Or, if your instructor suggests, write a few brief sentences to complete any of the statements. Of course, you may use the name of any sport in place of the one used in the sentences below.

1. I played well when . . .
2. Losing a game is not so bad if . . .
3. The most satisfying sport is . . .
4. A game I'll never forget was . . .
5. The value of sports is . . .
6. Jogging makes me feel . . .
7. One thing I hate about sports is . . .
8. Watching World Cup soccer makes me . . .
9. When my coach yelled at me, I was . . .
10. I wish my son (daughter) would play . . .
11. When I swim, I . . .
12. When it comes to riding horses, I . . .
13. When I won my first game, I felt . . .
14. On my first bicycle trip I . . .
15. For bodily fitness my exercise is _____ because . . .

Here are some students' responses:

> A dangerous sport I like is skiing because the cold mountain air, the steep slopes, and the heart-pounding speed make me feel alive.
>
> —*Richard Young*
>
> I wish my son would play basketball more for enjoyment rather than for a victory over the other team. He takes the sport too seriously, and he broods over a loss for days.
>
> —*Willa Brown*
>
> The most satisfying sport is cross-country running. I am never more at peace with myself than when I run for hours through the cool green countryside.
>
> —*Lola Argentino*

Expanding the Topic Sentence

You can limit your topic sentence if you name your topic specifically and if you give your opinion about the topic. (If you need a quick review, see Chapter 1.) But you can further limit the topic sentence—especially when you write a paragraph that tells a story—by showing where and when the event you are writing about takes place. By *where* we mean the room, the outdoor setting, the physical location in which the moment happened. By *when* we mean not the date but the season or month of the year, the part of the day, the day of the week. Sometimes a word of color or sound or touch helps the *when* and *where* details come to life. Here are two topic sentences that give the topic and opinion, that tell when or where, and that use a sense word.

[time]   [place]   [opinion]

One winter evening in our school gymnasium I learned the importance of teamwork in basketball as the final bell clanged to end the game.

[sound]

Topic: teamwork in basketball

[time]   [place]   [opinion]

Every morning in the park I experience the agony of the long distance runner as I jog ten miles through the grey dawn.

[color]

Topic: jogging ten miles

Step 1. Adding Details. Add details of time or place or both to the topic sentences listed in Column I and rewrite them under Column II. If possible, use a sound, color, or touch word.

I   *II*

Example
1. My husband loves the excitement of watching hockey.

    On weekend evenings in our living room my husband, lying on our green sofa, loves the excitement of watching hockey.

2. Our energetic cheerleaders always helped our teams to win.

3. Deep sea divers are usually very cautious people.

4. My coach embarrassed me in front of the other football players.

   _____
   _____
   _____
   _____
   _____

5. My father enjoys the peacefulness of trout fishing.

   _____
   _____
   _____
   _____

6. I am always excited by the fast pace of a horse race.

   _____
   _____
   _____
   _____

Step 2.   Writing Sentence Openers. For each subject in Column I write a topic sentence that includes time and place, gives an opinion, and appeals in some way to one of the senses. Try to put the words that tell *where* or *when* right at the beginning of the sentence.

I   *II*

Example
1. team practice sessions

   Every Saturday morning I hate dragging my football equipment to Washington Field to practice for the next week's game.

2. canoeing in the rapids

   _____
   _____

3. watching a champion boxer

   _____
   _____

4. playing a doubles tennis match

_____
_____
_____
_____
_____

5. learning to swim

_____
_____
_____
_____
_____

6. a terrible defeat

_____
_____
_____
_____

Step 3.   Analyzing the Topic Sentence. Turn to the top of page 9. Look at the topic sentences numbered 1 and 2. What words tell the time of the event? Which of the topic sentences tells *place*?

Chronology

Whenever you narrate events, they are most easily understood when you write of them in the time order in which they happened. The arrangement of details or events according to time is *chronology*. Look at the two paragraphs below. The sentences on the right present the events in their order of occurrence, while those on the left jump around without logic from event to event.

Confused

On Wednesday evenings my uncle and I spend an enjoyable hour playing racquetball. On the way home we sometimes stop for a beer or ice cream; of course, the loser always pays the bill. We usually go into the sauna for ten minutes before hitting the showers. We change our clothing in the locker room, and play an exciting but exhausting hour of racquetball. My uncle picks me up in his station

Chronological

On Wednesday evenings my uncle and I spend an enjoyable hour playing racquetball. After dinner, my uncle picks me up in his station wagon and we zoom over to the Bethpage Racquetball Center. After a quick change of clothing in the locker room, we play an exciting but exhausting hour of racquetball. Then we usually go into the sauna for ten minutes before hitting the showers.

Confused

wagon and we zoom over to the Bethpage Racquetball Center. When I get home, I'm ready for a good night's sleep.

Chronological

On the way home, we sometimes stop for beer or ice cream; of course, the loser always pays the bill. When I get home, I'm ready for a good night's sleep.

Step 1. Chronology. Write four sentences in chronological order about each subject named below.

1. catching a fish

   a. _____

   b. _____

   c. _____

   d. _____

2. changing a bicycle tire

   a. _____

   b. _____

   c. _____

   d. _____

3. setting up a campsite

   a. _____

   b. _____

   c. _____

   d. _____

4. studying for an exam

   a. _____

   b. _____

   c. _____

   d. _____

Step 2. Telling the Order. Here is a good topic sentence that calls for a paragraph in *chronological order*. Write six or seven sentences in which you tell details in the order in which they might have occurred. Use a separate sheet of paper.

Driving along frozen mountain passes can be a hazardous experience on a dark February morning.

Expanding Sentences

One way to avoid writing a paragraph whose sentences are too much alike is to start one or two of them with a word that ends in -*ly*. You have a number of these words (called *adverbs*) in your vocabulary already (*swiftly, slowly, annoyingly, suddenly*). Step 3 of the Vocabulary section introduces some new and more difficult -*ly* words.

Step 1.   -*ly* Words for Variety. On a separate sheet of paper use each -*ly* word in Step 3 of the Vocabulary section to open a sentence of your own.

Example
Brazenly, my cousin announced, "I'm the best!"

Step 2.   Two -*ly* Openers. A very effective technique for opening sentences is to use two -*ly* words at the beginning. Separate the -*ly* words either with a comma or with *and* or *but*. Don't use two -*ly* words that mean exactly the same thing.

Example
Slowly, annoyingly, the actor's voice filled the theater.
Strongly and cautiously, the lion stalked its prey.

Write a sentence about each subject indicated below, starting each sentence with two -*ly* words. Use words from your own vocabulary and from the words in Step 3 of the Vocabulary section. Use a separate sheet of paper.

1. a base runner stealing home
2. a racing car speeding out of control
3. getting out of bed in the morning
4. a cat licking its fur
5. sneaking twenty minutes late into a classroom

SOLVING PROBLEMS IN WRITING

Quotations

One way of adding life to your narrative is to use the words spoken by a person who plays some part in your paragraph. It's usually more realistic and more lively to use the person's specific words rather than an indirect quotation, a statement that only summarizes what was said. Look at the difference:

1. My father said that I might be a good basketball player, but that he wanted me to study for my exam tomorrow.

2. My father shouted, "You might be a hot-shot basketball player, but I want you to study for that exam tomorrow!"

Sentence 2 has more force because it is a direct quotation; it lets the reader hear the person's exact words. Now, of course, if you are writing about a moment that occurred a while ago, it's impossible to remember *exactly* what a person said. Still, if you recall the general idea of the person's words, you can construct a sentence so that the reader hears it as a quotation.

Correct punctuation of quotations—exact words—is sometimes tricky. Remember that most quotation sentences have two parts: one part tells who is talking and how the person says the words; another part tells what is being said. These parts must be separated by punctuation. Study the charts below.

I. EXACT WORDS AT THE END

[quotation marks]
[Capitalize first spoken word.]

My father shouted, "You might be a hot-shot basketball player, but I want you to study for that exam tomorrow!" [quotation marks]

[comma]   [end mark inside; period, question mark, or exclamation point]

Hint: If the same person speaks another sentence—without being interrupted—right after the first one, *don't* use another quotation mark. Put the last quotation mark after the very *last* word any one person speaks.

My father shouted, "You might be a hot-shot basketball player, but I want you to study for that exam tomorrow. I won't put up with any more failing grades."

Step 1. Correct Quotations. Put in the correct punctuation for these sentences.

1. The defendant shouted I am innocent of all these charges
2. Will Rogers said I never met a man I didn't like
3. The movie star insisted I never give interviews
4. The astronaut explained it was like nothing I ever felt before
5. The instructor asked did anyone do this assignment

II. EXACT WORDS AT THE BEGINNING

[quotation marks]
[capital letter]   [small letter]

"You might be a hot-shot basketball player, but I want you to study for that exam tomorrow," my father shouted. [period]

[comma, question mark, or exclamation point inside quotation mark: no period]

[quotation marks]

Step 2.   Writing Quotations. Put in the correct punctuation for these sentences.

1. This will teach you a sense of responsibility my father snapped
2. Nobody ever wants to go first the doctor complained
3. Will wonders never cease Sam asked
4. I hope Dad comes home soon my sister said
5. Doesn't anyone care about me anymore he demanded fearfully

---

III. EXACT WORDS BROKEN UP

[quotation marks]   [small letter—sentence is continued]   [small letter—sentence is continued]

[capital]

"You might be a hot-shot basketball player," my father shouted, "but I want you to study for that exam tomorrow."   [open quotation again]

[close quotes]   [close quotes]

[end mark]   [comma]   [comma]

Step 3.   Punctuating Quotations. Punctuate these sentences correctly.

1. Didn't you know Barbara asked that Jim is in the hospital
2. It will do you no good Pat insisted to apologize now
3. Never mind the dessert Don said where's the salad
4. Two's company Val said but three's a crowd
5. If Paul were here Richard said he would know what to do

Hint

The question mark goes at the end of the complete question.

Step 4.   Practice with Exact Words. In Column I, write three sentences you have heard spoken recently. In Column II, rewrite each sentence with correct punctuation to show who did the talking. Sometimes a word like *shouted, muttered, whispered,* or *cried* is more vivid than *said.* In other sentences, *said* is adequate because the words in the quotation itself tell the tone the speaker is using. In one sentence, use the spoken words at the beginning; in another, use the spoken words at the end. In one sentence, break up the spoken words as in Chart III, above. One of each appears in the examples below.

I   *II*

Examples

"Are you serious about joining the track team?"

"Hey, we'd better move or we'll be late for class."

"This cafeteria coffee is poisonous!"

Trying to stifle a laugh, my friend asked, "Are you serious about joining the track team?"

"Hey, we'd better move," someone insisted, "or we'll be late for class."

"This cafeteria coffee is poisonous!" gasped Peter, frowning.

1. _____   _____

   _____   _____

   _____   _____

   _____   _____

2. _____   _____

   _____   _____

   _____   _____

   _____   _____

3. _____   _____

   _____   _____

   _____   _____

Step 5.   Punctuation Review. Punctuate these sentences correctly. Both direct and indirect quotations are included.

1. Every morning my mother would switch on the lights and would shout rise and shine
2. In ten years as a gymnast Lydia insisted I've never seen a person as agile on the parallel bars as Terry
3. I've been told that when I was two years old my father threw me in the water and suggested that I learn how to swim
4. Tim called to me from behind the house I want to tell you something important
5. Come on up and see for yourself Henry shouted in front of his booth at the county fair

Sentence Fragments: Part I

The *fragment* is an incomplete part of a sentence used as though it were a sentence itself. Here are some fragments that are easy to recognize.

1. Over the curb and into the street.
2. Pushing angrily through the crowds.
3. Just to play his radio quietly.
4. Usually exhausted from lifting heavy cartons.

None of these fragments makes any real sense. Since a sentence contains a complete thought and has a subject and a verb (see the sentence review on pages 15–17), the word groups above are not sentences.

Fragment 1 has no subject or verb. *What* is being done over the curb and into the street? *Who* is doing it?

Fragment 2 has no subject (*Who* does the pushing?) and only a part of a verb—the word *pushing*.

Fragment 3 has no subject (*Who* plays the radio?) and only part of a verb—the infinitive *to play*. (You may recall that if *to* is used like this, what results is merely the starting point of a verb, not a verb itself.)

Fragment 4 has no subject (*Who* was exhausted after lifting heavy cartons?). The word group would also need a word like *is* or *was* in order to be complete. Here *exhausted* without a helper is no verb.

Each fragment, 1, 2, 3, 4 above, separated from the sentence that comes before it, is easy to recognize because it really makes no sense. But now look at the fragments as they appear as parts of paragraphs and read the explanations alongside.

Fragment	*Explanation*
1. *a.* In a square of pavement down the block a small dog played with a rubber ball, but it rolled out of his reach. *b.* He rushed after it. *c.* Over the curb and into the street.	Here a student might think that the subject *he* and the verb *rushed* in sentence *b* would also serve as subject and verb in word group *c*. But that is not the case. Word group *c* is a fragment because it lacks its own subject and verb. The capital letter in *over* and the period after *street* indicate that the writer thought the sentence a complete one.
2. *a.* Holiday shopping is always a difficult task. *b.* Every store I visit overflows with noisy shoppers. *c.* Pushing angrily through the crowds. *d.* I'll try to shop earlier next year.	Here, a student might think that the word *shoppers* in sentence *b* would serve as the subject in word group *c*. But word group *c* must have its own subject. Furthermore, the word *pushing* is not a verb: if *is* or *was* appeared before it, or if the word were *pushed* instead of *pushing*, it would be a verb. But as it stands, word group *c* is also a fragment because it lacks a verb.
3. *a.* It is important to understand that teenagers often require privacy. *b.* For an hour or two a boy wishes to be left alone in his room. *c.* Just to play his radio quietly.	Here, it is possible that an inexperienced writer would imagine the word *boy* in sentence *b* serves as the subject in word group *c*. But word group *c* must have its own subject to be complete. In addition, *to play* is no verb. We need to add a word such as *wants* or *likes* before the infinitive. Sometimes the infinitive can be changed to a verb: *plays, played,* or *is playing*. But as it stands, word group *c* is also a fragment because it lacks a verb.

4. *a.* My mother works very long hours to support our family. *b.* She trudges home at eight o'clock every evening. *c.* Usually exhausted from lifting heavy cartons. She falls asleep by nine-thirty.

Here, the writer gives no subject in word group *c*. Furthermore, *exhausted*—as it is used—is only a part of a verb. It must have *is* or *was* or some such word before it. So, word group *c* is also a fragment because it lacks a verb.

Fixing Fragments

Knowing that sentence fragments lack subjects, complete verbs, or both, you should not find this kind of sentence error difficult to correct.

1. Add a subject and a verb to make the sentence complete.

Correct this Fragment	*This Way*
Over the curb and into the street.	[added subject] The dog jumped over the curb and into the street. [added verb]
Pushing angrily through the crowds.	[subject] They are pushing angrily through the crowds. [word added to make verb] They push angrily through the crowds. [-*ing* word changed to verb]
Just to play his radio quietly.	[subject] He just wants to play his radio quietly. [word added to make verb] He just plays his radio quietly. [infinitive changed to verb]
Usually exhausted from lifting heavy cartons.	[subject] She is usually exhausted from lifting heavy cartons. [word added to make verb]

Step 1. Completing Sentences. The last word group in each item below is a fragment. Rewrite the fragment in the space provided and add a subject, a verb, or both in order to make the sentence complete. You may wish to change an *-ing* word or an infinitive to a verb; or you may wish to add a new verb as a helper.

1. I swaggered out of the classroom. Knowing that I passed the exam.

_____

_____

_____

2. Imagine my disappointment when I went to the refrigerator and looked for the apples. Already eaten by my brother Juan.

_____

_____

_____

3. Trevor finally got his pilot's license. Flying an average of ten hours a week.

_____

_____

_____

4. Millions of people are jogging. To stay fit and healthy.

_____

_____

_____

5. Jaime often asked questions during the game. To understand the rules better.

_____

_____

_____

2. Another way to fix the fragment is to connect it to the sentence that comes before it. In that way you legitimately give the fragment the subject and verb it needs by using words of another sentence. Notice how the last two sentences in 1, 2, and 3 on page 64 may be joined together to eliminate the fragment:

Correct the Fragment	*This Way*
He rushed after it. Over the curb and into the street.	[small letter] He rushed after it over the curb and into the street. [no period]
Every store I visit overflows with noisy shoppers. Pushing angrily through the crowds.	Every store I visit overflows with noisy shoppers, pushing angrily through the crowds. [no period] [small letter]
For an hour or two a boy wishes to be left alone in his room. Just to play his radio quietly.	For an hour or two a boy wishes to be left alone in his room just to play his radio quietly. [no period] [small letter]

3. A fragment may be corrected effectively by attaching it to the sentence that comes after it.

Correct the Fragment	*This Way*
Usually exhausted from lifting heavy cartons. She falls asleep by nine-thirty.	Usually exhausted from lifting heavy cartons, she falls asleep by nine-thirty. [comma] [small letter]

Here is another example:

Correct the Fragment	*This Way*
Hearing the photographer talk about his travels through Alaska. Audiences responded with enthusiasm.	Hearing the photographer talk about his travels through Alaska,[comma] audiences responded with enthusiasm. [small letter]

Hint

When you open a sentence with a fragment that contains an *-ing* verb part or an *-ed* verb part, follow the fragment with a comma.

Step 2. Correcting the Fragment. Each of these groups contains at least one fragment. Correct the error by adding the fragment either to the sentence that comes before or to the sentence that comes after. Write your new sentence in the blank spaces alongside.

Hint

Make sure that the new sentence you have written makes sense.

1. Going into the twentieth inning. I thought I would faint. Staring at the scoreboard. I actually wished the other team would hit a home run.

   _____
   _____
   _____
   _____

2. Just thirty minutes of yoga a day will keep you in good shape. Without too much strain. You will feel more alert, too.

   _____
   _____
   _____
   _____

3. It's no wonder people find it hard to be independent. Everywhere we turn someone gives us orders. At home, in school, on the job.

   _____
   _____
   _____
   _____

4. The large, gas-guzzling automobile will soon disappear. Replaced by smaller, more economical cars. Large vehicles are already losing popularity.

   _____
   _____
   _____

5. In America everyone recognizes the extent of the recession. Even the President and the members of Congress. But they cannot agree on how to end it.

_____
_____
_____
_____

Finding Fragments

Here are some suggestions for learning to recognize sentence fragments of the type described in this chapter.

1. Read your paragraph aloud. Learn to tell the difference between pauses between words and stops between sentences. A pause often requires a comma. A full stop requires a period or one of the other end marks, a question mark or an exclamation point. A semicolon may also indicate a complete stop between sentences.
2. Read the sentences of your paragraph from the last to the first. In that way you'll be listening for complete thoughts that make sense.
3. Look for an -ing word used incorrectly as the verb in a sentence.
4. Make sure every sentence has its own subject and its own verb. (See item 7 in the sentence review, page 17, for "understood" subjects.)
5. Make sure every sentence expresses a complete thought by itself.
6. Watch out for these "Fragment Stop Signs: Group I" because they are expressions that often open word groups that fail to include subjects and verbs.

Fragment Stop Signs: Group I

just	especially
for instance	for example
such as	like
also	mainly

If you open a sentence with one of these words or word combinations, be sure that a subject and verb come later on in the sentence.

Study the review chart below before moving on to the next steps.

A FRAGMENT FINDER

1. Read aloud. Listen for incomplete thoughts.
2. Look out for *-ing* words, especially when they start sentences.
3. Look for subject and verb in each sentence.
4. Read paragraph from last sentence to first. Stop after each sentence and ask: Is it a complete thought?
5. Know Group 1 of the Fragment Stop Signs:

just	mainly
especially	for instance
for example	like
also	such as

A FRAGMENT FIXER

1. Add subject, verb, or both.
2. Add fragment to sentence that comes before or sentence that comes after. Make sure final sentence makes sense.
3. Change an *-ing* word to a verb by using *is, was, are, were, am* in front of it. Or, change *-ing* word to a verb.
4. If you put an *-ing* fragment or another "verb-part" fragment in front of a complete sentence, use a comma after the fragment.
5. Change an infinitive to a verb by removing "to" and by using the correct form of the verb. Or, put one of these verbs before the infinitive: *like(s), want(s), plan(s), try(tries), is, was, were, are, am.*

Example

Fragment	**Corrected**
John works weekends. To earn money for college.	John works weekends. He *earns* money for college.
	OR
	John works weekends. *He likes* to earn money for college.

Step 1.   Eliminating Fragments. The sentence groups below contain *one or more* sentence fragments. Correct the fragments by using any of the methods you have learned so far. Cross out words, add words, change or remove punctuation. If the set of sentences is correct, mark it *C* Use a separate sheet of paper.

1. Watching my first rugby match. I thought of how easy this game makes American football look. As easy as pie. There is never a break in the action. Not even for an injury.

2. Watch out for words said in anger. They can hurt people, especially the ones you love.

3. Avitar XRC. A sports car to set you free. See it at your nearest dealer.

4. Old people face many terrible problems. For example, their dependence on fixed incomes. Poor medical care in nursing homes. Also, neglected by their own relatives.

5. I have trained to be a sprinter. My lungs no longer give way after a half-mile run.

6. Kathy walked to the foot of the bed. Gripped the bedposts. Looking concerned. "How are you feeling today?" she asked.

7. We gained much in the few months we were apart. Together vowing never to take each other for granted again.

8. Many athletic events attract large crowds only because the sports are violent and bloody. Such as ice hockey and boxing.

9. She lifted herself painfully from the chair. Like an old woman of eighty. She sighed and let her breath out slowly. To make us believe that she was really in pain.

10. The South is unlike the other sections of our country. In many ways. Its magnificent architecture is a blend of the past and the present. Modern skyscrapers soaring over quaint, wooden townhouses.

Step 2.   Avoiding the Fragment Error. Use each of these word groups to open a sentence of your own. Complete the sentence in the space provided.

Hint
If you follow the word group with a complete sentence, use a comma after the opening word group.

1. To smoke a cigarette

_____

_____

2. Stopped by a police officer

_____

_____

3. Running around in circles

_____

_____

4. Stuck by cactus needles

_____

_____

5. Bleeding from the cut on her leg

_____

_____

6. Storming into the classroom

_____

_____

7. Covered with mud

_____

_____

8. Laughing so hard

_____

_____

9. Sweating profusely

_____

_____

10. Depressed by low grades

_____

_____

Step 3. Correcting Fragments: A Review. Each of the following passages was written by a professional writer but has been altered to include sentence fragments. In each selection, correct the fragments, using any of the methods discussed in this chapter. Ask your instructor for a copy of the original passages to compare with your corrections.

1. This morning I got a note from my aunt. Asking me to come for lunch. I know what this means. Since I go there every Sunday for dinner and today is Wednesday, it can only mean one thing . . . .

—Walker Percy

2. Sula would come by of an afternoon. Walking along with her fluid stride. Wearing a plain yellow dress . . . .

—Toni Morrison

3. Just as he started to turn off the lamp. He thought he saw something in the hall . . . He leaned over. To look for something to throw.

—Raymond Carver

4. He was at his letter-writing desk. Again in the morning. The little desk at the window was black. Rivaling the blackness of his fire escape . . . .

—Saul Bellow

5. Once down at the creek. Blinking at the yellow-birds that fluttered and disappeared and reappeared above their heads. With his back against the big oak as usual. The old man would relax.

—Joyce Carol Oates

WRITING THE NARRATIVE PARAGRAPH

> ASSIGNMENT: Your assignment for this theme is to write a paragraph of at least twelve to fifteen sentences to narrate one moment in which you reveal some experience you had with exercise or with sports. To *narrate* means to tell the story of an event in such a way that your reader can easily follow the sequence of events of the experience you choose to relate. As with descriptive writing, narration also makes use of vivid and concrete details and images. Before you write, take a look at the checklist on pages 77–78.

As you write this narrative, confine the action to a single moment. These suggestions will help you:

1. A "moment" is a memorable instance in your life that illustrates some opinion or idea you want to write about.
2. A "moment" is limited as much as possible in time; it is a brief span of time that you recall sharply.
3. You must make this "moment" as vivid for your reader as it was for you when you experienced it. In order to do this, you need to fill in details with concrete sensory language. Remember that you create pictures (images) by using sensory words that will let the reader share your experience.
4. What kinds of details do you need to make the moment come alive? Show some images of the setting (where the moment occurs) through color, smell, touch, and sound; describe the people who participate in the moment (show their faces and actions); use bits of important dialogue that people speak as the moment develops.

Step 1.   Reading Samples. Read the paragraphs below, written by students in response to the same assignment. When you finish reading each paragraph, answer the questions on expanded topic sentences, sensory language, chronological order, and sentence variety.

Chicken

One hot July afternoon at Hecksher State Park Pool I finally tried diving but suffered defeat. I was in the water when I suddenly noticed someone on the diving platform. Quickly and gracefully the muscular young man bounced off the blue board. As he hit the water, a small splash leaped up. He made it seem so simple and so much fun that suddenly I wanted to try it. I could do it; I knew I could. Brazenly I scampered out of the water and ran across the hot concrete floor to the ladder, stepping in small puddles that I passed. As I looked up, I saw someone in a bright yellow bikini stepping down. She looked into my eyes and confessed, "I've changed my mind. That's too high and the water's too deep for me." "Chicken," I thought to myself and slowly climbed the steps one by one. Suddenly I thought to myself, "What if I don't make it? What if I drown? Think positive; you'll do it, and then you'll be able to dive every time you come to the pool." I kept repeating those words to myself as I nervously reached the top. I stood there proudly, yards above everyone at the pool. "Hey, everybody, look at me, I'm going to dive." Placing one foot in front of the other, I inched my way to the tip of the board. Looking down into the clear blue water, I saw my faint reflection. The water looked so cool and inviting as I felt the hot sun burning my back. The smell of chlorine drifted up as I heard the screams and laughter of the young children below me. As I glanced around, red and blue sun umbrellas whirled together in front of my eyes. "Hurry it up, will you," someone behind me said. "Okay, okay," I said, "here I go." I bounced once, then twice. I smiled as I swung my arms in front of me, still not daring to jump. I counted aloud, "One, two, three." Then suddenly I stopped bouncing, quickly balanced myself and did an about-face. Staggering back to the ladder, I pushed everyone aside as I stepped down. When I reached the hot pool deck, I realized what I had done. I looked into a pair of brown, sympathetic eyes and muttered, "I couldn't do it." Touching my shoulder, my sister replied, "Maybe some other time, Liz." "Yes, maybe," I said, but I thought to myself, "Chicken."

—*Elizabeth Santiago*

1. What is the topic of this paragraph? What is the writer's opinion about the topic?
2. Which quotation sentence is most realistic, one that includes words you think a person might really say in the situation?
3. Which image in the paragraph is most clear? Where has Elizabeth Santiago used color most effectively? Which actions are especially well presented?
4. Why is the title a good one?
5. What does *scampered* mean? Why does the writer say "scampered out of the water" instead of "went out of the water"?
6. Which sentence opens with two -*ly* words?
7. The events in the selection you read follow a strict chronological arrangement. Below, several important details from the selection are listed. But they appear in the wrong time sequence. Put number 1 in front of the first event that occurred; number 2 in front of the second; and so on.

_____ Liz pushed everyone aside as she stepped down.

_____ Liz heard the screams and laughter of the young children.

_____ Liz scampered out of the water and ran quickly over to the ladder.

_____ Liz said to her sister, "I couldn't do it."

_____ Liz saw the muscular young man bounce off the diving board.

Buck Fever

One blustery November morning I thought I would experience the thrill of shooting my first deer, but at the last moment I was seized by that dreaded hunter's ailment, buck fever. I was staying at my sister's house when, early in the morning, my brother-in-law Frank came into my room. The clumping of his boots on the bare wooden floors woke me in an instant. In a whisper Frank made my dream come true. "Do you want to go hunting with me this morning at the farm?" he asked. I leaped out of bed and jumped into my gray longjohns, my woolen hunting suit, and my orange plastic vest. Following Frank into his navy Ford pickup, I quickly pulled my yellow knit cap tightly over my head and ears. He started driving us over fifteen miles of slick, ice-covered country roads across the state line to Frank's father's farm. We parked behind the farmhouse and trudged through the snow-covered fields. The deep mysterious smell of the woods surrounded me, and as the pink light of dawn guided our way, I heard the wind rustle eerily through the bare birch and poplar trees. To encircle the meadow, we split up. Frank turned left and I trekked right. We had been apart for about fifteen minutes when I saw the soft, brown skin of a deer down in the creek bed at the bottom of the meadow. Stealthily, cautiously, I tiptoed forward so I wouldn't startle the deer, although I was sure that my heartbeat sounded like cannons firing. The small deer heard me and looked up. I even stopped breathing for fear he would run away. Luckily he lowered his head again and foraged for some sprouts of grass under the snow. At that, I brought my rifle up to my shoulder and took careful aim through the cold, steel sight. The deer brought his head up again and stared right at me. Through the sight I could see drops of moisture at the corners of his eyes. It was at that moment that buck fever struck me, the paralysis that comes when you think too much about the life you are about to take. It's the disease all hunters fear, and it overtook me so suddenly that I started shaking. I dropped the rifle from my shoulder to my side. The thump of the wood and metal slapping against my leg startled the deer who jumped in surprise and darted away through the woods. I never recovered from buck fever: I never went hunting again.

—*John Scoville*

1. What is your reaction to the topic sentence? Does it state the topic clearly? Does it give an opinion?
2. How does the title serve the writer's purpose in the paragraph?
3. Which images are most original? Identify pictures that appeal to the sense of sight, smell, and sound.
4. Is the sequence of events clear? Which transitions does the writer use to help the reader move easily through time?

Fishing with My Father

On an exciting summer day in mid-July in the middle of Sabago Lake my father helped me reel in my very first catch. At first, everything was quiet around us. There were no human voices, cars, or planes to break the silence of the still pond. It was a perfect day for fishing. The sky was a brighter blue than usual, and puffs of white clouds raced overhead. We sat hushed, afraid to talk, thinking that the fish would hear us and would stay away. As we sat there, my father, holding his pole in one hand, passed me some lunch. I put down my brown chipped rod to take a sandwich wrapped in tin foil from him. The foil reflected the bright sunlight onto the water. With my mouth filled with peanut butter, I whined, "When do you think the fish will bite? We've been in this boat forever." It was terribly hot, for the sun hung directly over us, and the mosquitoes had told me hours ago that they favored my blood the best. Buzz. Smack! Another body dropped to the bottom of the boat. "These things are eating me alive," I complained to my father. Suddenly my line tightened and my sinker moved. "Dad, it moved; what do I do now?" My father, now as excited as I was, crawled over to my side of the boat. Everything rocked. Little circles with white bubbles formed on the water. Dad took the rod from me and, grasping it firmly like a champion fisherman, pulled and reeled the line in. "First you pull a little to let it know who's boss," he explained excitedly. "Then you bring it in gradually." In complete control of the pole he alternately reeled and jerked the line. Finally, a six-inch silvery blue perch sailed through the air, dangling on my line. The fish landed on the seat of the boat, flapping wildly and gasping for air. I picked the perch up, looked into its gaping mouth, and then plopped the struggling body into a pail of water. The fish regained consciousness and swam around unharmed for the moment. I think it knew that it would be part of our dinner that night.

—*Lenora Hines*

1. What words in the topic sentence show Lenora Hines' attitude toward her fishing experience with her father?
2. Why does the writer say "on a warm summer day" and "in the middle of Sabago Lake" in the first sentence?
3. Why are the quotations particularly effective in this narration?
4. Which action words make this theme come alive?
5. Which words appeal to the reader's sense of sound and color?

Some Topics to Think About

In case you need help in finding a moment about which to write, perhaps one of these titles will give you an idea.

1. My Coach's Temper	11. Proving Myself
2. Training for Victory	12. Alone on a Run
3. A Special Win	13. The Agony of Jogging
4. Special Endurance	14. Skiing Thrills
5. A Crushing Defeat	15. Soccer and Me
6. The Meaning of Sportsmanship	16. Fishing with Friends
7. Runners-up	17. From the Grandstand
8. My Moment of Glory	18. Full Court Press
9. A Bicycle Ride I Won't Forget	19. Dead Last
10. Learning from Losing	20. In the Swim

For some more topic ideas turn to page 55 and reread the sentences in Step 1.

Prewriting

Another prewriting strategy (see page 39) to loosen up ideas on a topic is *brainstorming*. Brainstorming is usually a technique in which a group of people meet in order to stimulate thinking on some idea or problem. People who brainstorm ask lots of questions about the problem at hand, trying then to answer them. To brainstorm on your own about some topic you are considering, make up questions that can generate information and details. On a scratch page write the words *Who? What? Where? When? Why?* and *How?* Then, try to answer the questions in short word groups or in full sentences.

BRAINSTORMING

Topic: baseball game

Who? my brother Pete and I
What? helped lose the game
Where? Highland Park in Fairfield, New Jersey
When? last July, a humid afternoon
Why? both poor players, inexperienced, clumsy, nervous
How? I struck out 3 times, Pete dropped 2 fly balls
                                        —Jerome Haag

Another kind of brainstorming involves the writer in more detailed questioning about the topic. You think on paper in question form about all the various things you want to ask in regard to the subject you have identified.

BRAINSTORMING

Topic: learning to swim

When did I learn to swim? I was eight years old, and I remember
being scared. Why? Fell into the creek at Cole's Farm three
years before. Who helped me learn? My sister Bertie. How did
she get me to do it? Why was I stupid enough to try again,
being so scared? She dared me. When was this? June afternoon on
the way home from school on the very last day. We were at the
creek again. What did the scene look like? What did Bertie say?
How did I feel when she held me under my stomach, making me
kick my feet and move my arms? How did the water feel? What did
I smell, feel, hear at my first swimming lesson?
                                        —Wilma Hanson

Hint

In brainstorming activities concentrate on getting ideas down on paper. Don't worry about spelling or other matters of correctness. And don't censor any of your ideas.

As with any other prewriting activity, the exercise in brainstorming allows you to develop from it a rough draft that expands on some or all of the ideas you have generated. You might need to group some of the thoughts you've written in brainstorming before you attempt your first draft.

Step 1.   Stirring up Ideas. Write your exercise or sports topic in a word or two on the top of a blank page. Next, list at 2- or 3-inch intervals along the left-hand margin the questions *Who? What? Where? When? Why?* and *How?* Then start filling in your responses. Or, you might wish to generate more detailed questions about the topic, questions you try to answer after you write them. Look at the two samples above.

Progress Reminders: A Checklist

1. Have I carefully selected my topic so that it is limited to one   _____
    brief moment for narration? (Review the definition of
    moment on page 72.)
2. Have I included rich sensory detail to bring that moment to   _____
    life?
3. Have I used a prewriting strategy that was comfortable to   _____
    me, such as the brainstorming technique that answers the
    questions *Who? What? When? Where? Why?* and *How?* about a
    topic?
4. As I wrote various drafts, did I include more details to make   _____
    my ideas clearer to the reader?
5. Did I present a clear sequence of events as I narrated my   _____
    moment?
6. Did I use images of *color* in several places in the paragraph?   _____
7. Did I show people as they performed various actions?   _____
8. Did I pay particular attention to describing the faces of the   _____
    people I wrote about? The eyes are particularly easy to write
    about; you can combine color with another sense like touch
    (*moist, hard, soft,* and so on).
9. Did I use several words that appeal to the sense of *sound?*   _____
    The essay "Chicken" (pages 72–73) includes "screams and
    laughter of young children" and "Fishing with My Father"
    contains such words as *buzz* and *smack.*
10. Did I show details of *touch* and *smell* of the scene in which the
    moment occurs? They were

touch: _____

smell: _____

11. Did I write a topic sentence that states a limited topic   _____
    through some opinion or attitude word?

12. Did I name time (month, part of the day, season) and place   _____
    (a special room, a street, a sports arena, a gym) as soon as
    possible in my paragraph, preferably in the topic sentence?

13. Did I start at least one sentence with an *-ly* word? Did I start   _____
    another sentence with two *-ly* words separated by a comma
    or   *and?*   These   two   words   are _____ and
    _____ .

14. Did I attempt to use some of the new words on pages 52–53?   _____

15. Did I make sure to include at least one quotation sentence   _____
    that gives someone's exact words? (Check the review charts
    on pages 60–61 for correct punctuation.)

16. Did I check my theme for errors, especially the fragment   _____
    mistakes explained earlier in this chapter and the run-on
    error explained in Chapter 1? Did I examine my Theme
    Progress Sheet (page 523) and my Individual Spelling List
    (page 481)?

17. Did I proofread my paragraph at least twice: once *before* I   _____
    prepared my final manuscript and once *after* it?

18. Did I give my paragraph a lively title? See pages 109–110 for _____
    some help.

GETTING READER RESPONSE

Give a draft of your paragraph to a classmate along with the checklist below. Ask
him or her to fill it out as completely as possible after reading your paper. Read
the responses and then spend fifteen to twenty minutes brainstorming on each
of your paragraphs. "Yes and No" questions should be answered *Yes, No,* or
Unsure; other responses should be as detailed as possible.

1. Is the topic clearly stated?   _____

   The topic as I understand it is _____

   _____

2. Are the sensory images clear and specific?   _____

   The best sensory images are _____

3. Is the time sequence in the story clear enough?   _____

Is there any point where you are confused by a "jump" in the   _____
action?

4. Is the "moment" of the experience limited enough?   _____

5. Are the six brainstorming questions suggested on page 76
sufficiently answered for you? If not, which ones need to be

described in more detail?_____

THE PROFESSIONALS SPEAK

Significant experiences with sports or exercise are often the basis for dramatic
narratives by professional writers. These writers work from the same kinds of
experiences you have been asked to write from in this theme.

Step 1.   Reading Two Professional Samples. Read the excerpts below and
answer the questions after each selection.

SOME WORDS TO KNOW BEFORE YOU READ

sadistically: cruelly
discernible: capable of being seen
resilience: ability to bounce back, to return to original form
adept: skilled
osmosis: the gradual movement of a substance through some kind of barrier

An Important Lesson

It was an early September day, cool and bright and just right for running, and I
was in the first few miles of a 10½-mile race over a course sadistically boobytrapped
with steep, exhausting hills. Still, I felt rested and springy; despite the hills it was
going to be a fine run.

Just ahead of me was Peggy Mimno, a teacher from Mount Kisco, New York. She
too was running easily, moving along efficiently at my speed. The pace felt
comfortable, so I decided to stay where I was; why bother concentrating on pace
when she was setting such a nice one? I'd overtake her later on when she tired.

So I tucked in behind her. The course headed north for five miles, wandered west
for a hilly mile, then turned south again along a winding road. The race was getting
tougher. We had four miles left and already it was beginning to be real work. I was
breathing hard, and my legs were turning to mush.

Peggy overtook a young male runner. Apparently she knew him, for they
exchanged a few cheerful words as she passed him. Their exchange worried me. You
don't chat during a race unless you are feeling good, and Peggy plainly was. There
was still a discernible bounce in her stride, but whatever resilience I'd once possessed
had long since left me.

Still, I was close enough to overtake her if she tired, so I didn't give up hope completely. We were approaching a long, punishing hill now and it would be the test. We were a mile from the finish line, so whatever happened on the hill would almost certainly determine who crossed it first.

As I moved up the hill, working hard, my attention wandered for a few minutes. When I looked up, Peggy was moving away—first five yards, then ten, then more. Finally it was clear that there was no hope of catching her. She beat me decisively.

There is an important lesson in that race. Much of what you read about running makes a sharp distinction between the sexes. Women are assumed to be weaker, slower and not nearly as adept athletically. (For example, women are always being told how to place their feet and hold their arms; the assumption is that any man simply knows such things, perhaps through some kind of male osmosis.) Yet as Peggy Mimno so clearly demonstrated, the similarities between male and female runners are more important than the differences. I have run with a number of women, both in training and in competition, and I can testify that it is often hard work.

—*James F. Fixx*
The Complete Book of Running

1. Why does James Fixx use the narrative technique in the above excerpt?
2. Which sentence best states the main point of this selection?
3. Which words show most effectively the hard work involved in running a race?
4. Why is the first sentence an effective one?
5. What important lesson did Fixx learn from his race?

SOME WORDS TO KNOW BEFORE YOU READ

entourage: followers and friends
theoretically: in theory, not in reality
pseudopsychological: pertaining to false psychology
ferocity: fierceness -
unanimous: complete agreement

"Let's Call It a Day"

The blood was flowing from inside Joe Frazier's mouth and trickling from his nose. The skin was puffed under the right eye and both above and below the left eye, and as Frazier made his way back to his corner at the end of the fourteenth round, Eddie Futch, his manager, his trainer, and his friend, came to an immediate decision. "Let's call it a day," Futch said.

"Don't," Frazer said, "don't stop it." But there was no conviction in his words. Joe Frazier always listens to Eddie Futch, and now Futch was telling his fighter that his bid to become the third man ever to regain the heavyweight championship was ended, that once again, despite a display of courage that was awesome, Frazier had lost to the man he calls Cassius Clay.

Futch leaned over Frazier and pulled one of his strong fists toward him and took out a pair of scissors and began to cut away at Frazier's red eight-ounce boxing gloves. In front of the challenger, the referee, Carlos Padilla, Jr., saw Futch's action and waved his arms, signaling the end. Across the ring, Angelo Dundee caught the signal and shouted, "It's all over," and reached down and lifted his man, Muhammad Ali, off his stool.

And then as chaos broke loose in his corner, as the members of his entourage jostled for position the way they always do, Muhammad Ali lay down on the floor of the ring and caught his breath. He was still the champion of the world, the winner on a technical knockout in 14 rounds.

For the fourth time in this calendar year, he had successfully defended the title he took from George Foreman a year ago, but all the other victims together—Chuck Wepner, Ron Lyle, and Joe Bugner—didn't put up half the struggle Joe Frazier did in a magnificent prenoon battle in the sweltering heat of the theoretically air-conditioned Philippine Coliseum.

"I don't know how he stood up," said Ali after the fight. "I know I would have gone down under all those punches I threw. He is greater than I thought he was."

A few days ago, Ali was saying that the fight would end early, possibly even in the first round, that Frazier was slow and soft and finished, that the fight would not even be close. But this fight was close. There wasn't a knockdown, and even though all three officials, the Filipino referee and the two Filipino judges, had Ali ahead on points by a comfortable margin after 14 rounds, there were many at ringside who thought Frazier, the underdog, outweighed by about nine pounds, was leading or at least even.

A crowd of 25,000 that paid $1.5 million—both records for an indoor fight—watched a fight that begin with pseudopsychological warfare and ended with street slugging.

Frazier entered the ring first, wearing blue trunks with a dull finish and white piping. By the time he reached his corner, he was already drenched with sweat.

Then Ali came in, his trunks a shiny white with black piping, the glitter of his trunks and the dullness of Frazier's a perfect symbolic contrast. There was not a drop of sweat on Ali. He did not sweat at all until the fight began.

Someone brought into the ring a handsome trophy, and the ring announcer said that the trophy would be presented by President Ferdinand Marcos, who was in the audience, to the winner. Ali didn't wait. He scampered into the center of the ring, grabbed the trophy, and lugged it back to his corner, looking at Frazier defiantly, as if daring the challenger to come take it back.

And then the fight began and in the early rounds, the first two or three, Ali seemed to be in complete command, almost toying with Frazier, giving a boxing lesson. In the last 30 seconds of the first round, Ali rocked Frazier with a left hook and a few seconds later, connected with a straight right. When the round ended, Frazier gave the champion a little tap on the rear and walked back to his own corner with a sort of goofy smile on his face.

In the third round, for the first time, Frazier rocked Ali with a left hook, and the sound and ferocity of the blow drew oohs from the crowd. Ali, responding more to the crowd than to the punch, turned and made a face, opening his mouth wide, as if to say that sounded a lot tougher than it felt. He was making fun, Angelo Dundee said later. But it hurt him. I saw his legs when it landed.

In the middle rounds, from about the fourth through the eighth, Frazier was in charge most of the time. He was the aggressor, and even when Ali flurried and pounded him with combinations, Frazier kept boring in, kept punching. The goofy look was gone.

And in those middle rounds, a strange thing happened: Ali lost the crowd. Before the fifth round, he led his followers in chants of "Ali, Ali, Ali," but the men in

Frazier's corner came back with chants of "Joe, Joe, Joe," and then the crowd, basically Filipino, started shouting, "Frazier, Frazier, Frazier."

The feeling was by no means unanimous, but enough of the Filipinos felt that Ali was too *mayabang,* too cocky, for their tastes, and so they wanted the underdog, the less boostful man to win. Apparently, Filipinos admire cockiness when two cocks fight—not when two men fight.

By the eighth round, the blood began to roll out of Frazier's mouth, some of it staining Ali's white trunks. But Ali was accomplishing little in those rounds, often allowing Frazier to back him into a corner and pound away at him. His corner yelled instructions. "Stay there," meaning in the middle of the ring, and "Don't hook"—you never hook with a hooker, Dundee said later—but Ali seemed to ignore the counsel.

By the twelfth round, Ali was definitely running the show again, manipulating Frazier, dictating the pace and the fury of the fight. "We had an extra gas tank in the corner," said Dundee later, kidding. Then he turned serious and said, "Nobody can suck it up like my man."

Ali sucked it up, found new strength, and sapped Frazier's. The thirteenth and fourteenth rounds were exercises in punishment. Several times, Ali landed six, seven, eight punches in a row, rights and lefts, shattering combinations that sent the sweat flying off Frazier's face, the mouthpiece flying from his mouth, but couldn't send him down to the floor.

In the thirteenth round, Frazier slipped—helped by a flurry of Ali punches—and almost went down, but regained his balance. His eyes were beginning to close, and in the following round, he was squinting at Ali, making out mostly the form of red gloves, coming at his face, bouncing off his nose and his forehead and his cheeks, pounding and pounding and pounding.

"No," said Frazier at the end, facing the press with sunglasses hiding his eye, "I wouldn't say I was hurt. No, I wasn't hurt. Just banged up. Tomorrow, I'll be all good."

Then Joe Frazier took off his glasses, and the bumps under the right eye and over the left looked enormous. They looked almost as big as Joe Frazier's heart.

> *Dick Schaap*
> *"That Thrilla in Manila"*

1. In this selection by Dick Schaap there are several narrative elements. The piece starts with the story of the fourteenth round in a fight between Frazier and Muhammad Ali. Then, Schaap returns to the beginning of the fight and narrates it from start to finish. Why has the writer selected this method of presentation? Schaap writes for newspapers and sports magazines. What might that have to do with the way he presents his material?
2. What image of the fight stands out most vividly for you?
3. Read aloud several images that mention colors, that describe actions, that name sensations of touch.
4. What is Schaap's attitude toward Joe Frazier? How does the last sentence contribute to this attitude?
5. Why has Schaap written such short paragraphs? Try developing a topic and an opinion word for a topic sentence that could organize some of the short paragraphs into one longer paragraph.

REACHING HIGHER

Step 1. Photo into Words. Look at the photograph on page 51. Write a paragraph of at least ten sentences in which you narrate the scene suggested by the picture. Use details of color, of sound, of touch, of smell to make the scene come alive.

Step 2. Review. Read this paragraph for errors with fragments like those you have learned about so far. Correct mistakes directly on the page. There are nine sentence fragments.

The Last Ski Run

A light December snow speckles my ski goggles as I gaze down the experts' slope on Buttermilk Mountain. At the powdery whiteness below. The sun is dipping behind the jagged mountains. Surrounded by feathery clouds. Like a peacock's tail. The skiers in blue and red ahead of me start their graceful slide down the slope. Quickly disappearing in the late afternoon shadows. Exhausted after a full day on the slopes. I watch my warm breath turn into vapor in the brisk mountain air. To start my last run of the day. I finally plant my poles in the soft powder and surge forward. Realizing that my wife is probably beginning to worry about me. My legs stiffen in fear and sweat drips from under my hat. Especially at an icy patch or a sudden bump. At last I reach the bottom of the lift. To discover that I am the last skier on the mountain.

—*Mark Kent*

Step 3. Expanding a Poetic Moment. A valuable exercise in writing narrative is to select a poem that crystallizes a moment in time and to flesh out in your own language the scene the poet sketches. One of the outstanding qualities of good poetry is its ability to suggest scenes through economical use of language. Poets strive for *compression;* that is, they try to use as few and as carefully chosen words as possible to set scenes and to create emotional reactions in readers. Since all of us have different emotional states and different kinds of imaginations, what one person sees or feels after reading a poem is often quite unlike another person's responses.

As you read each of the following poems, think about the character of the person who speaks and of the other people in the poem. Then, by using sensory language, expand in a paragraph of your own the moment the poet presents. Try to suggest in the opening sentence or two the most important meaning of the poem. Describe the people as you see them, whether or not the poet has shown them clearly. Through color, sound, action, and images of smell and touch, paint a scene rich in details that your own imagination creates. Use comparisons (simile, metaphor, personification: look ahead to pages 134–137) for special vividness.

Read the poem below and then the paragraph written by a student as an example.

Lament

Listen, children:
Your father is dead.
From his old coats
I'll make you little jackets;
I'll make you little trousers
From his old pants.
There'll be in his pockets
Things he used to put there,
Keys and pennies
Covered with tobacco;
Dan shall have the pennies
To save in his bank;
Anne shall have the keys
To make a pretty noise with.
Life must go on,
And the dead be forgotten;
Life must go on,
Though good men die;
Anne, eat your breakfast;
Dan, take your medicine;
Life must go on;
I forget just why.
        —*Edna St. Vincent Millay*

The Meaning of Death

In "Lament" I see a sad mother who has lost her husband unsuccessfully trying to explain the meaning of death to her children in a cold dark kitchen. Sitting at the breakfast table one December morning, the mother in a faded robe runs her hand up and down the yellow plastic tablecloth. There are the morning smells of instant coffee, cereal, and orange juice, but she does not notice them. Her sorrowful brown eyes are small like little stones. Tiny lines of age and worry fill her face, and her hair, speckled with gray, falls sloppily onto her forehead. When she speaks to her ten-year-old son Dan, he stops tapping the table with his fork and listens. "Dan, even though your father is dead, I'll make you trousers from his old brown pants. You can keep the pennies in his pockets for your bank." Quickly, Dan looks away staring at a vitamin pill and his cough medicine, a red syrup in a clear glass bottle. "Anne," the mother says, "I'll give you Daddy's keys to play with." But the three-year-old in a wooden high chair just frowns and plays with the oatmeal in her little dish. The mother cannot soothe the children, though, because she herself is confused about the meaning of death. First she tries to comfort the children by keeping alive the father's memory. (That is why she talks of his keys with the pretty noise and his coins covered with tobacco.) But then she says just the opposite when she explains that the dead must be forgotten so life can go on. This contradiction is, I believe, the feeling many people experience in the loss of loved ones. We want to forget the person who died and to remember him as well. All the mother's sadness, bitterness, and confusion about death show in the last two lines: "Life must go on; I forget just why."

—*Sheila O'Connor*

Now read to yourself or listen as your instructor reads aloud the following poems. Then, using Sheila O'Connor's theme as an example, write your own paragraph that expands the scene from any one poem as you see it. You may wish to write about "Lament," if you prefer it to one of these.

Mother to Son

Well, son, I'll tell you:
Life for me ain't been no crystal stair.
It's had tacks in it,
And splinters,
And boards torn up,
And places with no carpet on the floor—
Bare.
But all the time
I'se been a-climbin' on,
And reachin' landin's,
And turnin' corners,
And sometimes goin' in the dark
Where there ain't been no light.
So, boy, don't you turn back.
Don't you set down on the steps
'Cause you finds it kinder hard.
Don't you fall now—
For I'se still goin', honey,
I'se still climbin',
And life for me ain't been no crystal stair.

—*Langston Hughes*

The Mole

"There goes The Mole!" Mother cried.
"You children look quick or you'll miss
him!" It was Father, disappearing down
the cellar stairs. Every day he'd retreat
to his radio shack, stay past midnight.

He'd built a rig others envied, came
from miles around to see. Every day
he'd jam the airwaves, ruin the block's TV.
Every day we'd hear him sit before the mike
calling "CQ, CQ, calling CQ" to whoever

listened at the other end. He once
claimed to reach Moscow. "Ralph's the handle,
calling from W3CAT, the Old Cat Station—
W-3-Cat-Alley-Tail." He was a handsome
cat; Mother once adored him, I know.

But what I'll never know is: Why he'd talk
to any stranger far away and not once
climb back up the stairs to the five of us
to say, "Hello...Hello...Hello...Hello."
                          —*Robert Phillips*

      My Papa's Waltz

The whiskey on your breath
Could make a small boy dizzy;
But I hung on like death:
Such waltzing was not easy

We romped until the pans
Slid from the kitchen shelf;
My mother's countenance
Could not unfrown itself.

The hand that held my wrist
Was battered on one knuckle;
At every step you missed
My right ear scraped a buckle.

You beat time on my head
With a palm caked hard by dirt,
Then waltzed me off to bed
Still clinging to your shirt.
                          —*Theodore Roethke*

CHAPTER 3

ILLUSTRATION:
Street Scenes and Sandlots, Memories of Youth

INTRODUCTION: USING EXAMPLES TO DEVELOP A PARAGRAPH

Each of us builds up unforgettable memories from childhood. These memories grow from experiences at school, from weekend trips in buses or cars or subways, from days in the country sun, or from sights on the city streets.

Often these events fall into a pattern so that we join together certain experiences under a single impression in our memories. We can recall, for example, a number of things that frightened us as children; we can point to a few occasions in which we learned how to speak up for what we wanted; we can remember the events that brought joy or pain or fear in our early years. Sometimes that single impression, which repeated experiences support, becomes a central thread in our own personalities. Because of a string of events, we may view ourselves forever as *insecure, shy, unloved, confident, independent, happy, angry*.

The scars and joys of your younger days will be the substance of the theme explored in this chapter. For this assignment you will present in a paragraph a number of experiences from your memories in order to suggest some general impression about your early life. To do so you will learn how to develop a paragraph by using *several* examples. Since each example represents an incident from your own experience, you will again turn to concrete sensory detail (see pages 6–7) to support your general statements, but not with as much complete-ness as you can achieve in a paragraph that narrates an event of a single moment (see page 72). When you use a number of examples to support a topic idea, you need to move the reader smoothly from one instance to another; therefore, you will examine further some important transition words.

VOCABULARY

Step 1.   Words for the Past. Each of the underlined words below can be helpful to you in writing about your childhood experiences. Try to determine the meaning of the word from the way it is used in the sentence. Circle the letter next to what you think is the best definition. Check the correct definitions in Appendix A.

1. When I <u>reminisce</u> about my childhood, I recall all my wonderful birthday parties.
    a. remember the past   *b.* ignore   *c.* think   *d.* cry
2. For example, my mother's pictures of my sweet sixteen party give me strong feelings of <u>nostalgia.</u>
    a. sorrow   *b.* desire to return to the past   *c.* illness   *d.* happiness
3. My tenth birthday was certainly my most <u>memorable</u> one, for my father presented me with a brown and white puppy named "Skippy."
    a. troublesome   *b.* exciting   *c.* happy   *d.* notable

4. The thought of Skippy licking my face with his hot, wet tongue <u>evokes</u> fond memories.
   a. produces   *b.* transfers   *c.* strikes   *d.* wipes away

5. I <u>recollect</u> how hilarious my tenth birthday party was; my school friends tossed balls of whipped cream at each other.
   a. forget   *b.* remember   *c.* become collected   *d.* fantasize

6. Surprisingly, I cannot clearly <u>discern</u> my eighteenth birthday party perhaps because both my parents had recently passed away.
   a. discuss   *b.* identify   *c.* forget   *d.* mention

7. There was a brief <u>interlude</u> after my eighteenth birthday when I thought it was silly and childish to celebrate any more of my birthdays.
   a. intermission   *b.* argument   *c.* period of time   *d.* event

8. Now that I am thirty, I realize that the <u>remembrance</u> of our past is a precious and important part of our lives.
   a. idea   *b.* discussion   *c.* situation   *d.* memory

9. Some people find it painful to <u>contemplate</u> the past because they are then more aware of the passing of the years.
   a. consider   *b.* talk about   *c.* sacrifice   *d.* manage

10. In <u>retrospect,</u> my past is indeed full of happy, tender memories that I will never forget.
    a. to come back   *b.* conclusion   *c.* tribute   *d.* review of earlier experiences

Step 2. Words for Unforgettable Personalities. These words are useful in describing those unforgettable personalities of your youth. Check them in the dictionary and write in definitions. For more help, see Appendix A.

1. compulsive _____

2. domineering _____

3. absurd _____

4. gregarious _____

5. volatile _____

Step 3. Using New Vocabulary. Fill in each blank with a word from the list in Step 2 so that the sentences make sense.

1. Her temper was so _____ that she would begin to scream at the slightest disturbance.

2. The _____ politician darted around the room, shaking hands and talking to small clusters of guests.

3. During the memorial service, his behavior was so _____ that he was asked to wait outside the chapel.

4. My father is very _____ ; he checks the locks frequently each day and he won't allow anyone except him to secure the doors of our house.

5. Donna was so _____ that she allowed her children very little opportunity to make their own decisions about anything important.

BUILDING COMPOSITION SKILLS

Finding the Topic

Step 1.   Getting Ideas. Complete any word group below by reading it aloud with your own ending. Then, in a few more sentences, explain what you said by giving two or three examples. Or, if your instructor suggests, write down in a few brief sentences your completion for any of the statements and then read aloud what you have written. Look at the examples.

1. My most important educational experience occurred when . . .
2. I lose my temper when . . .
3. The things that confused me as a child were . . .
4. I'm easily embarrassed when . . .
5. I can always please my parents (wife, husband) when . . .
6. I got into trouble when . . .
7. I was very frightened when . . .
8. My childhood was unusual because . . .
9. My first job taught me . . .
10. I used to be a bully, but . . .
11. As a youngster, I admired . . .
12. I remember learning about loneliness when . . .
13. Happy memories of my adolescence were . . .
14. When I returned to my old neighborhood, I . . .
15. My basic personality trait is . . .

Examples

My childhood was unusual because I lived in so many strange places. Since my father was an air force colonel, I lived for a time in Japan and Turkey. One summer I lived on a houseboat with my uncle, and the following winter at a remote radar station complex in Alaska.

—*Karen Youngman*

I'm easily embarrassed when I have to stand up in front of a group to speak. In science class when I had to make a report on the nervous system, I stammered nervously and felt my knees shake. And once in high school English I was so nervous that I dropped my note cards to the floor and had to slip back to my seat without finishing the report.

—*Helen Cendrowski*

Paragraph Unity: Subtopic Sentences

It's often helpful, especially when you use several examples to support your point, to remind the reader of the topic in several places in the paragraph. The subtopic sentence serves that function.

Here is a topic sentence that will obviously introduce a paragraph that uses several instances to support the topic:

When I was seven years old and the family moved from a small village in Puerto Rico to Manhattan, everyday city occasions frightened me.

This topic will deal with selected events of city life; the writer's opinion is that these events were frightening. The very next sentence would present the first subtopic:

The traffic noises scared me.

The word *scared* repeats the opinion of the topic sentence; *traffic noises* introduce one specific aspect of the topic for discussion. The next three or four sentences would explain how the traffic noises were frightening. Images filled with sensory language in those sentences would support this first unit of thought. After finishing this thought group, the writer would write another subtopic sentence:

I also didn't like the people I saw on the streets.

The words *people I saw on the streets* introduce another part of the topic for the writer to discuss. The words *didn't like* refer back to the opinion in the topic sentence. The next few sentences would illustrate the point of the subtopic with colors and sounds and actions. After this thought unit ends, another subtopic sentence would appear:

And every new thing I saw in Manhattan looked oversized and ugly.

The words *every new thing I saw in Manhattan* refer the reader back to the original topic; the words *oversized and ugly* report the writer's opinion toward the topic discussed in the paragraph. In this way the paragraph achieves unity—all the sentences will build upon the main idea.

Even paragraphs that do not give several incidents can benefit from subtopic sentences. Paragraphs of description (Chapter 1) and narration (Chapter 2) achieve unity too when subtopic sentences introduce major blocks of thought. Each subtopic sentence needs several sentences of support for whatever aspect of the topic the writer introduces. Here a topic sentence introduces a paragraph that narrates:

On a cold December morning I learned how dangerous skiing can be.

Here are two subtopic sentences:

1. *As I rode up the chairlift, the sun reflected off the icy surface of the slope.*
2. *Suddenly the hazardous rock loomed in front of me.*

What kind of information would you expect to find in the seven or eight sentences after subtopic sentence 1 above? After subtopic sentence 2? What words in each of the subtopic sentences remind the reader of the opinion expressed in the topic sentence?

SUBTOPIC SENTENCE CHART

Subtopic Sentence	Why
1. Introduces one aspect of the topic you want to discuss	So it's clear to the reader what proof you will use at a given point in the paragraph So it's clear to you what part of the topic you are treating at a given point in the paragraph
2. Uses a word similar to the "opinion" word in the topic sentence	So the reader is reminded of your position on the topic So that you remember that you're trying to prove only a certain feature about the topic So that the details in the sentences that follow the subtopic sentence all try to support the key impression you have given about the topic in the topic sentence

---

Step 1.   Finding Subtopics. Reread "The Gloom Room" on pages 35–36.

1. Copy here the first subtopic sentence, the sentence that introduces the one aspect of the topic that the writer will discuss first. _____

_____

2. Copy the second subtopic sentence. _____

_____

3. What details does Mr. Golden use to support the first subtopic sentence?

_____

_____

4. What details does he use to support the second subtopic sentence?

_____

_____

Step 2. Writing Subtopic Sentences. For each topic sentence below, write subtopic sentences. The numbers in parentheses tell you how many subtopic sentences to write. Use your own paper.

Hint

Each subtopic sentence:

a. introduces some aspect of the topic that can be discussed in a few sentences
b. may repeat some idea of the opinion word
c. must be followed by supporting details.

Example

At Springfield Gardens High School, trouble and I were never far away from each other! (3)

Subtopic sentence 1: Once I "borrowed" my homeroom teacher's key for a practical joke.

Subtopic sentence 2: To protest the awful cafeteria food, I caused a commotion.

Subtopic sentence 3: Finally, the Dean of Boys summoned me when he learned I had cut history eighteen times.

1. When I was seventeen, two friends had major effects on my way of thinking and behaving. (2)
2. During our trip to Washington, D.C., I had two shocking experiences. (2)
3. Travelling to another country can be an unforgettable experience. (2)
4. On the bus ride downtown yesterday, several passengers and the driver suffered in the rush-hour traffic. (2)
5. My first date was filled with embarrassment. (3)
6. I learned early how to survive in a rough neighborhood. (3)
7. The athletics program in my high school was a disaster. (2)
8. Although it is a good idea to keep trim, it is important not to become too underweight. (2)
9. I have never read a book as fascinating as _____. (3)

Hint

There is no set number of subtopic sentences to use for each paragraph. If you write only two subtopic sentences, each subtopic (thought unit) will need to be developed in greater detail. Write three subtopic sentences, and you will need to use fewer supporting details for each thought unit.

Several Examples without Subtopic Sentences

Sometimes a writer wishes to propose many instances to support the topic sentence in a paragraph. In that case, each instance is not highly developed—it is told in just a sentence or two—and a subtopic sentence to introduce each example is unnecessary. The paragraph below uses several instances to support the attitude in the topic sentence, but does not need subtopic sentences. The unity in the paragraph comes from repetition of key words (see pages 98–99).

SOME WORDS TO KNOW BEFORE YOU READ

downs: an area of low hills in South England
cricket: a popular English game; it is played by two teams, the ball hit along the ground
    with a kind of bat
sixpence: an English coin
newt: a salamander, a small lizardlike animal

Memories of Crossgates School

I have good memories of Crossgates, among a horde of bad ones. Sometimes on summer afternoons there were wonderful expeditions across the Downs, or to Beachy Head, where one bathed dangerously among the chalk boulders and came home covered with cuts. And there were still more wonderful midsummer evenings when, as a special treat, we were not driven off to bed as usual but allowed to wander about the grounds in the long twilight, ending up with a plunge into the swimming bath at about nine o'clock. There was the joy of waking early on summer mornings and getting in an hour's undisturbed reading (Ian Hay, Thackeray, Kipling and H. G. Wells were the favourite authors of my boyhood) in the sunlit, sleeping dormitory. There was also cricket, which I was no good at but with which I conducted a sort of hopeless love affair up to the age of about eighteen. And there was the pleasure of keeping caterpillars—the silky green and purple puss-moth, the ghostly green poplar-hawk, the privet hawk, large as one's third finger, specimens of which could be illicitly purchased for sixpence at a shop in the town—and, when one could escape long enough from the master who was "taking the walk," there was the excitement of dredging the dew-ponds on the Downs for enormous newts with orange-coloured bellies. This business of being out for a walk, coming across something of fascinating interest and then being dragged away from it by a yell from the master, like a dog jerked onwards by the leash, is an important feature of school life, and helps to build up the conviction, so strong in many children, that the things you most want to do are always unattainable.

—*George Orwell*
Such, Such Were the Joys

Arrangement of Details by Importance

In telling about an event, you know that the clearest way to present the moment is to give the details in chronological order—the order in which things occur. If you write a paragraph that gives several instances or examples to support the topic sentence, you can certainly write about them in the order in which they occurred. But another method is to tell the details in the order of their importance: tell about the least important thing first and the most important thing last. In this way you build up to the proof that has the most significance.

Suppose you wanted to write a paragraph for this topic sentence:

When I returned to my old neighborhood, I was sad to see how many things had changed.

Let's assume that you would develop these three incidents as illustrations in the paragraph:

1. *Mr. Lewis, my old history teacher, had died in a car accident.*
2. *Mike's Pizzeria, a local hangout, was destroyed in a fire.*
3. *The park bench where I spent hours reading was gone.*

From these incidents, although item 1 might have occurred first in time, because it seems to be the most important it would best be discussed last in the paragraph. Item 3 seems least important so it could be the first event discussed. Of course, only the writer himself could determine which was most or least significant.

Step 1.   Making the Order Count. In Column I, jot down three instances you might discuss and expand for each of these topic sentences. In Column II, arrange the details in order of importance.

I Instances   *II Order of importance*

1. Several good experiences in high school made me like my years there.

    a. _____   1. _____

    b. _____   2. _____

    c. _____   3. _____

2. Many things amuse me about my teenage daughter's behavior.

    a. _____   1. _____

    b. _____   2. _____

    c. _____   3. _____

3. The last time I got lost proved to me that I could find my way around a strange place on my own.

    a. _____   1. _____

    b. _____   2. _____

    c. _____   3. _____

Step 2.   Arranging Details by Importance. Instead of writing in detail about two or three instances, you can mention seven or eight instances, each in just a sentence or two. In Column I, list seven events that could be written to support the topic sentence as given. In Column II, arrange the details according to importance as *you* see it.

I Events

1. Choosing the kind of person to marry is a
   very difficult and important decision.

   a. _____
   b. _____
   c. _____
   d. _____
   e. _____
   f. _____
   g. _____

2. Living in cities has many advantages over
   living in other parts of the United States.

   a. _____
   b. _____
   c. _____
   d. _____
   e. _____

3. I was shocked the first time I watched boys
   and girls playing on the same baseball
   team.

   a. _____
   b. _____
   c. _____
   d. _____
   e. _____
   f. _____
   g. _____

II Order of Importance

   1. _____
   2. _____
   3. _____
   4. _____
   5. _____
   6. _____
   7. _____

   1. _____
   2. _____
   3. _____
   4. _____
   5. _____

   1. _____
   2. _____
   3. _____
   4. _____
   5. _____
   6. _____
   7. _____

Transitions

In Chapter 1 you learned about bridging thoughts through transitions—idea
connectors—that move the reader from place to place. But you can also join
ideas by means of other types of connecting words.

Connecting through Time

later on	suddenly	former
afterward	now	latter
years ago	some time later	in the first place
earlier	once	in the next place
before	often	further
next	yesterday	furthermore
first	today	meanwhile
second	tomorrow	previously
third	then	when
	in the past	at last
	thereafter	

Hint

These words help refer the reader to the idea that came directly before. The words suggest that the ideas are numbered.

Step 1. Using Time Connectors. Here are several ideas that could be used one after the other in a paragraph. They are not sentences. Using these details, connect the ideas with some of the time transitions above and write complete sentences in a paragraph. Use a separate sheet of paper.

means of effective transportation important to Americans

horses and single riders popular

covered wagons and carriages for more complex travel

go long distance with family's belongings

mass transportation by train important in travel history

bus, ship, airplane development

automobile single most popular form of transportation

relatively inexpensive means of going from one place to another

families everywhere consider car necessity

rising costs of oil question auto's continued use

turn to mass transportation

Connecting through Coordinators: *and, but, for, or, nor, yet*

You learned in an earlier chapter that these words could join sentences together. The words also serve to connect ideas in separate sentences. Notice how the sentence on the left below—a correct sentence grammatically—may be written as two sentences, the second of which makes a powerful transition to a new thought group.

Connie tried everything to stop smoking, yet she refused to give up her morning cigarette.	Connie tried everything to stop smoking. Yet she refused to give up her morning cigarette.

Hint

And, but, for, or, nor, or *yet* may be used at the beginning of a sentence. In your early years of school, you were probably warned against doing so because you may have started too many sentences with *and* or *so.* But, used carefully, coordinators open sentences effectively. Make sure a complete thought follows the coordinator. Make sure the sentence before is logically related to the sentence that follows the coordinator. Don't open more than one or two sentences in each paragraph in this way.

Step 2. Coordinators for Transition. Use a coordinator that makes sense as a sentence opener in each blank space below.

1. Many young people live for today. _____ who can tell what tomorrow may bring?
2. Raphael often stuttered when he talked to strangers. _____ when he sang on stage, he never stammered at all.
3. My sister pleaded with my father to allow her to go camping. _____ my father still refused to give her permission.
4. Tom refused to apologize to Michael. _____ Michael was as stubborn as Tom in refusing to settle their argument.
4. You can choose the chocolate cake for dessert. _____, if you want something even richer, ask for banana cream pie.
6. Never drink and drive. _____ you may seriously injure yourself and others.

Hint

See pages 19–20 for explanations of the meaning of coordinators such as *and, but, for, or, nor.*

Connecting through Repetition

Sometimes the repetition of a word or two at the beginning of or within a sentence helps join ideas together. Notice the repetition of the words *who* and *what* in the use of the angry questions below.

Who Are These Men?

Who are these men who defile the grassy borders of our roads and lanes, who pollute our ponds, who spoil the purity of our ocean beaches with the empty vessels of their thirst? Who are the men who make these vessels in millions and then say, "Drink—and discard"? What society is this that can afford to cast away a million tons of metal and to make of wild and fruitful land a garbage heap? What manner of men and women need thirty feet of steel and two hundred horsepower to take them, singly, to their small destinations? Who demand that what they eat is wrapped so that forests are cut down to make the paper that is thrown away, and what they smoke and chew is sealed so that the sealers can be tossed in gutters and caught in twigs and grass?

—*Marya Mannes*
More in Anger

Step 3.   Finding Connectors. Read "Memories of Crossgates School" on page 94. Circle the words repeated at the beginning of several sentences, words that help connect ideas through repetition.

Connecting through Pronouns

he	you	its
she	who	our
it	whom	their
we	his	your
they	her	whose

A pronoun takes the place of a noun. When you use a noun in one sentence, a pronoun that occurs later on in another sentence automatically refers the reader back to the original noun. In that way, you can help ideas move smoothly from one to the other.

Step 4.   Pronouns as Connectors. Circle the pronouns that help connect the sentences in this paragraph.

The Tailor Arrives

Almost instantly there was the sound of soft steady footsteps through the open doors, and from the back of the house through the hall following the manservant there came the tailor. He was a tall man, taller than the servant, middle-aged, his face quiet with a sort of closed tranquility. He wore a long robe of faded blue grasscloth, patched neatly at the elbows and very clean. Under his arm he carried a bundle wrapped in a white cloth. He bowed to the two white women and then squatting down put his bundle upon the floor of the veranda and untied its knots. Inside was a worn and frayed fashion book from some American company and a half-finished dress of a spotted blue-and-white silk. This dress he shook out carefully and held up for Mrs. Lowe to see.

—*Pearl S. Buck*
"The Frill"

Step 5. A Brief Paragraph with Pronoun Connectors. Write five sentences to describe the person sitting next to you in class. Mention the person's name in the first sentence. Connect the ideas in each succeeding sentence by using pronouns to bridge each complete thought. Use a separate sheet of paper.

Hint

It must always be clear to the reader just which noun the pronoun replaces. Consider this sentence:

The mother held the baby, and she laughed at her.

We don't know—because the pronouns are unclear—just who did the laughing at whom.

Subordination

In Chapter 1, pages 19–22, you learned how to combine sentences using coordination. Another way to join thoughts in paragraphs is to set up a relationship between two thoughts, a relationship in which one of the two ideas is stressed more than the other. For example, you can join two short sentences so that one of the thoughts gets more emphasis. Look at these two sentences (from "The Nursery," on page 19), which are then joined, using subordination:

He rests his head on the pillow. I tiptoe quietly to the door.
a. Because he rests his head on the pillow, I tiptoe quietly to the door.

The words *I tiptoe quietly to the door* express a complete thought and, as such, give the part of the sentence that has the most stress.

The words *because he rests his head on the pillow* are not a complete thought and, therefore, get less emphasis than the rest of the sentence. Those words give "background information": they tell *why* the writer tiptoed quietly to the door. But clearly, it is the tiptoeing to the door that the sentence stresses, and the writer shows that the baby's falling asleep brought about the action of leaving the child's room.

Now look at the sentences joined together in another way:

b. Because I tiptoe quietly to the door, he rests his head on the pillow.

Here, the words *he rests his head on the pillow* are the stressed part of the sentence because they can stand alone as a complete thought.

The words *Because I tiptoe quietly to the door* are not a complete thought. As "background information," they tell *why* the baby fell asleep. But it is the fact that the baby rests his head on the pillow that the sentence stresses. The writer shows that the action of tiptoeing to the door made the baby do what he did.

The technique that gives one part of a sentence more stress than another is *subordination*. Only the writer can decide which part of the sentence is less or more important. Completely different meanings are achieved by subordinating different word groups within a sentence: this is clear in sentences *a* and *b* above.

It's obvious that the word *because* is the word that brings about the subordination in sentences *a* and *b*. It is one word among many which are called *subordinators*. Although all subordinators connect the unstressed part of a sentence to the part that gets the emphasis, they explain different things about the emphasized part of the sentence.

If you want to show *why* the stressed part of the sentence occurred, use one of these to subordinate:

as	because	so that
since	in order that	as long as

Example

[This tells why the lateness occurred.]

Because the train was delayed, I arrived late to work.

[This is the stressed part of the sentence. It expresses a complete thought.]

Step 1.   Subordination to Tell Why. Make up a correct subordinate part to tell *why* for each of these complete thoughts. Use one of the subordinators in the boxed chart above. Be sure a subject and a verb come after the subordinator.

1. _____, I called for an ambulance.

2. _____, Mr. Bogan raced across the street.

3. _____, I listened closely to the news.

4. _____, Juanita played her best game ever.

5. _____, the child chewed his nails nervously.

If you want to show *when* the stressed part of the sentence occurred, use one of these to subordinate.

after	whenever
as	while
as soon as	until
before	once
since	provided
when	

Example

[This tells *when* the wish for
  popcorn occurred.]

After the movie began, we decided to have popcorn.

[This is the stressed part of the sentence.
It expresses a complete thought.]

Step 2. Subordination to Tell When. Make up a correct subordinate part to tell *when* for each of these complete thoughts. Use a subordinator from the chart above. Be sure a subject and verb follow the subordinator.

1. _____, the students gathered their books
   and bolted from the classroom.

2. _____, she locked the front door and
   trudged wearily up the stairs.

3. _____, my cousin laughed until she cried.

4. _____, Dominick decided to leave his job
   for good.

5. _____, Betty returned to her parents' farm
   near St. Louis.

If you want to show *where* or *how* the stressed part of the sentence occurred, use one of these to subordinate:

wherever   if   as if

where   how   as though

Examples

[This tells *where* forces of
     good work.]

Wherever evil appears, the forces of good will work against it.

[This stressed part of the
sentence is a complete thought.]

[This tells *how* Susan acted.]

As if she had never seen snow before, Susan dived madly into the drifts.

[The stressed part of the sentence:
it is a complete thought.]

Step 3. Completing Subordinated Sentences. Write the stressed part of the sentence for each subordinated word group below.

1. Wherever William looked, _____.

2. As though he had not eaten in a week, _____.

3. As if he had never driven a car, _____.

4. Where there is smoke, _____.

5. If you play Pac-Man too often, _____.

If you want to show *under what condition* the stressed part of the sentence occurred, use one of these to subordinate:

although	unless
if	provided
though	once

Examples

[You would not expect a tired person to run.] [This complete thought is what the sentence stresses.]

Although I was tired, I ran the ten blocks home.

[This tells *under what condition* the bills will be paid.]

Unless the check comes, I will not be able to pay my bills.

[This, a complete thought, is what the sentence stresses.]

Hint

Although introduces an idea that you would not expect to happen because of the information in the stressed part.

Step 4. Subordinators Tell Conditions. Complete the sentences below by adding a subordinated section that tells under what condition the main part of the sentence occurs. Use the subordinator as indicated.

1. Although _____, she still refuses to admit her mistake.

2. Once _____, I can feed the baby.

3. If _____, I will fail my psychology course.

4. Provided _____, we should be in Texas by nightfall.

5. Unless _____, you should not swim right after eating.

6. Once _____, it is impossible to replace.

Hint

Always use a comma after the subordinate part of the sentence when the subordinate part comes first.

[subordinate part]

As she arrived, we left.

[comma here]

Step 5.   Subordinating Your Sentences. For each topic below, write a sentence that uses subordination at the beginning of the sentence. Use as many sub-ordinators as you can from the four groups in Steps 1 to 4. Don't forget commas after the subordinated part.

Example
1. music   *After the music stopped, Carol and I sat down for a drink.*

_____

2. a pet _____

_____

3. starting a friendship _____

_____

4. a person you admire _____

_____

5. renting an apartment _____

_____

6. winter driving _____

_____

   Subordinated portions like the ones you've been writing may also appear at the ends of sentences. You generally do not use a comma before the subordinat-ed section if it comes at the end.

Example
I watched every game of the World Series because I love baseball.

Step 6.   Subordination to Join. Each item in Column 1 below contains two brief sentences. Subordinate one of the two sentences, and rewrite your new sentence in Column II. Then subordinate the other sentence, and write the new sentence in Column III. Look at the example.

I	*II*	*III*
1. I heard the telephone ring. I unlocked the door.	*As I unlocked the door, I heard the telephone ring.*	*As I heard the telephone ring, I unlocked the door.*
2. It began to rain. We rushed for shelter.		

3. The leaves were falling. I
   felt lonely.
   _____   _____

   _____   _____

   _____   _____

4. Ray and Tess met in
   Seattle. They now live in
   Syracuse.
   _____   _____

   _____   _____

   _____   _____

5. The cat hid under the
   bed. The dog barked.
   _____   _____

   _____   _____

   _____   _____

6. I wrote a letter to him.
   He sent a postcard to me.
   _____   _____

   _____   _____

   _____   _____

7. Alexis enjoys baking. Ian
   likes her bread.
   _____   _____

   _____   _____

   _____   _____

Hint

If the subordinated part—placed at the end—starts with *though* or *although*, use a comma.

Example

We read the whole book, though we were bored by it.
                    ↑[comma]

If in the subordinate part of the sentence you want to describe someone or something you have mentioned in the stressed part, use one of these:

who
whose   that
which

                    [This identifies the
                          woman.]

1. The woman whose purse was stolen called the police.

                         [This identifies the book.]

2. We bought the book which had the most pictures.

                    [This identifies the
                          man.]

3. The man who enjoys his work does the best job.

4. The Empire State Building, which is in New York, is no longer the tallest building.

(continued on next page)

(Chart continued)

Hint The word *which* never refers to a person, only places and things. Use *who, whom,* and *whose* to refer to people.

Wrong: The people which eat fast will be ill.

Correct: Those people *who* eat fast will be ill. The meat *which* we ate was tasty.

A Hint About Commas

Sentences 1 to 3 above do not use commas with the subordinate part because the subordinating sections identify some subject. Without the words *whose purse was stolen,* we cannot identify the woman. Without *which had the most pictures,* we cannot identify the book in sentence 2. Without *who enjoys his work* we have no idea of which man is being identified. *Because they are essential for proper meaning, subordinate sections that identify the subject don't need commas.*

However, when information is added in subordinate sections to describe further a subject already identified, you need to use commas as in sentence 4 above. This material is *nonessential:* the subordinate section merely adds information about a subject already named. (See pages 280–288 for more information on commas.)

[comma]   [comma]

Professor Barton, who teaches here, is ill.

[This *adds* information; the person is already identified.]

The girl who won the contest received $100.

[This identifies the girl: no commas.]

I admire John Steinbeck's novels, which are full of rich imagery.

[comma]   [This *adds* information; the novels have already been identified.]

Step 7. Practice with *Who, Whose, Which, What, That.* Add words to complete the subordinate section in each sentence below. Use commas where necessary.

1. The basketball star *who* _____ rammed the ball through the basket.

2. I live in a small town *that* _____.

3. The best crops grow in well-drained fields *which* _____

   _____.

4. The movie star *whose* _____ was no longer popular with the fans.

5. The time in my life that _____ will be my old age.

6. The Golden Gate Bridge *which* _____ is one of the major tourist attractions on the West Coast.

7. They are the only circus people *who* _____

   _____ .

8. The injured woman *whose* _____ waited
   for help more than an hour.

9. Health foods *that* _____ will make your
   skin look better.

10. John and Liz *who* _____ are getting di-
    vorced.

Step 8. Writing Sentences that Subordinate. For each of these subordinate
word groups, write a complete sentence that makes sense. Put the subordinated
part in the middle or at the end of the sentence; remember to put in commas
when necessary. Use a separate sheet of paper.

1. who never smiles   **6.** whose book was published
2. whose father makes clocks   **7.** which has never been opened
3. that looked too small   **8.** who never forgets my birthday
4. that made me happy   **9.** who was so boring
5. who loves me deeply   **10.** which disturbed our sleep

Step 9. Rewriting Coordinated Sentences. Although coordination is often
effective, subordination of ideas allows for much greater sentence variety. Many
beginning writers use coordination too frequently. Change each coordinated
sentence below to a sentence that uses subordination.

Examples
I like water skiing, but the speed frightens me.
Although I like water skiing, the speed frightens me.

_____

1. Kathy began to applaud, for the program amused her._____

   _____

2. Paco finally arrived, and we sat down to dinner. _____

   _____

3. Mr. Wong telephoned for an ambulance, and the three police officers

   administered first aid. _____

4. Gina arrived for class on time, but there was no one in the room. _____

5. You must exercise daily, or you may become ill. _____

   _____

Step 10.   Rewriting a Paragraph. On a separate sheet of paper, rewrite the paragraph "The Nursery" that appears on page 19. Use coordination and subordination to vary the sentence length and structure. Use coordination only once; use subordination at least three times.

Titles

The title is a helpful feature for the reader since titles give the first hint of what appears within the paragraph or essay.

HOW TO WRITE A STRONG TITLE	WHAT NOT TO DO IN A TITLE
1. Give the main idea of your paragraph in the title. **2.** If you don't want to tell the topic in your title, pick out a word or word group from the paragraph that will hint at the kind of topic you are treating. **3.** Arouse the reader's curiosity by the title. **4.** Write the title last, after you have finished the paragraph. **5.** If you can write an interesting, exciting title, good. If not, don't worry. It's better to be clear and to give a title that suits the paragraph than to be brilliant, clever, or original. **6.** When you write your title, put it on top of page one. Capitalize all important words. *Hint:* Do not capitalize words like *and, the, an, a, but,* or any of the short direction words like *in, on, to, for* unless one of these words is the first or last word in your title.	**1.** *Do not* make the title the only statement of the topic. *A title is not a topic sentence.* If you tell the topic in the title, repeat the topic in the topic sentence. **2.** *Do not* try to be cute. If you want a funny title, be sure your paragraph deals with a humorous subject. **3.** *Do not* use overworn expressions as your title: "A Stitch in Time Saves Nine" or "Love Makes the World Go Round" would be inappropriate titles for themes about prompt action and love because these titles are too familiar. **4.** *Do not* write titles that are too long. A long full sentence is rarely used as a title. **5.** *Do not* write a title that is too general. **6.** *Do not* use quotation marks or underlining in your title when it appears on your composition.

Step 1.   Seeing Effective Titles. Each statement in Column 1 is the topic sentence of a paragraph. Column II gives a title that is poor for one of the reasons explained in the boxed chart. In Column III, write why you think the title is poor; in Column IV, try to write your own title.

I	*II*	*III*	*IV*
1. Many members of my family contributed to my happiness as a child.	Relatives	*too general*	*Relatives and Childhood Pleasure*
2. One frightening experience I	Keeping Cool		

recall is the awful
time I was locked
in a butcher's
refrigerator for
three hours.

3. Keeping to a   I Keep to a
   schedule has   Schedule Every Day.
   allowed me to get
   more work done
   more easily each
   day.

4. Jon enjoyed   Digging Flicks
   seeing the movie
   Annie twice last
   month.

5. I learned the true   Dribble Trouble
   meaning of
   friendship while
   playing varsity
   basketball.

6. I remember the   Money Is the Root
   awful troubles I   of All Evil
   had working
   after school for
   Mr. Sanchez.

Step 2. More Practice with Titles. List titles of several books, motion pictures, or television shows. Explain why you think the titles are effective or why they lack appeal for you. What might you add to the titles to make them stronger?

SOLVING PROBLEMS IN WRITING

Sentence Fragments: Part II

The technique of subordination you learned earlier in this chapter is an essential characteristic of effective writing style. Used incorrectly, however, subordination gives rise to another type of *sentence fragment*. It's important to use the subordinating word group only when it can join on to a complete sentence, a word group that can make sense standing alone. These fragments appeared on student papers because the students forgot that subordinators must *join* ideas together:

1. **When** an empty shopping <u>cart</u> <u>soared</u> down the aisle.

2. **Who** really <u>looked</u> ridiculous.

3. **Unless** our <u>government</u> <u>gives</u> financial assistance.

The words in dark print are *subordinators*. Each one indicates that a major and complete idea will be expressed either earlier or later on in the sentence.

In number 1, the reader wants to know *what has happened* **when** that empty shopping cart soared down the aisle.

In number 2, the reader wants to know **who** looked ridiculous.

In number 3, the reader wants to know *what will happen* **unless** the government gives financial assistance.

It is true that each of the word groups does contain a subject and a verb (they are underlined in each case.) However, the use of the *subordinator* means that connection to a complete thought must be made for a correct sentence.

But these subordinator fragments are easy enough to recognize in isolation. Now look at them as they appear in parts of paragraphs.

Fragment	*Explanation*
a. (1) Parents should leave their children at home when shopping must be done. (2) One afternoon at the A&P I stood minding my own business at the corn counter. (3) *When an empty shopping cart soared down the aisle.* (4) I knew some little brat was to blame.	The word *when* here is a subordinator. It must connect all the words that follow it to a complete sentence. Since word group 3 is standing alone and *is not* connected to a complete thought, it is a *fragment*. The reader needs to know, within word group 3, what happened *when an empty shopping cart soared down the aisle.*
b. (1) All the children in the third grade danced in snowflake costumes on the auditorium stage. (2) Over to the left stood my cousin Tyrone. (3) *Who really looked ridiculous.* (4) He was covered with a big white sheet and he moved more like a hippo than a snowflake.	The word *who,* as it is used here, is a connector. It must join all the words that follow it to a complete sentence. In addition, the sentence that uses the word *who* must also identify the person that *who* refers to. It's not enough to use *Tyrone* at the end of sentence 2. Since word group 3 is standing alone and is not connected to a complete thought, it is a *fragment*.
c. (1) Our country's Olympic teams will be defeated. (2) *Unless our government gives financial assistance.* (3) American athletes cannot afford the time to train and compete.	The word *unless* is a subordinator. It must connect all the words that follow it to a complete sentence. Since word group 2 is standing alone and is not connected to a complete thought, it is a *fragment*. The reader needs to know, within word group 2, what will happen *unless our government gives financial assistance.*

FIXING THE SUBORDINATOR FRAGMENT: METHOD I

Join the fragment to the sentence before. In *a,* above, join 2 and 3.

One afternoon at the A&P I stood minding my
[no period]
own business at the corn counter when an
[small letter]
empty shopping cart soared down the aisle.

In *b,* above, join 2 and 3.

Over to the left stood my cousin Tyrone,
[comma]
[small letter]
who really looked ridiculous.

In *c,* above, join 1 and 2.

Our country's Olympic teams will be defeated,
[small letter]   [no period]
unless our government gives financial assistance.

Hint: A comma may be required when a subordinate word group is added at the end of a complete sentence. See pages 106–107.

Step 1.   Adding Fragments On: Method 1. Correct the selections below by adding the fragment onto the sentence that comes before it.

1. Our country will face an energy crisis in the near future. Unless we develop new resources in this century.
2. I greatly admire my Uncle George. A man who taught me to love the simple things in life.
3. Nothing new ever seems to happen in this town. As if we lived in a time warp.
4. Adjusting to a new city is not difficult for me. Because we often traveled when I was a child.
5. I never believe what I read in the newspapers. Until I can check a second source.

FIXING THE SUBORDINATOR FRAGMENT: METHOD II

Join the fragment to the sentence after.
In *c,* page 111, add 2 and 3.

Unless our government gives financial assist-
[comma]
ance, American athletes cannot afford the time to train and compete.

In *a,* page 111, add 3 and 4.

When an empty shopping cart soared down the aisle, I knew some little brat was to blame.
[comma]

Hint: When a subordinate word group comes first in a sentence, use a comma between it and the complete sentence that follows.

Step 2. Adding Fragments On: Method II. Correct the selections below by adding the fragment to the sentence that follows it. Add commas where needed.

1. Before my first child was born. I was afraid that I would be a poor parent.
2. Provided Brenda does well in the interview. She is assured of the job.
3. Because Hector is such a fine dancer. He will surely receive a scholarship.
4. Whenever I read a good book. I vow never to watch television again.
5. An event that I'll never forget. The day the first astronauts landed on the moon was a great achievement for all citizens of the earth.

   Hint

In trying to decide whether to add the fragment to the sentence before or after, first decide which way makes more sense. Add the fragment to the sentence to which it is most closely related in meaning.

FIXING THE SUBORDINATOR FRAGMENT: METHOD III

Add a new subject-verb word group to the fragment.
In *a*, page 111:   When an empty shopping cart soared down
                                              [added word group]
                             the aisle, I had to jump out of the way. I
                                       [subject]   [verb]
                             knew some little brat was to blame.

Step 3. Adding Words to Fragments Add the necessary words to these fragments and rewrite the correct sentence on the blank lines below. Remember punctuation.

1. As if it didn't matter. _____

   _____

2. That nearly won first prize. _____

   _____

3. Unless Sheila would rather spend the night. _____

   _____

4. If the drought continues. _____

   _____

5. When the play begins. _____

   _____

FIXING THE SUBORDINATOR FRAGMENT: METHOD IV

Sometimes you can take out the subordinator and some accompanying words in order to correct the fragment.
In *a*, page 111:

[Remove subordinator]

~~When~~ An empty shopping cart soared down the

aisle.　　[capital letter]

Sometimes it is necessary to add a new word, which will serve as the subject.
In *c*, page 111:

[added word; subject of *looked*]

He

~~Who~~ really looked ridiculous.

[Remove subordinator]

Hint: Use this method only when all others fail. It's best to incorporate the fragment into a complete sentence. In that way you will be improving your writing style by using subordination.

Step 4.　Dropping the Subordinator. Correct these fragments by removing the subordinator.

1. Although I applauded the actors and actresses.
2. The boy who fell into the Mississippi River.
3. While Julie walked around the museum.
4. The teacher who addressed me by my first name.
5. When the President visited our school.

Finding the Fragment

You can see that the only way to spot the subordinator fragment is to be thoroughly familiar with the list of subordinators you were asked to experiment with earlier in this chapter. Here again are most of the subordinators, this time in Stop-Sign warning charts. If you memorize these words, you'll know what causes most students to write fragments.

FRAGMENT STOP SIGNS

I

as long as	how
after	provided
although	if
as	since
as if	so that
as soon as	though
because	unless
before	until
whenever	when
once	where
while	whether

II

what	whoever
which	whomever
who	whatever
whose	
that	

Hint: Remember, do not avoid using these words. When used correctly, they add variety and clarity to your style.

REVIEW CHARTS: THE SUBORDINATOR FRAGMENT

A Fragment Finder

1. Learn the list of subordinators that frequently give rise to fragments (see above).
2. Read the sentences aloud; do not confuse a pause for breath (which may or may not be indicated by a comma) with a complete stop (indicated by a period, a semicolon, or some other end mark).
3. Read your sentences from the last one to the first, stopping after each sentence to see if a complete thought has been expressed.

A Fragment Fixer

1. Join the fragment to the sentence that comes before.
2. Join the fragment to the sentence that comes after.
3. Add a new subject-verb word group.
4. Remove the subordinator. Add any new words.

Step 1. Correcting Fragments. Most of the selections below contain fragments of the subordinator type. Correct the fragments in any of the ways you have learned. If the selection is correct, mark the sentence *C*.

1. After driving a taxi all night. I find it impossible to go right to sleep.
2. We camped out at Moon Lake. Where we steered our canoe amid churning white water.
3. Travelers' checks are very safe. Wherever people travel. Their money is secure. Even if it is lost or stolen.

4. Many people praised WABC-TV. The station that first reported the story. That showed the events of the crime.
5. Diets high in sodium are unhealthy. A special problem for people who have high blood pressure. Who have to watch salt intake.
6. Chicago has the reputation of being a dangerous city. Which it can be. But it is also a city of great business and culture.
7. Before I took the speed-reading course, I was a very slow reader. Now that I have finished the course, my reading speed has tripled.
8. My stepfather was late for dinner. Since he missed the bus. He had to walk home from work.
9. Dreams can be very mysterious. Whenever they occur. During the middle of the day or in the dead of the night.
10. Whenever I think of my Little League days. I remember playing third base in the World Series. That was held in Phoenix, Arizona.

Step 2. More Practice with Fragments. Study the fragment review charts on page 115. Then follow directions.

1. Write two sentences to tell something that you do each morning when you wake up. Use the words *when I get out of bed* in one of your sentences.

_____

_____

_____

2. Write one complete thought about a person who is always interrupting you. Use the words *who is always interrupting me* in your sentence.

_____

_____

3. Write two sentences that tell how you study for a final exam. Open one of your sentences with either of these word groups: *Whenever I have a final exam* or *Before a final exam.*

_____

_____

_____

_____

4. Write a sentence that tells what you do when a person you are meeting shows up late. Start your sentence with one of these words: *when, if, while.*

_____

_____

_____

5. Write a sentence or two about farming. Use the words *to plant* or *to drive a tractor* or *to plow the fields* somewhere in your sentence.

_____

_____

_____

_____

6. Write a sentence that tells your opinion of some course that you were asked to take in high school or college. Use the words *which is required* in your

sentence. _____

_____

_____

7. Write two sentences about the first motion picture you remember watching. Use the words *that I remember* in one of your sentences. _____

_____

_____

8. Write three sentences about people you know. Use one of these word groups in *each* sentence:

who smiles easily
who always buys me coffee
whom I have not seen in a long time

_____

_____

_____

_____

9. Write a sentence about a relative who looks like you. Use this word group in your sentence: *whom I greatly resemble.*

_____

_____

10. Write a sentence or two about some changes in your life-style as a result of your learning to drive. Use one of these word groups somewhere in your sentence: *because I learned to drive* or *since I learned to drive.*

_____

_____

_____

_____

11. Write a sentence that tells of some exotic ethnic food you like. Use this word group somewhere in your sentence: *whether or not it is spicy.*

_____

_____

_____

12. Write a sentence or two about people who sew their own clothes in order to save money. Start your sentence with these words: *When sewing to save money.* _____

_____

_____

_____

13. Write a sentence whose first word is *Whatever.* _____

_____

_____

14. Write two sentences, each one telling about electronic games that you like. Start the second sentence with *Also.* _____

_____

_____

15. Write two sentences about what you would do if you had to move out of your present home. Open one of the sentences with *If.* _____

_____

_____

_____

_____

Step 3. Look at Step 1 on pages 17–18. For each word group that is not a sentence, write a complete one by adding and/or changing words.

Plurals

Although the usual method of plural formation involves the addition of an -*s*, there are several variations. Study the review charts below, which show examples and state rules.

Regular Plurals

Add *-s* to the singular for most plurals

boy + *-s* = boys
pencil + *-s* = pencils
tree + *-s* = trees

Words Ending in Y

1. If a consonant comes before the *y*, change the *y* to *i* and add *-es*.

   cit (y) + *-s* = cities
   part (y) + *-s* = parties
2. If a vowel comes before the *y*, add only *-s*.

   day + *-s* = days
   key + *-s* = keys

Words Ending in F

1. Most words ending in *-f* form plurals by adding *s*:

   roof—roofs
   chief—chiefs
2. Some words ending in *f* change to *v* and add *-es*:

   leaf—leaves   wife—wives
   elf—elves   self—selves
   wolf—wolves   half—halves
   knife—knives   calf—calves
   shelf—shelves   loaf—loaves

Plurals That Stay the Same

Some words are the same in plural and singular:

cattle   series
deer   sheep
bass   wheat
corps   means
cod   dozen
            swine
one deer, many deer
a series, three series

Plurals That Add Syllables

If another syllable is added when you pronounce the plural, add *-es*. Words ending in *s, ss, ch, sh, tch, x, z* add another syllable and therefore add *-es*.

fox + *-es* = foxes
church + *-es* = churches
glass + *-es* = glasses

Words Ending in O

1. Add *-s* to most words ending in *-o*.

   piano + *-s* = pianos
   radio + *-s* = radios
2. Exceptions

   echoes   heroes   mulattoes
   potatoes   Negroes   mosquitoes
   tomatoes   torpedoes   mottoes

-en Plurals

Some words add *-en* to make plurals

ox—oxen
child—children

Inside Plurals

Some words show plurals by changing letters within the word:

mouse—mice
man—men
louse—lice
foot—feet
tooth—teeth
goose—geese

Words from Other Languages

Some words still keep the plural of the foreign language from which they originated:

alga   algae
oasis   oases
alumnus   alumni
alumna   alumnae

(continued on next page)

(Chart continued)

parenthesis	parentheses
thesis	theses
basis	bases
bacterium	bacteria
medium	media
phenomenon	phenomena
axis	axes
criterion	criteria
radius	radii
fungus	fungi
datum	data
stratum	strata

Combination Words

1. If a word is formed by combining two or three words, make a plural of the main word.

   son-in-law = sons-in-law   man-of-war = men-of-war
   editor-in-chief = editors-in-chief
   commander in chief = commanders in chief

2. If the combination is written as one word, add -*s* or -*es* to the end.

   suitcase = suitcases
   cupful = cupfuls

   Hint: Check a dictionary for plurals of combination words.

Step 1.   Plurals. Write the plurals of these words:

1. congresswoman	10. arch	18. soprano
2. task	11. valve	19. elf
3. halo	12. fistful	20. medium
4. corn	13. beauty	21. doe
5. pilot	14. mouse	22. crisis
6. dwarf	15. focus	23. high school
7. watch	16. belief	24. torpedo
8. Negro	17. child	25. Wednesday
9. bacterium		

Step 2.   Selecting Plurals. Change the words in parentheses to their plurals, and write them in the spaces provided.

1. Hosts at both (party) _____ served (cod) _____ with two (dozen) _____ different (loaf) _____ of bread.

2. Those (woman) _____ who are (alumna) _____ of the Uni-

versity of Texas are (editor-in-chief) _____ of their county newspapers.

3. The ship-to-shore (radio) _____ informed the marine (corps) _____ of the (torpedo) _____ headed their way.

4. The scientific (datum) _____ on the study of (mouse) _____ show that they can kill (themself) _____ by eating (cupful) _____ of a known poison.

5. The (economy) _____ of many (nation) _____ are tied to changing political (crisis) _____ and (phenomenon) _____.

6. The (wolf) _____ attacked the (sheep) _____, but the ranch-ers leaped to their (foot) _____ and became (hero) _____ by scaring the (animal) _____ away.

7. Although she is best known as one of Hollywood's prettiest (woman) _____, Marilyn Monroe was also among the best dramatic (actress) _____ of her day, as many of her more serious (movie) _____ prove.

8. The New York (Yankee) _____ defeated the Los Angeles (Dodger) in two consecutive World (Series) _____.

WRITING THE PARAGRAPH OF ILLUSTRATION

> **ASSIGNMENT:** Write a paragraph of twelve to fifteen sentences in which you provide examples to demonstate some general impression that you have about yourself from your childhood. To develop your paragraph through examples, choose some memo-ries of your youth as the basis of this written assignment. Express them by means of details of people, places, and actions. Try to select memories that fall into a pattern in order to suggest a single impression about your experiences. In that case you will develop your paragraph by offering several instances to support your topic sentence.

Student Samples

You may find it convenient to use subtopics if you offer a few well-detailed examples to support your topic. Read the student samples below; pay close attention to the use of subtopic sentences to introduce each new example. Then answer the questions that follow.

Childhood Mischief

I will never forget the mischievous things I used to do when my parents were not at home. Sliding across cool beige linoleum on a cushion of talcum was one exciting bit of mischief. I shook baby powder all over by bedroom floor unitl it looked as if it was covered with snow and was as slick as a sheet of ice. With white socks I became an ice skater gliding gracefully across a frozen pond. Feeling adventurous sometimes, I would run from the hall and slide into my room stopping within a few inches of my wooden dresser, which stands opposite the door. I did another really crazy thing on a night my older sisters babysat for my brother and me. Tired of minding us, Angela and Alethea sent us to bed, but we were not the least bit tired. To make our sisters mad, my brother and I sneaked past them into the kitchen. We each took a little bit of laundry detergent and put it in our noses. Slipping back into bed, we kept sneezing uncontrollably for fifteen minutes. We thought this was funny, and every time a sneeze did not come we laughed. This made my oldest sister Angela very angry. Annoyed, she yelled at us, "You two better stop that sneezing, or when Ma comes home I am going to tell her how you were behaving!" From that moment on we had to cover up our sneezes so we would not get into trouble. But the most mischievous thing I did was to throw heavy rocks at passing cars. My friends, my sister Alethea, and I would go to Crotona Park and would climb to the top of a steep, rocky hill that overlooked an exit off the Cross Bronx Expressway. Whenever we hit one of the speeding cars, we would run off somewhere and hide. One day my sister hit a new brown and white Mustang. She did not see a small angry man burst out of his car. All of us ran except Alethea. Cursing in a harsh voice, the man climbed up the hill behind her and almost grabbed her. She darted out of his reach just in time. That was the last time I ever threw rocks! In retrospect, all those mischievous things I did for fun could have caused me trouble not only with my parents but with other innocent people too.

—*Elaine Dawkins*

Horrors and High School Math

I will never forget my math teachers because I disliked most of them throughout my high school years. I remember my eleventh year math teacher vividly. She had a straight nose on which a pair of gold-rimmed glasses sat tightly at the end. Before each lesson began, she compelled me, her worst student, to erase long white columns from the chalkboards. Each day she gave pages of homework. I hated those assignments, so I just ignored them. In the end, of course, my reward was a *fifty* in red on my report card. Next, my geometry teacher stands out in my mind. Although Miss Carpenter was twenty-five, she acted like an old witch of a hundred. She wore the same dingy green dress each day. Sloppily, mousy brown hair hung in her eyes, and she scooped strands and curls off her forehead. Her voice, high-pitched, would screech across the classroom and down the hall. "Julius," I can still hear her squeak, her lips pinched in a little pink circle, "if you don't know about diameters, I'll have to fail you." But of all my math teachers, I disliked most the one who taught me algebra. A tall, lanky man, this teacher had an angry temper that kept most of us from asking questions. Once a girl in the last row asked timidly, "Will you explain that again please?" As Mr. Gilian's face grew scarlet, he plunged his hands into his black pants pockets. "Try paying attention," he barked, "and then you won't have to bother me with ridiculous questions." From my past unpleasant experiences with math teachers I have grown to dislike them all automatically; is it any wonder that my math grades never rise above C's and D's?

—*Julius Passero*

Step 1.   Reviewing What You Read. Discuss these questions.

1. What is the topic in each paragraph? What is the writer's opinion about the topic in each case?
2. Read aloud the subtopic sentences for each paragraph.
3. How are the details in each case arranged, chronologically or by importance? How do you know?
4. Which details of color, sound, and action do you find most original?

Listing Details: Examples without Subtopics

In the words below from "There Was a Child Went Forth," Walt Whitman, the nineteenth-century American poet, suggests that every experience a person meets in life becomes part of that person.

There was a child went forth every day,
And the first object he look'd upon, that object he became,
And that object became part of him for the day or a certain part of the day,
Or for many years or stretching cycles of years.
The early lilacs became part of this child,
And grass and white and red morning glories, and red clover, and the song of
   the phoebe-bird.

—*Walt Whitman*
"There Was a Child Went Forth"

Some events play more important parts than others in contributing to our development. For the child in the poem, lilacs, morning glories, clover, and a bird's song became part of him. What experiences do you remember that became part of you? Can you capture them in images? What details can you list in order to answer the question "What Am I?"

Step 2.   Using Details in Place of Subtopics. You need to recall the memories that are the deepest parts of yourself, the most vivid events (in your relations with people, parents, and the world) that you feel have become part of you. What you have seen and heard; what you have learned from others and seen in their faces; what smells you recall at unforgettable moments; the books you have read and the movies you watch: these all are the sources of defining your self.

In a paragraph that offers several details to support an idea, you do not need to use subtopics because you are presenting, almost as a list, a series of examples.

Use the following paragraph by Andrew Siscaretti as a model before you write. As he does, use only images in your paragraph: mention people and places by name. Use color and sound.

You might wish to prepare this assignment along with Step 2 of Reaching Higher; there you use Whitman's poem to make a collage.

What Am I? West, Clapton, and Flynn

I am the ringmaster of a three ring circus formally known as my family. I am the arguments between my brother and the whisperings of my sisters. I am the polluted, greyish-blue sky of Long Island City and the slimy, filthy waters of the East River and Newton's Creek. I am the limp in old Jack's leg or the large red girder that smashed down upon it. To my childhood companions, I was a real Casanova for going out with twin sisters at the same time and to those girls I am a devil. And I am the look that I still receive from their reddened blue eyes. To mom, I am still her blue-eyed bundle of joy, maybe growing up to wear the black robe of priesthood, while to pop, I am a future Jim Thorpe sprinting flat races, hurtling over large obstacles with a pole vault, and smacking through defenses for touchdowns. Or am I a future Jerry West, swishing the winning basket at the buzzer? On the football field, I am every player to hold a ball but after ripping my leg open, I change from a growling bear into a purring kitten waiting to die. In the hospital, I become the uncontaminated cleanliness and the antiseptic fragrance of the ward. I also become the lethal point of the syringe used to render me into the world of nod or the scent of flowers I receive from close friends. While listening to my stereo, I become Eric Clapton strumming "Layla" before close to thirty thousand screaming fans and I also become the tangy odor of marijuana that permeates Madison Square Garden. I become one of the fans smoking a joint in the front row. My gang thinks of me as just another head in the crowd, but I am still part of each one of them: one person's sneer, another one's smile, I am the hate and the love that exist among them. In the movies I become an Errol Flynn and a John Wayne who rescue the beautiful brown-eyed damsel and slay the cowardly rogue. I am the pebble in a little boy's shoe, a knife in a policeman's back, a dent on someone's car, a Hank Aaron homerun, my mother's teardrops, a bubble in Raquel Welch's bath, or a derelict stinking of alcohol. I am all of these things and many more. I am life.

—*Andrew Siscaretti*

Some Topics to Think About

In case you have trouble finding a topic, reread some of the sentences on page 90. Here are some other topics you might wish to write about:

1. doing things wrong (right)
2. my friendly disposition
3. my fantasies
4. dressing up
5. dangerous times
6. insecurity: my personality key
7. my strengths
8. three rules I hated to obey
9. competing with a brother (sister)
10. religion in my life
11. my temper
12. favorite toys
13. being independent
14. learning important lessons
15. my dreams
16. getting eyeglasses
17. experiences dating
18. embarrassment
19. rainy days
20. what I liked (disliked) about my parents

Prewriting: Free Association

In free association, you choose a topic and jot down on a piece of paper everything and anything about that topic that pops into your head. The ideas may be random and unrelated. The important thing is to let your thoughts run freely. Don't stop to correct the spelling of a word. When you are finished, look over your words and group related ideas together so that a pattern emerges. These ideas can serve as sources of details for your theme. Below is part of one student's attempt at free association. Examine his list of words and answer the questions that follow.

PREWRITING: FREE ASSOCIATION

Topic: my childhood behavior
sister's appendicitis: threw a tantrum in school
caught smoking in the junior high school bathroom
fishing trip with my father when I was five — I dumped all the bait overboard
happy Sunday mornings at home when I made pancakes and eggs for the whole family (pretty messy!)
bringing home stray parakeet
worm collection in a fish tank
draining a glass of wine from the dining room table (I was seven years old and I couldn't stop laughing)
Hallowe'en fun, howling like ghosts and waking all the neighborhood dogs
learning to swim at Riverhead
collecting money door-to-door for Muscular Dystrophy
sliding down Wilder Hill and knocking out a tooth
eating a whole bag of chocolate kisses.

— Michael D'Angelo

Step 1.   Exploring a Student's Free Associations. Look at the list above to answer these questions:

1. What associations on Mr. D'Angelo's list might you group together because they seem related in some way?
2. What general word or words could you use to describe some of the groups of details? Would you call any of the groups *dangerous? thoughtless? funny?*
3. What central personality thread might Mr. D'Angelo choose to develop on the basis of some of the items on this list?

Step 2.   Your Own Free Associations. Select one of the topics on page 124 (or select a topic of your own), and practice prewriting by using free association to shake loose some ideas about the subject. Use separate paper.

Step 3.   Associations on Tape. Some writers use a tape recorder for free-association techniques in prewriting. Once you have an idea of the topic you want to write about, speak for about twenty minutes into a tape recorder. Say whatever comes into your mind about the topic. Afterwards, with pencil and paper before you, play back the recording of your voice. Try to identify some thread running through your associations about your childhood. Then play the tape again, listening for those examples that support that central thread. Write down the examples with brief phrases; then try to arrange them in some order.

Progress Reminders: A Checklist of Questions

Follow these guidelines as you write a one-paragraph theme that in some way reveals some memorable features of your youth. Some of the questions call for a simple yes or no while others require that you fill in a short answer. Hand in the completed checklist with your final draft. Reread the samples on pages 121–124 before you begin.

1. Did I use a prewriting method to develop my ideas?   _____

2. Did I attempt to use free association to prewrite for this   _____
    essay?
    Was it more or less useful than the techniques I tried in   _____
    Chapters 1 and 2?

3. Did I choose to write a paragraph that employs two or three   _____
    instances to show something about my youth or a paragraph
    that offers a listing of details without subtopics?

4. Did I write a topic sentence (see pages 7–14) that announces   _____
    the subject of the paragraph and identifies my attitude or
    opinion toward the subject?

5. In my rough draft, did all the examples I offered—no   _____
    matter how many—support the personality thread I tried to
    identify?

6. Did I use subtopic sentences where necessary (see pages   _____
    91–93) to introduce each new aspect of the topic?

7. Did I use specific color imagery?   _____

    Color images included: _____

8. Did I use any images that named sounds?   _____

9. Did I use words that show lively actions?   _____

10. Did I remember to use at least one line of someone's spoken words? (See pages 60–62 for punctuating quotations.) _____

11. Did I show enough details of the scene, including a touch word and a word that appeals to the sense of smell? _____

12. Have I used effective transitions to tie my sentences together? (See pages 96–100.) _____

   Have I tried repeating a pronoun (page 99) and repeating the same word at the beginning of several sentences (page 98)? _____

13. Have I arranged the details of my paragraph either in chronological order or in order of importance? _____

14. Have I used some of the new vocabulary on pages 88–89? _____

15. Have I opened one sentence with a word that ends in -ly (see page 60)? _____

16. Did I start some sentences with different subordinators, explained on pages 100–109? _____

17. Did I use a semicolon correctly in at least one sentence (see page 272)? _____

18. As I proofread my essay, did I look especially for errors in run-ons, comma splices, fragments, and plurals? _____

19. After rereading my essay, am I satisfied that I have expressed a dominant impression about my experience? That impression is: _____ _____

20. Does my paragraph have a strong, lively title? _____

GETTING READER RESPONSE

Pair up with just one other person and read each other's drafts about memorable experiences of your youth. Immediately after you finish reading your partner's paper, write a critique about it. (A *critique* is a critical review or commentary.) In your critique, tell the writer how to improve the paragraph. If you are stuck, you might want to consider the following ideas:

1. What impressions did you get from the paragraph?
2. What more do you want to know about any of the examples?
3. Do the examples successfully demonstrate the general impression the writer tries to give of childhood?

   Return the critique to your partner, along with the essay. Use the critique you have received on your paper to produce your next draft.

THE PROFESSIONALS SPEAK

Step 1.   Authors Remember Their Youth. The selections below develop topics through the use of examples. Discuss the questions after you read the excerpts.

Down South

Down South seemed like a dream when I was on the train going back to New York. I saw a lot of things down South that I never saw in my whole life before and most of them I didn't ever want to see again. I saw a great big old burly black man hit a pig in the head with the back of an ax. The pig screamed, oink-oinked a few times, lay down, and started kicking and bleeding . . . and died. When he was real little, I used to chase him, catch him, pick him up, and play catch with him. He was a greedy old pig, but I used to like him. One day when it was real cold, I ate a piece of that pig, and I still liked him. One day I saw Grandma kill a rattlesnake with a hoe. She chopped the snake's head off in the front yard, and I sat on the porch and watched the snake's body keep wiggling till it was nighttime. And I saw an old brown hound dog named Old Joe eat a rat one day, right out in the front yard. He caught the rat in the woodpile and started tearing him open. Old Joe was eating everything in the rat. He ate something that looked like the yellow part in an egg, and I didn't eat eggs for a long time after that. I saw a lady rat have a lot of little baby rats on a pile of tobacco leaves. She had to be a lady, because my first-grade teacher told a girl that ladies don't cry about little things, and the rat had eleven little hairless pink rats, and she didn't even squeak about it.

I made a gun down South out of a piece of wood, some tape, a piece of tire-tube rubber, a nail, some wire, a piece of pipe, and a piece of door hinge. And I saw nothing but blood where my right thumbnail used to be after I shot it for the first time. That nail grew back, little by little. I saw a lot of people who had roots worked on them, but I never saw anybody getting roots worked on them.

Down South sure was a crazy place, and it was good to be going back to New York.

—Claude Brown
Manchild in the Promised Land

Boyhood Farm Days

As I have said, I spent some part of every year at the farm until I was twelve or thirteen years old. The life which I led there with my cousins was full of charm, and so is the memory of it yet. I know how the wild blackberries looked, and how they tasted, and the same with the pawpaws, the hazelnuts, and the persimmons; and I can feel the thumping rain, upon my head, of hickory nuts and walnuts when we were out in the frosty dawn to scramble for them with the pigs, and the gusts of wind loosed them and sent them down,. I know the stain of blackberries, and how pretty it is, and I know the stain of walnut hulls, and how little it minds soap and water, also what grudged experience it had of either of them. I know the taste of maple sap, and when to gather it, and how to arrange the troughs and the delivery tubes, and how to boil down the juice, and how to hook the sugar after it is made, also how much better hooked sugar tastes than any that is honestly come by, let bigots say what they will. I know how a prize watermelon looks when it is sunning its fat rotundity among pumpkin vines and "simblins"; I know how to tell when it is ripe without "plugging" it; I know how inviting it looks when it is cooling itself in a tub of water under the bed, waiting; I know how it looks when it lies on the table in the sheltered great floor space between house and kitchen, and the children gathered for the sacrifice and their mouths watering; I know the crackling sound it makes when the carving knife enters its end, and I can see the split fly along in front of the blade as the knife cleaves its way to the other end; I can see its halves fall apart and display the rich red meat and the black seeds, and the heart standing up, a luxury fit for the elect; I know how a boy looks behind a yard-long slice of that melon, and I know how he feels; for I have been there. I know the taste of the watermelon which has been honestly come by, and I know the taste of the watermelon which has been acquired by art. Both taste good, but the experienced know which tastes best. I know the look of green apples and peaches and pears on the trees, and I know how entertaining they are when they are inside of a person. I know how ripe ones look when they are piled in pyramids under the trees, and how pretty they are and how vivid their colors. I know how a frozen apple looks, in a barrel down cellar in the wintertime, and how hard it is to bite, and how the frost makes the teeth ache, and yet how good it is, notwithstanding. I know the disposition of elderly people to select the specked apples for the children, and I once knew ways to beat the game. I know the look of an apple that is roasting and sizzling on a hearth on a winter's evening, and I know the comfort that comes of eating it hot, along with some sugar and a drench of cream.

—*Mark Twain*
Autobiography

1. What topic does each writer attempt to support?
2. What examples does he present in order to develop the topic?
3. Which images of action are clearest?
4. What words serve as transitions through repetition in each selection?

Step 2. Reviewing a Professional Sample. Reread "Memories of Crossgates School" (page 94) by George Orwell. What topic does this paragraph develop? What examples does the writer give in order to support his point? Which details are most lively and original?

REACHING HIGHER

Step 1. Photo into Words. Look at the photograph on page 87. Write a topic sentence that introduces the main subject of the picture and some opinion you have about the subject. Write subtopic sentences—if necessary—to introduce each aspect of the topic; add details of color, sound, smell, touch, and action to support each subtopic sentence.

Step 2.   A Collage to Answer "What Am I?"   Read again the piece on page 123 from Walt Whitman's poem "There Was a Child Went Forth." This time, using old magazines, newspapers, paint, ink, pieces of advertisements, various other materials (foil, string, macaroni, photographs), make a *collage* that you think will present to the class a visual answer to the question "What Am I?" Select from the sources you use things that you believe have become part of you. Look at the "What Am I?" collage below by Jacqueline Boston.

After everyone has prepared collages, line them all up in front of the room so that nobody's name can be seen. One at a time, discuss the personality of the person who made each project. What specific feature of the collage tells you most about the person who made it?

Jacqueline Boston

CHAPTER 4

COMPARISON AND CONTRAST:
People You Know, Side by Side

INTRODUCTION TO COMPARISON AND CONTRAST

Hundreds of people brush past our lives every day: crowds at the shopping malls; long lines at restaurants and movie houses; bodies on campus running, strolling, laughing, pushing, drifting between classes; men and women and children in the family, on the block, in the homes of friends. With many of these people nothing more develops than a meeting of the eyes, then a quick glance away and a rapid forgetting. With others, relationships build, some with our delight and thanks, others against our own wills. As our experiences and memories collect faces, appearances, personalities of the people around us, we cannot help making comparisons and drawing contrasts, almost automatically. One woman's smile reminds us of another's. One child's delights make us wonder at another child's pains. One man's kindness and patience we lay alongside another man's anger and cruelty. In our minds' eyes we see side by side our relatives, our friends, our teachers, our colleagues, our enemies, our loves.

One of the best ways we have to analyze, understand, and evaluate is through comparison and contrast. It is second nature for us to compare one experience with another to see points of resemblance and difference. In writing, such a process adds force to your presentation; the reader comes to understand the value of your experiences as you yourself weave together the strands of comparison or contrast.

VOCABULARY

Step 1. Words for Opposite Qualities. These words will help you contrast people you may want to describe. In the blanks write definitions for the opposite—or nearly opposite—words in each set. Use a dictionary for assistance. (Check Appendix A for more help.)

1. *a.* dexterous _____   *b.* awkward _____

2. *a.* diminutive _____   *b.* massive _____

3. *a.* rotund _____   *b.* slender _____

4. *a.* conventional _____   *b.* rebellious _____

5. *a.* altruistic _____   *b.* egocentric _____

Step 2. Applying Meanings. From the words above select one to describe a person who

1. challenges rules _____   4. cares only about himself _____

2. is very tiny _____   5. is gracefully thin _____

3. does things in accepted ways _____   6. is bulky and solid _____

_____   7. is clumsy _____

8. has a plump shape _____

10. gives generously to others
_____

9. is skillful in the use of body or mind _____

Step 3.   Words for Contrasting Moods. Check the definitions of these words to describe moods. Write definitions that you understand in the blank spaces (see Appendix A).

"Up" Moods

1. content _____

2. confident _____

3. affectionate _____

4. pacific _____

5. exuberant _____

"Down" Moods

6. irate _____

7. apathetic _____

8. anxious _____

9. masochistic _____

10. depressed _____

Step 4.   Listening in on Moods. Each statement made below identifies a mood named in Step 3. Identify the mood that the person who speaks seems to be experiencing.

_____   1. "I feel very happy and feel that I have everything I need in life."

_____   2. "Let me kiss you again. I love to hold you."

_____   3. "If I get my hands on him, I'll kill him. I'll tear him limb from limb."

_____   4. "I'm so worried about everything, especially the test tomorrow."

_____   5. "I couldn't care less about my new job."

_____   6. "I feel so calm and peaceful."

_____   7. "I'll study until dawn. Unless I suffer, I'm not going to pass that final!"

_____   8. "I know I can do the job right."

_____   9. "I'm delighted at being alive. What a beautiful, wonderful, sunny day!"

_____   10. "I never felt so rotten in all my life."

BUILDING COMPOSITION SKILLS

Finding the Topic

Step 1.   Talking It Over. Using the suggestions below, speak for a minute or two about two people who are similar to or who are very different from each other. Show how your specific experiences with these people illustrate your point as Thomas Baim does in his talk below.

1. two friends you know
2. the way two salespeople treated you
3. two math or science teachers you liked (or disliked)
4. how your parents are alike (or different)
5. how your brothers (sisters, cousins) are different
6. the same news story as told by two different television announcers
7. two employers you worked for
8. two different boyfriends (girl friends)
9. a teacher who lectures as opposed to a teacher who guides class discussions
10. two aunts (or uncles) from different sides of your family
11. two coworkers: likenesses and differences
12. high school teachers versus college teachers
13. your son (daughter) at one age compared with the same child at another age
14. two neighborhood storekeepers: how they treat customers
15. two politicians

To me lectures are worthless; group discussions make much better and more interesting class sessions. Mr. Goldman, my junior history teacher at Park Lane High, lectured to us all the time. Even though he had a lively booming voice and a good knowledge of his subject, after thirty minutes, feet would shuffle on the floor, pencils would drop, girls would whisper and yawn as the teacher turned his back to write on the board. I loved history, but I found myself staring out the window at the sky or the clouds. But Mr. Rudnicki, my psychology teacher here at State, never lectures. Sure, he contributes information to our discussions—sometimes he talks for ten minutes straight—but lots of other people talk as well. It's much more exciting to hear different voices and different opinions. We all sit around with our chairs in a circle and usually more than half the class talks at each session. I know it's much harder to learn in this kind of class because you never really know what's "right" since there is often no definite information. But I find I'm always thinking about what went on in my psych class, and I can't wait to forget what I scribbled in my notebook during a lecture!

—*Thomas Baim*

Figures of Speech

An important way to improve your written expression is to make comparisons so that the reader sees clearly some picture you are describing. Notice how the picture in Column I below takes on new life in Column II by means of a comparison.

I	*II*
Her blue eyes sparkled.	Her eyes sparkled *like small blue circles of ice.*

By using the word *like* (or, often, *as*) in II above, the writer compares *eyes* to *small blue circles of ice.* Such a comparison, using *like* or *as*, is called a *simile.*

A *metaphor* is a comparison that leaves out the comparing word *like* or *as:*

Her eyes were *small blue circles of ice.*

This kind of comparison is often very forceful because it shows that the object is so much like the thing to which it is being compared that it almost becomes that thing. Look again at the difference.

Her eyes were *like small blue circles of ice.*	Her eyes *were small blue circles of ice.*
Here, a woman's eyes are compared to circles of ice, and there are two distinct features of the comparison, *eyes* and *blue circles of ice.*	Here, the woman's eyes are said to *be* those *blue circles of ice.* It is as if the eyes and the icy blue circles were one and the same; the eyes take on all the qualities of the ice.

Sometimes, to add liveliness, a writer can give some nonhuman object living qualities. The comparison between a nonhuman object and a living thing is called *personification:*

The hot day dragged its weary feet into the evening.

In this sentence, the *day,* a nonhuman object, is given the qualities of a person who is tired: the words *dragged its weary feet* express the human quality.

Step 1. Reading Lively Comparisons. Read aloud these comparisons by professional writers. Explain the meaning of the comparison. Which sentence lets you see most clearly what the writer had in mind? Which comparison is most original?

1. If dreams die, life is a broken-winged bird that cannot fly.
   —*Langston Hughes*

2. Out of the low vapor softly roofing the fields a gull came flying slowly over their heads.
   —*Constance Holme*

3. A sickly light, like yellow tinfoil, was slanting over the high walls into the jail yard.
   —*George Orwell*

4. The town hung like a bird's nest in the cliff, looking into the box canyon below, and beyond into the wide valley we call Cow Canyon, facing an ocean of clear air.
   —*Willa Cather*

5. The trailer was the most stable home he had ever known, and it rocked like a conoe in the ocean.
   —*Beth Weinstein*

6. His face was white as pie-dough and his arms were lank and white as peeled sticks.
   —*Robert Smith*

7. The mysterious East faced me, perfumed like a flower, silent like death, dark like a grave.

—*Joseph Conrad*

Step 2. Comparisons of Your Own. Using the word groups below, on separate paper write sentences that make a comparison in a vivid picture. Strive for originality, humor, beauty, clarity. Use any of the three types of comparisons you have learned so far—simile, metaphor, personification.

Example
rain

The rain hissed on the hot cabin roof, then slithered down the window in streams like transparent snakes.
—*Gerald Hull*

1. wheat fields
2. cemetery
3. a friend's smile
4. a rainy afternoon
5. the moon
6. a river
7. the fall
8. an old automobile
9. your kitchen table
10. an empty beach

Step 3. Metaphors for Abstract Words. Try to explain your view of some hard-to-define emotion, idea, or concept in a metaphor rich in sensory detail. Select a word such as *hope, love, fear, power, war, hate, hunger, life, sorrow, joy, death,* or any other abstract term. Look at the student samples below. Use your own paper.

Life is a rosebush growing in my garden, full of thorns but fragrant and lovely.
—*Alayne Finkelstein*

Fear is sitting in a creaking dentist's chair and seeing only the top of Dr. Rifkin's bald head as his trembling hand tries to zero in on a cavity.
—*Janet Hutter*

Life is an elusive, black fly buzzing through cool air, slipping past the blue-eyed youngster stalking him with a fly swatter.
—*Terry Sanders*

Step 4. Avoiding Trite Comparisons. When a comparison appears too frequently in language, it loses its originality. Any statement or expression that is overused is called *trite* or *hackneyed* because it is no longer original. Such expressions appear numbered from 1 to 10 below. For each one, rewrite the comparison to strengthen it. Use separate paper.

Example:
1. quiet as a mouse   *quiet as a schoolyard in a Sunday morning rain.*

2. red as a beet
3. white as a ghost or white as a sheet

4. fresh as a daisy
5. so hungry I could eat a horse
6. ugly as sin
7. as different as night and day

8. busy as a bee
9. happy as a lark
10. pretty as a picture

Transitions

As you may recall, certain words help one idea in a paragraph flow smoothly into the next idea. The *transition* words below, cementing together ideas so that the thoughts are related clearly, show relationships you might want to indicate in your paragraph.

Transition Words That Add One Thought to Another		*Transition Words to Compare Ideas (to Show Likenesses)*
in addition	likewise	in the same way
moreover	nor	similarly
and	further	likewise
and then	next	resembling
besides	last	alike
again	also	like
too		
furthermore		

Transition Words to Contrast Ideas or to Admit a Point (to Show Differences)

but	although	dissimilar
still	on the other hand	unalike
however	in contrast	differ(s) from
nevertheless	otherwise	difference
on the contrary	conversely	different
after all	while this may be true	
notwithstanding	yet	
even though	granted	
though	in spite of	

Transition Words to Show That One Idea Results from Another

as a result	accordingly
thus	therefore

because   consequently

since   then

hence

Step 1.   Transitions to Show Relationships. In this paragraph, fill in each blank with a transition word that will help move one idea smoothly into the next. The information at the left tells what kinds of transition words you need. Be sure that the word you select makes sense in the blank.

The True Musician

[contrast]   _____ Plato believed that music played a strong part in a man's education, he did not ignore other areas of learning. Music, through rhythm and
[add]   harmony, could bring grace to the soul _____ a man educated in
[result]   music could develop a true sense of judgment; _____ he would be able to recognize quality in art and nature and could respond with praise for
[compare]   good things. _____ a man who knew music could, without having to
[contrast]   think too long, give blame to any bad artistic works. _____ any man who devoted his life only to music risked the chance of becoming too softened
[result]   and soothed. _____ such a man would be a feeble warrior and of
[contrast]   little use to the Greeks. Someone who practiced gymnastics, _____, could fill himself with pride and could become twice the man that he
[compare] [admit was. _____ he could develop courage for battle. _____
            point] athletics made an essential part of the educated man, Plato also knew that too much focus on physical training could make a man excessively violent and
[add]   fierce. _____ he might come to hate philosophy and the art of
[compare]   persuasion in preference to battle. _____ such a man would live in
[result]   ignorance and would not be civilized. _____ Plato showed that the man who learned music and athletics in good balance was best; "He who mingles music with gymnastics in the fairest proportions . . . may be rightly called the true musician. . . ."

Transition Words That Summarize

therefore   consequently

in conclusion   thus

finally   to sum up

as a result   accordingly

in short   in brief

as I have [shown]   in other words

          [said]   all in all

          [stated]

Transition Words That Emphasize

surely   indeed

certainly   truly

to be sure   in fact   /

undoubtedly   without a doubt

Transition Words That Tell That an Example Will Follow

for example   specifically

for instance   as an illustration

as proof   to illustrate

Step 2.   Example, Summary, Emphasis: Transitions. From the three lists of transition words, select one word that will fit in the blank as a good transition. The words at the left tell the kinds of transition words you need.

[emphasizes]   1. Rock music is still extraordinarily popular. _____ it will maintain its hold on young people over the next decade.

[summary]   2. Recently many popular magazines have addressed the topic of nuclear war. _____, it is no longer an issue people are evading.

[example]   3. _____ the desire to be better educated is represented in the increase in community college enrollments.

[example]   4. Not all housework is tedious. _____ cooking, even though it can be a chore, is still an imaginative and creative one.

[summary]   5. He failed his driving test three times. _____ he could not use the family car all summer long.

[emphasis]   6. _____ there are many ways to save energy around the house.
[example]   _____, lowering the thermostat drops oil consumption remarkably.

[emphasis]   7. _____, she decided never to be a secretary again.
[summary]   8. He watched a total of six hours of television _____.

Step 3.   Checking More Transitions. Read "Different Roommates," page 146. Circle the transition words that add, compare, contrast, show result, summarize, or indicate example.

Expanding Quotation Sentences

A sentence in which you tell the exact words someone is saying adds life to a paragraph. Often you can expand a quotation sentence by using sensory language in order to paint a vivid picture of the speaker or the circumstances under which the speaking is done. By adding action words and appeals to color, smell, touch, or sound, you can create a full and satisfying image for your reader.

HOW TO BUILD A QUOTATION SENTENCE

1. Start with a lively, realistic quotation:

"Hurry up, you lazy slowpoke!"

2. Tell who talks:

"Hurry up, you lazy slowpoke!" Vivian shouted.
"Hurry up, you lazy slowpoke!" my sister said.

3. Tell *how, when* or *where* the words were spoken:

[where]
"Hurry up, you lazy slowpoke!" Vivian shouted at the door.
"Hurry up, you lazy slowpoke!" my sister said angrily.
[how]

4. Add a detail to describe some action or movement:

Pulling on her gloves at the door, Vivian shouted, "Hurry up, you lazy slowpoke!"
[action]

[action]
"Hurry up, you lazy slowpoke!" my sister said angrily as she stamped her foot on the floor.

5. Describe the speaker's face. Add a detail of color or touch or sound.

Pursing her lips and pulling on leather gloves at the door, Vivian shouted,
[description of speaker]   [touch word]
"Hurry up, you lazy slowpoke!"

[color]
"Hurry up, you lazy slowpoke!" my sister said angrily, her brown eyes flashing as she stamped her foot on the floor.
[description of speaker]

Hint

Review the correct punctuation of quotations on pages 60–62.

Step 1. Expanding Quotation Sentences. Expand each of these quotations by adding details in several steps like those in the boxed chart. Write your final sentence on the blank lines.

1. "I'm not interested in your opinion." _____

_____

2. "Close the door because it's freezing in here." _____

_____

3. "I just don't care anymore!" _____

_____

4. "It's not the heat but it's the humidity too." _____

_____

5. "This work must be finished by this afternoon." _____

_____

6. "I'm trying to say I'm sorry." _____

_____

7. "I'd rather do it myself." _____

_____

8. "Nothing ventured, nothing gained." _____

_____

9. "Let's get moving!" _____

_____

10. "I'd prefer to eat alone." _____

_____

Step 2.   Building Up Your Own Quotations. Return to Step 4 on pages 62–63. Expand in the manner described above each original sentence you wrote in Column II. Use separate paper.

COMPARISON AND CONTRAST: THREE PARAGRAPH PATTERNS

A favorite method of paragraph and essay development involves comparison and contrast. *Comparison* means showing how things are alike, and *contrast* means showing how things are different. Sometimes a paragraph may be developed through illustrations of how things are *different;* other paragraphs discuss *similarities* only; still others may treat both *likenesses and differences*. The writer decides which approach to take.

> *Hint*
>
> If you are asked to *compare* two things, you usually need to *contrast* them as well.

Whatever approach you choose, there are some patterns you can follow to make the comparison effective.

Likenesses *or* Differences

Pattern 1. In this kind of paragraph, first you discuss one of the two objects; then you discuss the other object.

You can single out one basic way in which the two objects are alike or different in order to limit your topic effectively. For example, you might decide to compare two people at work by discussing the way they do their jobs. The first part of the paragraph would show something about one person's approach to work; the next part of the paragraph would show something about the other person's approach.

However, instead of deciding on one basic way by which to compare the two things, you can choose to discuss a *few* points or ideas about the first object; then you can discuss a *few* points or ideas about the second. Here you do not use a single focus of comparison. For example, in a paragraph comparing two people in this manner, you might want to discuss these points:

1. the way they dress
2. the way they talk
3. how they behave under pressure

First you would discuss all those ideas in regard to one person; then, in the next part of the paragraph, you would discuss the same points in regard to the other person. In each part, of course, you would need to offer details to support your ideas.

SOME HINTS ABOUT PATTERN I

If you decide on a basic focus of comparison:

1. A subtopic sentence (see pages 91–93) will help you introduce the basic difference for each object.
2. You might wish to illustrate your point with *one specific instance* about one person and *one specific instance* about the other. Each instance would be a dramatic moment expanded by means of sensory language.
3. If you want to use more than one instance from your experience to illustrate each part of your point, you can also use sensory language. True, you will not be able to go into great detail for each instance, but you need to make the details as clear as possible.
4. You might wish to combine 2 and 3: state briefly several instances that illustrate your point about the first person; then focus on one dramatic moment that illustrates your point about the second person.

(continued on next page)

SOME HINTS ABOUT PATTERN I *(continued)*

If you decide to discuss a few points about each object:

1. A subtopic sentence can help you introduce each of the two people you are comparing.
2. You will not be able to go into great detail for each of the points. However, make sure that you can support each point with some kind of illustration.
3. You run the risk of writing a dull paragraph because each point is usually repeated twice, once for each object. Lively illustrations and varied vocabulary can help overcome dullness.

Step 1. **A Student's Theme.** Read the student sample below. Answer the questions after the paragraph.

The Two Willies

Only five years old, my son Willie tickles the family with opposite sides to his behavior. One piece of him is quiet and shy, especially when he is with strangers. Last month I had to drag him up the steps at Presbyterian Nursery School for his first day in class. Willie clutched at my leg in silent terror as we stood at the doorway to his room. Two little boys sat at a table near the window and played with green clay as they giggled to each other. Nearby a boy and girl dressed and undressed two rag dolls. "Well, so this is Willie," said his teacher, Miss Natalie, with a bright smile. "Come, let's say hello to the rest of the class." But she had to pry his fingers one by one off my skirt as he stared without a sound. When Miss Natalie led Willie from child to child, saying his name, Willie never breathed a word. Though his teacher says now that he is coming along, he is still the quietest boy in the class. But just let him loose in the backyard of our house and he turns into a wild man! Yesterday, a warm fall afternoon, he hung by his ankles from a limb of our elm as my heart pounded. Calling like a monkey and beating his chest, he swung back and forth, back and forth. Leaping down, he raced to the grey wooden fence and barked through it at my neighbor's German shepherd, who howled and rattled his pen. Then like a squirrel Willie dug a dozen holes in the lawn and buried whatever he could find, bottle caps, pieces of glass, leaves, cigarette butts, broken twigs. He's never quiet or shy! He chased flies, snorting through his nose. Off key he sang the *Sesame Street* song as he poked a pink worm with a rock. When Charlotte, my next-door neighbor's four-year-old, came to play, Willie screeched at her like a plane about to crash and pushed her to the grass. She cried miserably, but Willie showed no mercy. My psychology teacher assures me that my son is perfectly normal for his age, but he is not at all easy to understand at this stage.

—*Mollie Boone*

1. What is the basic focus to show the different qualities of Mollie Boone's son Willie?
2. What two moments does she use to illustrate her point?
3. Which, in your opinion, are the liveliest images of action? What details name sounds? Where is color used effectively?

4. Read each of the two subtopic sentences. What key words in the subtopic sentences suggest opposite meanings?

Step 2.   Using a Focus for Comparison. Assume that you would develop each topic in Column I in a comparison-contrast paragraph like Pattern 1 where you would use a single focus of comparison. In Column II, write down the basic way in which the two ideas are either alike or similar. In Column III, name two specific moments you might use to illustrate each object. Look at the example.

I *Topics to Compare*	*II* *Basic Focus of Comparison*	*III* *Two Illustrations*
1. baseball and football	*level of excitement (baseball: dull; football: exciting)*	*a. time I sat through an eleven inning no hitter.* *b. time I watched the Jets and Packers at Shea Stadium.*
2. two former teachers		
3. a blind date compared with a date I chose myself		
4. summer and winter		
5. a book I have read and the movie or play based on it		

Step 3.   Understanding Another Approach. Assume that you would develop each topic in Column I in a comparison-contrast paragraph that follows Pattern 1 where there is no basic focus but where, instead, a few points are discussed for each object. In Column II, list three significant points you might use to illustrate each part of the topic. Look at the example.

I	*II*
Topic for Comparison	**Discussion Points**

1. city and country winters

a. *transportation* _____
b. *ways of having fun* _____
c. *landscape* _____

2. waiters and waitresses

a. _____
b. _____
c. _____

3. close friends and casual acquaintances

a. _____
b. _____
c. _____

4. dressing casually and dressing up

a. _____
b. _____
c. _____

5. two neighbors

a. _____
b. _____
c. _____

Pattern 2. This pattern does not separate the two objects you are discussing. Instead, it treats both objects together for each point of comparison. For example, in a paragraph comparing two roommates, let's assume that a writer wants to discuss these three points:

1. their physical appearances
2. their interests
3. their approaches to schoolwork

After mentioning each point, the writer would discuss both roommates in relation to that point, in order to illustrate how they compare in physical appearance, how they compare in their interests, and, finally, how they compare in the way they do schoolwork.

HINTS ABOUT PATTERN 2

1. Ordering details by importance (see pages 94–96) is often the best plan for this pattern. You may wish, therefore, to discuss in less detail your first point or points so that you can concentrate more fully on the last point, the one that is most important to you.
2. The subtopic sentence helps you introduce each new point of comparison.
3. Transition words help you move easily from one point to the next.

Step 4.   A Point-by-Point Comparison. Read the paragraph below, developed by means of Pattern 2. Answer the questions that come after it.

Different Roommates

I am amazed myself at how little trouble it is living with and liking two such different roommates. Their physical appearances differ greatly. With small brown eyes and straight black hair to her shoulders, Julie is tall, lean, and statuesque. Pat, on the other hand, is tiny. Under five feet tall, she keeps her blonde hair short and fluffy. Looking out over a small nose, her large grey eyes are "funny looking," according to her. "They're all right if you like cats," she says grinning. These two girls also have different kinds of interests. Julie likes reading or relaxing quietly in front of the television set. She likes talking too; she will speak to me for hours about a feature in *People Magazine* or about a Marx Brothers' film she watched on Channel 4 until dawn. Her voice quivers with excitement. "Just listen to this," she will say, her eyes glowing, her warm fingers pressed to my palm to hold my attention. But for Pat the outdoor life holds more interest than books or screens. At six each morning, in a bright orange sweat suit, she is jogging merrily down University Drive, crunching through leaves for her usual four miles. She swims. She plays tennis. She is a terror at paddleball, smashing shots I have to groan to return. However, the most interesting difference between them is their approach to schoolwork. Julie grows tense before an exam. At her desk a small fluorescent lamp throws a pale light on her face as she sits for hours glaring nervously at a page in her biology book. She underlines words noisily and scrawls notes to herself in the margin with a yellow felt pen. Her lips say over and over some key words she wants to memorize. Because only "A" grades satisfy her, she works tirelessly. Pat, on the contrary, takes everything easy, and exams are no exception. Sprawled on the red and white print couch, she surrounds herself with cola, corn chips, chocolate bars, apples, and salted nuts. She jabbers endlessly and jumps up every few minutes to stare out the window, to do a few sit-ups or to splash herself with spicy cologne. Without much effort or anxiety she crams enough data into her head to earn grades that keep her happy. Since I can live in harmony with my two roommates in spite of their differences, I am confident that I will be able to get along with most people·anywhere.

—*Cecilia Richardson*

1. Pick out the three subtopic sentences.
2. Which details let you see best what Julie looks like? what Pat looks like? Which images do you find clearest and most memorable?

3. What is the main difference in the approaches to schoolwork each of the writer's roommates takes? What specific details best show the difference?
4. What order has Cecilia Richardson used to arrange the points in this comparison? Why has she chosen such an order?

Likenesses *and* Differences

Pattern 3. In this comparison and contrast paragraph, you discuss both likenesses *and* differences. You can decide on *one basic way* in which the two objects may be compared, or you can discuss a number of points for the two objects without naming some central focus (as in Pattern 1). The idea here is that both similaritics *and* dissimilarities appear in the paragraph. Of course, you will have to illustrate just *how* these two objects have some similar features and how they have different features. If you think the differences are more important, discuss the *similarities* first so that you may give the reader the most important idea *last* (see pages 94–96 for order of details). If you think the similarities are more important, discuss the differences first.

Let us assume that you want to compare two of your relatives and that you select *the way they disciplined you as a child* as the one basic point of comparison. Let's also assume that the differences in these methods of disciplining are what you think are most important. The first part of your paragraph could illustrate through vivid details one or more of these similarities:

1. your relatives' concern for your welfare
2. their strictness
3. their little speeches after you did something wrong

Then, you might focus on one or more of these differences:

1. the way the two relatives looked when they were angry
2. what they actually did to you
3. how long it took them to get over their anger

Determine the *number* of points you want to discuss by the nature of the details you wish to use. One dramatic, expanded illustration for *one* of the points would mean that fewer points would be treated in the paragraph.

HINTS ABOUT PATTERN 3

1. The topic sentence should indicate that your paragraph will treat *both* similarities and differences. Coordination or subordination may be effectively used in the topic sentence.

[subordinator]

Although my mother and father shared similar outlooks in rearing children and in disciplining them, mom took her responsibilities more seriously.

[coordinator]

Both my parents were very liberal in the way they reared their children, but my father's sudden loss of temper in moments of anger always scared me.

2. Remember, if differences are more important to you, discuss similarities first; if likenesses are more important, talk first about differences. Topic sentence I below stresses the major area of difference; topic sentence II stresses the major areas of likeness. The sentences deal with similar topics.

I	II
Although my mother and my grandmother supported strict rules in rearing young children, I could always count on grandma's understanding when I got in trouble at school.	Despite their different ways of showing approval or disapproval for my behavior, my mother and my grandmother supported strict rules in rearing children.
This paragraph will stress the differences in the degree of understanding the relatives showed toward school problems.	*This paragraph will stress the similarities in the support shown by the two relatives for strictness in raising children.*

3. Sometimes you do not need to explain both similarities and differences, even though you wish to make the point that likenesses and differences exist. You can assume that the reader understands, appreciates, or agrees with the part that you do not wish to explain. In this way you can use the paragraph to develop the more important element of your comparison. For example, in topic sentence 1 above, the writer could assume that readers would accept this part of the sentence: "my mother and my grandmother supported strict rules in rearing young children." The writer would not have to discuss these strict rules but could move right on to illustrate the differences as he or she sees them.

Step 5. Understanding the Pattern. For each subject of comparison or contrast in Column I list in Column II two or three similarities that might be expanded with details in a paragraph. In Column III list two or three differences between the two objects, differences that might also be expanded with details in the paragraph. Look at the example.

I *Topic for Comparison*	II *Some Similarities*	III *Some Differences*

1. cats and dogs as pets	a. *companionship*
	b. *owners develop a sense*
	  of responsibility
	c. *amusement*
		a. *cats are very easy to*
		  care for
		b. *cats often get in trouble*
		c. *cats are moody and*
		  unpredictable

2. ice skaters and roller skaters		
3. city children and rural children		
4. being the driver and being the passenger		
5. one friend's humor versus another friend's humor		

Step 6. Comparison and Contrast. Pattern 3: A Student Model. Read the student's paragraph below, which discusses likenesses and differences in two people who are close friends. In the margins are explanations of the various parts of the paragraph. Answer the questions that appear after Stacy Kissenger's theme.

Birds of a Feather?

[topic sentence
1. tells that similarities and differences will be discussed
2. tells that the *differences* are more important]

[subtopic sentence: tells that discussion of likenesses will follow]

Despite their close relationship my two friends Tammy Smith and Laurie Potter provide striking contrasts in their dispositions. Granted, there are many ways in which these friends are similar. Both born on farms,

[one similarity and instances to illustrate it]

[more points to finish discussion on similarities]

[details to show qualities for one person]

[closing sentence
1. uses transition "then"
2. restates main idea that two friends are alike yet have distinct personality differences
3. introduces a new but related idea: people do not have to have similar personalities in order to be close friends (see pages 205–208 for information on closing sentences.)]

Tammy and Laurie prefer fields of corn to buzzing city streets. Their love for farming unites them as together they lecture their city slicker friends like me about Guernseys and Holsteins or about the uses of cultivators. Both girls also share an interest in athletics. The two of them played on the high school basketball team and by their senior year had developed the flawless "Smith-Potter" rebounding method, which included elbowing and stomping on anyone separating them and the ball. Off the basketball court their fun-loving natures further reinforce each other as they tease and joke, often to the dismay of those around them. Once they convinced the shop teacher's daughter that rubber crowbars and metric screwdrivers really existed. But the personality differences between these two friends are much more outstanding than the likenesses. Laurie is carefree and easygoing with a well of cheerfulness within her. Her sapphire eyes twinkle brightly and the corners of her lips curl upward into a smile as she chats with her friends in the college hallways. When I am feeling miserable, she jokes and giggles to chase away the depression. Her own anger rarely surfaces. When everyone else rages, Laurie rarely shows hostility, except perhaps in her face. Angry, she retreats within herself. Her chatter ceases as the twinkle disappears from her eyes. Her jaw locks tightly, and every muscle tenses. The soft brown crop of curls and the light sprinkling of freckles across her nose suddenly make her face look sharp. But the anger passes quickly, and Laurie once again radiates warmth and excitement. Tammy, in contrast, is much less even-tempered. Though she is a warm and generous person, her moods often change drastically. Frequently she grows depressed and sulks for days at a time. Her forehead wrinkles with anxiety; her hazel eyes glare disgustedly, even at best friends. If Laurie or I try to find out why she is so angry, she growls, "Just leave me alone!" and stalks away. Once I watched her face flush with crimson as she snatched a phone book and hurled it, its pages flapping before it thudded against the floor like a dead bird. At another time I saw her kick the wall beside her bed, leaving a black heel mark just above her pillow. Neither people nor things are safe when one of her famous moods transforms Tammy into a monster! Despite some likenesses, then, these two contrasting personalities have convinced me that being birds of a feather is not essential for friendship; although their dispositions differ widely, Laurie and Tammy are each other's best friends.

—Stacy Kissenger

[another similarity (note transition "also" and reference to topic sentence with "Both girls share an interest") and a supporting example]

[subtopic sentence: tells that discussion of differences will follow]

[contrasting details to show qualities for other person (note transition "in contrast" and reminder of the differences between the two girls with "much less even-tempered")]

1. What is the basic feature of contrast between the two friends?
2. In what two ways are the girls alike? What details does Stacy Kissenger offer to support those likenesses?
3. How does she illustrate the major difference she sees between the two people she is discussing? Do you find her illustrations effective? Why or why not?
4. Discuss the images in the paragraph. Which pictures best use color and sound?

SOLVING PROBLEMS IN WRITING

Mirror Words II

Here are several more words that cause confusion because they look and sound similar.

QUIT   *QUIET*   *QUITE*

quit: to stop.

I *quit* my job last week.

quiet: silent; without noise or movement

A *quiet* room is restful.

quite: completely; rather.

He was *quite* disturbed at the accident.

Step 1. *Quit, Quiet, Quite?* Fill in the blank with *quit, quiet,* or *quite* so that the sentences make sense.

1. "That's _____ a _____ automobile you have there," the gas station attendant said with a grin.
2. In a _____ voice he mumbled that he would _____ as of tomorrow.
3. "I'm just looking for some peace and _____," he wearily told the desk clerk.
4. It takes _____ a bit of courage to change careers.
5. It's _____ a drive to Helena from Great Falls but perfect for a _____ Sunday morning.
6. When you _____ studying, take a long, _____ walk around the campus.
7. That was _____ a foolish thing to do.
8. Bill shouted angrily, "You haven't fired me. I _____!"

PRINCIPAL   *PRINCIPLE*

principal:

1. a head person at a school.

   The *principal* speaks to the students each day.

2. a major sum of money.

   The *principal* he invested earned $1,250 interest.

3. a descriptive word that means *most important.*

   Rice is still the *principal* food for many people.

principle: a rule, a major belief, a basic idea or truth

One *principle* for success is hard work.
As a man of *principle,* he refused a bribe.
The *principle* of atoms and molecules goes back to the early Greeks.

   Hint: Princip*le* and ru*le* both end in *-le:* if you use princip*le* make sure it means ru*le.*

Step 2.   Using *Principle* and *Principal*. Fill in the blanks with the letters *-le* or *-al* so that the word *principle* or *principal* correctly suits the meaning of the word group.

1. a woman of princip_____s

2. the high school princip_____

3. princip_____s of algebra

4. the princip_____ of the loan

5. princip_____ means of support

6. the princip_____of the matter

7. deep moral princip_____s

8. lost interest and princip_____

9. a speech from the princip_____

10. my princip_____ goal in life

LOOSE   *LOSE*

loose: rhymes with *moose.* It means *not tight, free;* sometimes it means *set free.*

A *loose* shoelace is dangerous.
You should *loose* the brake before driving your car

lose: rhymes with *whose.* It means *to misplace* or *not to win or keep.*

If you *lose* the registration form, you will have to pay another fee.

Step 3. *Lose or Loose?* Write in the correct word, *lose* or *loose*, so the word groups make sense.

1. _____ the track meet

2. a _____-leaf notebook

3. The child's tooth is _____

4. He will _____ the screw.

5. _____ his nerve

6. _____ -fitting jeans

7. turn it _____

8. snakes set _____

9. _____ your temper

10. Don't _____ your way in the woods.

NO   NOW   KNOW

no: negative; not any

I have *no* information about it.

now: at this time

Now you can understand his reasons.

know: to understand, to be acquainted with

I *know* the principles of chemistry.
They *know* the family next door.

Step 4. *No, Now, Know* for Proper Meaning. Fill in the blank spaces with the correct word, *no*, *now*, or *know*.

Many people _____ do not _____ where their ancestors came from. Yet _____ one can resist the urge to _____ his or her true beginnings. Men and women everywhere _____ longer ignore the past and _____ that if they ask questions _____ amount of effort is too much _____ to uncover family origins. To _____ one's past is to _____ oneself.

WERE   WHERE

were: the past tense plural form of the verb *to be*

> **Hint:** *Were* rhymes with *her*.

We *were* searching for our car.
They *were* laughing.

where: a word that tells a place or asks "in what place?"

> **Hint:** Pronounce the *wh* at the start of the word. *Where* rhymes with *care*.

In the city *where* I grew up many changes now appear.
Where did all that noise come from?

Step 5.   *Were* and *Where* in Action. Fill in the blanks with the correct word, *were* or *where*.

1. We _____ waiting for you to return.
2. The child did not know _____ to go.
3. Why _____ you late?
4. _____ you looking for me?
5. She never visited the place _____ her grandmother was born.

6. It's a resort _____ everyone eats health foods.
7. The mosquitoes _____ really biting last night!
8. _____ you trying to convince him to sing?
9. _____ is the best place to eat in this town?
10. _____ _____ you yesterday?

PIECE   PEACE

piece: a part or portion of something

One *piece* of glass cut his finger.

peace: without war; a state of restfulness

Peace is one of our noblest goals.

Step 6.   *Piece* or *Peace*? Fill in the blanks with *piece* or *peace*.

1. love and _____

2. world _____

3. a _____ of chicken

4. a _____ mission

5. _____ of mind

6. a _____ of writing

7. _____ in the Middle East

8. a _____ of trash

9. need some _____ and quiet

10 a _____ officer

THEN   THAN

then: at a certain time

The folksinger performed, and *then* we left the party.

than: a comparing word

She is taller *than* her brother.

Step 7.   Using *Then* and *Than*. Fill in the blank spaces with the letter *e* or *a* to make *then* or *than*, whichever the sentence requires.

1. better th____n a new house
2. waited until th____n
3. th____n she spoke
4. larger th____n life
5. more votes th____n her opponent

6. could not leave just th____n
7. Th____n the doctor walked in.
8. first lightning, th____n thunder
9. looked thinner th____n her sister
10. "I'll see you th____n."

LEAD   LED

lead:

1. rhymes with *weed*. It means *to show the way*.

A good instructor will *lead* you to discover important values.

The boy who *leads* must know the forest path.

2. rhymes with *fed*. It is a grayish metal.

A *lead* pencil contains graphite and no *lead* at all.

led: rhymes with *fed*, too. This *led* is the past tense of *lead*. It means *showed the way*.

He *led* us through the back alleys of Los Angeles.

Step 8.   Making Sense with *Lead* or *Led*. Fill in the blank spaces with *lead* or *led*, whichever makes sense.

1. Who will _____ our country into the twenty-first century?

2. After he had _____ the expedition for two weeks, he collapsed with exhaustion.

3. For years now, pencils have been made of graphite rather than _____.

4. Would you like to _____ a discussion on Vonnegut's new book?

5. Do felt-tipped pens _____ the _____ pencil in popularity?

6. As she _____ the troop through the woods, thunderclouds the color of _____ covered the sky.

7. I never thought I would _____ the league in home runs.

KNEW   NEW

knew: had knowledge about; was familiar with

They *knew* each other from childhood days.

new: the opposite of old

That *new* car has all the safety features.

Step 9. *Knew or New* **in Word Groups.** Write in *knew* or *new* so that the selection makes sense.

As soon as we entered Ed and Sally's apartment, we _____ nothing would ever be _____ in their lives. There was not one _____ piece of furniture anywhere. It was as if they _____ their lives would never change. We had hoped so much that this _____ place would be a _____ beginning for them.

CLOTHS   CLOTHES   CLOSE

cloths: woven or knitted material used to make a variety of items

Dry the dish*cloths* before using them.

clothes: what you wear

The *clothes* of today are lively and imaginative.

close: to shut; near

Please *close* the door. Stand *close* to me.

Step 10. *Cloths, Clothes, or Close?* Underline the correct word from the parentheses below.

1. Before you (clothes, close) the drawer, make sure your summer (cloths, clothes) are neatly in place.
2. Her (close, cloths, clothes) cost lots of money, but she never looks right in them.
3. If your (close, cloths, clothes) are dirty, light (cloths, clothes) may be used to wipe off the dust.
4. Don't (clothes, close) the closet door on those oil-soaked (clothes, close).
5. To save energy, make sure to (clothes, close) the (clothes, close) drier door tightly.

Step 11. Reviewing Troublesome Words. Fill in the blanks with proper letters in the sentences below.

There is nothing qui_____ so annoying as a high school princip_____ who claims to _____ow everything about keeping order in a school. When each _____ew student received a p_____ce of paper entitled "_____ew Princip_____s of Order at Melville High," we _____ew something was very wrong. It was bad enough that there w_____re ten more hair and cl_____s regulations th_____n last year, but the regulations w_____re also full of corny old sayings. One said, "L_____se lips sink ships." My dad said it was something from World War II. The _____ew regulations told us there was n_____ talking in the halls, _____o slamming doors, and n_____ wearing jeans to assemblies. He was practically telling us w_____re to sit. Th_____n, when the Handi-Wipe cl_____s started showing up near bathroom sinks, I thought I would l_____se my mind! It's one thing to want p_____ce and qu_____ in a school, but attending Melville High was beginning to cl_____ in on me. It was enough to make me want to qu_____ school altogether. Well, to sum it all up, we got tired of being l_____d around by our noses; _____ow we're taking the l_____d and calling a strike until the princip_____ changes his princip_____s. After all, we've got nothing to l_____se.

Agreement of Subject and Verb

You probably know already that a verb can tell time, so to speak, because it indicates whether an action has already happened, will happen soon, or is in the process of happening.

The girl spoke *in a loud voice* shows, through the verb *spoke,* that the action happened in the *past.*
The girl will speak *in a loud voice* shows, through the verb *will speak,* that the action is going to occur sometime in the *future.*
The girl speaks *in a loud voice* shows, through the verb *speaks,* that the action is happening at *present.*

The quality of telling time that verbs illustrate is called *tense:* past, future, and present are three of the main tenses in the English language. In using the present tense, problems in agreement arise.

AGREEMENT DEFINED

When a subject is singular, the verb must be singular.
When a subject is plural, the verb must be plural.

The girl speaks in a loud voice

[singular   [singular verb
(no -*s*   (-*s* ending)]
ending)]

The girls speak in a loud voice.

[plural   [plural verb
subject   (no -*s* ending)]
(-*s* ending)]

     Hint: The letter *s* is often a clue to proper agreement.

---

(1) Singular Subjects	**Singular Verbs**	**(2) Plural Subjects**	**Plural Verbs**
(which usually do $\left\{ {go \atop with} \right\}$ not end in **s**)	(which usually do end in **s**)	(which usually do $\left\{ {go \atop with} \right\}$ end in **s**)	which usually do not end in **s**

A teacher works hard.
      [no *s* to show
      singular subject]

A safe driver moves carefully
      [no *s* to show
      singular subject]

Teachers work hard.
      [no *s* to show
      plural verb]

Safe drivers move carefully
      [no *s* to show
      plural verb]

     Remember: Some subjects form plurals in ways other than adding an -*s (children, men, mice)*. See pages 118–121.

Step 1. Verb and Subject in Agreement. Select a subject from Column I and a verb that agrees with that subject from Column II. Write the words in Column III. In Column IV tell whether the subject and verb are singular or plural. Then write a sentence with each subject-verb combination below. Look at the example.

I	II	III		IV
Example:		*Subject*	*Verb*	
		daisies	*grow*	*plural*
women	grow			
horses	laughs	_____	_____	_____
ballerina	break			
glasses	learn	_____	_____	_____

I	II	III		IV
Example:		*Subject*	*Verb*	
daisies	gallop			
blood	flows	_____	_____	_____
people	speak	_____	_____	_____
students	study	_____	_____	_____
	dances	_____	_____	_____
	work	_____	_____	_____
		_____	_____	_____

1. *White daisies grow wild along Harden Creek.* _____

_____

2. _____

_____

3. _____

_____

4. _____

_____

5. _____

_____

6. _____

_____

7. _____

_____

8. _____

_____

PRONOUNS AND AGREEMENT PROBLEMS

A singular pronoun works with a singular verb.
A plural pronoun works with a plural verb.

    Pronouns used as subjects do not end in **s**, so the letter **s** cannot serve as a clue to agreement as far as the subject is concerned. But because a singular *verb* in the present tense usually ends in **s**, look for an **s** at the end of the verb used with a singular pronoun subject.

Singular Pronoun Subjects		*Plural Pronoun Subjects*	
I	it	we	you
he	you	they	
she	who		

It crawls along the ground.
[singular   [s ending on verb]
pronoun]

They crawl along the ground.
[plural   [no s]
pronoun]

Exceptions

1. *I*, even though it is singular, is always used with a verb that does NOT have the singular **s** at the end.
   I sing   NOT   I sing**s**
   I run   NOT   I run**s**
2. *You*, even though it can be used as singular or plural, is always followed by a verb that does NOT have the singular **s** at the end.
   You sing   NOT   You sing**s**
   You run   NOT   You run**s**

Step 2. Plural to Singular. Rewrite each sentence below, changing the plural subject to a singular pronoun subject. In most cases you will have to change the verb too so that it agrees with the new subject. *Do not add* -ed *to the verb:* that will *avoid* the agreement error by shifting into the past tense where there are few problems in agreement! Study the example. All subjects and verbs are underlined.

1. <u>Cats</u> <u>run</u> wild in the hot city streets.
   It runs wild in the hot city streets. _____

2. The <u>children</u> <u>want</u> dinner too early in the day.

   _____

3. <u>Soap</u> <u>operas</u> <u>give</u> viewers unrealistic ideas about love.

   _____

4. <u>Calculators</u> <u>make</u> taking math tests very easy.

   _____

5. For car repairs my <u>friends</u> <u>use</u> Anthony's Service Station.

   _____

6. My <u>cousins</u> <u>buy</u> cherries from a farm stand.

   _____

7. Those <u>men</u> <u>speak</u> softly.

   _____

8. My <u>teachers</u> <u>try</u> to return papers quickly.

9. The <u>lakes</u> <u>ripple</u> when the <u>boys</u> <u>cast</u> the fishing lines.

   _____

10. The harvesting <u>machines</u> <u>roar</u> from morning to night during October.

    _____

Step 3. Verbs That Work with Pronouns. Draw a line through any verb that does not work correctly with the pronoun in each group below. Look at the example.

1. They
   ~~sings~~   laugh   speak   ~~listens~~   ~~votes~~   complain   ~~jumps~~

2. She
   studies   read   hikes   draw   runs   spell   spill

3. He
   questions   read   acts   decide   appear   go   have

4. I
   study   tries   work   plan   decides   asks   has

5. We
   jump   eats   remain   swims   attends   want   does

6. It
   break   sparkles   cut   squeaks   shine   falls   slice

7. You
   explain   drives   try   work   finish   remembers   goes

8. Who
   speaks   lose   know   reads   smoke   leaves   kisses

Step 4. Sentences with Correct Verbs and Pronouns. For any *five* correct combinations of pronoun subject and verb that appear in Step 3 above write an original sentence. Use separate paper.

Example

They complain whenever the temperature drops below seventy degrees.

Some Special Pronouns and Agreement

Even though they may seem plural to you, some pronouns, when used as subjects, are singular and always go with singular verbs. Although people do not usually keep to this rule when they speak, formal writing still requires that you use singular verbs with these subjects.

Singular Pronouns

anybody	somebody	neither
anyone	everybody	either
nobody	someone	everything
no one	everyone	nothing
none	each	something

Examples

[singular verb (*s* ending)]

Singular   Anybody believes a sincere speaker.
Subject   Everyone tries hard.

[singular verb (*s* ending)]

Step 5. In the following sentences, fill in the correct form of the verb in parentheses.

1. Nothing ever (to happen) _____ in this quiet town.

2. Everyone (to want) _____ to believe the president's speech, but no one (to do) _____.

3. Each (to feel) _____ the argument was the other's fault.

4. Everything (to go) _____ wrong just before closing time.

5. Somebody (to phone) _____ me every night at midnight.

Step 6. Sentences of Your Own. On a separate sheet of paper write a sentence for each singular pronoun listed above. Be sure that the verb is singular (check for the *s* ending) and that the tense is present (don't add *-ed*).

Examples
Each of the boys drifts off on his own.
Everyone buys a newspaper.

FOUR TROUBLESOME VERBS

I. *TO BE*

Singular Forms

am: Use with *I* only
is: use with all singular subjects (except *you*)

I *am* tired today.
It *is* late.
The wind *is* blowing.

Plural Form

are: use with all plural subjects and with *you*

You *are* attractive.
The students *are* busy.
They *are* all outside.

> **Hint:** Do not use *be* with any subject.

It *is* late.   NOT   It *be* late.
They *are* at the movies.
         NOT
They *be* at the movies.

This verb has agreement problems in the past tense as well.

Past Singular

was: use with all singular subjects (including *I*)
except *you*
I *was* awake early.
         NOT
I *were* awake early.
He *was* seated in the rear.
         NOT
He *were* seated in the rear.

Past Plural

were: use with all plural subjects and with *you*
They *were* singing.
         NOT
They *was* singing.
You *were* lucky to miss being drafted.
         NOT
You *was* lucky to miss being drafted.

II. *TO HAVE*

Singular Form

has: use with all singular subjects except *I* and *you*

He *has* a cold.
The book *has* a torn page.
It *has* a bright red cover.

Plural Form

have: use with all plural subjects and *I* and *you*

I *have* five dollars.
You *have* a cold.
The women *have* new cars.

> **Hint:** If the subject is singular, the verb usually ends in *s*. If the subject is plural, the verb usually does not end in *s*.

(continued on next page)

FOUR TROUBLESOME VERBS (continued)

III. *TO GO*

Singular Form

goes: use with all singular subjects except *I* and *you*

She *goes* to sleep early.

The dog *goes* out before dinner.

It *goes* to its favorite tree.

Plural Form

go: use with all plural subjects and *I* and *you*

I *go* to the garage daily.

The men *go* this way.

You *go* too far when you drive.

Hint: If the subject is singular, the verb usually ends in *s*. If the subject is plural, the verb usually does not end in *s*.

IV. *TO DO*

Singular Form

does: use with all singular subjects except *I* and *you*

She *does* important work.

It *does* not look right.

Plural Form

do: use with all plural subjects and *I* and *you*

You *do* the work!

I *do* too much driving.

Hint: If the subject is singular, the verb usually ends in *s*. If the subject is plural, the verb usually does not end in *s*.

Another Hint: Although you should usually avoid contractions in formal writing, contractions with some of these verbs and the word *not* can cause many agreement problems. To select the correct form of the verb, separate the contraction into two words.

doesn't: does not   Use with singular.

                                            He doesn't work.
                                              (does not)

don't: do not   Use with plurals, *I,* and *you.*

                                            They don't work.
                                              (do not)

wasn't: was not   Use with singular (and *I*).

                                            The doctor wasn't in.
                                              (was not)

weren't: were not   Use with plurals and *you.*

                                            You weren't ill.
                                              (were not)

Step 7. Picking Correct Verbs. Circle the correct forms of the verbs in each sentence below. Then write the subjects and the verbs in the appropriate columns alongside each sentence.

Subject	*Verb*	
1. _____ _____ _____	1. _____ _____ _____	1. When I (be, am, is) alone, I (have, has) to listen to music or I (go, goes) crazy!
2. _____ _____ _____	2. _____ _____ _____	2. He (has, have) to go to school today, but if he (does, do), he (is, be) in trouble on his job.
3. _____ _____ _____	3. _____ _____ _____	3. If it (doesn't, don't) matter to you, tell us where you (was, were) before you (has, have) to leave again.
4. _____ _____ _____	4. _____ _____ _____	4. When she (go, goes) on a construction job, she (does, do) the work quickly; when her assistant (has, have) the job, though, he (doesn't, don't) ever work fast.
5. _____ _____	5. _____ _____	5. Where (do, does) you (have, has) your vacation home?
6. _____ _____ _____	6. _____ _____ _____	6. They (was, were) very lucky; the fire (weren't, wasn't) very extensive, and their insurance policy (don't, doesn't) cover such accidents.
7. _____ _____ _____	7. _____ _____ _____	7. Do you (has, have) to make so much noise when you (does, do) your exercises? Couldn't you (go, goes) into another room?
8. _____ _____ _____	8. _____ _____ _____	8. This book (be, is) too long to read by Friday; however, I (has, have) a report due, so it (don't, doesn't) do any good to complain.

MORE THAN ONE SUBJECT *(compound subjects)*

    [Subject is plural]   [plural verb]

A desk and an old lamp stand in the room.

      Since *desk* and *lamp* both make up the subject, the subject is plural; therefore the sentence requires a plural verb.

When   ⎰ either . . . or   ⎱   join subjects, the verb agrees with the
             neither . . . nor   subject that stands close to the verb.
             or
             nor
             not only . . . but also

Either the manufacturers or the driver is at fault.

                    [closer subject: [verb: singular]
                    singular]

Either the manufacturer or the drivers are at fault.

                    [closer subject: [verb: plural]
                    plural]

Step 8. More than One Subject. Use the expressions indicated to open each sentence. Then use the correct form of the verb in parentheses to finish a sentence of your own. *Do not use the past tense:* use only the present.

Example

1. Television or radio (to play)

   Television or radio plays in my house most of the day.

2. Not only my sisters but also my cousins (to be)

   _____

3. Air pollution and water pollution (to destroy)

   _____

4. A sunset and a sunrise (to inspire)

   _____

5. Neither Pac-Man nor Space Invaders (to interest)

   _____

6. In my class neither the women nor the one man (to have)

   _____

7. Either the table or the chairs (to do)

   _____

8. A bed and a dresser (to stand)

   _____

9. A boy and his father (to sit)

_____

10. Neither that course nor those books

_____

IS, ARE, WAS, AND *WERE* WITH *IT, HERE, WHERE,* AND *THERE*

To start a sentence correctly with *Here is, There is,* or *Where is,* remember that *here, there,* and *where* are not subjects: subjects in these sentences always come after the verb.

    [not the subject]   [subject (singular)]

    Here is an old maple tree.

        [verb: singular]

    [not the subject]   [subject (plural)]

    There are dead lilacs on the lawn.

       [verb: plural]

It is followed by a singular verb, *is,* even when the word it refers to is plural.

    It is an important idea.

          [singular]

    It is ideas like these that we need.

      [plural]

Step 9. Special Openers. Use the words given below as the subject for each sentence. Open each sentence with *it, here, where,* or *there* and the verb that agrees with the subject: *is, are, was,* or *were.*

Example

1. two open doors *There were two open doors in the hallway.*

_____

2. a cactus _____

3. mountains _____

4. some apples _____

5. love _____

6. cigarettes _____

WORDS THAT GET IN THE WAY

Don't be confused by singular or plural words that appear between the subject and the verb in a sentence.

[Although this word is plural and close to the verb, it is *not* the subject.]

The rain (on the rooftops) is causing trouble.

[singular subject]   [singular verb]

[Although this word is plural and close to the verb, it is *not* the subject.]

A group (of students) was here before you.

[singular subject]   [singular verb]

Don't be confused by certain words that join with the subject: *together with, as well as, in addition to, along with* do not affect the subject.

[These words do not affect the subject.]

The banker, (together with his partners), was arrested for theft.

[singular verb]

Step 10. Verbs That Agree. Circle the correct form of the verb.

1. A set of fine glasses (look, looks) lovely on the shelf.
2. The talk about important Indian tribes (was, were) interesting.
3. Nancy, as well as her twin, (take, takes) evening classes.
4. The best groomed of the horses (were, was) awarded first prize.
5. Life among carnival workers (is, are) always exciting.
6. Creativity, together with technical training, (make, makes) a good photographer.
7. The pieces of chocolate cake (has, have) icing.
8. The book as well as the magazines (was, were) ruined.
9. One of the girls (was, were) expected to drive.
10. Ideas, in addition to action, (require, requires) attention.

PLURAL WORDS THAT ACT AS SINGULAR

Some words, though they look plural, always take singular verbs:

physics	Amounts of weight, height or length, time and
economics	money.
civics	Three ounces *is* a small amount.
mathematics	Six feet *is* very tall.
news	Three hours *was* not enough time.
measles	Five dollars *is* what I am paid each day.

Economics *is* difficult.

Measles *is* a childhood disease.

Titles, though they may be plural, take singular verbs.

Star Wars was an exciting film.

Hint: These words are always plural and take plural verbs:

scissors	trousers
glasses	means
riches	pants

The scissors *are* on the table.

WORDS BOTH SINGULAR AND PLURAL

Words like *committee, group, team, family,* and *class,* when referring to an action by the group as a whole, take singular verbs.
     When you want to stress that each individual in the group does something, use a plural verb.

The committee *are* leaving the work until tomorrow.	The committee *is* leaving the work until tomorrow.
The plural verb *are* stresses individuals leaving the work.	Here you are showing that the committee acts as a whole in leaving the work.

Step 11. Singular or Plural Verbs? Write the correct form of the verb in parentheses.

(to buy)   1. Five dollars _____ very little these days.

(to use)   2. Modern mathematics still _____ many principles developed centuries ago.

(to play)   3. That family _____ in a band together.

(to fly)   4. Two hours _____ quickly when you are happy.

(to be)   5. The news _____ good from England.

(to look)   6. The scissors _____ sharp.

(to be)   7. *Star Wars* _____ still a very popular film.

(to practice)   8. The team _____ on the parade ground every Saturday morning.

AGREEMENT WITH WHO, THAT, WHICH

The words *who, that,* and *which* are singular *or* plural depending on the words they refer to.

The boy who finds the money keeps it.
    [*Who* is singular   [singular because
    because it refers   *who* is singular]
    to *boy*, a
    singular word.]

One of the pages that appear looked badly torn.
    [*That* is plural   [plural because *that*
    because it refers   is plural]
    to *pages*, a
    plural word.]

Step 12. Agreement with *Who, That, Which*. Circle the correct form of the verb.

1. My father is one of those people who (is, are) very strict.
2. One of the women who (work, works) with me received a promotion.
3. Darrel is one of the boys who never (come, comes) late.
4. Aspirin is one of the drugs that (require, requires) careful use.
5. Betsy Leung is one of those women who (work, works) while others play.
6. Two of the plays that (open, opens) tomorrow are comedies.
7. The students who (talk, talks) least are often the smartest.
8. The green glasses, which (seem, seems) most precious, are not crystal.

Step 13. Reviewing Agreement Problems. Finish each incomplete sentence below so that agreement is correct. Use the verbs in the columns.

is	go	speak
are	goes	speaks
was	do	stand

were	does	stands
looks	have	sit
look	has	sits
taste	laugh	feel
tastes	laughs	feels
want	speed	throw
wants	speeds	throws

Example

1. A cup and saucer *sit on the table.* _____

2. Ten years _____

3. One of my neighbors _____

4. German measles _____

5. Drivers who _____

6. Connie, along with her sisters, _____

7. Anyone who _____

8. Either a car or a motorcycle _____

9. Neither frankfurters nor salami _____

10. Twenty-five cents _____

Step 14. More Review. Circle the correct form of the verb.

1. Every Sunday she (goes, go) to the park.
2. One of the children (has, have) a cold.
3. Three bottles of milk (costs, cost) too much.
4. Gypsy moths on the trees (eats, eat) away the leaves.
5. There (is, are) the sandwiches you ordered.
6. Neither the bicycle nor the toys (belongs, belong) here.
7. The teacher (doesn't, don't) accept themes written in pencil.
8. The team (travel, travels) by bus to all their games.
9. The team (sleep, sleeps) in separate hotels.
10. That (is, be, are) the strangest exercise I have ever seen.
11. In high school, economics (was, were) my best subject.
12. Fifty pounds (is, are) too much weight to lose.
13. The street (has, have) garbage everywhere.
14. One of the old posters, which (hang, hangs) in the bedroom, (is, are) torn.
15. Somebody always (help, helps) me when I ask for directions.

WRITING THE COMPARISON-CONTRAST PARAGRAPH

ASSIGNMENT: Write a paragraph that compares and (or) contrasts two people you know well. Use the patterns discussed on pages 142–151 as models for your paper. Remember that complete details and examples will make your essay more vivid and particular.

Of course, any two people (like any two objects or ideas) may be contrasted in some way. To say that two people are different is not really saying much. The point in a paper that emphasizes contrasts is to present two subjects that do not *seem* dissimilar and then to make a case for their differences. In like manner, in a comparison paper the point is to select two subjects that do not seem to be alike and then to make a case for their similarities. Also, the reason for the comparison and contrast must be clear to the reader, and you must balance your presentation by giving equal time to each element in your topic.

Think about some of the people you know, and, using any one of the several methods of paragraph development explained in this chapter, write a composition that in some way uses the technique of comparison and contrast. Read the student themes on pages 143, 146, and 149–150 in order to review the approaches you might use. Look at the suggested topic ideas below and at the ideas on page 134 to help you along. If you would like to write about a topic that suggests comparisons between subjects other than people, see page 181 for suggestions.

Topic Ideas: Comparing People

Use any topic of your own, of course, but in case you are stuck for ideas, you might find one of these titles helpful as you think about comparing or contrasting two people.

1. My Daughter (Son): Two Different Personalities
2. Discipline: Mother's Style, Father's Style
3. How My Cousins Are Alike
4. Two Bosses: A Study in Contrasts
5. Two Teaching Styles
6. My Two Boyfriends (Girl Friends)
7. Puppy Love Versus Lasting Love
8. Roommates
9. Politicians: A Conservative and a Liberal
10. Two Teachers

11. Two Neighbors I Know
12. Good Friends
13. Two Children on the Block
14. Birds of a Feather
15. My Two Grandmothers (Grandfathers)
16. Two Rock Guitar Players
17. Two Shopkeepers
18. My Brother, Before and After
19. A Doctor I Liked; A Doctor I Disliked
20. Good Service and Bad: Two Waiters in Contrast

Prewriting

As a way of exploring and grouping information on a topic, the *informal outline* (sometimes called a rough or a scratch outline) can be helpful before you prepare your first draft. With an informal outline you lay out in groups or categories various thoughts you intend to develop in your paper. Under each group or category you jot down a few words or phrases that will help you expand ideas into sentences. For extensive assignments or for complicated topics the more formal *sentence outline* may serve you better. (See pages 515–516 in the Minibook.)

Preparing an outline is not a prewriting activity like list making or brainstorming or free association. Those help you to uncover ideas about topics and to discover what you know or what you need to find out when you are stuck for ideas. Outlining, however, demands that you already know in some detail what you want to write about. Of course, an outline should be highly flexible so that you can eliminate idea groups or can add to them as you write your first draft.

Because a comparison-contrast theme usually involves balanced parts that can be separated easily—you deal with one object, then another; or you deal with one point as it relates to two objects before you go on to another point about the objects—informal outlines can help you, once you have stated and limited your topic. Look at this informal outline by Cecilia Richardson for her paragraph "Different Roommates" on page 146. Notice how she uses numbers (1, 2, 3) and letters (a, b, c) to organize her material easily. Although numbers and letters are not *required* in a scratch outline, many writers find them convenient.

PREWRITING: A SCRATCH OUTLINE

Topic: Contrasts between my roommates
            Pat and Julie ←—[topic already limited]
            1. Physical appearances ←——[first thought group]
            → a. Pat—small, blonde, funny- ←—[details to be
[objects writer   looking grey eyes   developed in the paragraph]
will discuss]
            → b. Julie—tall and lean, straight black←
               hair
            2. Attitude toward school work
               a. J.
               tense before exams   [second thought group
               studies for hours   ←   divided into objects
               takes notes carefully   for discussion, details
                                               under each]
               b. P.
               takes things easy before tests
               surrounds herself with food
            3. Interests ←—[third thought group]
               a. J.
               inactive type—reads, watches
               T.V., likes talking
               b. P.
               "outdoors" type
               jogger, swimmer
               beats me at paddleball
                                        —Cecilia Richardson

Step 1. Comparing Paragraph to Outline. Reread "Different Roommates" on page 146. Comparing it to the outline above, answer these questions. Use separate paper.

1. How does the topic sentence compare with the statement of topic in the outline?
2. What new order does the writer present in her paragraph for the thought groups numbered 1, 2, and 3 in the outline? Why do you think she has made the change?
3. The outline is not consistent in the order of discussion of the two objects. Under 1, Pat comes first; under 2, Julie comes first. Why has Cecilia Richardson changed this situation in the paragraph so that she discusses the same person, Julie, first each time?

Step 2. Practice with Informal Outlines. Look at the topics you developed in Step 2 or 3 on pages 144–145. On a separate page prepare a scratch outline for any of the topics and their accompanying illustrations or discussion points. Be sure to include in your outline some details you might use to develop the thought groups.

Step 3.   An Outline for Your Paragraph. If your instructor requests it, prepare an informal outline after you have decided on your own comparison and contrast topic and before you write your first draft. Use separate paper, and hand in your outline when you hand in your theme for evaluation. Use Cecilia Richardson's outline (page 174) as a model, but take whatever liberties you need with it so that the outline works for you. Remember, this is a *rough* outline. Its main purpose is to help you write your paper successfully.

Progress Reminders: A Checklist of Questions

While preparing your outline and your first and later drafts, but before writing your final copy, use this checklist for your paragraph so that you will follow as many of the suggestions as possible. After you prepare your final copy, fill in the checklist and submit it to your instructor along with your theme.

1. Did I spend time thinking about the topic in some prewrit-   _____
   ing activity that works well for me? (See page 39.)
2. Did I use a scratch outline to help me organize ideas?   _____

3. Did I write a rough draft and any other needed drafts   _____
   before making my final copy? Did I make changes in my
   rough drafts so that I expressed thoughts clearly and
   smoothly? Does my final copy follow correct manuscript
   form?
4. Did I write a topic sentence that makes clear what I want my   _____
   paragraph to deal with and that states some dominant
   impression I have about the subject? (See pages 7–14.)
5. Did I use subtopic sentences and transitional expressions or   _____
   both to help the ideas move smoothly from one to the other?
   (See pages 91–93 and pages 137–139.) Here are two transitional expressions that appear in my theme:

   a. _____

   b. _____
6. Does my paragraph contain several word pictures that use   _____
   sound, color, smell, and touch? Here is one image that uses
   sound:

   _____

7. Did I use two or three comparisons (see pages 134–137) in   _____
   my paragraph?
8. Did I follow one of the patterns of comparison outlined on   _____
   pages 141–151? The pattern that I followed most closely was

   _____

9. Does my paragraph distinctly stress either similarities or   _____
differences between my subjects? It stresses

_____

10. If I stressed differences, have I included any similarities for   _____
a balanced essay (or, if I stressed similarities, did I include
differences)?

11. Is there a clear enough *reason* or *basis* for my comparison or   _____
contrast?

12. Did I try to use words from the new vocabulary on pages   _____
132–133? Here is one word I used:

_____

13. After making changes in my drafts for clarity and smooth-   _____
ness, did I check my Theme Progress Sheet (page 523) and
proofread the draft before my final draft? Did I check   _____
especially for the run-on and fragment errors? Did I
proofread again before I submitted my final draft?

14. Did I examine my theme for any mistakes in agreement?   _____
Have I checked carefully for words I may have confused,
like those explained on pages 151–157?   _____

15. Did I look in a dictionary for any words that troubled me as   _____
I spelled them?

16. Did I use a variety of sentence types: subordination; coordi-   _____
nation; sentences that open with words that end in *-ly*?

17. Did I try to write one expanded quotation sentence that   _____
through strong images includes details of the speaker? (See
pages 139–141.) In "Different Roommates," Cecilia Richardson writes: "'Just listen to this,' she will say, her eyes
glowing, her warm fingers pressed to my palm to hold my
attention."

18. Did I write at least twelve sentences, about three hundred   _____
words?

GETTING READER RESPONSE

After you write your first draft, pair up with one other student in the class and read his or her paragraph carefully a couple of times until you understand it well. Then prepare a simple outline of that paragraph as it is written. The outline should show the balanced parts of the work as they appear to you. Use numbers and letters to organize the material you have read. (You might want to review pages 173–175 in this chapter.) Using this outline, write a few sentences of suggestions that can help the writer produce the next draft.

When your classmate returns the outline of your paragraph and the suggestions, use them to write your next draft. Are there any inconsistencies between your paragraph and the outline? Does the outline indicate any lapses in logic—things you thought were clear but which the reader did not understand? Do the parts of your paragraph balance, or do you have to add details or remove any?

THE PROFESSIONALS SPEAK

Read the selection below. It describes the experiences of two students at an integrated high school where a riot closed the school. Keep in mind the use of comparison-contrast techniques.

SOME WORDS TO KNOW BEFORE YOU READ

animosity: feeling of bad will
serene: peaceful
pun: a humorous use of a word, which brings out unexpected meanings
verbatim: in exactly the same words
cytology: the study of cells
din: loud, confused noise
tonnage: the carrying capacity of a ship

Black and White at Madison High

Socially, the races have almost no contact. There are no school dances, no picnics, trips, clambakes. After school, the blacks troop over to Nostrand Avenue to wait for the city buses back to the ghetto. There is, of course, no interracial dating, and even an after-school friendship is something rare and unusual.

"When I first came here as a sophomore, I was petrified of them," says 16-year-old Pierre Socolow, a white senior who lives near the school. "If I'd see them all going out one exit, I'd find another one to go out of. But now I've gotten over that. If they're standing by a door, I just go out right past them. But maybe that's because I'm a senior." Other than the exits, just about the only place even to meet blacks in the school is the one period a day when everyone goes to gym. "In gym you get friendly with them and they become familiar faces," says David Chase, another white senior, who wants to study biochemistry at Cornell University. "Then, the next time in the hall if you see him, you can say, 'Hi, see you in gym.' But you wouldn't see them after school."

A majority of the blacks come to the school with crushing academic problems, many reading two to five years below grade level. And a lot of the separation has as much to do with class and educational differences as with race. "I looked at the black kids with the same regard as the whites in the business and commercial course," says Charles Schumer, a Madison graduate who was elected the district's State Assemblyman last fall, his first year out of law school. "There was no animosity or anything. They were just different; they were not the kinds of kids who were friends."

Assemblyman Schumer's younger brother, Robert, is a 17-year-old senior at Madison now and will graduate in June. He lives with his family half a block from the school in a tidy white stucco house on a serene, tree-lined street. Over the livingroom fireplace is an 18-by-22-inch color photograph of the three Schumer children: Charles, who went to Harvard and Harvard Law School; Fran, also a Madison graduate, who went to Radcliffe and is now working in North Carolina as a reporter on *The Charlotte Observer*; and Robert. Robert, whose father runs an exterminator business in Bedford-Stuyvesant, ranks 26th in his class out of 850 but doesn't think he's going to make Harvard. He scored only 1150 on the Standard Achievement Test and might have to settle for the University of Michigan. His brother had scored 1535 out of a possible 1600, and Robert feels a certain pressure to succeed in similar fashion. "It's not overt, but it's there," he says. "They don't think I work hard enough. If my mother doesn't see me doing my homework all the time, she gets annoyed." For practice, Robert spent six weeks last summer taking college courses at Cornell. It was his brother's idea, he said, "but I really liked it."

Ernest Drew is also 17 and a classmate of Robert's. Ernest lives in Brownsville on a block of Bergen Street that has abandoned cars, a gutted factory and boarded-up tenements. He is one of seven children. His mother is from British Honduras and speaks halting English; his father, a Jamaican, has a job as an ironworker. Whereas Robert prepared for Madison at Cunningham Junior High School, which, academically, ranks ninth in the city out of 168, Ernest went to Intermediate School 55, which ranks 13th from the bottom and where only 9 per cent of the graduates can read at their proper grade level. To get to Madison, Ernest has to get up at 6 A.M. and spend nearly an hour on two different buses, standing all the way. His classes on the G track are mostly all black, while Robert's are Honors sections and almost totally white. But the color difference pales beside the one of content.

Robert's Honors English is a creative-writing class where students learn imagery from Dostoevski and D. H. Lawrence and read Carl Jung for his theory on the creative process. The teacher, Robert Anker, is chairman of the English department and a student favorite who dishes out a breezy lecture punctuated by cheerful if nauseating puns ("Yes, that's Shakespeare's omelet," he says of Ophelia's lover, "a good egg but a little yellow") that keep the class in stitches. The discussion rests on much of what the students have read on their own. At one point, for example, a student in the back says, yes, he agrees with Carl Jung and points out that it was only after Thomas Wolfe lived in Europe that he could write about his experience of growing up in America.

Ernest's G class is called Power English. There, the students plod through vocabulary books, pondering words like "vague" and "gesture." They, too, read books, but ones written for black high-school students such as "Black Pimps," "My Daddy Was a Numbers Runner" and "Mr. and Mrs. Bo Jones," which is a tale of highschool pregnancy. To pass the course, Ernest has to read five books and hand in a one-paragraph book report on each. Here is a report on "Black Pimps," in its entirety and verbatim, done by an 18-year-old girl in Ernest's class: "The book Black Pimps is about pimps, ho, prostitutes and hustler, the games they pull. How they commute with one another. Also how the contract their pimps or players. There use of slang words of the ghetto. What their style are or the way in which they are made."

The teacher is Robert Greenman, Ernest's favorite. "To go over every mistake on that paper, I'd have to spend a whole period," he says, "so what I do is pick out five mistakes and let it go at that. It's just not possible to grade some of these kids. They would never get a passing mark."

For science, Robert has already had introductory biology and this year is taking a college-level course that concentrates on physiology, cytolpgy and genetics. Ernest takes "General Science," a sort of grab bag of information about everything from atoms to astronomy, much of it lost somewhere between the teacher and her students. "Ernest," asks the teacher, "what do you use to measure carpeting: meters, grams or liters?"

Ernest stares, mute.

"She's messing with you, man," whispers a classmate. After a bit, the teacher asks the question of another student.

"Some teachers you just have to speak up and say you don't know," says Ernest. "But with her, you just stare at her."

The class moves on to oxygen. "Would it be a good thing if all the plants in the world died?" the teacher asks a girl on the other side of the room.

"Yes," says the girl. Then, quickly, "No!"

"Why not?"

"Because . . . it just wouldn't," the girl replies.

In mathematics, Robert is up to calculus. That day the teacher is sick, so the class is taught by a fellow student. Ernest has two math classes. One, a math workshop, uses minicomputers paid for by the Federal Government to help students as they puzzle out 8 into 48 and 7 into 49. The teacher asks about a cut on his lip, and Ernest, who is in the class for his third go-around, explains that he was mugged over the weekend near his home. "Some of these kids are five years behind," says the teacher, "but we try to improve their skills. I say we try. We don't always succeed." Ernest's other math class is Business Math, where he learns the arithmetic of borrowing money and paying taxes.

Both youths take American History II, which deals with immigrant groups and foreign policy, but there the similarity ends. In Robert's—he has had to sign up for a Regular class, since the Honors section would interfere with calculus—the emphasis is on learning history. In Ernest's, it is on using history to have another go at reading, writing and arithmetic. That day, Ernest's teacher is trying over the general din to shout some information about a graph showing construction of American ship tonnage before and during World War II. The point here is not to learn about shipbuilding but to see how to read a graph.

Ernest's attention wanders to a friend outside the room who is making gestures through a window in the door, indicating that Ernest should cut his next class and "party" out on the sidewalk. The friend has a green jewel in his left ear and a rabbit-fur jacket which, Ernest explains later, cost $167 and was paid for by one of his girl friends. The teacher is now completely drowned out by boys and girls yelling at one another. A girl named Fern is quietly playing with jacks.

"What kind of religion did the Indians have?" the teacher shouts in desperation.

"Voodoo," one boy calls back.

The teacher asks Fern to *please* put away her jacks. The whistle sounds—an ear-goring electronic noise transmitted over a loudspeaker—and the class is dismissed.

Though at opposite academic poles, both boys say they're glad they went to Madison, Robert for its good college preparation and Ernest because it's a "together" school. It also provided Ernest a welcome alternative to Boys' High, an all-black school in Bedford-Stuyvesant that his mother was afraid would lead him into taking hard drugs. The two boys, of course, do not know each other, although both have acquaintances of the opposite race. Ernest knows a white boy named Kenny, he says, whom he "parties" with outside when both cut classes. Robert's black friends are mostly from his gym class. "It's an in-school relationship," he says. "I'm friendly with them, but after school it drops there."

After June, both will go their separate ways.

Robert, who worked in his brother's campaign last fall, hopes to go on to law school and then maybe into politics. Ernest has a six-course deficit from subjects he flunked but thinks he can make it up by going to night school in his neighborhood and still graduate in June. Students get a diploma from Madison if they pass enough courses and can show they read at the eighth-grade level. As for the future, Ernest is taking welding lessons from a friend and maybe, he says, he will become a welder.

—Bruce Porter
"It Was a Good School to Integrate . . ."

Step 1. Understanding the Selection. Discuss these questions.

1. How do the family and social backgrounds of the two boys, Robert Schumer and Ernest Drew, compare? What are the major differences between them?
2. How do the experiences in various high school classrooms show the sharp contrast in what and how the boys learn? Discuss the classes in English, science, mathematics, and history.
3. Why are both boys glad they chose Madison High?
4. How do you account for the differences in the boys' future plans?
5. The Human Rights Commission, in its investigation of Madison High School, said that the riots that erupted at the school were completely predictable and stemmed from the school's failure to assimilate—to take in and make as its own—black students into the life of the school. How does the author's contrast between the students demonstrate that failure?

REACHING HIGHER

Step 1. Pictures to Words. Look at the photograph on page 131. Write a paragraph that compares and contrasts any two of the faces you see there. Use concrete sensory language to fill in details. Write a topic sentence that states the comparison clearly.

Step 2. Other Topics. Several other topics for comparison and contrast appear below. Write a paragraph about any one of them.

1. interesting and uninteresting writing
2. summer in the city and summer in the country
3. two female rock singers
4. store-bought and homemade Christmas gifts
5. extremely hot or cold weather
6. two different dances you do ,
7. spring and autumn in the garden
8. marijuana and alcohol
9. high school classes and college classes
10. two television comedies (dramas, "specials," movies)
11. travel by train and travel by car
12. summer sports and winter sports
13. American and foreign cars
14. two poems you read
15. women's roles: old and new
16. poverty today and yesterday
17. geniuses and lunatics
18. city ghettos and suburban ghettos
19. two concerts you heard
20. picnics and dinners at home

Step 3. Two Special Comparison and Contrast Papers.

1. The Mood Sketch

An imaginative paragraph is one in which you compare and contrast one of your inner moods with the actual moment in which you were experiencing that mood. In this type of paragraph, you set up a contrast between your inner emotions and the world around you. You need to use a number of concrete details to make the scene rich in sensory appeal; and you need to mix in those details with the thoughts and feelings that reflect the mood you are experiencing.

A mood, as you know, is some state of feeling at a given time. Each of us lives through a number of moods each day: happiness, boredom, loneliness, fear, excitement, depression, sorrow, anger, discomfort, relaxation, tiredness. The point of this writing assignment is to set the mood in a specific place at a specific time and to weave in the details of the setting with your own inner state.

Read the theme below as an example. Then look at the hints and the suggested topics.

Waking on a Monday Morning

I hear an innocent click and then, "It's seven fifteen on a bee-yoo-tiful Monday morning here on WABC" blares out of my clock radio on my bedroom dresser; "Oh damn, it's Monday!" I think with a groan. Lifting out of bed with the grace of a sick hippo, I manage to turn the volume down. Resting my weight on my dresser, I grope for the light switch. In an instant the bulb flashes on and knocks me with its glare right back into bed. I weigh in my mind what I have to do. "Damn, I don't feel like getting up, and I don't feel like going to work, and I don't feel like going to school." I smile to myself. I'd sure hate to have to put up with me in the morning! Finally pushing my better judgment to the top, I stumble into the bathroom, banging my knee on the door. After I wash with icy water, I return to the closet for a faded pair of jeans and an ugly old sweatshirt. "The sun is out strong," the disc jockey screams, in a rapturous voice, "and it's a perfect November morning." Ugh! I look out the window; the early morning cloudiness hangs like a grey film on everything in sight. "How the hell can anyone enjoy Mondays?" I mutter to the plastic face of the radio. It sneers at me. "Sure, what does that announcer care?" I figure to myself. "He works four hours a day and earns fifty grand a year. No wonder he's so happy!" I notice I've buttoned my shirt wrong. I do it all over again, cursing. When I move lazily into the kitchen I grab a chipped bowl and a box of Rice Krispies from the cabinet above the sink. Setting my breakfast on the table, I try to pour the cereal into the plate, but the cereal has its own thoughts and tumbles onto the tablecloth, onto my lap, onto the floor. "Damn these rice thingees! We ought to declare war on China or Japan or wherever we get rice from!" Cleaning up the mess, I return hungry to my room where the skinny white hands of my clock tell the whole story. "Seven forty-five. I'd better move it." Scooping up a fistful of change, I release the nickels and quarters into my pocket with a jingle. I snatch my jacket and pull it around me, glancing at my face in the mirror. Awful! I look at the clothes and papers and books strewn haphazardly everywhere in my room. Awful! Quickly I zoom out the front door, slamming it behind me. A cool morning breeze and the sun rising above the roof across the street suddenly make me feel better. Trapping that ugly part of myself within, I say aloud, "Okay Monday, we're on neutral grounds now. I'm ready to take you on!"

—*Ronald Gross*

HINTS ABOUT THE MOOD PARAGRAPH

1. Tell the major feeling in the opening sentence.
2. Identify the setting as soon as possible. Ronald Gross mentions the clock radio on his bedroom dresser in order to locate the scene for the reader.
3. Show the thoughts that go through your mind as the mood develops. *At the same time,* show the details of the moment. These details of the outside world keep mixing in with your inner world of feelings. Notice in "Waking on a Monday Morning" how the voice of the disc jockey interrupts a mood.
4. Use eight or ten lively images of concrete details.
5. Use quotation sentences to identify thoughts.
6. Use comparisons like those explained on pages 134–137. Find a simile in the above theme.

Here are several moods that students have felt at some time. Perhaps one mood here might suggest to you possibilities for a paragraph. The key in selecting a proper mood for writing is to try to remember a brief moment you experienced recently in which your feelings were all one major kind.

1. boredom in class
2. Sunday evening depression
3. fear in nature
4. ignorance at a lecture
5. innocence in a group
6. excitement at a concert
7. dislike of a teacher
8. waiting for a date
9. nervousness at the birth of a child
10. anxiety in the middle of the night
11. loneliness in a forest
12. confusion toward a friend
13. love for a spouse
14. sorrow at a loss of a relative
15. pity for a beggar
16. pride at some achievement
17. tiredness after exercise
18. pleasure during a good meal
19. feeling important on the job
20. closeness to God in church or synagogue

2. The Analogy

An analogy is a special kind of comparison. It relates two things that seem to be very different on the surface by showing that there are many things these two objects have in common. The paragraph sample below is developed through analogy. What does the topic sentence announce as the terms of the analogy? Which details of color, sound, and touch make the comparison most vivid?

Biology Jailhouse

Professor Diedrich's biology class on the Monday morning of midterm day at Prep is a prison scene. First we convicts stand uncomfortably outside the classroom door in our dismal winter coats in brown and grey, whispering behind our hands or staring nervously down the empty hall. This is leisure time for the prisoners. Some men squat on the floor and frown; others lean against the ugly green walls near the lab; others drag deeply on stubs of cigarettes. A black film of unshaved whiskers sits like coal dust on every face. Sullenly, my friend Tony says "You wanna butt?" He pushes a pack of Lucky Strikes at me, but I shake my head no. Suddenly footsteps sound on the stairway around the bend. The warden, Professor Diedrich, marches firmly to the door and shouts, "Let's go!" We all snap to attention and, still slouching, march single file into the lecture hall. "Take every other seat. Skip two rows between you and the person in front of you. When the examination begins, there's to be no talking or smoking." I fall into my seat, thinking, "I wish I could break out of this place." But I know I'm just paying for my crime: everyone warned me not to take biology in my freshman year. Suddenly two guards—assistant examiners—burst through the doors with cartons of test booklets and question sheets. Taking a handful of books and question pages, the guards stamp between the rows, tossing out the equipment solemnly. "Nobody writes," barks the professor, "until eight o'clock sharp!" He scribbles in yellow chalk the time the exam begins, the time it ends, and the time it is now, measuring out a life's sentence for the prisoners before him. At eight o'clock the bell howls like a siren; everyone jumps and writes a name across the first page of the examination blue book. Occasionally, nervously, someone glances up at the beady-eyed guards who watch us without a smile. But I know my parole will begin just one hour from now. If I pass this awful exam, maybe I will not be a two-time loser like most of my friends, just an "ex-con" who learned his lessons and never returned to the biology jailhouse.

—*Charles Gomez*

Here are some other analogies you may wish to develop in a paragraph. As your instructor directs, select one of them for your theme assignment. Better yet, make up your *own* analogy to develop in a paragraph.

1. reading is like traveling
2. learning is a baseball game
3. leaving home: my private war
4. campus personalities and colors
5. home is like a zoo
6. books as people
7. the college exam room as hospital
8. working as slave labor
9. the principal's office as courtroom
10. a date is like a card game

Step 4. Exploring Contrasts Visually. Select two related objects that you might compare or contrast. With a camera, take several pictures that explore the relationship between the two objects. Mount your pictures and then arrange them in an effective order. Patterns 1, 2, and 3 on pages 141–151 will help you decide on an effective arrangement even though you are now working with visual images. You might want to select from this list of possible topics:

youth and old age	wealth and poverty
houses and apartments	work and play
love and hate	men and women
fear and courage	joy and sorrow
night and day	dawn and dusk
boys and men	city streets and country roads

CHAPTER 5

USING EXPERT TESTIMONY:
Spotlight on Jobs

INTRODUCTION

In the 1980s, different forces have had a stunning impact on America's labor scene. Economic uncertainty, unexpected population shifts, the growth of new technologies and the decline of others—all have made the choice of a career increasingly difficult for today's student. Opportunity and dead ends confront anyone who is trying to plan for future work. Which course of study do you take to prepare for a job that you will like and that will assure you some financial security throughout your life? What career options can you plan for in case there are no job openings in your chosen field when you graduate? What jobs are likely to be in great demand over the next decade, and which jobs will be plentiful?

Of course no one has the exact answers to these questions, but experts—researchers, writers, statisticians—provide enough material to help take some of the guesswork out of job- and career-related issues.

Investigating what experts say on various topics and recording what you find in clear, logical writing are two of the most important tasks for students throughout their course work. Using data on jobs and careers, this chapter asks you to turn from your own experiences as a source for supporting ideas to another vital source: research.

Throughout this book, you have learned how to develop topics through sensory detail. Although your own experiences (told through the clear language of the senses) always make for exciting and informative paragraphs, often you must write about subjects outside your own life. Writing about World War I in history class, about the varieties of cell reproduction in biology, about the social status of the American Indian in sociology—for these kinds of assignments you need some source of detail other than your own experience. Research leads you to knowledge beyond your own life; the information you find in books, in periodicals (magazines and newspapers), or on the television or the movie screen serves well as the basis of support for ideas you wish to develop.

In this chapter, you will examine data related to the job scene, and you will see how writers use data as sources for detail in their own writing. You'll practice reading information that experts present, and you'll practice making statements that accurately reflect their positions. In your own writing, you'll learn how to use statistics and cases from reliable sources and how to quote, directly or through paraphrase, information that you have read or heard from someone else. Also, to practice integrating expert testimony into your own writing, you will write a paragraph from a list of data on some aspect of jobs and careers.

VOCABULARY

Some Words for the Business Scene

Step 1.   Meanings from Context. Try to use clues in the sentences below to determine the meanings of the words that appear in italics. Write your definitions in the spaces provided; then check Appendix A to see if you are correct.

1. Current advances in *technology* support the idea that science can be applied to commercial or industrial objectives.

   technology means _____

2. The letters from Mr. Green and several other *correspondents* proved the success of the new product.

   correspondent means _____

3. So many *liabilities* meant one thing to the president of the company: she would have to take money from her own personal account in order to pay what she owed.

   liabilities means _____

4. It is not the slow-moving and lazy person who achieves in business, but rather the *dynamo*.

   dynamo means _____

5. Neither a policy of very active government control in business nor a policy of *laissez-faire* will end the depression; probably a path somewhere in the middle will best succeed.

   laissez-faire means _____

6. The modern day *entrepreneur*—anyone who boldly undertakes a business venture—must often make enemies on his way to success.

   entrepreneur means _____

7. Several thousand dollars worth of bonds, a large holding of land in Arizona, a million-dollar building in Trenton: these *assets* give the Marion family a leading voice in the business community.

   assets means _____

8. Before choosing a career, try to explore the *trends* in the occupation of your choice so that you know the general direction or tendencies that that career seems to be taking.

   trends means _____

9. Just what an employee brings forth on the job, his *productivity*, is what often determines his future with the corporation.

   productivity means _____

10. The company's *insolvency* shocked everyone; but the notice of bankruptcy in the papers did not lie.

    insolvency means _____

Words for the Job Situation

Step 2. Checking Definitions. In the blank spaces, write definitions for the words listed below. Use your dictionary for those you do not know; then check Appendix A.

What employers look for in workers:

1. compatibility _____

2. initiative _____

3. assiduity _____

4. integrity _____

5. loyalty _____

What workers look for in employers:

1. inspiration _____

2. generosity _____

3. compassion _____

4. amity _____

5. indulgence _____

Step 3. A Dialogue with New Vocabulary. Read the sentences below that employer or employee might speak and, from the new vocabulary in Step 2, select the word you think describes the missing character trait each complains about.

1. Employer: He puts other interests ahead of the company's, and so I do question his _____.
   Employee: Perhaps if you gave him a raise or a bonus every now and then—showed more _____—he might find it easier to be faithful to your organization.

2. Employer: That fellow in Department C does not follow a reasonable code of behavior. He lacks _____.

Employee: Well, if you gave in more to his shortcomings or to the little things he did wrong—showed more _____—then perhaps he would show more honesty.

3. Employer: I like a worker who sets her own tasks for herself, someone who takes the lead on her own. This is a woman with _____.
Employee: It might be easier for your workers to do that if you stimulated them by your own excitement for the work, if you could arouse a strong, positive feeling in them. You ought to be an _____ to your workers.

4. Employee: You never understand that I have my own problems and that these sometimes affect my work. When someone is suffering you should show more _____.
Employer: I try to respect your problems, but you always seem so disagreeable. I guess there is no _____ between us since we don't seem to work in harmony with each other.

5. Employee: I'll never understand why you display such a feeling of _____ for Smith. If you are not equally friendly to all your workers, don't you think they will be jealous?
Employer: I am naturally friendly to hard workers, Smith's _____ makes me particularly friendly.

-ing Words for Liveliness

Step 4. Checking Meanings. The words below, in their *ing* forms, will help you improve your writing style (see pages 208–211). Check a dictionary for any you don't know; write the definition in the blank space (see Appendix A for more help).

Hint

Look up the word in its infinitive form. Look up *sputter,* not *sputtering,* for example.

1. sputtering _____

2. asserting _____

3. familiarizing _____

4. lauding _____

5. assenting _____

Step 5. Naming the Action. From the list above, write in each blank a word that would show:

1. that someone was praising something _____
2. agreement _____
3. someone becoming acquainted with information _____

4. a manner of excited and unclear speech _____
5. someone making a statement she thought was true _____

BUILDING COMPOSITION SKILLS

Step 1. Sharing Ideas. Below are several statements about jobs and careers. Pick one or two statements with which you agree or disagree and discuss your opinions briefly, giving reasons to support your point of view.

1. Computer technology will make more and more jobs available over the years.
2. The only important quality employees look for in a job is financial security.
3. Summer job opportunities for college students are practically nonexistent.
4. Government-sponsored training programs are very important in giving disadvantaged people access to jobs.
5. Government-sponsored training programs are badly administered and are wasteful of taxpayers' dollars.
6. A liberal arts degree makes a college student well suited for a variety of jobs.
7. Affirmative-action rules for the employment of minorities have had little impact on jobs in America.
8. Physicians and dentists are the highest-paid workers in our society.
9. A career in show business is filled with enormous problems despite the glamour associated with singers, dancers, and actors.
10. College programs should have one main goal only: preparing students for their careers after graduation.

Statistics and Cases

You might support many of the ideas in Step 1 above by recalling instances from your own experiences. But another way to back up your position on a topic is to use statistics or cases as supporting evidence. *Statistics* may be thought of as facts, the numbers and examples revealed through responsible investigation. By offering comparisons between figures in charts, tables, and graphs, statistics make impressive evidence for backing up ideas.

A *case* is a specific incident involving real people and events. It is another kind of factual evidence that writers offer to support topics.

Of course, you must realize that even when presenting facts, writers often weight the evidence in favor of a particular point of view. Writers who are biased—that is, who have strong opinions about an idea—sometimes do not present complete information; or they may interpret the facts to suit a conclusion they have already reached.

GUIDELINES: STATISTICS AND CASES FOR STRONG DETAILS

In order to use statistics and cases wisely, make sure that you
1. select them from reliable, unbiased sources; this means that you often must check more than one source for data about the same issue.
2. present them in clear language.
3. give information honestly; do not leave out important records because they do not agree with the point you wish to make.
4. acknowledge your sources—that is, be sure to say where you took your information from.

Step 1.   Statistics and Cases as Supporting Detail. Read the following excerpt, in which the writer uses statistics and cases to support her point about the earnings of stockbrokers. Answer the questions after you read.

SOME WORDS TO KNOW BEFORE YOU READ

bail out: to leave quickly when conditions become adverse
commodities: economic goods, especially agricultural and mining products
options: the rights to buy or sell securities or commodities
gross: overall total, exclusive of deductions
revenue: income from an investment
generate: to create or bring into existence
commission: a fee paid for transacting business

Selling Stocks and Bonds

For most of the past decade, selling stocks and bonds was a tough way to make a living. After stock prices collapsed from their highs in the late 1960s, investors fled the market, and in many cases their brokers were right on their heels. Between 1969 and 1974, nearly 20,000 registered representatives at New York Stock Exchange member firms—about 35 percent of the total—bailed out of the business.

But for those brokers who managed to ride out the stormy Seventies, 1980 came as a rich and glorious reward. As stock prices rose sharply (Standard & Poor's 500-stock index was up 26 percent for the year), wealthy individual investors returned to the market, and trading volume soared to record highs. The newer lines of retail business, such as commodities and options, were booming too. *Fortune* estimates that the average broker rang up between $140,000 and $150,000 in gross commissions last year. That's about 30 percent better than in 1979, and considerably higher than any year in the Sixties. Since a broker's income is tied to his commission volume, the rise in revenues had a profound effect on take-home pay. Most firms allow their brokers to keep 35 to 40 percent of the commissions they generate. Which means that the average broker pocketed close to $60,000 last year.

The top "producers"—as they are called on Wall Street—did immensely better than that. *Fortune* estimates that over 100 brokers grossed in excess of $1 million last year. Steve Karelitz, 46, pulled in $2.5 million in commissions at Shearson Loeb

Rhoade's Boston office, netting himself close to $1 million. A main reason for his success, says Karelitz, is the long list of clients he has built up during 20 years in the business. At last count the list held more than 3,000 names. While many of these customers stayed in the market through the lean times, Karelitz heard last year from scores of customers who hadn't called in years.

In contrast to Karelitz's mass-market approach, Fred Berens, a 38-year-old Cuban émigré in the Miami office of Bache Halsey Stuart Shields, has only about 500 accounts. But many of these are big ones—wealthy individuals in Central and South America who last year found the U.S. securities markets particularly attractive. They helped Berens pull in $1.7 million in commissions, of which he netted well over $600,000. At Morgan Stanley, which caters mostly to very rich clients, roughly a quarter of the 80 retail brokers were above or near the $1 million commission level last year. A better racket than pro sports.

—Linda Hayes
"Boom Time for Brokers"
Fortune

1. Which statistics in paragraphs 1, 2, or 3 do you find most impressive or surprising?
2. What sources does Hayes cite for the statistics on brokers' earnings? the decline of registered representatives? the rise of stock prices?
3. What cases does the writer present to support her point about brokers' earnings?
4. What is Hayes' main point here? That is, what idea does she attempt to support with statistics and cases?
5. What does the last sentence of the last paragraph tell you about how Hayes wants you to view the data she is presenting?

Reading Tables, Charts, and Graphs

Often data that you find to support a topic appear in the form of tables, charts, and graphs. These visual presentations are designed to help you see relationships among numbers and what they pertain to.

In a diagram, statistics stand out dramatically and make it easier for the reader to identify trends and patterns, to make comparisons and contrasts, and to see the scope of an issue that the use of numbers alone can often minimize.

When you examine tables, charts, and graphs, your purpose is to note the relationship between the figures for individual items as well as the larger concern identified in the diagram.

To achieve this, do the following:

• *Read the title and the headings carefully.* The title explains the purpose of the table, chart, or graph and lets you know the key point that the figures support.

Projected Employment Changes in the Eighties

Projected change in employment, 1978–90 (millions)

| | −2 | 0 | 2 | 4 | 6 |

Professional and technical workers

Managers and administrators

Sales workers

Clerical workers

Craft workers

Operatives, except transport

Transport equipment operatives

Non-farm laborers

Private household workers

Service workers, except private household

Farm workers

■ Employment decline   □ Growth

Source: Bureau of Labor Statistics

In the bar graph above, the title tells you that the purpose of the illustration is to show projected changes in employment among different working groups.

- *Study the legend.* The legend is the caption that explains the illustrations. In a bar graph, for example, the legend will show what the differently shaded or designed bars illustrate. In the graph above, the black bars show employment decline, and the white bars show employment growth.
- *Take note of the numerical categories represented by the figures.* Often numbers will be stated simply, such as "4" or "-2" or "24.8." However, such numbers may represent much larger numbers, like hundreds of thousands, millions, or even billions. In the graph above, the numbers that the bars illustrate are in millions. (The heading above the numbers indicates "millions" in parentheses.) Thus, the first bar signifies a growth of about 2 *million* jobs in the field of professional and technical workers.
- *Translate the figures into verbal statements.* As you examine a table, a chart, or a graph, try to draw conclusions about the concepts represented by the figures. The best way to do this is to weigh carefully the relationships suggested by the numbers and the accompanying illustrations and to produce statements about the data in your own language. From the preceding graph, you could state, for

example, that between 1978 and 1990, jobs for professional and technical workers will increase by about two million, but this growth will be less than half the growth of clerical workers. In making that statement, you would have to make the connection yourself between the figures represented by the first bar and the fourth bar on the graph.

SOME POINTERS FOR WRITING STATISTICS CORRECTLY

1. Use numbers for percent.

18% or 18 percent

2. Use numbers for dates.

May 15, 1971

3. To show sums of money:
   a. If you need two words or fewer (*not* counting the word *cents* or *dollars*), write out the words for the numbers.

   three hundred dollars
   forty-two cents an hour
   eight billion

   b. If you need three or more words, use the numbers.

   $8.76 $8,487 $62,908,433

   c. For a series of numbers, use the figures, not the words.
4. Two-word fractions are written like this:

seven-tenths of all students
one-ninth of student drivers

Step 2.   Statements About Data. Examine the following graph and then answer the questions.

Causes of Job Openings in the Eighties

Job openings 1978–90 (millions)

```
        −5        0        5       10       15       20
```

Professional and technical workers	
Managers and administrators	
Sales workers	
Clerical workers	
Craft workers	
Operatives, except transport	
Transport equipment operatives	
Non-farm laborers	
Private household workers	
Service workers	
Farm workers	

▨ Employment decline   ■ Growth   ▢ Deaths and retirements

Source: Bureau of Labor Statistics

1. Based on the title, what is the purpose of this graph? _____

_____

_____

2. What does the black area signify? _____

_____

the white? _____

the striped? _____

3. For the following statements, put a plus sign (+) next to any conclusions that you could draw correctly from the graph and a minus sign (−) next to conclusions that the graph does not suggest.

_____ a. Growth in jobs for private household workers will be completely offset by employment decline.

_____ b. Deaths and retirements will produce more job openings than employment growth in all categories *except* for clerical workers.

_____ c. The decline in opportunities for farm workers will be offset by jobs made available through retirements or deaths.

_____ d. More than five million jobs will be open for non-farm laborers.

_____ e. There will be six million jobs open for clerical workers.

_____ f. Jobs for sales workers, transport-equipment operators, farm and non-farm workers, and private household workers all fall below five million.

_____ g. In all of the categories, death and retirement account for more openings than does job growth.

After you gather data on your topic, you will want to present it selectively when you write.

HINTS FOR USING CASES AND STATISTICS IN YOUR WRITING

1. When you collect data from charts, graphs, and tables, be sure that you understand what the various figures and numbers mean.
2. Don't just pile up a series of numbers as statistical information or your reader will lose interest. Make sure that you present your statistics in a clear and honest way. Often an image adds life to a paragraph built upon facts and figures.
3. In using cases, identify as much as possible the people, the events, the specific families or groups whose experiences support your idea.
4. Always select your statistics and cases from reliable sources. And be sure to name whatever sources you use for your information. The chart on page 205 suggests ways for telling the reader what materials you used as the basis for your facts.
5. Make sure that your statistics are not one-sided. By leaving out information or by "loading" evidence to give an incomplete picture, a writer can bias information. See pages 381–383 for other propaganda techniques to avoid.

Step 3. Graphs and Tables: Making Your Own Statements. Examine the circle and line graphs and the table on careers in the 1980s. Following instructions given in the box and on pages 192–194, note relationships among items identified in the illustrations. Then, for each of the three presentations, write in your own language at least three statements about the data. Use separate paper.

A. Circle graph
Projected Distribution of Employment by Occupation in 1990

Workers (millions)

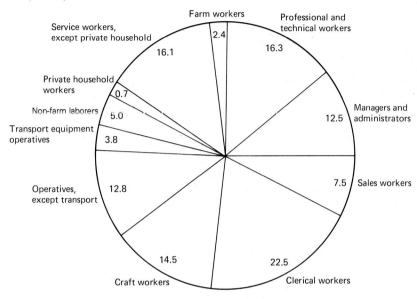

Source: Bureau of Labor Statistics

B. Line graph

Industries Providing Services Will Continue to Employ More People than Those Providing Goods

Workers (millions)[1]

Service producing:
  Transportation
    and public utilities
  Trade
  Finance, insurance,
    and real estate
  Services
  Government

Goods producing:
  Agriculture
  Mining
  Contract
    construction
  Manufacturing

80

60

40

20

0

Service producing

Goods producing

1960   1965   1970   1975   1980   1985   1990

[1] Wage and salary workers, except for agriculture, which includes self-employed and unpaid family workers.

Source: Bureau of Labor Statistics

C. Table

CAREERS IN THE EIGHTIES (FROM BEST TO WORST)

Occupation (1978 Employment)	Estimated Growth in Jobs to 1990	Prospects for Job Seekers	Starting Salary	Mid-career Salary	
The Sunniest					
Computer systems analyst (182,000)	37%	Excellent	$16,500	$34,000	Add management skills and you can write your own program for advancement.
Doctor (405,000)	38%	Good	$45,000	$82,000	Best of both worlds: the demand is in small towns, the money is in big cities.
Health service administrator (180,000)	57%	Good	$18,000	$37,500	Health care is booming, but a master's in business or health management is a must.
Geologist (31,000)	36%	Good	$17,600	$31,000	Domestic oil exploration will easily soak up the supply of degree holders.
Engineer (1,136,000)	27%	Good	$19,200	$35,000	Energy specialists strike a gusher, but budget cuts cap need for civil engineers.
Dentist (120,000)	29%	Good	$27,000	$53,000	New bridges to prosperity: corporate dental plans and in-store offices.
The Variables					
Dietitian (35,000)	43%	Good	$14,000	$25,000	Nutrition-consciousness feeds ample growth, but salaries are far from fat.
Economist (130,000)	39%	Good	$14,500	$45,000	Bad times are good for the dismal science, but beginners start low.
Banker (330,000)	55%	Good	$12,500	$27,000	Plenty of security, but when it comes to pay, the money stays in the vault.

CAREERS IN THE EIGHTIES (FROM BEST TO WORST)

Occupation (1978 Employment)	Estimated Growth in Jobs to 1990	Prospects for Job Seekers	Starting Salary	Mid-career Salary	
The Variables					
Accountant (985,000)	29%	Good	$14,000	$31,000	In a money-maddened era, starting out is easy, but management spots are elusive.
Personnel administrator (405,000)	17%	Good	$12,500	$29,500	Job growth may be even faster than expected, but competition may be stiff.
Physicist (44,000)	9%	Good	$16,000	$30,400	Bad news: jobs are few. Good news: number of qualified grads is fewer.
The Cloudiest					
Teacher (2,409,000)	2%	Poor	$11,000	$17,000	Budget cuts and declining enrollments teach a bitter lesson to newcomers.
Military officer (272,530)	1%	Good	$10,000	$22,000	Housing and living allowances (not included) won't shore up sorry pay scales.
Newspaper reporter (45,000)	20%	Poor	$12,500	$25,000	Writers blocked: Woodward, Bernstein and company inspired too many.
Public relations manager (131,000)	24%	Poor	$12,000	$32,000	When the economic news turns sour, the publicity people are the first to go.
Lawyer (487,000)	25%	Poor	$18,000	$50,000	Verdict: oversupply; sentence: less courtly compensation for years to come.
Architect (54,000)	43%	Poor	$12,000	$28,700	Some room at the top, but ground-level jobs are scarce and pay is poor.

Source: *Money Magazine*, May, 1980.

Quotations and Paraphrase as Details

Another source for supporting topic and subtopic sentences in your paragraph is quoted material from books, magazines, newspapers, radio, and television. By quoting, you use someone else's words and ideas to support your own opinion on a given subject. Of course, if you read something or hear it on the radio, it is not necessarily true; however, by using reliable sources, you can impress your reader with the strength of your position.

If, in your reading or listening, you discover some ideas that you want to use *exactly* as you have read or heard them, you can quote the material just as it was presented by giving the source of your information and by using quotation marks around the material. In that way you tell your reader that somebody else first stated the ideas you are writing about and that they are not original with you.

If you do not wish to use the information exactly as you have read or heard it, you may *paraphrase*—that is, you can use your own words to give an idea of what someone else wrote or said, especially if you want to summarize the idea. You do not need quotation marks, but here too you must identify the source of your information.

Step 1.   Effective Quotations. Read the following selection (taken from a longer work) that uses quoted material. Answer the questions that appear after it.

SOME WORDS TO KNOW BEFORE YOU READ

propagate: spread a report or an idea from person to person
assertion: an unsupported statement put forward as being true
distortion: a twisting out of shape; misrepresentation
prevalence: widespread or in general use or acceptance

Racism in Education

Since racism is the philosophy of the Establishment and is propagated in the institutions of higher learning and by the mass media which they control through ownership, it is not surprising to observe that "a vast majority of the white population south of the Mason-Dixon Line, and large numbers, probably a majority elsewhere, are firmly of the belief that Negroes are subhuman or only semi-human, despite the positive assertions of biology and anthropology to the contrary." (*The Rich and the Super-Rich,* by Ferdinand Lundberg).

The Black parent knows his child is "educable" in spite of all the funded programs and studies to the contrary. Dishonesty and distortions in intelligence tests are common. The literature on such tests shows that when "two groups of whites differ in their IQ's, the explanation of the difference is immediately sought in schooling, environment, economic position of parents. However, when Blacks and whites differ in precisely the same way the different is said to be genetic." (*The Study of Race,* by Sherwood L. Washburn). There are other instances which show the prevalence of racism. Trade schools (located in all industrial centers) have a long history of excluding Blacks. However, a Black occasionally slips through the net, after which the net is thoroughly examined to see how it happened. The trustees of these trade schools include the conservative officials of craft unions which exclude Blacks from membership. A classic example involved the Sheet Metal Workers Union Local 28 in New York. There were 3,300 white members in the union, but no Blacks. Apprenticeship was reserved almost exclusively for relatives of members. Finally, the State Commission on Human Rights found the local union guilty, and the union agreed that "henceforth every applicant for membership would be judged solely on an aptitude test administered by the New York Testing and Advisement Center."

—Maude White Katz
"End Racism in Education:
A Concerned Parent Speaks"

1. What is the source of each of the quotations in the above selection?
2. What *case* does the writer offer to make her point that racism spreads to trade unions? How is the writer's discussion of that case an example of *paraphrase*?
3. Why does the writer talk of a "net" in the second paragraph? How does the word help build an image?
4. What does the writer imply about jobs for minorities as sheet metal workers? Does racism still exist in certain careers? How could you go about finding data to support your point?

Integrating Testimony Into Your Own Writing (see also pages 499–500, Quoting From Books)

After you do research on a topic and after you collect notes that include statistics, exact quotations, and paraphrases (see pages 191–201), you will have to select from all your information those details that best support the point you want to make in your paper. As you do prewriting and, later, as you prepare your draft, you will be making those selections, choosing one set of dramatic figures over another, or choosing one quotation over others for its clarity and reliablility.

Integrating someone else's ideas into your own writing requires special attention.

It is perfectly all right to use someone else's ideas, statements, or conclusions to support your own point in a paragraph or an essay. However, you must always mention the source of your information. Any time you use someone else's words or ideas without giving credit to the person who first presented them, you are guilty of *plagiarism.* Although plagiarism is a serious offense, students often plagiarize merely through oversight or through a misunderstanding of the way to present research findings.

If you use statistics that you have gathered from reading charts, graphs, and tables in books or periodicals, you must state the source of your figures. Often you will see the source named at the bottom of a graph or a table. As you see on pages 195–197, "Source: Bureau of Labor Statistics" appears below many of the illustrations. If no source is named, you can assume that the writer of the book or article that you are using has collected original data. If you cite those data, name the author and the title of the piece as your source. Thus, if you wanted to cite figures from the graph on page 197 in your own paragraph, you might do it this way: "According to the Bureau of Labor Statistics, jobs for professional and technical workers will increase by about two million between 1978 and 1990" or "More than five million jobs will be available to clerical workers by 1990, reports the Bureau of Labor Statistics."

Step 1. Practice Citing Sources for Statistics. Return to Step 3 on pages 196–199. Select any three statements you developed from the data and incorporate the name of your source in each case. Use the lines below.

1. _____

_____

_____

_____

2. _____

_____

_____

_____

3. _____

_____

_____

_____

When you want to quote someone else's words, you must state them exactly, you must put those words in quotation marks, and you must name your source. Look at this selection from *Overseas Summer Jobs,* by D. J. Woodworth:

The best opportunities for work in Spain are in hotels and letters to the recently built hotels could result in an offer of a job. As most of these hotels cater for tourists from Northern Europe, a good knowledge of languages such as German, Dutch, French and English will be a great advantage to foreign workers, for whom there remains a good demand despite high local unemployment.

It should be remembered that hotel workers in Spain work very long hours during the summer months and foreign workers will be required to do likewise. In most cases hotel and restaurant staff work a minimum of 10 hours per day and bar staff may work even longer hours. A 7 day week is regarded as perfectly normal during the summer.

Suppose you were writing a paragraph on summer work in Europe and you wanted to quote from this selection. (Be sure to review pages 60–62 and 270 if you are unsure of how to use quotation marks correctly.) You would have to use quotation marks to separate someone else's ideas from your own, and you would have to cite your source. The trick is to blend your own words and the words of the writer you are quoting to produce a smooth, graceful sentence. Look at these two examples:

1. D. J. Woodworth in *Overseas Summer Jobs* says, "In most cases hotel and restaurant staff work a minimum of ten hours per day and bar staff may work even longer hours."
2. Workers in resorts overseas have no easy time. "In most cases," writes D. J. Woodworth *(Overseas Summer Jobs, page 103)* "hotel and restaurant staff work a minimum of ten hours per day and bar staff may work even longer hours."

Notice in the second example above how the writer makes a statement of his own (sentence 1) and then quotes his source. By breaking up the quotation with the words "writes D. J. Woodworth," the writer further weaves his own words into the statement he wants to quote exactly.

If you want to leave out part of the sentence you are quoting because it is too long or because some of the information might not serve your point, use an ellipsis. An *ellipsis* is a punctuation mark made up of three periods with spaces between them. Look at this example:

D. J. Woodworth points out in *Overseas Summer Jobs* that summer restaurant workers in Spain have ten-hour days and that "In most cases . . . bar staff may work even longer hours."

Above, the three spaced periods (the ellipsis) mark the omission of the words "hotel and restaurant staff work a minimum of ten hours per day and."

If you choose to start your quote with a word that does not begin a sentence in the original, however, you do not need an ellipsis.

In *Overseas Summer Jobs* D. J. Woodworth reminds us "that hotel workers in Spain work very long hours during the summer months. . . ."

In the example above, no ellipsis appears before "that," even though the writer left out the words "It should be remembered." The lower case *t* on "that" tells the reader that the quote is beginning in the middle of a sentence from the original. The four spaced periods after *months,* however, are required. The ellipsis here indicates that the writer left out the words "and foreign workers will be required to do likewise." The fourth period signifies the end of a sentence in the original.

If you wanted to put any of the ideas you read from Woodworth into your own words—that is, if you wanted to *paraphrase* the writer—you would still have to name your source, but you would not need quotation marks. Your paraphrase might look something like this:

According to D. J. Woodworth in *Overseas Summer Jobs* (page 103), hotel workers in Spain work very long hours. A ten-hour day, seven days a week is not at all an unusual schedule for a summer job.

In the paraphrase above, the writer put the sense of Woodworth's paragraph into the writer's own words. None of Woodworth's phrases appears in the new statement; the writer has simply paraphrased the ideas of this source and has acknowledged where they came from.

However, if the writer used any of Woodworth's own phrases, they would require quotation marks.

In *Overseas Summer Jobs,* D. J. Woodworth says that hotel workers put in "a minimum of ten hours per day" and that it is "perfectly normal during the summer" to work seven days a week.

In the example above, the writer has paraphrased part of Woodworth's sentences, but the quotation marks around exact phrases taken from the original are required to avoid a charge of plagiarism.

Sometimes writers want to quote an authority whom they have interviewed personally or have heard speak. In those cases, the writer usually names the authority and the person's position or credentials.

"We can't afford some top soloists for our subscription season any more," says Harold Lawrence, president and executive director of the Oakland Symphony. "We engage them only for galas with high priced tickets."

Sampson Field, the president of the New York Philharmonic, concurs. "Artists can raise their prices. We can't. We can't price ourselves out of the field or limit ourselves only to the very wealthy."

—Harold C. Schonberg
The New York Times

QUOTING AND PARAPHRASING: TIPS AND POINTERS

1. Always name your sources if you quote or paraphrase.
   a. Cite the source internally—that is, directly within the sentence you are writing. Your instructor may require a range of information in those internal citations, such as publisher's name, city of publication, date of publication, or page number on which the quotation appears. If you quote or paraphrase parts of an article in a periodical, you'll need the name of the article and of the newspaper or magazine, along with the date of publication. On pages 203–204 you saw several different models for internal citations.
   b. Cite the source in a footnote directly after quoted or paraphrased material. If your instructor requires footnotes, you must follow an accepted form for writing them. See the section called Writing Simple Footnotes, pages 497–499.
   c. Name your sources in a bibliography. A bibliography is a list of books used in the preparation of a research report. If your instructor requires a bibliography, use the correct form explained in the section called Preparing a Bibliography, pages 495–497.
2. Use quotation marks around all quoted materials, whether you quote full sentences or brief phrases. Review the correct use of quotation marks on pages 60–62 and on pages 270–271.
3. Integrate quotations smoothly into your own writing.
4. Do not load your paragraph with too many quotations or with one quotation that is too long. (If you must use a long quotation, set it off according to the instructions on pages 499–500.) Usually, in paragraphs and essays based upon research, about one-fourth of the writing should be made up of quoted material.
5. Use your own clear language in preference to quoting ordinary material. A sentence or two of your own to summarize a long or complicated point is a good way to offer important information.
6. Always select material from reliable sources.
7. Check unfamiliar words. Be sure that you know the meanings of any words that you quote or paraphrase.
8. Offer your thoughts and opinions based on the data you provide. Readers expect you to evaluate the expert testimony you present. Offer your own insights, but be sure the data support your opinions.

Ending a Paragraph

A paragraph must have some kind of closing, some indication that the writer has finished developing ideas and has not simply run out of things to say. In one-paragraph papers, the closing may be made effectively in just one sentence. Often two or three sentences may conclude the paragraph. Here are a few pointers to help you write closing sentences:

1. The closing sentence should leave no doubt in the reader's mind that you are finished with the paragraph.

2. The closing sentence should leave the reader with a feeling that you have done what you intended to do. It should clinch the main point of your theme.
3. The closing sentence should perform one or a combination of these functions:

   a. Restate the main idea by referring back to the topic sentence

   Hint

   You do not have to use the same words that appear in the topic sentence. Find synonyms for the opinion word and the words that state the topic.

   b. Summarize one or more of the subtopics
   c. Give the dominant impression of the experience being described
   d. Suggest some action that could be taken based on the paragraph
   e. Form a judgment based upon information in the paragraph
4. Use transition words to help you conclude: *therefore, as a result, consequently,* and a number of others explained in previous chapters are, good for concluding, summarizing, and showing results.
5. Make the conclusion fit the tone of the paragraph. A funny, brief, clever conclusion might suit a humorous paragraph about jobs. But a serious paragraph about employment problems would require something more formal.

Here are the things you should *not* do in closing sentences:

1. Don't start a new topic.
2. Don't contradict the point you have tried to make. A one-paragraph paper that tries to show why factory workers dislike their jobs should not end in the way that one student chose: "Some of them like their job, however."
3. Don't make statements that are obvious or overused. A paragraph dealing with the high costs of job training would gain little by a conclusion like this: "Money is the root of all evil."
4. Don't apologize for your lack of knowledge, lack of resources, or lack of interest. If you are not qualified to write about the topic, select a topic for which you are qualified.
5. Don't end with a hasty statement that indicates that your paragraph is over. *Avoid* endings like these:

And that's all I have to say.	You see what I mean.
The end.	That's all.
That's how it happened.	It may sound unbelievable but it's true.
I hope you have enjoyed my story.	Therefore what I have said is true.

6. Don't use too many words. Be brief, to the point, and clear.

7. Don't make any sweeping statements that admit no possibilities of other ideas or actions. To conclude a paragraph with "Therefore, all workers can learn to improve their job performance" overstates your case by an *absolute* conclusion, that is, a conclusion that has no conditions or possible exceptions or limitations. Try to soften your point with words that permit other possibilities: *perhaps, it seems, we may conclude, I am in favor, a good suggestion is.*

8. Don't make your closing statement too obvious by saying things like: "As I have shown you in my paragraph . . . ." or "So my closing sentence is . . . ."

Step 1. Picking Good Endings. Column I gives the topic sentence of a paragraph. Circle, in Column II, the closing sentence you think would best suit the paragraph. Explain your choice.

I

1. Students realistically must take into account the job market when choosing a major, but they must also choose careers that will be emotionally satisfying.

2. Our society must realize that children have legal job rights that must not be ignored.

3. The job forecast for humanities or creative-arts majors is rather bleak for the 1980s.

II

1.
  a. But some students are just out for big money.
  b. As I have indicated to you, emotions are important, too.
  c. We may conclude that a blend of financial and emotional considerations is the best way to choose a major.

2.
  a. Since I am not a lawyer, I don't know all the legal rights of children, but something should be done.
  b. As I have shown you in the above paragraph, this is a serious problem.
  c. Therefore, the legal rights of our children as American workers must be upheld.

3.
  a. It is unfortunate that many qualified writers, philosophers, and artists may be unemployed in the next decade.
  b. However, a rolling stone gathers no moss and so future employees must continue to search everywhere for jobs.
  c. Since I don't really know anything about art, I don't know how bad the situation really will be in the 1980s.

Step 2. Rewriting Closing Sentences. Answer the following questions.

1. Reread "Childhood Mischief," pages 121–122. How does the closing sentence *summarize* the various subtopics? _____

_____

Write a different closing sentence that will *suggest some consequence of the actions told about in the paragraph.* _____

_____

2. Reread "The Gloom Room," on pages 35–36. How does the closing sentence give the *dominant impression of the experience?* _____

_____

Write a different closing sentence that will *summarize* the main point.

_____

3. Reread "Waking on Monday Morning," on pages 181–182. How does the closing sentence *restate the main idea* and *suggest some action that could be taken* based upon the ideas expressed in the paragraph? _____

_____

Rewrite the closing sentences so that it *forms a judgment* based upon the information in the paragraph. _____

_____

_____

Expanding Sentences: Verb-Part Openers

You can improve sentence variety by opening a sentence with a verb part or with a group of words containing part of a verb. You have already dealt with two verb parts: the *infinitive* and the *-ing* word.

Using the *-ing* Opener

An *-ing* word—called a *present participle*—used without a helping word (see page 17) is not a verb, but it may be used effectively to open a sentence that contains a "legitimate" verb. Here is a complete sentence that contains a verb and a subject:

A young boy read *Robin Hood.*

An *-ing* word may be added at the beginning.

[comma here]
Whistling, a young boy read *Robin Hood.*

Hint

A comma must come after an introductory *-ing* word or an introductory group of words that contain an *-ing* word.

A word that tells *how, when,* or *where* may be placed after the *-ing* word.

[how]   [comma here]
Whistling softly, a young boy read *Robin Hood.*

A group of words that tell *why* or *how* or *where* or *when* may now be added after the *-ly* word.

[These words tell where.]   [comma here]
Whistling softly *in a hard brown chair,* a young boy read *Robin Hood.*

Sometimes a subordinator (see pages 100–109) may appear as the first word in a verb-part opener:

[subordinator]   [comma here]
While whistling softly in a hard brown chair, a young boy read *Robin Hood.*

Hint

Make sure that the first two or three words after the comma tell *who* or *what* is doing the action of the *-ing* word with which you have opened the sentence. See pages 213–215 for some work with incorrect verb-part openers.

Step 1. Opening a Sentence Strongly. Add opening word groups to the complete sentences that follow by selecting an item first from Column I, then from Column II, then from Column III. You should have three new sentences for each statement below.

I (*-ing* word)	II (one word to tell *how, when, where*)	III (a word group to tell *how, when, where, why*)
trembling	gracefully	in the sky
leaping	noisily	below the hill
soaring	clumsily	near me
roaring	there	through an open window
speeding	yesterday	in darkness
moaning	above	on a warm summer night
creeping	innocently	with a whine
dancing	swiftly	beyond the gray mountains
cheering	today	at noon

I (-*ing* word)	**II** (one word to tell *how, when, where*)	**III** (a word group to tell *how, when, where, why*)
speaking	slowly	beneath a pale cloud
crying	excitedly	across a stream
hurtling	softly	from their seats
drifting		at the campfire
		beside an old oak

Example

The boat returned home.

a. *Speeding, the boat returned home.*

b. *Trembling noisily, the boat returned home.*

c. *Drifting slowly across a stream, the boat returned home.*

1. A truck rumbled down Route 84.

    a. _____

    b. _____

    c. _____

2. My sister felt very content.

    a. _____

    b. _____

    c. _____

3. The ballet dancer gave his best performance ever.

    a. _____

    b. _____

    c. _____

4. The children laughed loudly.

    a. _____

    b. _____

    c. _____

5. The cat sprang quickly away.

    a. _____

b. _____

c. _____

Step 2.   Using New Words. Use the words given in the new *-ing* vocabulary (on page 189) to open three sentences of your own. Use separate paper.

Step 3.   *-ing* at the End. The *-ing* construction works nicely at the end of sentences too. On a separate sheet of paper, rewrite any five sentences you wrote in Step 1 or Step 2 above, this time placing the *-ing* word group at the end.

Sentence from Step 1: Drifting slowly across a stream, the boat returned quietly.
Rewritten sentence: The boat returned quietly, *drifting slowly across a stream.*

Step 4.   Two *-ing* Words. Two *-ing* words at the beginning produce an effective sentence. Complete each sentence below that begins with a double *-ing* construction by adding your own complete thought.

Example
Laughing and smiling,
Laughing and smiling, the children shouted, "Trick or Treat!"
_____

_____

   Hint
The first few words after the comma must tell who or what does the action of the *-ing* words. See pages 213–215 for errors that may arise in the use of the *-ing* opener.

1. Smoking and drinking,

   _____

2. Slamming the brakes and hitting the clutch,

   _____

3. Brushing his hair and smiling into the mirror,

   _____

4. Holding her stomach and gasping for breath,

   _____

5. Groping in the dark and calling her name,

   _____

6. Daydreaming and imagining new careers,

   _____

Infinitives as Openers

If you want to tell *why* the subject of a sentence performs some action, you can open the sentence with a word group that starts with an infinitive. (An infinitive is made up of the word *to* and the present tense of the verb: *to hope, to sing, to laugh* are just three examples.)

[This tells *why* he had the tires checked.]
To ensure the safety of his car, he had the tires checked carefully.
[comma here]

Step 5. Using Infinitives as Openers. Use each of the following infinitive word groups in front of your own complete sentence.

Hint
Use a comma after an infinitive word group when a complete sentence follows it.

Example
1. To achieve high grades

   To achieve high grades, a student needs discipline.

2. To run a marathon

   _____

3. To change jobs

   _____

4. To write well

   _____

5. To learn computer programming

   _____

Other Verb Parts as Openers

Word groups with verb parts that end in *-ed, -n, -en,* or *-t* (*past participles*) may also be used to start sentences. Again, a comma must come after the introductory word group, and the first words after the comma must tell who performs the action of the verb part used in that introductory word group.

Spoken in a loud voice, the announcer's words reached the whole audience.
[verb part]   [comma here]   [This tells *what*
                                      was spoken.]

[verb part]

Concerned about her choice of medical schools, Joyce consulted her academic adviser.

                              [comma]   [This tells *who* was concerned.]

Step 6. Using Other Verb Parts as Openers. Begin a sentence of your own with the following verb-part openers. Be sure you study the examples given above.

1. Pleased with his behavior

_____

2. Taken by surprise

_____

3. Greeted by her friends

_____

4. Exhausted from the hike

_____

5. Delighted with the good news

_____

Avoiding Errors with Verb-Part Openers

When you use verb-part openers, you must remember to name the correct subject (the person or thing that performs the action of the verb part) in the first few words after the opening word group. Whether or not it is intended, the first noun or pronoun after the verb-part opener is automatically the subject; this often yields strange and humorous sentences. Look at the columns below.

I *Correct*	*II* *Incorrect*
1. While dressed in a new overcoat, [This tells who was dressed in an overcoat.] I brushed against a bus and soiled my sleeve.	**1.** While dressed in a new overcoat, [This shows that the bus was dressed in an overcoat.] a bus brushed against me and soiled my sleeve.
2. Feeling fine, the little old man [This tells that the man was feeling fine.] smiled at the trees and flowers.	**2.** Feeling fine, the trees and flowers [These words tell that the trees and flowers felt fine.] made the little old man smile.

It is obvious that the sentences in Column II do not say what the writer wants them to say (a *bus* dressed in an overcoat? *trees* feeling fine?).

TO CORRECT THE ERROR MADE WITH VERB-PART OPENERS

1. Ask *who* or *what* is performing the action indicated by the verb part.

Who is dressed in a new overcoat?

Who is feeling fine?

If necessary, rewrite the sentence so that the words that answer that question appear within the first few words after the verb-part opener.

2. Rewrite the sentence so that the subject is included in the opening word group. You will have to add a word to make a complete verb.

Sentence 1 in Column II could be rewritten in this way:

[added word to make a verb]

While I was dressed in a new overcoat, a bus brushed against me and soiled my

[subject now included in opening word group]

sleeve.

Sentence 2 in Column II could be written in this way:

[added word to make a verb]

Since the little old man was feeling fine, the trees and flowers made him smile.

[subject now included in opening word group]

Although this second option helps you correct errors, it also removes the *-ing* structure from the beginning of the sentence. Because *-ing* words are valuable in varying your style, try to keep them by naming the subject right after the verb-part opener, as explained in Column I on page 213.

Step 7. Making Sense with *-ing* Words. For each item below, draw an arrow from the verb part to the person or thing that the *sentence says* is the subject. Then, rewrite the sentence so that it makes sense. If the sentence is already correct, mark it *C.*

Example

1. After failing the final exam, her father scolded her. *After she failed the final exam, her father scolded her.*

2. Running for the bus, my books fell out of my arms. _____

_____

3. Spilling milk all over the table, my shirt and pants were drenched. _____

_____

4. While biting my nails nervously, the judge called my name. _____

_____

5. While waiting for the train to Cheyenne, I read my textbook from cover to

cover. _____

_____

6. Gazing sadly out the window, the heavy rain turned my garden into

mud. _____

_____

7. While shopping for Christmas presents, the fire engines raced down the

street. _____

_____

8. After undressing completely, the doctor examined me. _____

_____

9. Running like a demon, the door smashed my nose. _____

_____

10. After waiting impatiently for two hours, my desire to see Cathy increased

greatly. _____

_____

Step 8. Checking Your Sentences. Examine the sentences you wrote in Steps 1 through 7 on the previous pages. Have you made any errors with verb-part openers? Does the sentence state clearly the subject you intended for the verb part? Correct any problems you find.

SOLVING PROBLEMS IN WRITING

Capital Letters

Step 1. What Do You Remember? Write a *full* sentence response to each question below.

1. If you were writing a job application letter to someone named Jeanne Gilbert, how would you open the letter? How would you close it?

_____

2. What river runs through your state?

_____

3. What are three subjects you enjoy at college?

_____

4. Which relative do you most enjoy visiting?

_____

5. If you could board a plane and fly anywhere, in which direction would you go?

_____

6. Which animal in the zoo do you think is funniest?

_____

7. What high school did you attend (write the words *high school* as part of your answer)?

_____

8. Which war do you think was the bloodiest?

_____

9. Which president do you think did the most for our country?

_____

10. What is the name of your favorite book, and who is its author?

_____

If you could not make up your mind about the spelling of some of your answers, study the reference charts on capital letters on pages 218–219.

Step 2.   Making Sense with Capitals. In each of the following sentences, the first letter of several words is omitted. Decide whether you need a capital or a small letter and then fill in the blank spaces.

1. My _____unt left her job at the _____nion _____avings and _____oan _____ompany to attend _____arvard _____aw _____chool this _____all.
2. Last _____ummer one of my _____eachers organized a trip to the _____est
3. When the _____rooklyn _____odgers moved _____est to _____os _____ngeles, it was a sad day in _____ay for my _____ncle _____harlie.
4. The _____hopwell _____upermarket, located on _____iverside _____rive between _____enth and _____ak _____treets, is the busiest _____tore in our _____own.
5. When writing _____usiness letters, I prefer to see "_____ear _____iss _____ones" rather than "_____y _____ear _____iss _____ones"; in closing, I use a simple "_____ours _____ruly."
6. If you like _____merican _____istory, you should know the role of the _____rench _____overnment during the _____evolutionary _____ar.
7. It is not true that science—_____iology, _____hemistry, _____hysics,

_____sychology—denies the existence of _____od; it is possible to be-lieve, for example, in _____reudian ideas and the _____ible as well.

8. Last _____pril just before _____aster, the _____epublican _____arty held a banquet at the _____ilton _____otor _____nn in _____ochester, a _____ity in _____estern _____ew _____ork _____tate.

9. _____he _____wilight _____one is still one of the best shows on _____elevision; that _____od _____erling was a great writer.

10. The _____ayor was late for the dinner given by the _____rban _____eague because her car broke down at the old _____ndicott-_____ohnson _____hoe _____actory.

Step 3. Correcting Your Errors. Return to Step 1, pages 215–216. Make corrections in what you wrote, based upon the reference chart on pages 218–219.

Step 4. Finding Mistakes with Capitals. Each sentence below has the number of errors with capitals indicated in parentheses. Make the corrections directly on the page.

1. Even though i live just Twenty miles West of st. Louis, I have never driven to see my aunt harriet, who teaches Philosophy at the University. (8)
2. my Dear ms. stromberg,

   I would like you to know that I received dr. weber's offer of a Teaching Position in the english department to teach three sections of creative writing 127. I accept with pleasure.

   Sincerely Yours,
tess carver, ph.D.   (16)

3. i would like to play Baseball for the chicago white soxs, but my Father insists that I become a Lawyer and work for the law firm of davis and rutter in seattle. (10)
4. San francisco's chinatown has a number of Schools where, even during the Summer months, students can study English, Mathematics, and History. (6)
5. when i saw the President of First National bank at a Baseball game in Shea stadium one hot august day, i was surprised because i thought he was visiting his Daughter in the midwest. (11).

Formal and Informal Language

Formal English is the language of professional journals, formal speeches, and most serious college writing. Informal English (the English you speak each day) is found in parts of novels, short stories, letters, books, most newspapers, articles for general readership, and advertisements. *Colloquialisms* (informal expressions used in speaking but generally not in writing) and *slang* (vivid words or phrases used because they are brief, "loose," and colorful) mark informal language and are perfectly acceptable in informal situations. Although it is effective to use such

QUICK REFERENCE CHARTS: WHEN AND WHEN NOT TO CAPITALIZE

Geography

Russian River
Rocky Mountains
BUT
a tall **m**ountain

Salt Lake City
BUT
our **c**ity

Yellowstone National Park
Market Street
BUT
a noisy **s**treet

Historical Occurrences, Names, and Writings

Tonkin Resolution
Boston Tea Party
Seward's Folly
Fifth Amendment
the Constitution

The Family

I get along with Mom.
OR
I get along with mom.
This is Aunt Celia.

No capitals to show relationship.

That is my **s**ister.
Our **u**ncle is generous.
My **a**unt is very helpful.

Buildings and Organizations

Dime Savings Bank
Sears Roebuck and Company
Brookdale Hospital
Pathmark Supermarket
Republican Party
San Francisco Giants
Girl Scouts

The Word "I"

Always capitalize the word *I*

When *I* saw her, *I* was delighted.

Days, Months, Seasons, Celebrations

Monday
April
not seasons
spring, **s**ummer, **f**all, **a**utumn, **w**inter
Election Day
Festival of Lights
New Year's Eve

Religion, Race, Nationality

God, Lord
Bible, Genesis
New Testament
bless His Name
the Egyptian gods
Catholicism
the Jewish religion
Protestant beliefs
Negro, Indian
Dutch Reformed Church

Titles
Books, Stories, Shows, Poems

"Oh Captain, My Captain"
Love Story
A Tale of Two Cities
BUT
a **b**ook by Dickens

The Washington Post
All in the Family
"The Legend of Sleepy Hollow"

Titles
People

President Carter
Judge Black
Dr. Bracken
He is the president of the company.
Mr. Davis, President of the company
OR
Mr. Davis, president of the company
Harriet Parsons, Ph.D.
BUT
a **t**eacher, a **l**awyer, a **p**rofessor

Hint: If the title takes the place of a person's name, use a capital.
The Mayor arrived late.
The **m**ayor's job is difficult.

(continued on next page)

QUICK REFERENCE CHARTS: WHEN AND WHEN NOT TO CAPITALIZE (continued)

School Things

LaGuardia Community
College
    BUT
a new college

Mohawk High School
    BUT
our old high school

Coleman Junior High
School
    BUT
a junior high school

English, Spanish, French
    BUT
American history
economics, biology, business

Hint: Languages are always capitalized. Other subjects are not, except when specific courses (usually indicated by numbers) are meant.

Economics 13.2

History 64

a sophomore in college
the senior class

Writing Letters

Opening: Capitals for first word and any names.
    Dear Mr. Stevenson:
    My dear Miss Trumball:
    Dear Jerry,
Closing: First word only:
    Sincerely yours,
    Yours truly,
    Very truly yours,

Areas and Directions

Lower East Side
East-West relations
Far East
Midwest
lives in the West
    but not for
    directions

New York is six miles east
of here.

They drove north across
the bridge.

**No Capitals for Plants,
Animals, Games**

daisies	a vicious lion
sycamore tree	baseball
an old oak	football
bananas	swimming
a bluebird	monkeys
six sparrows	apple

informality for special effects in your writing or as part of the quoted words you show someone speaking, for the most part informal language should be avoided in your compositions. And very often informal expressions change so rapidly that acceptable words one year are no longer used at a later time.

But be careful! Do not substitute for an informal expression something stuffy, unnatural, and jarring to the ears. Usually, however, students are too *in*formal in their writing.

Here are some informal expressions used in student themes and some alternatives that could be used.

Informal	*Example*	*More Formal Expression*
cool; way out; super; swell; together	It was a *cool* movie.	excellent; effective; remarkable; superior; relaxed; provocative
fun (used to describe)	We had a *fun* time.	enjoyable; uproarious; amusing; hilarious
sort of (a) kind of (a)	That policeman was *kind of* strange.	rather; somewhat
a couple of	Bring me *a couple of* books.	some; several; a few
dig on groove on	My girl friend and I were *grooving on* a record.	enjoy; respond; appreciate; love; listen
lousy	What a *lousy* time we had.	dull; depressing
enthused	The singer was *enthused* about the piano player.	enthusiastic about or over; excited
a lot, lots of	I have *lots of* time.	much; a great deal
a fix	What a *fix* I got into with this car! I'll *fix* you!	complication; troublesome time; awkward event punish
myself yourself } used as himself } subjects	Mary and *myself* were late.	I you he
real; mighty; awfully; plenty	He was *real* annoyed at me.	very; extremely; strongly
faze	It didn't *faze* me in the least.	bother; disturb; annoy
sure	*Sure* I wanted to leave the house.	certainly; indeed; surely; absolutely
drag	Biology is a *drag*.	boring; uninteresting
do a number	My girl friend *did a number* on me.	cheat, confuse, betray

Hint

If occasionally you want to use some informal word for special effect, put the word in quotation marks:

Because of so much construction and repairs, no one but the builders can "dig" Atlanta any more.

See also "Biology Jailhouse," pages 183–184, last sentence.

USING CONTRACTIONS

Putting words together by replacing letters with an apostrophe helps writers record accurately the words people speak. Thus, hearing *can't, isn't, it's, could've,* and other contractions, writers attempting to produce on paper a direct quotation would write exactly what they hear.

Contractions are also acceptable in informal writing, even when no speaker is being quoted. Therefore, in newspapers, popular magazines, and textbooks aiming for a conversational tone, contractions work well—though never when they are excessive.

However, most formal writing for your college courses demands that you avoid contractions wherever you can. Use the two words that led to the contraction rather than the abbreviated form of the word. Here are some examples:

Informal	*Formal*
She *didn't* look up from her page of notes.	She *did not* look up from her page of notes.
They'd have phoned if they *could've.*	They *would have* phoned if they *could have.*

Instead of these contractions:	*Write the words out:*
I'm	I am
isn't	is not
wasn't	was not
weren't	were not
aren't	are not
don't	do not
couldn't	could not

Step 1. Informal to Formal. Rewrite each of the sentence examples of informal usage on page 200 into more formal language. Be careful not to make your new sentences sound too high-flown. Use separate paper.

Step 2. More Informal Sentences. Here are several more sentences using informal language. Discuss how you would change them into sentences that would be acceptable in a formal writing activity. Do not write anything too stiff.

1. They're a cool bunch to hang out with, but my old lady flipped when she caught me.
2. I pick up lots of foxy ladies who groove on the disco scene and fancy threads.
3. For sure, that scene was so outrageous we all got kinda wasted.
4. My lousy gig is such a drag, but I really need the bread.
5. Sure, Pop gave the wheels plenty of juice, but we couldn't jive those cops out of a ticket nohow.

6. I figure I should talk turkey if my old man hangs the accident on me. Otherwise he might think I was strung out or something, and then it's painsville for me.
7. My chick was sort of uptight when she met the tough dudes I hang out with.

Step 3.   A "Square" Dictionary. Write your own dictionary of several more informal expressions (slang, colloquialisms) that you define for someone who might not "dig" your language. Write a definition for each word; use each word in a colloquial sentence that you might speak or write; give one or two alternate words that could be used for the same effect; then, rewrite your original sentence in more formal English. You might want to define colloquial and slang expressions like *dough, kookie, wicked, uptight, with it, right on, boss, bread, gig, gross, airhead*. Make a chart like the one below. Follow the example.

A "SQUARE" DICTIONARY

Informal Expression	Definition	My Own Sentence	Alternate Words	More Formal English
uptight	to be nervous	I was all uptight about the driving test.	anxious, worried, troubled, nervous	I was nervous about the driving test.

Abbreviations and Numbers

When you take notes, it's often convenient to use some sign or shortened form of a word to save time. But in formal writing, you should avoid abbreviated forms of words.

What Not to Use	What to Use Instead
& or ✄ or &	and
Feb., Apr., Wed.	February, April, Wednesday Write out the word for the day or month.
bio, psych, eco	biology, psychology, economics Write out the word for all school subjects.
thru, tho, boro nite, lite, brite	through, though, borough night, light, bright Don't leave off the ends of words or make up short forms.
st., h'way., ave., blvd., rd., co.	street, highway avenue, boulevard } Always write these out. road, company

What Not to Use	What to Use Instead	
ch., p., pp.	chapter ⎫ page ⎬ pages ⎭	Write these out, except in footnotes or bibliography.
lbs., oz., ft., in.	pounds, ounces ⎫ feet, inches ⎭	Measurements are spelled out.
L.A., Ill., Calif., Rocky Mts.	Los Angeles Illinois California Rocky Mountains ⎫⎬⎭	Names of states, countries, cities, geographical places are not abbreviated. (For addresses on envelopes, however, established post office abbreviations are required.)
e.g.	for example	
no., #	number	
and etc. or ect.	etc. This is the abbreviation for *et cetera*. Do not use *ect.* or *and etc.*	

Hint

Use *etc.* very infrequently.

WHEN YOU CAN USE SHORTENED FORMS

1. &, &, Co., Inc.

1. only when part of an official name: A&P, Tiffany & Co.

2. Mr., Mrs., Dr.

2. only immediately before someone's name

3. Jr., Sr.,

3. only immediately after someone's name is mentioned

4. Ph.D., M.D., M.A.

4. only immediately after someone's name

5. FBI, NAACP, UN

5. Some organizations and government departments are usually referred to by initials. No periods are necessary after the letters.

6. A.M., P.M.
(or a.m., p.m.)

6. when numbers appear directly before: 8:15 P.M.

> **Hint:** If you use the word *o'clock*, write out the number: ten o'clock *not* 10 o'clock.

7. $, No.

7. when numbers come after: $5.00, Booth No. 6,

Hint

1. Abbreviations usually require periods.
2. If you don't know what an abbreviation means, consult any dictionary.
3. It's better, in general, not to use abbreviations.

DO'S AND DON'TS ABOUT NUMBERS

Don't use the number if you can write it out in one or two words.

fifty	*not*	50
three hundred	*not*	300
eighty-eight	*not*	88
nineteenth	*not*	19th
eightieth	*not*	80th

Do use the number if more than two words are needed to write it out.

654   *not*   six hundred and fifty-four

Do use the number for the year and day of a date.

February *2, 1971*

Hint: Don't use *-st, -th, -nd, -rd* after any number in a date.

Do use numbers if you need to mention a series of numbers.

On the rack hung *50* red dresses, *340* skirts, and *15* vests.

Do use the number for percentages and decimals.

Of the students, *45%* were boys.

The paper measures *8.73* inches in length.

Do use the number for items in street addresses.

480 Rockaway Parkway

1874 Ninth Avenue

Hint: If the street itself is named by a number, write the word out if the number is below ten. Otherwise, use the number, *without -st, -th, -nd, -rd* at the end.

251 East 91 Street

1880 18 Street

37 Fifth Avenue

Do use the number for parts of a book.

On page *18* the author presents a graph to illustrate his point.

Don't start a sentence with a number.

Nine parents attended not *9 parents attended.*

The room held 350 seats not *350 seats were in the room.*

Step 1.   Correcting Abbreviations. In each sentence below, correct whatever errors you find in regard to abbreviations. The numbers in parentheses tell how many errors there are.

1. I have lived at 1092 1st. Ave. in L.A. a no. of yrs., but I have never visited northern Calif.   (6)
2. On the 2nd Thurs. nite of every month I take a bio. class at Drs. Hospital located on Madison H'way.   (6)
3. Every nite I pray that when I wake up & weigh myself I will have lost at least 10 lbs. and grown at least 4 in.   (6)
4. Getting thru eco 101 is my #1 concern in school this yr.   (6)
5. 1,000,000 people turned out for the anti-nuclear rally in NYC last June 11th, tho the newspapers reported much fewer.   (4)
6. On April 6, 1975, 5 children earned grades of forty-five% on their arith. tests; but Mark's bro, 8 years old, missed only No. 4.   (6)

WRITING A PARAGRAPH FROM DATA

> ASSIGNMENT: Write a paragraph about jobs and careers, using as supporting detail the data that appear in any one of the data clusters on pages 226–235.

Each of the following clusters of information contain data on current careers. Study the information and try first to make some generalization about it. A *generalization* is a broad or extended meaning drawn from specific information. When you generalize, you develop a concept or a rule that goes beyond the data at hand and yet is based on that data.

You can use the generalization to write a strong topic sentence that both introduces the topic and gives an opinion about it. In addressing the subject that the data supports, your generalization will, of course, name the topic, the first requirement of a topic sentence. Next, when you generalize, you do offer an opinion of sorts because the generalization represents your individual reaction to the information you've read. You might want to emphasize your reaction to the information by using words that convey a stronger sense of opinion, but the generalization itself does imply an opinion. Thus, by generalizing, you produce a topic sentence for your paragraph.

Support the generalization in your topic sentence with a paragraph of solid details. Draw upon the expert testimony in the cluster you've chosen. Be sure to study the checklist on page 238. And, examine the sample paragraph, "Teenagers as Part-Time Workers," written by a student who studied Data Cluster 3.

If your instructor suggests, you may do research on your own to supplement the data here or to explore other topic ideas.

DATA CLUSTER 1: WHAT GOVERNMENT WORKERS DO

Nearly 1 million civilian employees in 1977 worked for Federal agencies concerned with national defense and international relations. Principal occupations that deal with these functions included administrative and clerical workers, health workers, teachers, engineers, scientists, technicians, and craft and other manual workers. People in these jobs work in offices, research laboratories, navy yards, arsenals, and missile launching sites and in hospitals and schools run by the military services.

Another 1.5 million workers provided health services and staffed hospitals, primarily for State and local governments. Many workers also were employed in housing and community development, police and fire protection, social security and public welfare services, transportation and public utilities, financial administration, general administrative functions, and judicial and legislative activities. The majority of these workers also were State and local government employees. All of the 650,000 government workers in postal services and a majority of the nearly 500,000 workers in natural resources, such as those in the National Park Service and the Forest Service, were employed by the Federal Government.

Source: U.S. Department of Labor, Bureau of Labor Statistics, *Occupational Outlook Handbook, 1980–1981 Edition* (Washington, D.C.: Government Printing Office, 1980), p. 614.

PERCENT DISTRIBUTION OF EMPLOYMENT IN GOVERNMENT AND PRIVATE INDUSTRY BY OCCUPATION, 1978

Occupation	Government	Private Industry
Total	100	100
White-collar workers	67	46
Professional and technical	35	11
Managers and administrators	8	11
Clerical	24	17
Sales	(2)	7
Blue-collar workers	14	37
Craft and related workers	6	14
Transport equipment operatives	3	4
Other equipment operatives	1	14
Non-farm laborers	4	5
Service workers	19	13
Farm workers	(2)	4

Excludes Federal employment overseas
Source: Bureau of Labor Statistics

Government Workers

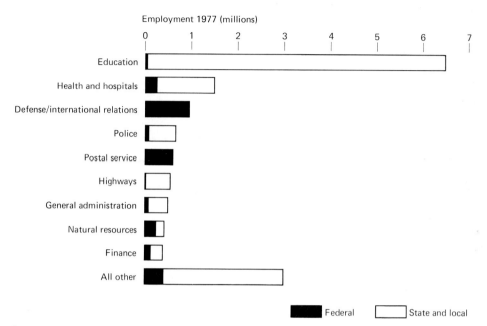

Employment 1977 (millions)

Federal   State and local

Source: Bureau of the Census

DATA CLUSTER 2: WHAT GOVERNMENT WORKERS ARE PAID

Over half of all Federal workers are paid under the General Schedule (GS), a pay scale for workers in professional, administrative, technical, and clerical jobs, and for workers such as guards and messengers. General Schedule jobs are classified by the U.S. Office of Personnel Management in 1 of 18 grades, according to the difficulty of duties and responsibilities, and the knowledge, experience, and skills required of the workers. GS pay rates are set by Congress and apply to government workers nationwide. They are reviewed annually to see whether they are comparable with salaries in private industry. [See table on next page.]

Source: U.S. Department of Labor, Bureau of Labor Statistics, *Occupational Outlook Handbook, 1980–1981 Edition* (Washington, D.C.: Government Printing Office, 1980), p. 617.

Every November, a favorite theme of most political speeches is the need to control the federal bureaucracy. Some politicians stress the difficulty of making it more responsive to the people, others, the importance of diminishing its size. Rarely, however, does anyone mention the delicate topic of rapidly rising pay rates in the federal civil service. One reason is that very few politicians want to be on record as opposing raises for 3 million voters; another is that, like most of us, politicians can't believe that bureaucrats could actually be overpaid.

DISTRIBUTION OF FULL-TIME FEDERAL EMPLOYEES UNDER THE GENERAL SCHEDULE BY GRADE LEVEL, MARCH 31, 1978, AND SALARY SCALE EFFECTIVE OCT. 7, 1979

General Schedule (GS)	Employees		Salaries		
	Number	Percent	Entrance	Periodic increase	Maximum
Total, all grades	1,396,265	100.0			
1	1,593	0.1	$ 7,210	$ 240	$ 9,126
2	22,635	1.6	8,128	271	10,327
3	94,786	6.8	8,952	298	11,634
4	176,286	12.6	10,049	335	13,064
5	188,366	13.5	11,243	375	14,618
6	87,392	6.3	12,531	418	16,293
7	129,205	9.3	13,925	464	18,101
8	27,911	2.0	15,423	514	20,049
9	140,986	10.1	17,035	568	22,147
10	26,724	1.9	18,760	625	24,385
11	153,468	11.0	20,611	687	26,794
12	150,686	10.8	24,703	823	32,110
13	108,852	7.8	29,375	979	38,186
14	55,164	4.0	34,713	1,157	45,126
15	27,251	2.0	40,832	1,361	[2]53,081
16	3,456	0.2	47,889	1,596	—
17	1,097	0.1	[2]56,099	—	—
18	407	[1]	[2]65,750	—	—

[1]Less than 0.05 percent

[2]The rate of basic pay for employees at these rates is limited by section 5308 of title 5 of the United States Code to $50,112.50 as of the above date.

Source: U.S. Office of Personnel Management

In November 1980, for example, the president's Advisory Committee on Federal Pay reported, just as earlier panels have, that the salaries of federal white-collar workers were lagging behind those in the private sector. In some cases the differences were very small—1 percent for clerks, typists and technicians; 2 percent for beginning accountants, attorneys, and engineers—but at many higher level positions there was a 7 percent gap, and at the top, government executives earned as much as 46 percent less than their counterparts in private industry. The report also stated that since 1970 white-collar salary scales rose 73 percent in the federal bureaucracy but 92 percent in the private sector. Although the government's own statistics indicate that the average white-collar federal employee earns $5,000 more than the average worker in private industry, the panel pointed out that the very high percentage of skilled people in the federal work force made such comparisons unfair.

But comparisons have been the crucial element in determining federal pay rates since 1970, when Congress passed a law guaranteeing government employees salaries comparable to those of private industry workers doing similar jobs. This was simple enough to implement for blue-collar workers because union contracts spell out, often in great detail, wage rates and job responsibilities. Establishing comparability standards for white-collar employees, however, has proved extremely difficult despite an elaborate monitoring system set up by the Bureau of Labor Statistics. Moreover, in recent years several economists, notably Yale Brozen and Edward Plazear of the University of Chicago, have challenged the bureau's methods of evaluating federal pay and have determined that federal workers are in fact more generously rewarded than private-industry workers.

Source: John W. Wright, *The American Almanac of Jobs and Salaries* (New York: Avon, 1982), pp. 100–101.

Any impression of civil servants being society's ragamuffins would be hard to reconcile with the data compiled in the July 1979 "Survey of Current Business," which shows that in 1978, federal employees earned an average of $18,988 compared with an all-industry composite average of $13,275.

Officials of the federal Office of Personnel Management (OPM) dismiss this comparison as an apples-and-oranges thing—the apples being working Americans at large and the oranges the federal force, which has a much higher component of professional and administrative personnel.

But for those who were born earlier than yesterday, the explanation is a cop-out. Since 1962, the great increase in federal programming has not been in research and development, where professionals dominate, but in routine payment social programs which require hives of clerical worker bees. Yet, during that same period, the superiority of the federal pay average over the all-industry average steadily increased from 27 percent in 1962 to 44 percent in 1978.

Back when men wore watch chains across their vests, compensation for federal employment was something less than lavish. But by mid-century, government salaries had moved up substantially and in 1962 Congress formally established the principle of "comparability" between federal jobs and equivalent work in the business world. The Bureau of Labor Statistics (BLS) was charged with designing annual surveys to provide information on salaries in the private sector for use as a yardstick against those in the federal service. Nobody apparently gave much thought to the fact that BLS is composed of government workers whose salaries would be directly affected by the results of annual surveys—and that these results would be worked into a recommended scale of pay increases by other government people in what is now OPM. This is not to suggest any dishonest number-switching on the part of the officials concerned; it is to suggest a built-in bias that has ample room for expression in the arcane method by which "comparable" federal pay formulas are determined.

"Comparability" does not mean that accountants, engineers, editors, secretaries and bottle-washers in government are paid on the basis of what their counterparts in industry earn. As one official of OPM admitted, "We are not trying to see that a secretary at the GS-7 level has the same salary as a secretary in a business office who does essentially the same work."

Instead, the government compares federal to private jobs using a medium called the federal "job standard." Job standards are lists of criteria and responsibilities that describe the various grades in the civil service.

The theory is simple: If the job standards describe the level of skill and responsibility of a GS-14, all BLS has to do is find the private-sector employees whose jobs match that same standard. Things equal to the same thing will be equal to each other.

But they are not equal. On the private side of the equation, BLS goes out and visits employees, observing their actual duties. On the government side, what is matched to the job standards is that flight of the federal imagination known as the "job description." That is like equating the military knowledge of Clausewitz with that of the fellow in the loony bin who says he is Napoleon.

Relatively few government workers have the responsibilities, make the kinds of decisions or exercise the latitude that their job description attributes to them. The writing of the job description is a practiced art—and the higher the grade, the greater the scope for what one OPM official referred to as "journalistic freedom" in describing the alleged duties that justify a given level of pay. If you take what a job description says a federal manager does, and find someone in the private sector who does those things, you'll discover he has a high salary indeed.

Source: Leonard Reed, "The Hokum of Comparing Pay: Why Federal Pay Levels Should Be Cut," *Washington Monthly*, May, 1980.

DATA CLUSTER 3: A QUICK PORTRAIT OF PART-TIME WORKERS

A. SENIOR WORKERS (55 Years and Older) IN PART-TIME JOBS

- *How many?* 2,200,000 (1976)
- *Why work?* income supplement
- *Which jobs?*

    1. *Men* in this age group work as bridge tenders or as school crossing guards; (more than 50% of these workers come from the senior age group); others work in cleaning or food services; others farm.

Senior Workers, Part-Time

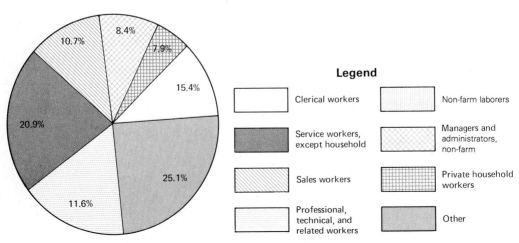

Legend

☐ Clerical workers

☐ Service workers, except household

☐ Sales workers

☐ Professional, technical, and related workers

☐ Non-farm laborers

☐ Managers and administrators, non-farm

☐ Private household workers

☐ Other

2. *Women* with high school education work in secretarial, bookkeeping, or clerical jobs or as household servants or as dressmakers (not in factories).

B. WORKERS 20 TO 55 YEARS OLD IN PART-TIME JOBS

- *How many?* 6,800,000 (1976): 85% women
- *Why work?* income supplement
- *Which jobs?*

1. *Men* in this age group make up about 75% of part-time musicians and about 50% of part-time teachers in colleges and universities. Other job categories: service workers (cleaning, food, and so on).

2. *Women:* more than one-quarter are clerical workers (receptionists and bookkeepers, for example); about one-quarter are service workers (hairdressers, baby-sitters, and so on); less than one-quarter are nurses, teachers, and other professional and technical workers. About 50% of part-time real estate agents and bus drivers are women in this age group.

20- to 55-Year-Old Workers, Part-Time

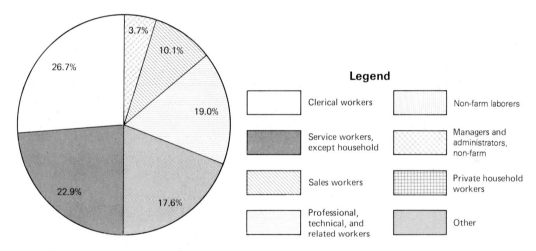

C. TEENAGE PART-TIME WORKERS

- *How many?* 4,000,000: 50% male, 50% female
- *Why work?* for work experience or for extra money (education, miscellaneous expenses)
- *Which jobs?* Generally, service jobs: 50% of all part-time food service workers; 33% of all part-time cleaning workers.

1. *Men* serve as dining-room workers, cooks, dishwashers, laborers, operatives, cleaning workers.

2. *Women* work as sales clerks, household employees, waitresses, child-care workers, and cashiers.

Teenage Workers, Part-Time

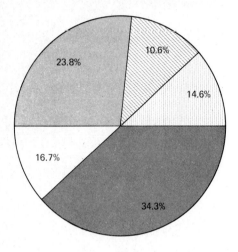

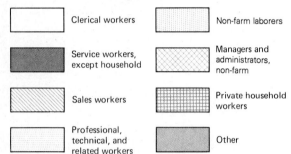

Legend

☐ Clerical workers	▦ Non-farm laborers
▨ Service workers, except household	▦ Managers and administrators, non-farm
▨ Sales workers	▦ Private household workers
▨ Professional, technical, and related workers	▨ Other

Source: U.S. Department of Labor, Bureau of Labor Statistics, *Occupational Outlook Quarterly* (Washington, D.C.: Government Printing Office, Summer, 1979).

Given the grim reality of inflation that just won't quit, it's not surprising that women in so-called typical American families have entered the labor force in record numbers in recent years. After all, what family can't use help in meeting the monthly rent or mortgage payments? Who wouldn't like to be able to worry less about how to pay for food and clothing, heating oil or gas, electricity, medical and dental care, cars and auto maintenance, gasoline, insurance, education, and all the other expenses that take an ever-larger bite out of our annual incomes?

Considering the skyrocketing costs of the essentials, it's no wonder that for millions of American families, such extras as yearly vacations and occasional weekend trips, new cars every few years, and even beef for dinner have rapidly become out-and-out luxuries. For countless families, the only way to obtain these now-elusive extravagances has been to find a source of additional income. And for most of these families, that has meant Mom goes out to get a paying job.

Yet it's certainly not only married people heading that increasingly atypical "typical American family" who find themselves in a financial bind. Single heads of households (usually unmarried or divorced women who receive little, if any, child support) are perpetually strapped. So are students—young people in their teens or early twenties who often must provide at least a portion of their support in addition to attending classes and studying at home. Older teenagers and young adults who plan to continue their formal education, for example, must contend with tuition, room and board payments, and the cost of books for classes. Even if a student has parents who are willing and able to pick up most of the tab or has found other sources of financial assistance, there is still the matter of everyday living expenses. Most of those aren't covered by financial grants. Younger teenagers, such as the sixteen-year-old who must buy his own clothes or the thirteen-year-old who must pay for her own record albums or roller skates, need to earn quite a bit of money, too.

Today's families and young students certainly are hard-pressed for money. Yet the group that unquestionably suffers most in periods of high inflation is senior citizens, particularly those living on fixed incomes. Clearly, yesterday's comfortable "nest egg for the future" barely covers today's food, rent, and utility payments—if, indeed, it covers all three. Consequently, more and more senior citizens are delaying their retirements, and growing numbers of men and women over fifty-five, and even over sixty-five, are looking for work.

Source: JoAnne Alter, *A Part-Time Career for a Full Time You* (Boston: Houghton-Mifflin Company, 1982), pp. 7, 10.

DATA CLUSTER 4: SECRETARIAL JOBS

She is 21 years old, has no college degree and has worked for only a year and a half. Yet Carmela Girello makes more than $300 a week, about $2,000 a year more than the average recent college graduate, and her salary is likely to keep rising.

Carmela Girello is bright, personable, articulate, and skilled, and these qualities all work to her advantage. But she is in high demand primarily because of her field. She is a secretary—and right now a good one seems almost as hard to find as a parking space on Wall Street.

When Miss Girello accepted a job at Chemical Bank last month, her decision brought a relieved "Thank God" from her new boss, Walter Kehoe, a divisional director.

Nationwide, secretarial training schools now graduate only two-thirds of the secretaries needed to fill 305,000 openings each year, according to the United States Labor Department's Bureau of Labor Statistics. And the problem is growing. Between 1978 and 1990, demand is expected to increase 45 percent, more than twice the rate for all other occupations. The need for all office support personnel, including clerks, bookkeepers, typists, and machine operators, may rise 28 percent, the Labor Department reports.

The problem is due to a rise in office paperwork, especially in growing fields like finance, insurance and real estate, at a time when women, who make up 98 percent of the secretarial force, are moving into other occupations.

According to the Katherine Gibbs School, where Miss Girello got her training, graduates get so many offers that they can virtually select the location where they want to work.

And hiring officers throughout the United States are feeling the squeeze.

"Secretaries just aren't walking in like they used to," said Janet Marsh, an employment officer at the Hewlett-Packard Company in Palo Alto, California. "There's a lot of competition in the Bay area. I'll interview someone and another company will swipe her first. They'll tell her we don't pay as much as they do, even though it isn't true."

In New York, Chemical Bank is one of the employers hit by the shortage. Deborah Karsai, an assistant vice president in charge of clerical employment, said, "We continuously have 20 percent more jobs open than we have candidates to fill them."

Secretaries in the metropolitan area earned an average of $261.50 a week last year, up 7 percent from the year before, according to the Labor Department. Weekly earnings ranged from an average of $147.50 for a file clerk to $330 for an executive secretary for a top executive. Secretaries trained in word processing, personnel officers say, often earn a 20 to 25 percent premium.

Source: "Secretaries Have Pick of Jobs: Demand is Rising, Pulling Up Salaries," *The New York Times,* March 10, 1981.

Advertised Salary Offers for Secretaries

A. By experience

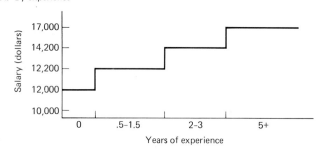

B. By speed of typing

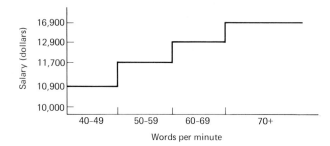

Source: *New York Times,* 1980

Generally, graduation from high school is required for a job as a secretary or stenographer. Many employers prefer applicants who have additional secretarial training at a college or private business school. Courses vary from a few months' instruction in basic shorthand and typing to longer programs teaching specialized skills such as shorthand reporting or legal or medical secretarial work. Shorthand reporters generally must complete a 2-year course in shorthand reporting school.

An increasing number of private firms and government agencies have their own training facilities where employees can upgrade their skills and broaden their knowledge of the organization. Also, many State and local governments sponsor programs to train unemployed and low-skilled workers for entry-level jobs as secretaries.

Several States require each court reporter to be a Certified Shorthand Reporter (CSR). A certification test is administered by a board of examiners in each of the States that have CSR laws. The National Shorthand Reporters Association confers the designation Registered Professional Reporter (RPR) upon those who pass a two-part examination and participate in continuing education programs. The RPR designation is recognized as the mark of excellence in the profession.

Employers usually have no preferences among the many different shorthand methods. For court reporters, however, the preference is for stenotype (machine shorthand), not only because reporters can write faster using stenotype, but also because they can feed stenotype notes to a computer for high-speed transcription. The most important factors in hiring and promotion are speed and accuracy. To qualify for jobs in the Federal Government, stenographers must be able to take dictation at a minimum of 80 words per minute and type at least 40 words per minute. Workers must achieve higher rates to advance to more responsible positions. In private firms the requirements vary, but applicants with the best speed and accuracy will receive first consideration in hiring. Many shorthand reporting jobs require more than 225 words of dictation per minute; shorthand reporters in the Federal Government generally must take 175 words a minute.

Secretaries and stenographers should have good hearing; a knowledge of spelling, punctuation, grammar, and a good vocabulary are essential. The ability to concentrate amid distractions is vital for shorthand reporters. Employers look for persons who are poised and alert, and who have pleasant personalities. Discretion, judgment, and initiative are important for the more responsible secretarial positions.

Many stenographers who improve their skills advance to secretarial jobs; others who acquire the necessary speed through additional training can become shorthand reporters. Secretaries can increase their skills and broaden their knowledge of their company's operations by taking courses offered by the company or by local business schools, colleges, and universities. As secretaries gain knowledge and experience, they can qualify for the designation Certified Professional Secretary (CPS) by passing a series of exams given by the National Secretaries Association. This designation is recognized by a growing number of employers as the mark of achievement in the secretarial field. Many executive secretaries are promoted to management positions because of their extensive knowledge of their employer's operations.

Source: U.S. Department of Labor, Bureau of Labor Statistics, *Occupational Outlook Handbook, 1980-1981 Edition* (Washington, D.C.: Government Printing Office, 1980), pp. 89-90.

Learning From Other Students

Read the paragraph below written from the information in Data Cluster 3. Discuss the answers to the questions after you read.

Teenagers as Part-Time Workers

Many teenagers who need money are solving their financial problems by holding one of a variety of part-time jobs. According to the United States Department of Labor's Bureau of Labor Statistics, teenagers say that they work to earn money to meet general expenses or expenses for their education, although many young people do work to get job experience as well. Writing in *A Part-Time Career for a Full Time You*, JoAnne Alter points out that part-time employment can help thirteen- and sixteen-year-olds earn extra money for luxuries like roller skates, new clothing, and records. Among older teenagers, though, students have particular problems. As Alter shows, many of them "must provide at least a portion of their support in addition to attending classes and studying at home." Students continuing their education "must contend with tuition, room and board payments, and the cost of books for classes." Even if the student's parents provide financial support, Alter says, or if the student has found some other source of income, "there is still the matter of everyday living expenses" and "most of those aren't covered by financial grants." Further, the government has cut back sharply on these grants. It should be no surprise then that about four million teenagers, half of them male and half female, worked part-time in 1976 at different kinds of jobs. The Bureau of Labor Statistics reports that men worked as dining-room or kitchen staff, as laborers, operatives, and cleaning workers. Women worked as clerks, cashiers, waitresses, household employees, or day-care workers. Of all those teenagers working part-time 16.7% were clerical workers, 14.6% were non-farm laborers and 34.3% were service workers. Half of all food-service workers are teenagers. Next time you place your order at McDonald's or Burger King you might remember that the cheerful teenager who wraps your burger or who salts your French fries may be a student who needs extra money for school.

—*Chris Donovan*

Step 1. Paragraph Review.

1. What generality has Chris Donovan drawn from the data she examined? Does her topic sentence state the generalization adequately?
2. What sources does she cite in this paragraph?
3. Where does she quote a source directly? Where does she paraphrase?
4. Where does she convert statistics from a graph into her own language? What other statistics does she use?
5. At one point the writer says that the government has cut back on financial grants. Why do you think that she did not cite a source for that statement? *Should* she have cited a source for it? Where might she have found a source to cite for that information?
6. Comment on the closing sentence of the paragraph.

Prewriting

You saw earlier how to brainstorm on a topic on your own (see pages 75–76), but brainstorming is also very useful when you work in small groups of people discussing the same idea or issue. Thus, you have a chance to share your impressions, to talk through any thoughts that develop in conversation, and to see how other people are thinking about the topic. Group collaboration can help you formulate one or more generalizations from a collection of data and can help you focus on the specific details that gave rise to the generalization and that support it. Also, questions people raise about your points in discussion can help you see what questions *readers* might have if you wrote those points in a paper. Thus, discussion groups are testing grounds for your own developing ideas, ideas that group conversation can influence, shape, and direct. And, if each small group reports back to the larger group—your whole class, for example— you get a chance to hear many different points of view.

When you brainstorm in groups you can discuss a topic in a variety of ways. Have an open-ended discussion—that is, let everyone say whatever comes to mind about the topic—and allow free interaction among group members who may raise questions or may interrupt with fresh insights. Or, structure the discussion in advance with a set of questions everyone will try to answer. With either approach, it's always valuable to ask each group member to *write* down ideas for a few minutes before discussion begins.

GUIDELINES FOR BRAINSTORMING IN GROUP SETTINGS

1. Select someone to act as recorder. This person should summarize the main conclusions drawn by the group and should report back to the class on those conclusions.
2. Require each person to write for a few minutes before discussion begins.
3. Limit the size of the group to from three to five members. Larger groups discourage everyone from talking, and some people will not have a chance to contribute.
4. Limit discussion time. Fifteen or twenty minutes is enough time for developing useful insights on a topic.
5. Decide on a format:

   • Prepare a list of questions or guidelines.
   • Run an open-ended discussion.

Step 1. Collaborating in Groups. Divide the class into groups of no more than five people each, and ask each group to select one of the four data clusters on pages 226–235. It's all right if more than one group works from the same cluster. Try to come up with as many generalizations as you can about information in the cluster. Each group should report back to the class on discussion highlights. Follow the guidelines above.

Progress Reminders: A Checklist

As you write your various drafts, keep in mind these pointers—phrased as questions—to help you prepare a strong paragraph based on research. Fill in the questionnaire, and submit it with your final manuscript.

1. Did I examine the data clusters carefully, and did I select one that interested me? _____

2. Did I read the graphs, tables, and charts carefully, and did I try to state in my own language the numerical relationships indicated in those diagrams? _____

3. Did I use whatever prewriting strategies work for me? _____

   Did I share my ideas in a group of people who discussed one of the data clusters? _____

4. Did I state some generalization in my topic sentence? Does my topic sentence state the topic clearly and my opinion or attitude about it? _____ _____

5. Did I use adequate detail—statistics, cases, quotations, paraphrases, sensory images, or a combination of these—to support my generalization? _____

6. Did I integrate smoothly any quotations I selected from other sources by following the pointers on pages 201–205? _____

7. Did I organize my material before writing a rough draft? _____

   Did I change language and sentence structure in later drafts? Does my final copy follow correct manuscript form? _____

8. Did I use subtopic sentences, when necessary, to introduce each new feature of the topic? Do my details support the specific points of the subtopics? _____ _____

9. Did I use transitions to connect my ideas smoothly and logically? _____

10. Did I use a variety of sentence types? Did I open sentence with subordinators (pages 100–109); -*ing* words; infinitives and other verb parts (pages 208–213); and one or two -*ly* words (page 60)? _____

11. Did I read the theme on page 236 as a model for my paragraph? _____

12. Did I cite sources that I used for statistics or quotations? Did I follow the guidelines on page 191 for writing statistics correctly and on pages 60–62, 270, and 499–500 for writing quotations correctly? _____ _____

13. Did I proofread my paper carefully both before and after I prepared my final draft? Did I look especially for errors in _____ _____

agreement; for run-ons and fragments; for errors in capitalization, plurals, and careless errors typical of my usual   _____
mistakes? Did I check my Theme Progress Sheet (page 523)?

14. Did I write a strong title for my paragraph?   _____

GETTING READER RESPONSE

When you write your draft, return to the same groups you formed to brainstorm
on the data cluster that you wrote about. Each group member should read his or
her paper aloud as the others in the group take notes. Discuss each paper in
regard to the following points in particular:

1. Is the generalization stated clearly in the topic sentence?
2. Do statistics, cases, quotations, or paraphrases support the topic?
3. Are quotations integrated smoothly?
4. Are facts presented accurately with appropriate citations?
5. Is the paragraph logical and easy to follow? Where should the writer clarify
   and simplify language?

   Use comments made after you read your paper to help you produce the
next draft.

THE PROFESSIONALS SPEAK

Read the essay titled "The Right Stuff for Careers in the Eighties," paying special
attention to the writer's use of statistics, cases, and quotations to make interesting
assertions about careers in the next decade. Answer the questions that come
after the selection.

SOME WORDS TO KNOW BEFORE YOU READ

somber: of a serious or gloomy nature
proliferating: growing and spreading rapidly
insatiable: incapable of being satisfied
catastrophic: disastrous
obsolescence: the process or condition of becoming outdated
dour: gloomy
glutted: became so available that supply exceeds demand
generalist: a person capable in several different fields or aptitudes
flux: continuous change; fluctuation

The Right Stuff for
Careers in the Eighties

Success in the '80s will require an unusual degree of education, initiative—or plain luck. In the view of labor and career specialists, many people will have to settle for less than they expect in the way of pay, promotions and satisfaction. During this decade, the babies of the postwar boom will reach their working prime in massive numbers, jamming the paths to promotion. At the same time, the economy's growth will probably slow down. A sharp recession or continued double-digit inflation or both, as well as interruptions in oil supplies and policy flip-flops in Washington, could limit career prospects.

Even if the economy provides 20 million new civilian jobs by 1990, raising the total to 114 million, as the Bureau of Labor Statistics estimates, more than half the openings will be routine and low paying. Throughout the economy, routine jobs are multiplying faster than more rewarding ones. For example, employment in the labor-intensive service businesses has lately been growing faster than in the higher-paying manufacturing and mining industries.

In its forthcoming *Occupational Outlook Handbook,* the BLS estimates that twice as many new clerks as managers will be needed in the 1980's. Jobs for cashiers and janitors will grow faster than openings for professional and technical employees. The professions used to be the fastest-growing group, but that trend ended early in the 1970s, mainly because school enrollments dropped and college expansion slowed, creating a huge surplus of teachers.

These somewhat somber tidings are statistical generalities. The real job market has infinite variety—and doesn't necessarily conform to the forecasts. There will, as always, be tremendous opportunities for people who choose the right career, the right employer or the right part of the country—preferably all three. Furthermore, there are two big pieces of good news:

- As the 1980s progress, young people should be able to find entry-level jobs more easily than they can now. Because of the drop in the birth rate since the 1950s, smaller and smaller numbers of youngsters will reach working age. For example, there will be 400,000 fewer in 1985 than in 1980 and 800,000 fewer in 1990, a reduction in 10 years of more than 20%. That should make teenage unemployment, now 15.9%, less acute.
- The demand for engineers is exceptionally strong. As a heritage of the hiring slump in the early 1970s and the resulting drop in student enrollments, engineers are in short supply. "Engineers will be kings of the job market until the mid-1980s," says Van Evans, president of Deutsch Shea & Evans Inc., a manpower consulting firm in New York.

Even if the market fades—and engineering does tend to have ups and downs—engineers who specialize in computer science should do well. The computer industry will remain uniquely promising through the 1980s and perhaps beyond.

Just as the number of memory cells that can fit on a silicon chip multiplied from 256 to 64,000 during the 1970s (and may quadruple by the middle of this decade), so the uses of computers are proliferating in office, factory, store, school, car and home. Working out the applications of this enormous amount of cheap computer power requires several times more systems analysts and programmers than colleges are producing. "We've seen this demand coming for a long time, but we are not prepared," says John Hamblen, chairman of computer science at the University of Missouri at Rolla. "The job market is just going wild."

Hamblen figures that the 12,000 to 14,000 new bachelors of computer science who graduate this year will have a choice of 55,000 jobs; the 3,000 new masters of computer science and the 300 Ph.D.s will be able to choose from 30,000 and 1,300 openings, respectively. Salaries for graduates of the better-known colleges start in the low $20,000s for those with bachelor's degrees and in the low $30,000s for Ph.D.s.

"We would kill to get more programmers," jokes a manpower specialist in a major consulting firm. Industry's needs seem insatiable. Bell Laboratories, for example, expects more than 30% of the professionals it hires this year to have degrees in computer science. Lower-level programmers trained, typically, at a two-year college aren't scarce, but Hamblen says the supply of programmers with four-year degrees probably won't match demand until the end of the decade.

Engineers with energy specialties have even hotter prospects right now than computer scientists. Among this year's crop of bachelors, reports the College Placement Council, petroleum engineers are being offered an average of $23,800 and chemical engineers $21,300. Experienced engineers in most fields are scarce too. Van Evans of Deutsch Shea & Evans says the "high-technology recruitment" index that his company keeps has never been so consistently strong as in the past two years.

Old engineering specialties are reviving to meet new demands. Since the country needs to burn more coal, jobs for mining engineers are expected to multiply faster than for any other kinds of engineers; however, the number of openings won't be large. After being grounded through most of the '70s, aerospace engineers have been put back in the cockpit by a healthy volume of orders for aircraft. A decade ago, Boeing's layoffs in Seattle were catastrophic. But recently, to get through a peak of work readying its 767 and 757 commercial jets for their maiden flights in 1981 and 1982, the company borrowed engineers from Britain and Canada.

The current enthusiasm of recruiters shouldn't lull engineers into forgetting that they're in a cyclical profession, dependent on the state of the economy and political moods, or that their training sometimes leads to dead-end jobs and early obsolescence. An engineer who keeps abreast of changes in his field and looks for opportunities in management, or is willing to move around the country, runs less risk of a stunted career.

Corporate managers are much in demand at the moment, whether they're new graduates of business schools, middle managers or senior executives. Recruiters don't seem to be digging in yet for a recession. But during the 1980s, as the baby-boom crowd advances into middle age, the number of Americans in the 35-to-44 age group will grow 50%, to 37 million. The implications for ambitious workers approaching mid-career are sobering. The number of people in these prime years for promotion will be increasing 2½ times as fast as the number of good management and professional jobs. That means it will be more than twice as hard to rise to, say, vice president in this decade as it was in the '70s.

Pearl Meyer, executive vice president of the New York management consulting firm of Handy Associates, doesn't see a problem for talented people. She argues that "the failure of our educational and value systems" will make good managers scarce because fewer people have a strong work ethic or a sound education. But Mrs. Meyer is decidedly in a minority. A more dour—and more typical—opinion comes from Roderic Hodgins, a psychologist in Cambridge, Mass. who specializes in career problems. Says he: "It's going to be one sweet scrimmage."

To make matters worse, American colleges will continue to turn out more graduates than the economy needs. The BLS estimates that in the 1980s, as in the 1970s, one in four college graduates will have to take a job beneath his expectations. This disturbing trend began in the 1970s, when graduates who got professional and managerial jobs dropped from 90% to 66%, and some 30% had to accept clerical, sales and unskilled blue-collar jobs. In the 1960s, only 7% of college graduates settled for such positions.

In his recent book, *Good Jobs, Bad Jobs, No Jobs* (1979), Columbia economist Eli Ginzberg writes: "To the extent that large numbers of graduates are forced into accepting second-best or even third-best jobs, the odds are strong that their work behavior will reflect their restiveness and disenchantment. . . . Some will overcome their disappointment and frustration, many others are likely to carry them to their grave."

This scrimmage for jobs will come at a particularly bad time for women and blacks. Far more women broke into professions and management in the 1970s than ever before. To a lesser extent, so did more blacks. A few stars achieved highly visible positions at the top. The question for the 1980s: Having opened the doors to women and blacks, will business now invite them upstairs in significant numbers? They should by rights now start moving up to middle and upper management. But they'll be fighting the population bulge, a slowing economy and resistance from the white males who dominate some industries.

Several specialists in minority employment told *Money* they thought progress in the 1980s might be disappointing. Betty Vetter, head of the private Scientific Manpower Commission in Washington, says women are welcomed into engineering with starting salaries a shade higher than men's. But then the climb gets tougher. "Many men go into engineering because they think it's manly," she asserts. "Men in that field are assumed to be competent, but women have to prove it over and over." Unfortunately, quite a few male executives in a variety of companies still believe they are taking a risk when they promote a woman.

The job market of the '80s will put a particular premium on people who pick the best industry, company and region to work in. Health services, for example, will expand vigorously while manufacturing jobs will barely increase. Banking, retailing, insurance and real estate will need more new people than will government, which must hold down spending to bring inflation under control and appease taxpayers.

Today's graduates tend to be particularly choosy about where in the U.S. they want to work. They can improve their prospects by being flexible. Whether they are bankers or broadcasters, they are more likely to prosper in regions or cities where the economy is growing faster than average.

The Sunbelt will continue to attract more business than the colder, costlier Northeast. When the top managers of electronics firms outside Boston want to expand, they quite likely will look south. Many mid-size American cities, inside and outside the Sunbelt, will offer expansive opportunities. Van Evans of Deutsch Shea & Evans expects strong growth in cities such as Austin, Charlotte, Raleigh, Tucson, Tulsa and others with metropolitan-area populations of around half a million. California still beckons to people in high-technology industries such as the computer, office equipment, communications and aerospace. But hiring in most other businesses there is slack and likely to remain so. Slower overall growth and the painfully high price of housing are taking some of the glow out of the Golden State.

Inflation complicates the choice of a career. A few strong unions have contracts with escalators almost fully tied to the consumer price index, but most employers don't come close to keeping up with today's high inflation. Last year's average pay increase for white-shirt workers from clerks to presidents was 7.9%, while the CPI went up 13.3%. Jay Engel, compensation specialist for the American Management Association, says most employers will not normally give more than a 10% raise in recognition both of merit and the rising cost of living. If a promotion is involved, the total could be 15%. Employees of nonprofit or government-regulated organizations, such as hospitals, schools, colleges and utilities, probably won't get even that much. But it is easier for professionals to adjust to inflation. Lawyers, doctors, accountants and consultants can simply raise their fees—within reason.

The most crucial choice of all is what to study and where. In a job market glutted with college graduates, achieving a good record at a highly regarded college and picking the right specialties for the '80s becomes supremely important. For example, corporations have a growing need for people who know about corporate-government relations, international business and personnel work, which now goes by the puffy title of "human resources management." The Harvard Business School, among others, has expanded the instruction it offers in all three fields.

In spite of the advantage enjoyed now by business and engineering school graduates, there is a strong case for a liberal arts education. True, few recruiters chase the humanities major. If he lands a first job with any promise at all, it will pay on average $11,800, which is less than apprentice plumbers get in many cities. But, says James O'Toole, a business professor at the University of Southern California, "The initial advantage of the specialist disappears quickly. Someone like a mechanical engineer may end up being a mechanical engineer all his life. Generalists have greater mobility and options." The board chairman, college president or magazine editor, adds O'Toole, is more likely to be a generalist than a specialist. Robert Schrank, a Ford Foundation authority on careers, believes that success in English studies is the best long-run predictor of overall success.

In pure economic terms, it may be more tempting than ever during the 1980s to skip college and choose a blue-collar trade instead. The demand for many skilled craftsmen, such as business-machine and computer repairers, iron- and sheet-metal workers, tool-and-die makers and boilermakers, is growing rapidly. Those skills can be learned during a paid apprenticeship, or at a vocational school or a two-year college. A skilled worker with a strong union behind him can well earn $20,000 to $30,000 a year; long-haul truck drivers are paid $30,000 or more. The average male college graduate earned about $22,500 last year, and women graduates averaged $13,300.

In blue-collar careers, James O'Toole of Southern Cal reports a gathering trend: more and more businesses are being started by young people of entrepreneurial spirit who don't want to go to college but don't want to limit their ambitions either. In six months to a year they can learn a skill such as repairing roofs or installing swimming pools. Then, instead of going to work for someone else, they set up their own business. "Some of them are millionaires by the time they are 30," says O'Toole.

In a way, these "wealthy dropouts" illustrate what it takes to be successful in the 1980s. They've seen an opportunity and grabbed it. The '80s are likely to be hard on those who can't adjust. If that sounds unsettling, it is. Accelerating technological change will hasten the obsolescence of some jobs and the creation of others. Like our way of living, our way of working is in flux. Few people will stick to one career all their lives. Says management consultant Pearl Meyer half seriously: "I am told by the sociologists that the typical new executive will have two families and three career cycles."

—*Jeremy Main*

1. What is Jeremy Main's major point in this essay?
2. What sources does he use? Make a list of the experts from whom he draws data.
3. What statistics does he provide to support the following points:
    a. that routine and low-paying jobs will be more plentiful than others
    b. that young people should find entry-level jobs more easily in the 1980s
    c. that computer-science engineers will do well
    d. that many college graduates will have to take jobs beneath their experience
4. The writer quotes John Hamblen from the University of Missouri but names no book or article as a source. What can you assume about the source of this quotation then? Where does Main mention a book or an article as a source for a quotation?
5. Find an example of paraphrasing in the essay.

REACHING HIGHER

Step 1. Investigating Jobs. Check your local newspapers and magazines for articles on job availability in your area, and draw some generalization about what you read. Then write a paragraph in which you offer expert testimony to support your generalization.

Step 2. Reading the Want Ads. Examine the want ads over several days in a newspaper of your choice, focusing on a particular occupation that interests you—accounting, secretarial, editorial, computer technology, health, sales, or any other field. Using the information you find in the advertisements, write a paragraph about the job. Draw a generalization from the data, and support it with details from the newspaper ads. As subtopics in your paragraph, you might deal with job qualifications, salaries, conditions, benefits, or any other categories you find repeated.

CHAPTER 6

WRITING ESSAYS:
A Place of Spirit

INTRODUCTION TO WRITING ESSAYS

There is a place every one of us carries in our personal memories. Sometimes you cannot forget a place because you know it so well, see it so often and closely: the train station where you catch the local for school each day; a picnic site along the river; the empty lot on the corner where you played your daily game of baseball; a piece of prairie just beyond your house or town; the doctor's office with its smell of alcohol and iodine, its sounds of babies' cries. Perhaps it is a place you have not seen often, but one clear in your mind because of what happened to you there: the lake where you caught your first fish; the stable where you saddled your first horse; the hospital emergency room; the principal's office in high school.

Your first essay assignment—a longer composition of four paragraphs—asks that you select for exploration some place both important and unforgettable to you. (If it is a place you can visit again before you write, so much the better; then, you will be able to jot down on paper the sights, colors, sounds, smells, and actions that give the place its character.) You will be able again to use your skills at narration and description—in fact, any of the paragraphs you learned about in the first part of this book can be helpful in your essay. And you will learn how to plan an essay, to avoid problems you might have had about organizing and finding enough to write. In its attempt to help you clear up problems in language, this chapter will look at some difficulties writers often have with pronouns and with punctuation.

VOCABULARY

The words in this activity will help you name sizes and shapes of things more specifically.

Step 1. Learning Words for Shape and Size. Check in a dictionary those words below that you do not know (Appendix A will help you, too). Write definitions you understand in the blanks next to the words.

1. vast _____   4. voluminous _____

2. miniscule _____   5. amorphous _____

3. towering _____

Step 2. Sizing It Up. Write in the blanks the words from the above list that you might use to describe:

1. the sky _____   4. a speck of dust _____

2. a flat tire _____   5. the Swiss Alps _____

3. the inside of an athletic stadium _____

Step 3.   Sharpening the Senses. These words help name sensations of touch and smell. Check their definitions in a good dictionary (or see Appendix A for assistance) and write them in the blank lines.

Smell   *Touch*

1. savory _____   6. pliant _____

2. putrid _____   7. clammy _____

3. musty _____   8. gossamer _____

4. pungent _____   9. rigid _____

5. medicinal _____   10. sinewy _____

Step 4.   Applying New Words. From the vocabulary above, select a word that best describes each of the following:

1. a plant of soft wood _____

2. vinegar _____

3. a solid steel door _____

4. the arm of an athlete _____

5. spoiled milk _____

6. turkey roasting in an oven _____

7. the feel of perspiration on a cool day _____

8. a spider's web _____

9. an old trunk opened after many years _____

10. a hospital corridor _____

BUILDING COMPOSITION SKILLS

Step 1.   Talking It Through. Complete aloud with one of your own endings any of these sentences about a place. Then speak a few more sentences to expand what you said for the rest of the class. Mention some sound or smell that you remember about the place.

1. The place to have most fun in this town is . . .
2. Our campus is . . .
3. The most elegant restaurant I ever ate in is . . .
4. If you saw my old house you would . . .
5. A place that always scared me was . . .
6. My brother's (sister's) room is . . .
7. For me the park is . . .
8. Wide open fields are . . .
9. One place I enjoy is . . .
10. When I want peace and quiet I go to . . .

Here is one student's response to 6:

My sister's room is a pig sty! Silver hair pins are piled in a heap on the dresser. Most of the drawers are opened and blouses and underwear hang out. A pile of dirty skirts sits in the corner and ten or twenty books lie all over the linoleum floor. But no one can reason with my thirteen-year-old sister Karen, the family know-it-all!

—*Diane Carter*

Hints for Strong Descriptions

In earlier chapters you learned and practiced how to build images with concrete sensory detail and how to use specific words that present a scene exactly. Here are other qualities of words and some techniques for using them that will help you build strong descriptions.

Denotation and Connotation

Words mean more than their dictionary definitions. (The dictionary definition of a word is called its *denotation*.) A word can also suggest meanings to us by appealing to our emotions or by arousing associations we make about that word. (The implied meaning of a word is called its *connotation*.)

Writers who know what certain words connote can use those words to advantage, compelling a reader to respond in exactly the manner the writer wishes.

Look at these sentences:

She lifted the *glass* slowly.
She lifted the *goblet* slowly.
She lifted the *chalice* slowly.

Glasses, goblets, and chalices have very similar denotative meaning—they are vessels to drink from. But the writer who says *goblet* suggests something more elegant about the action than the writer who says *glass*. With the word *chalice*, the writer creates an even more romantic and poetic—even religious—situation: it's not an everyday drink one sips from a fine cup. By using one of these related words, a writer can create essential conditions without having to use too many modifiers.

Step 1. Explaining Connotations. The words in each numbered item have similar denotations but different connotations. Explain what each word in each group connotes. If you need to, use a dictionary.

1. job, profession, position
2. novel, romance, potboiler
3. child, youngster, adolescent
4. actor, ham, thespian
5. advisor, counsellor, psychologist
6. coach, carriage, chariot
7. assistant, servant, maid
8. rot, decay, decompose

Step 2. Comparing Meanings. For each word below write a denotative definition. Then, explain the possible connotations for the word.

1. love _____

2. racism _____

3. courage _____

4. communist _____

5. cure-all _____

Step 3. Using Exact Meanings. In the sentences below the words in parentheses have similar denotations. However, because of what the words connote, only one of the pair is appropriate. Circle the word that suits the meaning of the sentence. Use a dictionary if you need help.

1. When Leslie was saving for her vacation, she tried to be more (economical, stingy) by bringing her lunch to school.
2. The fashion designers admired the model's (exotic, odd) clothes.
3. When Paul popped his gum in the theater, his friend criticized his (youthful, immature) behavior.
4. The (stench, fragrance) from the gym locker was nauseating.
5. The diplomats attempted to (bargain, negotiate) a peace settlement.

Showing versus Telling

Writers must always resist *telling* a reader how to react when they can better *show* details with strong images. Instead of using words that interpret, writers try to describe clearly by naming colors, sounds, actions, sensations of touch, smell, and taste. In these two sentences, notice how the first makes a judgment whereas the second compels readers to make their own judgments based upon the detail:

He had an ugly smile.
He smiled a cold, toothless grin.

With a word like *ugly*—or any such judgmental word, for that matter—the writer is never sure that the reader sees exactly what the writer had intended. After all, what is ugly to one person may not be ugly to another.

Step 4.   Showing with Clear Images. For each item below write an original image that changes the word in italics into descriptive details. Add other words if necessary. Use separate paper.

Example
The child was *happy*.
The child giggled as she shook her rattle playfully.

1. She bought a *simple* dress.
2. Joseph has *attractive* eyes.
3. The child had a *pretty* smile.
4. A *beautiful* tree grew on the hill.
5. The motel room was badly *run down*.

Avoiding Too Many Modifiers

You already know how important it is to select highly specific words in order to build successful images. Using a word like *rose* instead of *flower* or *pudding* instead of *dessert* helps you avoid using descriptive words you might not need.

But the temptation to overuse modifiers is great among beginning writers. In general, you should be cautious about using too many modifying words for the objects or people you are trying to describe. A typically weak sentence will pile up a number of descriptive words in front of a noun.

The *tall, dark-haired, blue-eyed,* quarterback spoke to his fans.

The modifiers (in italics) smother the noun *quarterback*. The sentence overwhelms the reader with detail; the reader cannot take so much in all at once in this way. By using a modifier after the noun or by expanding a modifier into a word group, the writer achieves a more desired effect.

With blue eyes smiling the tall, dark-haired quarterback spoke to his fans.

Removing some modifiers completely is usually one of the best ways to avoid overwhelming your reader with detail.

Step 5.   Cutting Down on Modifiers. Rewrite the sentences below so that the modifiers do not all appear before the words they are describing. In some cases just shift the modifiers around. In other cases expand some of them into word groups. In others simply remove the modifier. All describing words appear in italics.

1. *A quiet, tired, dirty, young* marine wrote *a long, passionate, overdue* letter to his girl friend. _____

_____

2. Compared to *sedate, charming, gracious* San Francisco, we were shocked by *busy, smoggy, unsavory* Los Angeles. _____

_____

3. *A long, black, chauffeur-driven* Cadillac screeched to a stop in front of *a brand new modern glass and steel* hotel. _____

_____

4. Next to the *weather-beaten, falling-down, rotted* old shack was a *beautiful, colorful, blooming* lilac bush. _____

_____

5. On a sizzling July afternoon at *approximately twelve* noon, I shoved aboard *a crowded, musty, gray and black graffiti colored subway* train headed east.

_____

_____

_____

Essay Form

The basic difference between the theme of one long paragraph and the theme that is a four-paragraph essay is simply one of length and proportion. An essay of four paragraphs allows you to develop your ideas more, to use more details, to bring in other information you might have left out of a single-paragraph composition so it would not be too long.

For every part of the paragraph there is a similar part of the essay. In a one-paragraph theme a *topic sentence* tells the subject and your opinion about that subject. In a four-paragraph essay an *introductory paragraph* gives you more space to build up to the topic you want to discuss. One sentence of this introductory paragraph (often the last sentence) generally announces what the whole essay will be about. This is the *thesis* or *proposal sentence:* it is usually more general than a topic sentence because it must tell what the *whole* essay will deal with.

In a one-paragraph theme the first subtopic sentence introduces one aspect of the topic. In the four-paragraph essay the first subtopic sentence becomes the topic sentence of its own paragraph. It requires a transition to the proposal sentence. You develop the paragraph by using details from your own experience or from what you have read or heard. This second paragraph of your essay is the first *body* paragraph: it is the first paragraph that tries to support some aspect of the topic.

In a one-paragraph theme a *second* subtopic sentence introduces another aspect of the topic. In a four-paragraph essay, the second subtopic sentence becomes the topic sentence of its own paragraph. This topic sentence requires some brief reference to the previous paragraph for an effective transition. You develop the paragraph with the kinds of details that best support your point.

In a one-paragraph theme you need a closing sentence to tell the reader that you have achieved the purpose of the paragraph. In the four-paragraph essay you need a conclusion, a whole new paragraph that allows you more space to develop an idea related to your dominant impression.

The following chart shows how a one-paragraph theme compares with a four-paragraph essay.

FROM PARAGRAPH TO ESSAY

The One-Paragraph Theme	*The Essay*

Topic Sentence　　　　　　　　　　　　P A R A G R A P H 1

Introduction: A Paragraph

1. Give background to your topic.
2. Make your readers feel that what you are going to say will be of importance and interest to them.
3. Set the stage for the one sentence that will tell the readers what the whole essay will be about (*proposal sentence*).
4. For your own convenience, put the proposal sentence *last* in the introductory paragraph; make sure that the proposal sentence allows you to discuss *two* aspects of the topic.
5. Take as much time with the proposal sentence as you took with the topic sentence.

(continued on next page)

FROM PARAGRAPH TO ESSAY *(continued)*

Subtopic Sentence 1

Supporting Details
Closing Sentence

PARAGRAPH 2

Topic Sentence of Paragraph 2

1. Relate this sentence in some way to the proposal (repeat key words, use words that mean the same, use transition words, and so on).
2. Announce the one aspect of the topic that you will discuss in this paragraph.

Supporting Details

Closing Sentence: Let the reader know you have finished with the subject of this paragraph. Bring all the information together.

Subtopic Sentence 2

The Body Paragraphs

PARAGRAPH 3

Topic Sentence of Paragraph 3

1. This sentence must relate to the proposal (the last sentence in the introductory paragraph).
2. It must tell the reader the aspect of the proposal that you will discuss in this paragraph.
3. It must also remind the reader of what you discussed in the paragraph before (paragraph 2).

Supporting Details

Closing Sentence: Let the reader know that this paragraph is finished.

Supporting Details
Closing Sentence

PARAGRAPH 4

Conclusion: A Paragraph

1. Summarize by briefly commenting on your topic (your proposal).
2. Bring in a related idea.
3. Give a dominant impression.

Paragraph to Essay

Step 1.   Reviewing Paragraph and Essay Form. The first student sample you read in this book—"The Gloom Room" by Harry Golden—appears here for review. It is followed by Mr. Golden's four-paragraph essay on exactly the same topic. These pages should help you see clearly the basic differences between the one-paragraph theme and the four-paragraph essay. Discuss the questions after you read the two pieces.

The Gloom Room

On this dreary October afternoon in my writing class here on the second floor of Boylan Hall at Brooklyn College, a shadow of gloom hangs over the people and things that surround me. The atmosphere is depressing. There is an old brown chair beside the teacher's desk, a mahogany bookcase with a missing shelf, and this ugly desk of mine filled with holes and scratches. As I rub my hand across its surface, there is a feeling of coldness. Even the gray walls and the rumble of thunder outside reflect the atmosphere of seriousness as we write our first theme of the semester. When some air sails through an open window beside me, there is the annoying smell of coffee grounds from a garbage pail not far off. My classmates, too, show the mood of tension. Mary, a slim blonde at my right, chews frantically the inside of her lower lip. Only one or two words in blue ink stand upon her clean white page. David Harris, slouched in his seat in the third row, nibbles each finger of each hand. Then he plays inaudibly with a black collar button that stands open on the top of his red plaid shirt. There is a thump as he uncrosses his legs and his scuffed shoe hits the floor. A painful cough slices the air from behind me. I hear a woman's heels click from the hall beyond the closed door and a car engine whine annoyingly from Bedford Avenue. If a college classroom should be a place of delight and pleasure, that could never be proved by the tension in this room.

—*Harry Golden*

The Gloom Room

October often looks and feels dreary because school is by then in full swing. Today, a rainy Thursday, is no different. What makes it worse is that I am forced to sit in my writing class on the second floor of Boylan Hall at Brooklyn College and write a theme. It is no wonder that a shadow of gloom hangs over the things and the people that surround me in this room.

[the proposal: it tells what the whole essay will be about]

[the topic sentence (paragraph 2): it tells what this paragraph will be about] →   [As I look around, I see that the surroundings are old and depressing.] There is a broken brown chair beside the teacher's desk; no one will sit in it for fear of leaning back and toppling over onto the floor. There is also a mahogany bookcase with a missing shelf, and all the books are piled on the bottom in a stack of blue and yellow covers, instead of standing in a straight row. This ugly desk of mine is filled with holes and scratches

[details: these give concrete sensory

because other impatient students, no doubt, lost their tempers and took out their anger on the wooden surface. As I rub my hand across it, I feel coldness. Even the gray walls and the rumble of thunder outside reflect the atmosphere of seriousness as we write our first theme of the semester. When some air sails through an open window beside me, there is the annoying smell of coffee grounds from a garbage pail not far off. (The smell is a perfect indication of our discomfort!)

[language, statistics, cases, quotations, paraphrase, or imagery to illustrate your point]

[closing sentence: it shows you are finished with this paragraph]

[This part of the topic sentence reminds the reader about what you wrote in the last paragraph.] →

[Aside from the unattractive surroundings,] ⟨the people around me show this mood of tension and displeasure.⟩ Mary, a slim blonde at my right, chews the inside of her lower lip. I can see by the way her forehead is wrinkled that she is having quite a bit of trouble. Because only one or two words in blue ink stand upon her clean white page, she looks around the room fearfully for some new ideas. Slouching in his seat in the third row, David Harris nibbles each finger of each hand. Then he plays with a black collar button that stands open on the top of his red plaid shirt. The tension gets to him too; drops of perspiration run slowly down his cheeks. I hear a thump as he uncrosses his legs and his scuffed shoe hits the floor. A painful cough slices the air from behind me. I hear a woman's heels click from the hall beyond the closed door and a car engine whine annoyingly from Bedford Avenue. All these signs of gloom do not help my mood at all.

[This part of the topic sentence tells the reader what you will discuss in this paragraph.]

[details: these illustrate the point of the topic sentence]

These last few painful moments make me wonder if what my friends told me about college was all true. Where are all the beautiful girls I'm supposed to be meeting and talking to in every room? Where are the freedom and relaxed atmosphere my friends bragged about? I'm supposed to be enjoying myself instead of suffering! Everybody seems to have forgotten that college is hard work too. My first days in writing class prove that delight and pleasure often disappear when assignments are due!

—Harry Golden

[conclusion:
1. may summarize
2. makes transition by referring to an idea in the introduction
3. may give a dominant impression
4. may bring in a new—but related—idea]

1. What is the difference between the opening sentence in Mr. Golden's one-paragraph theme and the opening paragraph in his essay?
2. How are the proposal sentence in the essay and the topic sentence in the one-paragraph theme alike?
3. How does subtopic sentence 1 in "The Gloom Room" paragraph compare to the topic sentence of paragraph 2 in "The Gloom Room" essay?
4. How do the details coming after subtopic sentence 1 in the one-paragraph composition compare with the details in paragraph 2 of the essay?
5. How does Mr. Golden's second subtopic sentence compare with the opening sentence of paragraph 3 in his essay?

6. How do the details after subtopic sentence 2 in his one-paragraph theme compare with the details in the third paragraph of Mr. Golden's essay?
7. Read the last sentence of paragraph 2 and that of paragraph 3. Are they effective as closing sentences? Why?
8. What part of the first sentence of the conclusion in Mr. Golden's essay refers back to the main idea of the essay?
9. Where in the conclusion does Mr. Golden bring in a new but related idea?
10. How does the closing sentence of Mr. Golden's one-paragraph composition compare with the concluding paragraph of his four-paragraph essay?

Proposal (Thesis) Sentences

The *proposal* (or *thesis*) *sentence*—the sentence in the essay that tells what you propose or intend to discuss in the remaining paragraphs—is the most important sentence in the essay. It controls and limits your entire composition. As a good writer, you will write only about what the proposal *says* you will write about.

GUIDELINES FOR GOOD PROPOSALS

1. Make sure your proposal sentence allows you to discuss what you want to. It should announce the topic clearly. It should express an opinion. If you find as you are writing that you no longer are discussing the topic you set for yourself, *go back and change the proposal sentence.*
2. The proposal should allow you to discuss at least two specific aspects of the topic. Notice how Mr. Golden's proposal tells *specifically* the two parts of the topic: the gloom surrounding the people and the gloom surrounding the things in his classrooom. Each body paragraph, then, can pick up *one* aspect of that topic. Paragraph 2 focuses on things. Paragraph 3 focuses on people.

    But it is not essential to mention in the proposal just what each paragraph will say. An alternate proposal for Mr. Golden's essay might be this:

    It is no wonder that gloominess is everywhere.

    Notice how, in this proposal, the reader has no idea of exactly what kind of treatment Mr. Golden's essay will offer of gloominess. But still, this alternate proposal permits the writer to discuss in one body paragraph the gloomy surroundings and in the other body paragraph the gloomy people.
3. A proposal sentence may appear anywhere in the introduction, but it is much easier for you if you write it as the *last* sentence of the introduction for several reasons:
    a. You can return to it often if you know exactly where it appears; by reading the proposal often while you write, you can make sure that you are staying on the topic.
    b. You can make the transition between the proposal and the opening sentence of paragraph 2 easily because the idea you must refer back to comes directly above your opening sentence. Mr. Golden's proposal mentions that he is in a room. The first words of paragraph 2 say "As I look around"; and because this looking around takes place in the room mentioned in the previous paragraph, the two paragraphs are thereby brought together smoothly.

Step 1. Preparing Proposals. Column I suggests the subject of an essay. In Column II, write a proposal that you think would serve to develop the ideas.

Hint

You do not need to state in the proposal exactly what each paragraph will illustrate. Just state the main purpose of your essay, the idea your whole essay will be about.

I

II

Example

This essay intends to show that the writer loves the thrill of skiing although she realizes the dangers that exist.

Although the slopes of Vail, Colorado, present certain dangers, the thrill a skier experiences is worth the risks.

1. This student wants to explain that family reunions can be very joyous affairs but also can be very distressing.

2. This essay attempts to show how proper exercise and good nutrition add years to a person's life.

3. This writer will show the pleasures and pains of raising a child.

4. This essay will defend work-study programs in colleges. Its first body paragraph will discuss the advantages for the student who comes to a college having such a program. The next body paragraph will illustrate the advantages of such programs to our society.

5. This essay will describe the differences between two friends' study habits.

6. This essay will show how the writer's kitchen is a place of great activity and also a

place where the family irons out many of
its problems together.

_____

_____

Step 2. Predicting Body Paragraphs from Proposals. These proposals all
come from student's papers. Basing your selection on the topic stated in the
proposal, tell briefly what you would discuss in each of the two body paragraphs.

Example

I feel that religion serves two essential functions in our society.

Main point of paragraph 2:
religion binds a family together

_____

Main point of paragraph 3:
religion teaches children values

_____

1. I now realize the many problems that
parents face.

Main point of paragraph 2:

_____

Main point of paragraph 3:

_____

2. Although the majority of Americans live
in big cities, many people are realizing the
advantages of living on a farm.

Main point of paragraph 2:

_____

Main point of paragraph 3:

_____

3. In recent years, the major television networks have been criticized severely by
their viewers.

Main point of paragraph 2:

_____

Main point of paragraph 3:

_____

4. The first three years of a person's life
strongly influence the sort of adult he or
she becomes.

Main point of paragraph 2:

_____

Main point of paragraph 3:

_____

_____

5. I learned some very important lessons on the day I spent with a handicapped friend.

Main point of paragraph 2:

_____

_____

Main point of paragraph 3:

_____

_____

6. My visits to art museums have helped me realize my own creativity.

Main point of paragraph 2:

_____

_____

Main point of paragraph 3:

_____

_____

Introductions

Aside from its purpose as the paragraph that gets the essay started by stating the topic in the proposal sentence, the introductory paragraph must make readers interested enough in what you have to say to make them want to read on. Any one of the suggestions in the following list can help you write an effective introduction to the proposal statement. Each suggestion is followed by a sample.

> **Hint**
> Always write the proposal sentence before you write the introductory paragraph.

1. Tell the reader why your topic is important.

   Sample: For fifteen years I lived on East 92nd Street in Brooklyn. I made friends there, earned bloody noses, broke Mrs. Segal's window playing stickball, and nursed back to health a small, frightened sparrow in a shoe box. That block was mother and father to me in a way, presenting a number of unexpected experiences that are so important in the life of someone growing up without "at-home" parents—my father ran away when I was six and my mother worked most of the day. So the block was my teacher, and in several ways the lessons I learned there taught me how to think fast to survive.

2. Give background information on your topic so that readers know when they get to your proposal the ideas and conditions that led you to consider the point you are treating in the essay.

Sample: Our house was built in 1950, part of a development of small one-family homes in Bellmore, New York, not far from the Great South Bay. Two other families lived in this house before us, and the man who sold the place to my father in 1972 was an old eccentric. He had painted all the walls a creamy blue color so that everywhere the vast, empty look of open sky surrounded us. The kitchen was ancient; the garage was a mess of boxes, old tools, and broken furniture; the basement would fill up with water with the slightest rain. This house on Poplar Drive needed lots of work, and I recall two large-scale projects our family undertook together with very amusing results.

3. Show what many people now believe is true if your proposal will attempt to suggest something else.

Sample: Education is the process by which the young people of today are trained to become functioning members of their society. This process is generally accomplished in institutions known as schools where young people become acquainted with all phases of knowledge and, after a few years, are thought ready to accept responsibility as adults. In college the usual picture is a classroom filled with excited, bright-eyed youths soaking up important lessons for living. However, the American school system has failed miserably in trying to accomplish what it sets out to do; our system of higher education does not provide a person with the necessary training to take a rightful place in society.

4. State several points that may contradict, disagree with, or disprove the point you want the rest of the essay to make.

Sample: Working hard from his childhood on, my father has grown into a hard man. He is strict and overprotective, and he screams when I tiptoe into the house at two in the morning on a Saturday. He threatens to disconnect my extension phone so he can get to make a call, but he will never give me the satisfaction of having my own number. I rarely sit down to chat with him because his opinions are so one-sided; besides, when I rush into my room and toss my books on the bed at seven o'clock after my last class, Dad's loud harsh snore already echoes through the house. Despite these difficult qualities, I am still Daddy's little girl and always will be; I am not ashamed that I have grown to love my father very much.

5. Ask questions to arouse the reader's interest.

Sample: Can a black lawyer, a Chinese fashion designer, and a white school teacher live happily side by side as neighbors? Can a racially integrated community achieve the dream of brotherhood and understanding? An experiment in a small town in Connecticut is providing some extraordinary answers.

6. Use an interesting quotation that helps you build toward your proposal sentence (see pages 60–62 and page 270 for writing quotations correctly).

Sample: Kahlil Gibran in *A Tear and a Smile* writes, "I looked toward nature . . . and found therein . . . a thing that endures and lives in the spring and comes to fruit in summer days. Therein I found love." This I believe to be true, because people do not "fall in love"; love that lasts is a feeling that must come gradually over a period of time and must develop only with emotional maturity.

Hint

Use quotations from your own reading of newspapers, magazines, and books, or from television, radio, or the movies. Books like *Bartlett's Familiar Quotations* and the *Oxford Dictionary of Quotations* have many quotations arranged according to subjects; often you can find a meaningful quotation there to use in your introduction.

7. Tell a brief story—an incident that helps set the stage for your proposal. Make sure that the story suits the purpose of your essay: don't be funny or "cute" unless you expect to deal with matters that are not serious or unless you can work humor into your point.

Sample: A man with one shoe and a face filled with red sores wobbles down the summer morning street cursing to himself. From his back pocket he snatches a paper bag, uncaps the bottle inside, raises it to his lips, and takes a long gulp. Then, he drops down against a brick wall and, still cursing, closes his eyes. This is skid row, the place of the drunkard, a place of horrors. But urban police are now trying to reach out to these fallen men and women.

8. Tell what each body paragraph will deal with.

Sample: Solar energy devices will one day adequately replace our fossil fuels. Moreover, wind-driven turbines will also provide us with a reliable, economical source of power. Together these two important natural resources will meet the future energy needs of America.

Hint

Sentence 1 in the above introduction tells what the writer expects to develop in the first body paragraph (paragraph 2 of the essay). Sentence 2 tells the purpose of the second body paragraph. The writer has divided the topic for the reader.

9. Use a series of images to build up to your proposal.

Sample: Rocks tossed from behind trees; bottles broken on our blacktop driveway; whispering voices behind wrinkled hands at the A&P; taunts of "Kyke" and "There's a Jew" sailing at my back as I march to school alone: a

Jew growing up in a small Midwestern town learns how to hate very early in life.

10. Show different aspects of the topic that you will not consider in the essay, as you lead up to the topic that you will consider.

Sample: In our society, discimination has many different forms. There is age discrimination, which prevents a seventeen-year-old from buying a bottle of gin, and racial discrimination, which denies a black youth a job in a labor union. But another form of discrimination that faces many women starting careers today is sexual discrimination.

AVOIDING PITFALLS IN INTRODUCTIONS

1. Don't make your introduction too long. If each of your body paragraphs contains ten or fewer sentences, your introduction usually needs no more than four or five sentences. Longer body paragraphs may mean that longer introductions are acceptable.
2. Don't apologize for what you do not know, for your lack of experience, or for your limited abilities. Even if you do have limitations, to mention them in your paragraph is to make the reader feel that you do not know what you are talking about. Don't make any of these statements:

   "Although I am not qualified to discuss this . . ."

   "My knowledge is limited so . . ."

   "Many people who know more than I do would disagree, but . . ."

3. Don't think of the reader as someone who is sitting next to you as you write. Don't say "Now I will tell you . . ." or "Now I am going to show you . . ."
4. Don't talk about the parts of the essay in your composition. Don't say "In my next paragraph, I . . ." or "My introduction and my conclusion will try to show . . ."
5. Don't write an introduction that wastes words, one that you have just thrown ahead of your body paragraphs to fulfill the requirements of essay form. Your introduction should be an important part of the essay itself.
6. Don't use overworked expressions—trite sayings or quotations that have lost their meaning because of overuse. Don't use quotations or expressions that are too general or that could be applied to hundreds of situations. To say "Too many cooks spoil the broth" in an essay about too many men at the top and giving orders in government would not really add anything of significance.
7. Don't say the same thing over and over again. If you don't have much to say by way of introduction, write only the proposal in a clear, well-planned sentence or two of some length.
8. Don't refer to your title in the introduction. A student whose essay title was "How to Save Our National Parks" would be mistaken to start the introduction this way: "It is possible in a number of ways."

Step 1.   Writing Introductions to Proposals. Using any three of the proposal sentences from Step 2 on pages 260–261, write three introductions. Put the proposal sentence last. Try to write a different kind of introduction for each proposal: check the ideas for starting essays on pages 261–264. And, make sure you avoid the errors explained above.

Step 2.   Reading More Introductions. Discuss the introductory paragraphs for the essays whose titles and page numbers are listed below. Are the introductions effective? Which of the items on pages 261–264 does each introduction seem to follow? How might you improve each introduction?

1. "Memories of the Australian Bush," pages 295–296
2. "Ironing for Food," page 330
3. "Deprived Children," pages 405–406
4. "Women: Fragile Flowers?" pages 408–409
5. "Working Mothers," pages 407–408

Step 3.   Introductions: You Be the Judge. Decide whether the introductions below would be good first paragraphs for essays. Defend your opinions. Then, make any corrections that you feel will improve the introductory paragraphs. In some cases you may have to rewrite the paragraph completely. Use separate paper.

1. Swimming is an important activity for a healthy life. I was a swimmer in high school, in college, and I will continue to swim as long as I am physically able. This essay will try to show how important swimming is and how swimmers benefit from swimming.
2. I don't drink liquor so my knowledge of its effects is limited to what I have observed at parties. Although doctors know more about this subject than I do, I would like to discuss the terrible problem of alcoholism, especially among our young people.
3. Are you fed up with street riots and automobile fumes? Are you trying to escape the summer heat of Newark and the noisy crowds that shove their way across Market Street? Well then pack a tent and a four-burner stove and head for the nearest camping grounds. Outdoor living for summer vacation is a relaxing and unusual way to spend some time with nature.
4. A young boy cowers in the corner whenever he enters a room full of adults. A little girl refuses to talk with her teacher, the school nurse, or the principal. A five-year-old boy refuses assistance from a park attendant as he tries to climb on to the jungle jim. A red-haired, big-eyed seven-year-old girl would rather eat lunch alone than join a group of "grown-ups." Are these children simply cautious? No, they are the fearful victims of child abuse. Fortunately, a national campaign to alert the public about the horrors of child abuse is now under way.
5. You just won't believe how sloppy my brother can keep his room. First, I'm going to show you his dresser drawers. Then, I'll show you what a mess his closet is. And to top it all off, you won't believe how he makes his bed.
6. I always have trouble telling people about my vacation in Europe. I try to tell

them about the Eiffel Tower and the Coliseum and the Parthenon, but they never seem to understand. I just can't seem to put anything in words. So, I've decided to show them my slides. As everybody knows, "One picture is worth a thousand words."

Step 4. More Work on Introductions. For any three of the proposals you wrote in Step 1, pages 259–260, write three good introductions using any of the suggestions you studied.

Then take any topic sentence you wrote for any theme assignment in Part I of this book, and assume that it is the proposal sentence of an essay. Write a good introduction following the advice you learned in this chapter.

Step 5. You Judge the Professionals. Select two introductions to articles by professional writers and bring the introductions to class. One introduction should represent what you consider a good introductory paragraph; the other should represent a poor introduction. Be ready to read them to the class and to point out the specifics that support your opinions.

Combining Sentences

In earlier exercises on coordination and subordination (pages 19–20 and 100–109), you learned how combining sentences often helps you relate ideas more closely. Another advantage of combining sentences is that the new word group you have created usually expresses its point more precisely and with fewer words than the original.

When two consecutive sentences discuss the same object and the purpose of one of the two is to describe the object, to identify it, or to add information about it, you can often combine the two sentences into one. Writers have many ways to achieve this effect. Sometimes words like *who, which,* or *that* help join the sentences (see pages 106–107). Sometimes special verb parts make the combination effective (see pages 208–213).

At other times a change in punctuation and the removal of some words allow you to put ideas together in a meaningful way. Look at these sets of examples.

A	B
(1) Henry Chin plays basketball for the county team. (2) He is a tall and supple athlete.	(1) Across Oakland Drive hobbled an old man. (2) He was our former gardener.

Notice how in example *A* the writer can use fewer words and can bring the descriptive details closer to the person he wants to describe:

                        ,[comma]   [comma]

(3) Henry Chin, *a tall and supple athlete,* plays basketball for the county team.

Because the words from sentence (2) now interrupt the main idea of sentence (1), the writer uses commas to signal that interruption (see pages 284–285).

Details from sentence (2) could also be added to the beginning of (1) with slightly different results:

(4) *A tall and supple athlete,* Henry Chin plays basketball for the county team.
   [comma]

In example *B* you can put at the end of sentence (1) the words from (2) in order to identify the old man:

[comma]
(5) Across Oakland Drive hobbled an old man, *our former gardener.*

You could write the sentence in this way too:

(6) Across Oakland Drive hobbled our former gardener, *an old man.*

In sentences (4), (5), and (6) a comma sets off the added details from the main idea of the sentence.

Hint

You cannot combine the sentences in examples *A* and *B* simply by removing the period between (1) and (2). That would yield run-on sentences. Why? See pages 27–29.

Step 1. Practice in Combining Sentences. In each set below, material in one of the two sentences may be incorporated into the other sentence in order to add information about or to describe an object or an idea. Using sentences (3), (4), (5), and (6) above as models, combine the two sentences into one, and write your new sentence on the blank lines. Place new material *after* the word you want to describe or identify. Use commas where you need them. Look at the example.

1. The insect repellent works well. It is a white cream.

   The insect repellent, a white cream, works well. _____

2. Three pine trees stand in front of our house. The trees are very tall and are bathed in sunlight.

   _____

   _____

3. The rooms in this apartment do not suit our needs. They are too small.

   _____

   _____

4. The badlands section of South Dakota is magnificent. The area is vast and colorful.

   _____

   _____

5. My employer bought a new pen. It is a special instrument with a built-in calculator.

   _____

   _____

6. The instructor stood angrily before the class as he announced the results of our chemistry midterm. The instructor's name is Mr. Hassan.

   _____

   _____

7. A tornado whipped across the northern plains states. It was violent and dangerous.

   _____

   _____

8. It is hard to compare my two sisters. They are both hard-working and intelligent doctors at St. Jude's Hospital.

   _____

   _____

9. You can get hoisin sauce at Kam Kuo. It is a market that sells many Oriental foods.

   _____

   _____

10. Maria sang last night at The Music Box. She is a fine jazz singer.

    _____

    _____

SOLVING PROBLEMS IN WRITING

Punctuation Guidelines

AIDS TO PUNCTUATION: END MARKS

The Period (.)

1. Use a period after a sentence that makes a statement.

I watched a crow circle over a twisted oak.

Everyone was tired.

2. Use a period after a sentence that makes a mild command.

Take the bus into Austin.

Buy United States savings bonds.

3. Use periods after initials.

Robert E. Lee

John F. Kennedy

4. Use periods after most abbreviations.

Ph.D., N.J.

Exceptions

1. Most government agencies use no periods in abbreviations.

FBI, CIA

2. tv or TV
3. Business companies

IBM, A&P

The Question Mark (?)

1. Use question marks at the end of sentences that clearly ask questions.
Who wrote *A Farewell to Arms?* ← [question mark: end of question]

"Can't you hear me?" David shouted.
[end of sentence: no question mark.]

2. Some sentences, though they mention that a question is being asked, do not ask the question themselves. Such *indirect questions* are not followed by question marks.
She wondered why he did not call. ← [Period]
He asked who brought the station wagon. ← [Period]

The Exclamation Point (!)

1. Use the exclamation point at the end of a sentence that shows strong emotion, sharp surprise, forceful command, or strong emphasis.

I hate all men!

I don't believe it!

Call the police!

I meant what I said!

2. Certain words and expressions, like *what, oh, alas, hurray, bravo,* often introduce exclamations.

Oh! What am I going to do?

What! You stole that car?

3. Only the individual writer can determine which sentences are spoken with strong emotion. *Do not overuse the exclamation point!*

Step 1. A Variety of Endings. Put in correct end marks in the paragraph below. Use a capital letter to show the start of a new sentence.

My Fear of Flying

Why was I boarding this massive TWA jet that loomed ahead of me on the icy runway did I really have to fly to Washington, DC, on such a stormy day of course I did I couldn't miss my own sister's wedding she would never forgive me for not attending I wonder why I didn't take the train at least they were showing during the flight highlights of the NFL game of the week although an old W C Fields movie would have made me more relaxed, I could not concentrate on any movie Oh God I was scared suddenly the captain's voice said, "Please fasten your seatbelts" in any case, I was trapped my body tensed, my eyes stared straight ahead, and my clammy hands squeezed the armrests I would never fly again

---

QUOTATION MARKS (" ")

(See pages 60–62)
  1. Use quotation marks to show someone's exact words.

  "Roller skating is great!" Jane shouted excitedly.
  "When I'm in a big city," she admitted, "I miss my father's farm."
  "Why is the sky blue?" his son asked.

  Hint: The exact words may be repeating what someone said in speaking; or the exact words may be a statement quoted from a book. In any case, quotation marks are needed.

  2. Use quotation marks to set off the names of short stories, poems, chapters, articles, or essays that are parts of books, magazines, or newspapers.

  I read a column called "The Presidency" in *Time* magazine.

  The anonymous poem "Frankie and Johnnie" appears in *Understanding Poetry* by Brooks and Warren.

UNDERLINING (ITALICIZING)

Underlining is used in handwritten sentences to show when italics are needed.

1. Underline all titles of books, magazines, movies, TV shows, and newspapers to show that these titles should be in italics.

   Most people still enjoy <u>*Gone with the Wind*</u>.

   If the sentence were printed, it would look like this:

   Most people still enjoy *Gone with the Wind*.

2. Underline names of ships, trains, and airplanes.

   My parents just returned from Bermuda on the <u>*Oceanic*</u>.

Step 2.   Quotation Marks and Italics. Put in quotation marks or use underlining where required in the sentences below.

1. The Deerhunter was supposed to be such a sensitive film, my sister complained, but I thought it was macho garbage!
2. Is traveling on the Orient Express still as elegant as it used to be? my aunt asked.
3. Was it still raining, asked Phil, when you came in?
4. On the Merv Griffin show last night, Peter Benchley, author of the novel Jaws, discussed an article that appeared in The New York Times.
5. John Updike's short story A & P, which appears in the collection Pigeon Feathers, is especially appealing to young adults.

USING SEMICOLONS (;)

1. Use a semicolon to separate two complete sentences that are closely related (see page 20).

   The landlord painted the fence; now he is painting the steps.

2. Use semicolons instead of commas to separate items in a series if some of the items contain commas themselves. See page 280.

   [comma]   [comma]

   At our picnic Lynette brought a whole chicken which, because of deep frying, was a

   [end of first item in series;
   semicolon used because commas
   already appear within the item]   [end of second item in series]

   rich golden brown; two pounds of potato salad that her mother prepared; and a basket of cold, ripe apples.

3. Use semicolons instead of commas (see page 283) occasionally before coordinators that join complete thoughts that already contain commas.

   [semicolon instead of comma]

   The landlord painted the fence around my patio; but, even if he agrees to fix the plaster and repaint the whole apartment, I still intend to move.

HOW TO USE THE COLON (:)

1. A colon comes
   a. after the opening in a formal letter.

      Dear Ms. Stevenson:

      Gentlemen:

      Use a comma after informal openings.

      Dear Steve,

   b. between the hour and the minute when you write the time in numbers.

      The plane left at 6:18 P.M.

(continued on next page)

HOW TO USE THE COLON (:) (continued)

      c. between the number of the chapter and verse in the Bible.

      Matthew 6:12 is inspiring.

      d. in a title, to separate the main name of the selection from a subtitle (see page 247 for example).

      e. between act and scene in a play.

      Macbeth II:iii

2. Use a colon when you introduce a long or detailed list of items.

                                                      [colon]

Remember to bring to registration the following: two sharpened pencils with erasers, your admissions letter, your IBM registration card, and a check for $36.00 for student fees.   [Commas separate items in series.]

    Hint: Don't use the colon for a simple listing.

                  [no colon]

     We bought shoes, gloves, and jeans.

3. Use a colon whenever you want to force the reader's attention to the statement that comes after the colon. That statement usually explains or clarifies the opening part of the sentence.

                                       [This part of the sentence

               [Colon pushes emphasis to   explains the what comes after.]   first part.]

Of this I am sure: I do not want any more life insurance.

4. Use a colon before you introduce a formal quotation.

                                   [colon]

About greatness, Ralph Waldo Emerson said: "Every human being has a right to it, and in the pursuit we do not stand in each other's way."

Step 3. **Semicolons and Colons in Practice.** Use the semicolon or colon correctly in each sentence below. Be prepared to explain your answer.

1. The wedding will begin at 730 I will not be able to arrive on time.
2. In Shakespeare's *Hamlet* IIii, Hamlet speaks these famous words "The play's

the thing wherein I'll catch the conscience of the king."

3. There is one rule in tennis that must be remembered never take your eye off the ball.
4. Before you begin painting your apartment, make sure to have the following items available a large drop cloth, brushes of various sizes, rollers and pans, wooden or plastic stirrers, and, of course, a few gallons of paint.
5. The pastor referred us to Matthew 83 he felt it would give us something to think about.
6. Gentlemen

   Kindly send me three red, all-wool long johns two navy-blue, 100%-cotton kerchiefs and one green-plaid, chamois shirt.

PARENTHESES ( )

Parentheses are used to set off words or word groups that are not so important as the rest of the sentence. *Parenthetical expressions* add information and/or make some side comment on or about the material in the sentence.

[The information in parentheses is a side comment that adds information.]

Abandoned automobiles (and there are thousands throughout the country) line our roads and highways.

[The information in parentheses is a side comment.]

If you have seen Woody Allen's *Zelig* (certainly you have), you know how important a good director is.

[The information in parentheses adds information about the author's birth and death.]

{ Dylan Thomas (1914–1953) read his own poetry brilliantly.

Hint: 1. Although parentheses indicate less important information, do not ignore or fail to read what appears in parentheses.
2. Commas also set off parenthetical information, but commas give the material more importance.

   a. That old man (a carpenter) works hard.

   b. That old man, a carpenter, works hard.

   The words *a carpenter* are parenthetical in both sentences, but the commas in *b* make that parenthetical information more important than it is in *a*.
3. Don't use parentheses too often in your writing.

Step 4. Your Statements in Parentheses. Add your own parenthetical information to the blank spaces in the following sentences. Use parentheses (or commas) as explained above.

1. The Equal Rights Amendment _____ was immediately reintroduced in Congress.

2. The once beautiful Dwight Building _____ is now a burned-out shell.

3. Many clichés _____ are based in time-honored truths.

4. The inflation rate _____ rose sharply in 1979.

5. The fields of corn _____ filled the Oklahoma landscape in every direction.

6. Our natural resources _____ may be seriously depleted by the end of the century.

THE DASH FOR INTERRUPTION AND SUMMARY

1. Use a pair of dashes to set off a sudden shift in thought or structure of the sentence.

[This question breaks into the complete thought expressed in the sentence.]

That old maple—did you see it?—lost all its leaves in June.

Hint: Parentheses could be used here as well. But the dash makes the information more important and stresses its sudden break into the main idea of the sentence.

2. Use a single dash before a summary of details mentioned earlier in the sentence.

Running a mile each day, exercising in a careful program, choosing food thoughtfully—these are the ways to keep weight down.

[This part of the sentence briefly summarizes the meaning of the details in the first part.]

3. Don't use the dash too often in your writing.

Step 5. Using the Dash. Use dashes correctly in the sentences below.

1. "He is too oh, you know what I mean too quiet and unfriendly," Marie said.
2. Life, liberty, and the pursuit of happiness these rights are granted to every

American.
3. The airplane crash a horrible thing to witness destroyed three private homes.
4. He ran after her a little too late begging her forgiveness.
5. Lowering taxes, increasing defense spending, lifting government regulations these were all part of Reagan's economic program.
6. *E.T., Star Wars, Close Encounters* each one was a staggering financial success.

THE HYPHEN AS DIVIDER

  1. Use a hyphen to separate parts of certain compound words (words that are made by putting together other words.)

time-consuming	president-elect
thirty-one	well-bred
self-assurance	brother-in-law

  2. Use a hyphen to divide a word when there is no room on the line to finish the word.

[hyphen]

After the union leaders approved the contract, the members voted it quickly into effect.

  3. Use a hyphen to separate the years of birth and death of some important figure.

Rudyard Kipling (1865–1936)

When dividing words, observe the following:

  1. Don't separate the word if you can avoid it.
  2. Do put the hyphen at the end of the first line, *never* at the beginning of the next line.

approved the con-	*not*	approved the con
tract		-tract

  3. Do separate the word at the end of a syllable and nowhere else.

be-lieve	*not*	beli-eve
re-call	*not*	rec-all
per-mit-ting	*not*	pe-rmit-ting

  Hint

Check a dictionary for proper syllables in words (see page 482, "How to Read a Dictionary Entry").

  4. Do divide the word, if pronunciation allows, so that a consonant starts the part of the word that appears on the next line.

writ-ten   stop-ping

but

leop-ard   knowl-edge

5. Don't divide words of one syllable: *laugh, called, brought.*
6. Don't leave just one letter of a word at the end of the line. Write the entire word on the next line.

not   He tried to e-   *but*   He tried to
         rase his mistake.   erase his mistake.

7. Don't carry over to the next line brief word endings like *-ly* (happi*ly*), *-ed* (hint*ed*), or *-ing* (sing*ing*).
8. Don't divide people's names.

Harry, Barbara   *not*   Har-   Bar-
                        ry   bara

9. Do leave a space at the end of a line rather than fill the space with part of a word that is incorrectly broken.
10. Do learn the difference between hyphen and dash.

In Writing by Hand

The hyphen is a short line (-). The dash is a longer line, about the length of three hyphens (—).

In Typing

The hyphen is a short line (-). The dash is typed as two hyphens with no spaces before or after them (--).

Step 6. Breaking Up Words. In the blank spaces, rewrite the words that appear below to show where you would use hyphens to break the word at the end of a line. Put an X after those words you would not divide.

1. neglect _____

2. innocent _____

3. spilled _____

4. spectacle_____

5. evidence _____

6. want _____

7. possessive _____

8. manly _____

9. Sarah _____

10. knowledge _____

THREE USES FOR APOSTROPHES (')

1. Possession (see pages 322–329)

   a. If a word *does not* end in *s*, in order to show ownership add an apostrophe *s* ('s).

     boy + 's = the boy's hat

     men + 's = the men's club

   b. If a word *does* end in *s*, in order to show ownership add only an apostrophe (').

     ladies + '   The ladies' coats were soiled.

     boys + '   The boys' bicycles all fell down.

    Hint: If a person's name ends in *s* and the name is to indicate possession, add *either* apostrophe *s* or just an apostrophe. Whichever you choose, however, be consistent throughout your writing.

Doris' book   OR   Doris's book

2. Contractions

   To show where letters are omitted in words that are combined in contractions, use an apostrophe.

    it's = it is   I'll = I will

    doesn't = does not   you're = you are

    hasn't = has not   I've = I have

    Hint: Contractions are usually informal words and should be avoided in formal compositions. Write out the two words in your themes.

3. Special plurals

   To show the plurals of numbers, letters, and symbols, use an apostrophe *s* ('s).

    There are two *t*'s in committee.

    Our address has three *5*'s in it.

    All &'s should be written as *and*.

    Hint: Aside from these special cases, *do not* use apostrophes to show plurals.

Step 7. Correct Apostrophes. For each word in parentheses, add an apostrophe or apostrophe *s* so that the sentence is correct, and write the new word in the blank. If the word needs no apostrophe, put an *X* in the blank.

1. _____ (Its) a shame that the disco had to close because of _____ (its) faulty electrical wiring.

2. The _____ (children) toys were left behind at Aunt _____ (Phyllis) house.

3. The preschool child practiced writing her _____(s) and _____(w).

4. The _____ (women) letters of protest _____ (werent) even read by the _____ (committee) chairperson.

5. "_____ (Youll) just have to move your _____ (father) car for him," the officer instructed me.

6. _____ (Ross) books were stolen from his _____ (boss) office, and he _____ (doesnt) have a clue as to the identity of the thief.

7. The _____ (company) profits decreased last year.

8. Ms. _____ (Jones) mother _____ (couldnt) climb the stairs to our apartment because _____ (shes) a woman in her _____ (nineties).

9. _____ (Ive) never gotten it straight how many _____ (s), _____ (i), or _____ (p) there are in *Mississippi*.

Step 8. A Punctuation Review. Use correct punctuation in the following paragraph. Although the ends of sentences are indicated by periods, sometimes you will have to change them to exclamation or question marks. The following list indicates what punctuation you will need. Do not add commas.

colons: 3

quotation marks: 4 pairs

exclamation marks: 1

question marks: 1

semicolons: 2

periods: 4

underlining (italics): 3

hyphens: 2

apostrophes: 3

dashes: 1 pair

parentheses: 2 pairs

Conrad's Photographic Eye

One of the masters of sensory images is Joseph Conrad 1857 1925. Pictures rich in color and sound, pictures of the sea in all its beauty these fill the pages of Conrads works. Born in Poland, he settled in England in the 1890s at the age of thirty seven. Conrad came to love about the English language its musical qualities its sweet, yet harsh, sounds its rich, lively, fluid motion. Conrad knew no one can deny it the importance of the senses in creating word pictures. *My task which I am trying to achieve is, he wrote, by the power of the written word to make you hear, to make you feel—it is, before all, to make you see.** How could that be more clearly expressed. It is Conrad's power to make readers see that has led many MA and PhD students to study his novels like Lord Jim and Nostromo. What marvelous use he makes of the language. In the description of a railroad changing from the short story Heart of Darkness he says *A slight clinking behind me made me turn my head. Six black men advanced in a file, toiling up the path. They walked erect and slow, balancing small baskets full of earth on their heads, and the clink kept time with their footsteps. Black rags were wound around their loins, and the short ends behind waggled to and fro like tails. I could see every rib, the joints of their limbs were like knots in a rope; each had an iron collar on his neck, and all were connected together with a chain whose bights swung between them, rhythmically clinking.** It must be a scene like this that John Galsworthy who, incidentally, was a writer and fellow traveler journeying on Conrad's ship the Torrens thought of when he wrote *Conrads eyes never ceased snapshotting; and the millions of photographs they took were laid away by him to draw on.**

*Start of quote.
**End of quote.

Commas

Commas have two basic functions within our punctuation signal system. First, they help us to separate main sentence parts. Second, they help us enclose interrupters within the sentence. The following seven sections on commas illustrate those two basic functions.

I. TO SEPARATE ITEMS IN A SERIES

A. We bought eggs, bread, and cereal.
B. My mother rushed to the garage, to the car, and then to the library.
C. Larry bought a Mustang, Gina bought an old Pontiac, but Andrew bought a sleek new motorcycle.

                1   2   3
D. He was a tall, handsome, and hardworking man.

    Words 1, 2, and 3 above describe "man." Since they are equally important, can be written in any order, and would make sense if the word *and* appeared between them (He was a tall *and* handsome *and* hardworking man), you need to use commas.

                    1   2   3
    However, in this sentence, *Steve ate four small chocolate candies,* commas are not needed. You could not reverse the order of the describing words, nor could you make sense if you used *and* between the words (Steve ate four *and* small *and* chocolate candies).

Hints: 1. Each item can be either one word (as in A above) or a group of words (as in B or C above).
      2. There must be at least three items in the series.
      3. The comma before *and* or *but* is *NOT* required.
      4. To determine whether you need commas between describing words:
         a. Try to reverse their order in the sentence.
         b. Try to use *and* between the describing words.
         If you can do *a* and *b*, use commas.

Step 1. Commas and Series. Use commas where they belong. If a sentence is correct, mark it *C*.

1. The radiator transmission and fuel pump all have to be fixed on my old Ford.
2. To create a good impression on a job interview dress neatly be courteous and be confident.
3. Don simply went out to buy iced coffee and dessert but returned with a new freezer chest a coffee grinder and a vast assortment of pastries.
4. When proofreading your essay it is best to read through it once to put it aside for a while and then to reread it thoroughly.
5. Down the dark wooden staircase through the empty hallways past the musty living room the old man hobbled with his cane.

II. TO SET OFF A DIRECT QUOTATION (SEE PAGE 270)

I said, "Sit down!"
"I'm not tired," she replied.
"But a person needs rest," I said, "even if she's not tired."

Hint: If you use a question mark or an exclamation mark after a quotation, do not use a comma too.

"Where were you?" he asked.
"Stand up!" she screamed.

Step 2. Commas and Quotations. Use commas correctly in these sentences. If the sentence is already correct, mark it *C*.

1. Sadly, Senator Davis announced "I will not run for a third term."
2. "Chicago is lovely this time of year" he admitted "but I miss the serenity of the country."
3. "Where did Daddy go?" John asked with a tear in his eye.
4. "Pull over" commanded the police officer "and show me your license."
5. "Please" she shouted "don't go!"

III. TO SET OFF INTRODUCTORY SECTIONS

A. *Certain Transitions as Openers* (one word or several words).

[comma]
Nevertheless, try to speak in a loud voice.

In other words, be careful!
[comma]

B. *Certain Conversational Words* (to set off *yes, no, oh well, why,* and *now* used in conversation).

[comma] [comma] [comma]
Yes, he will be there. *Why,* how did that happen? *Oh,* that is awful!

C. *-ing Word or Other Verb-Part Openers* (see pages 208–213).

[-ing ⟶ *Sailing along the lake,* I felt peace and contentment.
opener] [comma]

[verb-part ⟶ *To reach the top of the shelf,* the child stood on a chair.
opener] [comma]

⟶ *Scribbled quickly,* the note was hard to read.
[comma]

D. *Subordinated Word Groups as Openers.*

[subordinator]
Although the moon hung in the sky, the sun still shone.
[comma]

Because the vocabulary confused us, we used a dictionary to check definitions.
[subordinator] [comma]

Hint: Brief opening-word groups not covered in A, B, and C above usually do not have commas after them.

[no comma]
In a few months I will be twenty.

[no comma]
Beyond the tree stands a small house.

If the introductory subordinated word group is brief, you may omit the comma.
When he sang I left the room.
[no comma]

Step 3. Commas after Openers. Put in commas where they belong. Mark the sentence *C* if it requires no commas.

1. Across the horizon flew the jumbo jet.
2. Wandering down the quaint old streets of Quebec I found my uncle's antique shop.
3. All in all there must be a better way to earn a living.
4. Sailing across Lake Ontario we suddenly lost radar contact with shore.
5. On the other hand we do carry a selection of Italian sweaters.
6. Without a substantial increase in salary John will quit his job.
7. Therefore I don't think Mr. Ross is guilty.
8. Provided he could get a visa Michael planned to fly to Paris on Tuesday.
9. My goodness you look wonderful!

IV. TO HELP SEPARATE TWO COMPLETE THOUGHTS WHEN A COORDINATOR IS EXPRESSED (see pages 19–20)

> **Hint 1:** Coordinators are *and, or, nor, but, for.*

[comma]

Many people believe that Memphis is a large city, but it has few problems of traffic congestion.

[comma]

Just turn the key, and you will see when the engine starts that this car is like no other you have ever driven.

> **Hint 2:** The comma may be left out when the two complete thoughts are very brief.

[no comma]

We ate and they drank.
They flew but we drove there.

[no comma]

Step 4. Commas and Coordinators. Select a sentence from Column I and coordinate it sensibly on separate paper with a sentence in Column II, using one of the five coordinators. Use a comma when necessary.

I	*II*
1. I swim as often as possible.	1. My mother was born in Vietnam.
2. I enjoy a good cry.	2. You can fail the exam.
3. Fred bought a very expensive shirt.	3. It is excellent exercise.
4. My father was born in China.	4. Its colors faded after the third washing.
5. You can study hard.	5. I always feel better afterward.

V. TO SEPARATE WORDS OR WORD GROUPS THAT INTERRUPT THE MAIN IDEA OF THE SENTENCE

A. *Transition Words to Interrupt.*

We felt, however, that whitewall tires were unnecessary.

[commas here]

But the kangaroo, to be sure, is an unusual animal.

B. *Subordinating Word Groups to Interrupt.*

That old truck, which has ignition trouble, is hard to start.

[commas here]

Mr. Davis, who drives to work, always complains about the traffic.

[commas]

Caroline, whose voice is soft, is really charming.

The subordinated word groups in B do not give information to identify the subject, and they could be removed from the sentences without changing the meaning. We know which truck is hard to start (*that old one*) without the interrupter. We know who complains about traffic (*Mr. Davis*) without the interrupter. We know who is charming (*Caroline*) without the interrupter. Therefore, commas are needed to set off the added information.

But if the subordinating word group is needed to identify the subject, commas are not required.

[no comma]   [no comma]

A truck that has ignition trouble is hard to start.

[These words identify the truck.
Without these words, we don't
know which truck is hard to
start.]

[no comma]   [no comma]

People who drive to work always complain about the traffic.

[Without these words, it
would seem that all
people complain about
the traffic.]

[no comma]   [no comma]

A girl whose voice is soft is speaking on the telephone.

[Without these words,
we don't know which
girl is speaking.]

Hint: If *that* opens the subordinating word group, you usually do not need commas.

(continued on next page)

**V. TO SEPARATE WORDS OR WORD GROUPS THAT
INTERRUPT THE MAIN IDEA OF THE SENTENCE (continued)**

C. *Interrupters That Describe*
   1. *-ing* word groups to interrupt

          [commas here]
     A shaky station wagon, laboring up the hill, backfired in a crash.

       [commas]
     The puppy, trembling, drew close to its mother.

   2. Interrupters starting with *-ed* words or other verb parts.

     [comma]   [verb part] [comma]
     Miss Kelly, *dressed* in red, ran for the bus.

     [comma]   [verb part (infinitive)]
     The dog, *to get* his food, barked wildly.

     [comma] [verb part] [comma]
     A mirror, *broken* in small pieces, lay on the street.

   Hint: The interrupting words in 1 and 2 just add information about the subject. They could be left out of the sentence without disturbing the meaning. Therefore, commas are needed. However, when interrupting word groups like those above identify the subject, commas are not used.

[Not just any wagon backfires: this word group identifies the wagon and is essential to the meaning of the sentence.]

A wagon laboring up a hill can backfire.
   [no commas]

[It is only the woman dressed in red who is attractive according to this sentence. This word group identifies the subject.]

The woman dressed in red is attractive.
   [no commas]

   3. Other describing words

[These words describe the driver. They could be left out of the sentence.]

     The driver, a doctor, was not injured.

     [commas]
     The Mustang, a new white convertible, crashed into a pole.

[These words describe the car, which has already been identified. The words could be left out of the sentence.]

Step 5. Commas for Interrupters. Select from Column II an interrupter that could be used sensibly within each complete thought in Column I. Decide whether or not commas are needed. Then, write each new sentence on the blank lines provided.

I

A student will fail.
My history textbook is unpleasant to read.
A news story is unprofessional.
An energy program is practical.
My father just retired.
Jimmy Carter was defeated in his 1980 bid for reelection.
My girl friend is practically blind.

II

a history professor
without her glasses
which contains sexist ideas
that contains the reporter's opinion
who doesn't study
our thirty-ninth President
that relies on solar energy

Example

1. *A student who doesn't study will fail.* _____

2. _____

3. _____

4. _____

5. _____

6. _____

7. _____

VI. SEVEN FAMILIAR PLACES FOR COMMAS

1. In dates, after everything but the month

On April 7, 1980, my life began.
         ↑   ↑
      [commas]

On Saturday, May 7, 1981, Alexander's Department Store had a sale on men's suits.
              └──[commas]──┘

2. In an address

                              [comma]
A riot occurred in Brooklyn, New York.

Atlanta, Georgia, has many qualities of Northern big cities.
       ↑   ↑
     [commas]

(continued on next page)

VI. SEVEN FAMILIAR PLACES FOR COMMAS (continued)

3. Before and after someone's title if the title comes after the name

[commas]
Carl Berkson, Ph.D., practices psychology in Los Angeles.

[no comma]
Dr. Smithers has retired.

4. To set off someone's name, if that person is being spoken to in the sentence

Carol, why don't you do your assignment?

[commas]
I understand, Mr. Harrington, that you cannot pay this last installment.

5. In informal letters, after the opening words and the words before the signature.

Dear Martin,
Dear Carl,
Yours sincerely, [comma]
Very truly yours,

Hint: In a formal letter, use a colon after the salutation.
Dear Mr. Porter:
Dear Senator Byrd:

6. To indicate that words are left out.

[Comma here shows that the words "man owns" are omitted.]
The older man owns the sedan; the younger, the convertible.

7. To set off a variety of numbers

[comma]
volume four, page eighteen

[comma]
six feet, three inches

19,385 students
[comma]

Step 6. Using Commas in Seven Ways. Fill in the commas where they are needed.

1. The lucky winner of our September 18 1979 contest is Jules Ramon M.D. who lives at 458 South Street San Francisco California.
2. Henry Davis the superintendent lives in building four apartment 12A.
3. "Would you explain Mr. Kingsley what 2 meters 50 centimeters is equal to in American feet and inches?"

4. Dear Hong Wei
> The information you asked for is in volume 3 page 8 paragraph 6.
>> Sincerely
>> Jerry

5. Jose why don't you just stay with us?

VII. THREE PLACES NOT TO USE COMMAS

Excessive use of commas distracts the reader, especially when the writer places commas incorrectly. Based upon errors made on the papers of beginning writers, these suggestions will help you avoid using commas unnecessarily:

1. DO NOT use commas to separate subject and verb.

INCORRECT: A small violet, grew beneath the elm.
CORRECT: A small violet grew beneath the elm.

2. DO NOT use commas after short word groups, even if they are introductory, unless they are transitional words like *in fact, for example, however* or unless confusion might otherwise result.

INCORRECT: Beside the fence, a calf stood grazing under a blue sky.
CORRECT: Beside the fence a calf stood grazing under a blue sky.
CORRECT: In fact, the child arrived after noon.
CORRECT: From the ceiling, light bits of plaster fell.
[Without the comma, readers would read *ceiling light.*]

3. DO NOT use commas before coordinators when the subject of the following complete sentence is not stated.

INCORRECT: She dug a deep hole, and planted a fir tree
                   [no subject here]
CORRECT: She dug a deep hole, and she planted a fir tree.
               She dug a deep hole and planted a fir tree.

Step 7. Avoiding Excess Commas. Correct any errors with commas in the following sentences. Mark correct sentences *C*.

1. She saw the film, on Saturday, and failed to enjoy it.
2. Across the vacant meadow, the wind howled like a hurt dog.
3. Listening to the radio, stimulates my imagination more than watching television does.
4. Rosa took down the license-plate number, and tried to remember the model and make of the car.
5. That tall, graceful man, is my husband, but I am not surprised that you did not recognize him.

6. In any case, discarded bottles are dangerous, and are ugly to look at.
7. Cold water and other liquids help reduce fever.
8. Breathing heavily, she whispered sweet nothings into his ear.
9. For example many grocery stores, now use laser beams to detect price codes.
10. Neatly piled stones formed an effective breakwater.

Step 8. Comma Review. Here are some sentences written by professional writers. All the commas have been left out. Put in the commas where you think they belong. In each blank space, write in the number of the review chart on pages 280–288 that tells why the comma (or commas) is needed.

_____ 1. The drama like the symphony does not teach anything.
                                        —*John Millington Synge*

_____ 2. God heals and the doctor takes the fee.
                                        —*Benjamin Franklin*

_____ 3. To be sure in all ages people have been afraid of loneliness and have tried to escape it.
                                        —*Rollo May*

_____ 4. All words grouping themselves round the concepts of liberty and equality for instance were contained in the single word *crimethink* while all words grouping themselves round the concepts of objectivity and rationalism were contained in the single word *oldthink.*
                                        —*George Orwell*

_____ 5. She drove up over a rise and suddenly looming out of the mist the deer was there.
                                        —*Jayne Anne Phillips*

_____ 6. Stopping in her tracks she first extended her arm bent her elbow and leaned forward from the hips—all to examine the watch strapped to her wrist; then she gave a loud double-rap on the door.
                                        —*Eudora Welty*

_____ 7. In a way I suppose that the little I recall of my early childhood in Russia my first eight years sums up my beginnings what now are called the formative years.
                                        —*Golda Meir*

_____ 8. I have now spoken of the education of the scholar by nature by books and by action
                                        —*Ralph Waldo Emerson*

_____ 9. On that bleak hill top the earth was hard with a black frost and the air made me shiver through every limb.
                                        —*Emily Brontë*

_____ 10. It reasons that the present is undefined the future has no other reality than as present hope and the past is no more than present memory.
                                        —*Jorge Luis Borges*

Step 9. **More Review.** Follow directions. Use separate paper.

1. Write a sentence that you heard someone say in the classroom. Identify the speaker at the beginning of the sentence.
2. Write a complete sentence that tells your street address, your city, and your state.
3. Write a sentence that tells the name of some important artist or performer. Use the words *an important artist* after the person's name.
4. Write two *complete* sentences about a peaceful place that you visit regularly. Use the words *and* or *but* to separate the sentences.
5. Write a complete sentence that lists your *three* favorite actresses. Use the word *and* only once.
6. Write a complete sentence about your boyfriend or girl friend, your husband or your wife. Use the words *who I love* somewhere in the sentence.
7. Write a quotation sentence about something you argued about recently. Use the words *I said* in the middle of the sentence.
8. Write a sentence about life in a small town. Use the word *although, when, if, while,* or *because* at the beginning of the sentence.
9. Write a sentence of advice to someone who has never driven in rush-hour traffic. Start your sentence with either of these word groups: *Driving in rush-hour traffic* or *To drive in rush-hour traffic.*
10. Use the word *however, nevertheless, on the other hand,* or *besides* in the middle of a sentence that describes how you feel about the current administration in Washington.

WRITING THE DESCRIPTIVE ESSAY

ASSIGNMENT: Write a four-paragraph essay describing a special place. Remember that good description relies on concrete sensory details. As a refresher, you might want to refer back to the section called Essay Form (pages 253–266).

Think about some particular place that has some significance in your life: a room, an office, a school yard, a country cabin, a farm, or any other memorable place. Make sure that there are two specific aspects of this place that you can write about—one in each body paragraph. Make sure that you have a strong enough feeling about the place so that you can write an effective proposal sentence. And use your highest level of concrete sensory language for details: color, sound, touch, smell, images of action will be the essential sources of support for the points you wish to make.

Suggestions for Thinking It Through

You remember that the first five chapters of this book introduced some ways paragraphs may be organized. Essays, since they are composed of paragraphs, may be organized in similar ways, each paragraph following a pattern of organization that suits the topic. Comparison, contrast, narration, several instances to support topic ideas, description, analogy, mood sketches: all these paragraph types may be extended to the essay itself. The table below makes suggestions for ways in which you can develop and organize your essay and gives you some sample proposals other students have written for the various developments suggested. But feel free to use any method that you think best suits the topic you are writing about.

Possible Plan for Body Paragraphs	Paragraph Development	Sample Proposal
1. Tell about two special moments you remember about the place, one in each paragraph.	Narration through chronology? Mood sketches? Analogy in one of the paragraphs?	1. In the school yard at the back of this public school in Cincinnati, I remember two important lessons in sportsmanship.
2. *a.* Compare and contrast the appearance of the place at two different times OR *b.* Compare and contrast the place you remember with some other place you remember.	Narration through chronology? Comparison-contrast? Definition in images? (See pages 464–465.)	2. *a.* The corner at Pitkin and Howard Avenues during July is two different places, one in the morning and another in the early evening. *b.* When I think back to the kitchen in our old apartment house, I realize how modern things are here in Springfield Gardens.
3. One paragraph to show *several* instances that support one aspect of the place you are discussing and *a.* the other paragraph to tell *one specific moment* that illustrates another aspect of the place OR *b.* the other paragraph *also* to show several instances that support another aspect of the place you are discussing.	Three instances arranged through importance? Three instances arranged through chronology? Listing of instances? Narration through chronology? Mood sketch? Instances arranged through importance? Instances arranged through chronology?	3. Not only did I learn in Cook County Hospital that nurses and doctors are really interested in patients, but I also saw that the patients themselves look after one another.
4. Describe the place fully in one paragraph. Tell in the next paragraph about a vivid moment that occurred at the place.	Description using transitions by place? Narration through chronology? Mood sketch?	4. The desert near El Paso is a beautiful place, but one experience I had there points to its hidden dangers.

TOPIC TIPS FOR IMPACT

1. Select a place that is particularly clear and important to you. Perhaps you can even return there briefly before you begin writing.
2. Write about your impressions of the sounds you hear; the smells and sensations of touch you experience; the actions and colors you observe. Show the reader through details why the place is special.
3. Try to recall bits of dialogue, people's words as they participate in the place you are writing about.
4. Keep in mind the proportion of your paragraphs. Generally, introduction and conclusion should be about the same length, and both of these paragraphs should be shorter (or at least not longer!) than the body paragraphs. A long introduction or conclusion requires substantial body paragraphs as well. If you try *generally* for four to six sentences in your introduction and conclusion and ten to twelve sentences in each of the body paragraphs, you will have set a reasonable and workable goal for yourself.
5. If one of your paragraphs is straight description:
    a. Describe the scene from one point of view: decide where you as reporter and observer are located and show all the details from that position.
    b. Name the place, the time, and the season in which your scene takes place.
    c. Build your description by moving from objects farthest away from you to objects that are closest.
    d. Use strong and active verbs.
    e. Avoid too many modifiers.

Learning from Other Students

Step 1.   An Essay on Place. Read the following sample, an essay about a place a student remembered vividly. Answer the questions that come afterward.

Uncle Del's Barn

I remember the big, red barn on my Uncle Del's farm in Montana with great fondness. The sight of its sprawling outline etched against the sky was the first thing I'd look for as we pulled into the road leading to my uncle's house. The barn's weathered sides needed painting badly. Once the proud home of cattle and horses, now chickens, cats, equipment, and dust took over as farm life had changed. Cool and dry inside, the barn lit up only occasionally as beams of yellow light from holes in the roof broke the darkness. Sunlight fell in patches on the floor, which was soft and springy from many layers of dust and straw. Walking along, I heard the wind moan through the chinks in the walls and the doors creak on their hinges. I had many adventures inside the barn and delighted in watching and playing with the animals who made their homes there.

The barn was an ideal place for a child to find adventure. Filled with junk and old tools, this hideaway offered hours of enjoyment. I would tiptoe between the piles of old harnesses and broken rakes and shovels, ever watchful for the imaginary bandits hiding just out of my sight, waiting to jump me the moment I turned my back. I stalked Billy the Kid, Jesse James, and the Sundance Kid, and I whooped and hollered after them, a toy silver gun in my leather holster. Now I was a brave pioneer, blazing a trail through the wilderness of plows and bales. I hid from attacking Blackfeet and built a homestead out of some loose planks, bits of hay, and an old green horse blanket. At other times I was a big game hunter, capturing lions, tigers, and exotic birds for the big circus across the sea. I pretended that the floor was a river filled with crocodiles and that I had to race across it with a rifle high above my head. Time flowed like molasses as I drifted from one adventure to another, lost in my daydreams.

Sharing in these adventures were the animals who lived in the barn, and they are as much a part of my memories as the barn itself. Hoping that I had a saucer of cream or a scrap of meat for them, barn cats and their new kittens ran to meet me as I opened the heavy wooden door. If I tried to reach out to pet them, they would run away, meowing just outside my reach. Half wild, the kittens trembled and shook those few times I did manage to catch them. As I explored the nooks and crannies and piles of straw, I startled many a chicken guarding her hidden nest. Squawking, with wings flapping, they fluttered off. Peeking at the spot an old hen had abandoned, I saw a pile of straw and feathers with a cluster of creamy-brown eggs. Once in a while, I would see a fluffy, yellow chick only a day or two old, cheeping furiously at his mother's rude departure. My search through the barn for hidden treasures always brought me to the pigs' pen sooner or later, their snuffles and grunts attracting me. I loved to watch them as they lumbered around on their stubby legs. Sniffing at their slop, they would saunter out the door to the muddy creek to flop down in its cool, slimy mud. The sight of a hefty porker trying to heave himself out of the goo was enough to send me into gales of laughter.

Even today, I can close my eyes and recall the good times I had playing in the old, weathered barn, the smell of Aunt Annabelle's fragrant spice cake filling the air, Uncle Del's rusty plow sitting on the barn floor, the chicks and kittens and pigs moving freely about. I consider myself fortunate to have experienced a piece of life in decline in America today. Up against high interest rates and soaring costs for equipment, many small farmers (my Uncle Del is no exception) sell out to big businesses with interest only in making money. For Uncle Del and Aunt Annabelle, and for me, too as I now think back, the small Montana farm was a way of life. Even when I knew it, the old barn was past its useful life, but it gave me many joys as a child. I'm sure that barn is long gone now, yet it will always be a symbol in my mind for the carefree, happy, innocent kind of life that is not easy to find these days.

—*Yvonne Wortman*

1. Put a check next to the proposal sentence. Is it specific or general?
2. Comment on the introductory paragraph. Is it effective? Does it tell the writer's attitude or why the topic is important to her?
3. What action do you see most clearly in this essay? Where has the writer appealed to our sense of touch and smell?
4. Underline all of the -*ing* openers in this essay. Are they effective? Why?
5. How do the last sentences in paragraph 2 and in paragraph 3 serve each moment being described?
6. What part of the opening sentence of paragraph 3 tells the topic of that paragraph? What part of the same sentence refers the reader back to paragraph 2?
7. What is your opinion of the conclusion?

Step 2. Other Samples. After you read the following student essays, discuss the questions for each.

Practice in the High School Gym

All my life I have loved baseball. As a little boy I stood at the iron schoolyard gates and watched the ninth graders zip around the bases. I sit glued to the television and suffer with the Mets as their pitchers go limp on the mound. It is easy to understand, then, why when March comes around I look forward to the start of baseball practice in my high school gym. What I liked most about senior practice was the thrill of all my friends around me in the locker room and the activity on the gym floor.

As I dressed in the locker room, I felt the warmth and enjoyment of all my friends who played on the team with me in the previous year. Bob on my left dressed hurriedly to rush out to the gym; as team captain, he rapped on the metal lockers and yelled, "Let's get the lead out! Cut the talk and let's move!" Richard on my right stuffed his red flannel shirt and his copy of *Hamlet* into the locker as he dressed, talking continuously about winning a school championship. As I looked around, I saw all the new fellows. Trying out for the team for the first time, they struggled with their uniforms. They were so nervous that they could not even put their bright yellow shirts on straight. Then I saw Coach O'Neill flying out of his office. Even he looked excited for the oncoming season, which would last until June, and the championship games. As he dashed out the door to the gym, he looked at me and smiled as if to say, "Isn't it great to be back with the team again?"

Then, when all the fun in the locker room was over, we charged out onto the shellacked floor of the gym. As we stood waiting for the coach to finish checking the new bats and uniforms, I could not help thinking how I felt like a father to all the new boys on the team. I looked at the brown painted stands halfway pushed out, but before we even got near to sit down, Coach O'Neill grabbed the silver whistle dangling from his neck and blew hard. His gray eyes looked mean as he barked out the drills we had to do. Then we started calisthenics because the coach said they would make us loose. As I did my push-ups to Coach O'Neill's crisp "One-two-three-four," I saw the yellow floor with its black stripes from the basketball court. Blood rushed up to my head, making me feel weak, but I still continued. Next we ran laps around the gym. As I ran I could see the huge panes of glass from the roof of the gym, the sun blinding me every time I looked up. After a loud blast from a whistle, the coach told us to stop running and to take a rest. Five minutes later we ended the workout with wind sprints in the hallway to make room in the gym for the football team on its workout session. These activities in the gym made me feel happy and healthy.

Because I have so much fun in the gym, to me exercise is a wonderful part of living. I was surprised to read in the papers about "Flabby Americans" and of the poor physical condition so many people today are in because of little activity. Maybe some worthwhile exercises and exciting workouts in high school would start more people on physical fitness programs. My friends in public school say that gym teachers leave uninterested students pretty much alone to sit and talk on the sidelines as long as there is no trouble. But I think that this is wrong: physical education teachers should be convincing all those sideline talkers that participating is the greatest part of sports.

—*Thomas Albanese*

Memories of the Australian Bush

From a very early age I had the urge to see what was beyond my native territory in Australia. At the tender age of eighteen I traveled half way around the world to live in the United States. Love, a new family, and boundless opportunities greeted me in this foreign country. But, I will never forget the land of my birth—Australia. There, I grew up among shady gum trees with wide open spaces for my playground. My home, a sheep station where sheep are raised for their wool, is a beautiful place to me and holds many happy memories of my childhood.

For instance, September to my sister, brother and me meant the delights of crayfishing or "yabbying" as we called it. After school we grabbed long lengths of rough, brown string, a dish of meat chunks, a chicken wire basket, and an old iron bucket. Arriving at the nearest dam, we tore off our shoes and socks. We tied large pieces of the fatty red meat securely to one end of the string. Clutching the makeshift fishing lines, we tiptoed into the mud, smooth red slime oozing around our feet and ankles. I deftly tossed the string into a dark, murky hole, causing ripples in concentric circles to break the surface of the water. Shivering with cold and anticipation, I watched and waited for a tug on the string. "I've got one!" squealed my sister Helen. All thoughts of my own catch vanished. I dashed for the wire basket while my brother David aided my sister in the delicate process of pulling the crayfish, inch by inch, out of his hole to where I could scoop him up with my net. We repeated this process until the bucket overflowed with shining blue, purple brown and green claws angrily snapping at each other. At this point we gloated over our fine catch; then we gleefully flung the crayfish back into the water. Tired, happy and dirty, we trudged back across the paddocks, knowing that all too soon the fierce summer sun would bake the mud dry, forcing the yabbies further into the depths of their cool, dark dungeons.

Besides the crayfishing expeditions, I loved to go out with my father on frosty June mornings to inspect the newborn lambs. Bundled up warmly in woolen hat and mittens, I sat silently as the blue utility truck bounced over the red dirt track. Arriving at a sheep camp, we slowly circled the mob, which was still dozing in the semi-darkness. Peering out from my father's brown wizened face, his bright blue eyes darted back and forth between the sleeping animals. Now and then, the urgent, high pitched bleat of a lost lamb broke the stillness of the dawn. Scurrying from one ewe to another, the lamb searched for its mother. When the comforting low reply of "Baa" sounded in the distance, I breathed a sigh of relief. That meant one less meal for the hungry foxes this morning. Suddenly, the truck stopped as my father's practiced eye discerned trouble. We plodded through the long, wet grass towards a ewe that was lying on her side with her legs flailing wildly in the air. Foxes had ripped off her udder to drink the warm, sweet milk, leaving the ewe bleeding in agony. While my father attended to the heartbreaking task of slitting the ewe's throat, I busied myself by trying to find her lamb. Huddled beside a burntout log, the little creature sat shaking, cold and damp with dew. As I carried it home, cradling the orphan in my arms, I pressed my cheek against the soft fuzz of its ear and smelt the musty odor of wet wool. Many times I returned from these trips bearing such a bundle, and each time I felt joyous to have a baby lamb to nurture and care for and, eventually, to profit from.

These and other fond memories I store away to relate to my children and grandchildren. It is very important for a person to have a sense of where she has come from in order to know where she is going. Pride in one's roots creates a feeling of self-worth and sets a level of attainment for each individual. It is also reflected in the way one relates to other people. Some day (before my daughter is too old) I hope to introduce her to the pleasures of living in the Australian bush.

—*Muriel Guba*

1. How does the proposal sentence allow for the development of two parts of the topic in the body paragraphs?
2. How does the introduction serve to involve the reader?
3. What transitions in the opening sentence connect paragraph 2 to paragraph 1? paragraph 3 to paragraph 2?
4. How does the conclusion suit the essay? Does the closing paragraph grow logically from the main idea of the essay?

More Topics to Think About

If you have trouble thinking about a topic for your first essay on a place, try one of these as a starting point

1. wrong place, right time
2. hamburger stand versus a "fancy" restaurant
3. camping in high mountains
4. street-corner lessons
5. your town beach or pool
6. the room in which you met your boyfriend's (or girl friend's) parents
7. your "hangout": bar, candy store, soda shop, street corner
8. an airport or a dock
9. sunrise in the desert
10. a farm you know
11. the supermarket: two experiences
12. a run-down neighborhood
13. your street at night
14. an old-fashioned bookstore
15. a day in court
16. rock dancing in a club
17. the town shopping center
18. the subway car: morning and evening rush hours
19. an electronic-games arcade
20. a hospital room you remember

Prewriting

Timed writing is another technique that you can use to stimulate ideas. First, decide on a topic; then without pausing to correct spelling errors or to ponder an idea, write continuously for five minutes. The object is to fill up a page with complete sentences that are related to the topic. Remember, don't stop writing! If you can't think of anything to write, write "I can't think of anything" as many times as you have to. Let your ideas flow naturally. Look at one student's timed-writing exercise below.

PREWRITING: A TIMED-WRITING EXERCISE

Topic: The IRT Subway

I ride the IRT subway everyday into Manhattan. The people are jammed together like sardines. Everyone reads the morning newspaper, afraid to make eye contact. Some people doze. All types of people ride the trains: drunks, pretty, young secretaries, businessmen in their look-a-like pin-striped suits. I don't know what to write. People look fresh and alert in the morning, but are sweaty and grumpy in the evening. I don't know what to write. I don't know what to write. A man once had a heart attack on the train. His wife was screaming. All the people started to push and shove. I felt trapped. Someone pulled the emergency brake and the train slammed to a stop. The noise was terrible. The air conditioners weren't working; my clothes were soaked with perspiration. I don't know what to write. So many things happen everyday. I hate the trains. They make me feel small and less than human. People get angry at each other for nothing. A guy throws a punch if someone steps on his foot. I remember the black-out in the city. I was trapped in the subway for over three hours. But that was O.K. People were friendly. Everyone helped one another. We shared someone's Coke. Kids played a guitar and we sang songs such as "A Hundred Bottles of Beer." People took turns standing up. The cops did a great job leading us through the black, stinking tunnels to the next station. I was proud to be a New Yorker. Time's almost up. I think I hate most the screeching of the wheels as the train turns and twists under Manhattan. I wish people were more friendly than they are. No one says good morning. They sit in tight little balls as if to say "Don't touch me!"

—Robert Sirola

Step 1.   Reviewing Timed Writing. Answer the questions below based on the preceding paragraph of timed writing.

1. Although many ideas are mentioned in Robert Sirola's timed-writing paragraph, what two ideas might be suitable for an essay on place?
2. What are Robert Sirola's feelings about the IRT subway? Which images do you see most clearly?

Step 2.   Using Timed Writing. Choose some place that you see clearly and about which you have strong feelings. Then write continuously about that place for five minutes. Use your own paper.

Progress Reminders: A Checklist of Questions

As you think about this essay on place and as you plan and write your rough and final drafts, use this questionnaire as a guide.

When you have prepared your manuscript, write *yes* or *no* in the blank spaces. If you have two or more no's, you should attempt another revision.

1. Did I think the topic through carefully? Did I follow some   _____
   prewriting activity that works for me, perhaps *timed writing?*
   (See page 39 and above.)
2. Did I prepare a rough draft and any other needed drafts?   _____
   Did I make changes in language and ideas on my rough
   draft in order to make my ideas clearer?
3. After making changes in content, form, and sentence struc-   _____
   ture, did I check my draft over by proofreading carefully
   for my usual mistakes? Did I check especially for errors in
   punctuation?
4. Do I have a four-paragraph essay, each body paragraph no   _____
   fewer than ten sentences, the introduction and conclusion in
   proportion to the rest of the essay?
5. Am I sure that I understand the way an essay is put   _____
   together, having studied the chart From Paragraph to Essay
   (pages 254–255) and the sample essay written from a
   one-paragraph theme (pages 256–257)?
6. Have I prepared carefully a proposal sentence that will let   _____
   me discuss *two* aspects of my topic?
   This is my proposal sentence: _____

   _____

7. Did I write an introduction *after* my proposal was clear to   _____
   me? Did I follow any of the suggestions in the ideas for
   starting essays on pages 261–264?
8. Have I planned out the essay according to one of the   _____
   suggestions on page 291 or have I used a logical plan of my
   own?
9. Have I introduced the topic of each body paragraph in the   _____
   first sentence? Have I used transitions in those sentences?

   The topics of each paragraph are

   paragraph 2: _____
   paragraph 3: _____

   The transitions are

   paragraph 2: _____
   paragraph 3: _____

10. Have I used lively, colorful language rich in sound, smell,   _____

touch, and images that use color? Do I name people, places, and times of events specifically?

11. Have I used a variety of sentence patterns?　　　　　_____

    a. Do I have several subordinated sentences?　　　_____

    b. Do I have coordinated sentences?　　　　　　_____

    c. Have I used a semicolon correctly?　　　　　_____

    d. Have I opened some sentences with words that end in　_____
      -ing or *-ly?*

    e. Do I have a quotation sentence using someone's exact　_____
      words?

    f. Did I use correctly punctuation such as the colon, the　_____
      dash, the parentheses?

12. Did I try to combine sentences for tight descriptions (as　_____
explained on pages 266–268)?

13. Have I used correctly some of the new vocabulary intro-　_____
duced on pages 248–249 of this chapter?

14. Have I proofread (see pages 42–43) my essay very carefully,　_____
looking for the errors that appear most often on my Theme
Progress Sheet? Did I check for run-on errors, sentence
fragments, spelling mistakes, and especially for the kinds of
punctuation errors explained in this chapter?

15. In rereading my essay, am I satisfied that I have sufficiently　_____
supported the strong feeling described in my proposal
sentence?

16. Have I written a strong title (see pages 109–110)?　　　_____

17. Have I written a concluding paragraph?　　　　　_____

GETTING READER RESPONSE

After you have prepared a draft of your essay, pair up with someone in the class and exchange your work. Read the essay carefully, and then write a paragraph in which you offer advice about what the writer should do to improve the draft. In your critique, try to address these questions, among any others you can think of:

1. Is the topic clearly stated in the proposal?
2. Are the details clear and adequate?
3. Is the logic clear? What parts don't you understand?
4. Do transitions connect the parts of the essay smoothly?
5. Do the introduction and the conclusion hold your interest? Do they suit the writer's purpose?
6. What single comment can you make to help the writer improve the draft?

THE PROFESSIONALS SPEAK

The following selection describes, in rich detail, a walk down a towpath—a path used by animals towing boats along a path or a river—in Maryland.

SOME WORDS TO KNOW BEFORE YOU READ

salvage: something extracted as valuable or useful
piecemeal: piece by piece; gradually
obliteration: being wiped out or destroyed
locks: part of a canal closed off by gates and in which a ship or a boat may be raised or lowered by raising or lowering the water level in that part of the canal.
coterie: a group whose members associate with each other frequently
culvert: a sewer or drain crossing under a road
catwalk: a narrow platform or pathway

A Walk on the Towpath

I was down in Washington around the middle of March, and smelling spring in the air, I gave myself the pleasure of a walk in the country to meet it. The walk I chose was along the towpath of the derelict Chesapeake & Ohio Canal. Situated on the Maryland bank of the Potomac River, the C. & O. Canal extends from the Georgetown section of Washington to a natural passage in the Appalachians at Cumberland, a distance of a hundred and eighty-four miles. The C. & O. is an old canal—one of the oldest lock and mule-drawn-boat canals in the United States. It is also almost the only one of which more than a trace survives. It was begun in 1828, it was completed in 1850, and it remained in operation until shortly after the First World War. The last boats moved through its locks in 1924. It was then stripped of its salvage and abandoned. The depression saved it from piecemeal sale and certain obliteration, and in 1938, through a freak of chance and charity, it was acquired by the federal government. The oldest section of the canal—some twenty wandering miles between the terminus at Georgetown and a point known as Violet's Lock—is now a part of the Washington park system. Its decline has been arrested, and its several locks and lock tenders' houses have all been fully restored. The rest, though reserved as a national monument, has been left to the wild and the weather, and it was there I chose to walk.

I began my walk by car. There is no other ready way to reach the canal once it emerges from the city. A friend with whom I was staying drove me out on his way to work. We passed for a time through an open countryside of rolling pastures and white paddock fences. Then the fences wheeled away and the fields roughened into brush and woods. We came to the head of a rutted lane that wound down the side of a ridge. My friend pulled over and stopped.

"Here you are," he said. "You'll hit the canal just down and around that bend."

I got out. He passed me a lunch that his wife had packed, and a leather-covered flask. I stowed them away in my jacket. "Where am I?" I said.

"Lock 22," he said. "Pennifield's Lock, they call it. Violet's Lock is the next lock up—about three miles from here. Then comes Seneca Creek and Seneca Lock and Aqueduct. That's another mile. After that, it's wilderness all the way to what used to be Edward's Ferry. You won't want to go any farther than that. Edward's Ferry is a good eight miles above Seneca. Maybe more. I'll pick you up there around five." He raised his hand. "Get going," he said, and drove off.

I watched him out of sight, and then headed down the lane. It had rained in the night, and the lane was awash with thin red mud, and puddles stood in the ruts and potholes. It was steep, wet, slippery walking. And cold. Under the trees the morning air had a bite. It felt more like fall than spring. But from what I could see of the sky overhead, the clouds were beginning to break and lift, and there was a hint of a watery sun. I slid down the lane to the foot of the ridge. A coterie of chickadees burst up from a thicket and scattered like a handful of gravel. The lane cut sharply to the left and emerged in a little meadow. At the edge of the meadow stretched the canal. Some fifty feet wide, the color of mud, and flanked by head-high banks, it looked like a sunken road. The towpath followed the farther bank, and beyond it, through a heavy screen of trees, I caught a distant glimpse and murmur of the river. The canal lay as still as a pond. I found a pebble and tossed it in. It sank with a throaty plunk. I guessed the water to be five or six feet deep. About a hundred yards downstream, the canal funneled into a kind of open culvert, which was bridged by a railed catwalk. Facing it, on the towpath side, sat a small white-washed stone house with two stone chimneys and a pitched roof of corrugated iron. That would have been the lock tender's house. The culvert was the lock.

I walked out on the bridge and looked down at the lock. The canal flowed into the lock through a sprung wooden gate just under the bridge. It ran between two narrowly confining walls for about a hundred feet. Then, with a sudden boil and bubble, it broke against another gate, spilled through, and resumed its sluggish course. The walls of the lock were faced with big blocks of rust-red sandstone. Some of the stones were so huge they could have been hoisted into place only with a block and tackle. It was beautiful stone, and it had been beautifully finished and fitted. Time had merely softened it. Here and there along the courses I could even make out the remains of a mason's mark. One device was quite distinct—a double-headed arrow. Another appeared to be two overlapping equilateral triangles. I went on across the bridge to the house. The windows were shuttered and boarded up, and the door was locked. No matter. It was enough just to stand and look at it. It was a lovely house, as beautifully made as the lock, and as firmly designed for function. It gave me a pang to think that there had once been a time when even a lock tender could have so handsome a house. A phoebe called from a sweet-gum tree in the dooryard. Far away, somewhere down by the river, a mourning dove gave an answering sigh. I looked at my watch. It was ten minutes after ten. I started up the towpath.

The sun was still no more than a promise, but the air had lost its chill. It was going to be a spring day after all. The signs of it abounded. Most of the trees that lined the path—sycamore, dogwood, sweet gum, hickory, elm—were coming into bud. Only the oaks still had the wrought-iron look of winter. Some creeping vine—Virginia creeper or honeysuckle—was even in leaf. And everywhere there were birds in sight or sound. Robins hopped and stood and listened at intervals along the way. A woodpecker drummed. A blue jay raced from tree to tree, screaming a wild alarm. There was a flash of cardinal red across the canal. I turned—but too late. It was gone. And so were the lock and the house. They had vanished around a bend. There was nothing behind me but water and woods. It gave me a curious sensation. I felt for the first time completely alone, but I didn't feel lonely. It was an exhilarating loneliness. It was solitude. I took a deep breath and lighted a cigarette. I felt at peace with the world.

—Berton Roueché
What's Left

Step 1.   Exploring the Essay.

1. Which details of sight, sound, color, action, and smell make this scene come alive for you?
2. What similes and metaphors (see pages 134–135) add visual qualities to the essay?
3. In the last paragraph of this excerpt, Roueché names particular trees, vines, and birds. Why? What does the naming add to the essay?
4. How has the writer arranged details here? Which transitions help move the reader from one sentence to another? from one paragraph to another?

REACHING HIGHER

Step 1.   Describing Your Street. In one narrative paragraph (see Chapter 2 for review), give an impression of your street at one particular time during one particular day. Use details of color, sound, smell, and touch as Berton Roueché does in "A Walk on the Towpath." Try to present dialogue as you hear it on your block. Look at the student's sample below. How has Ms. Boardley individualized Tompkins Avenue?

The Watermelon Man

The most pleasant memory of my youth in the slum section of Bedford-Stuyvesant in Brooklyn is the scene of the watermelon man and his crew when he drove into our neighborhood on a summer Saturday. His horse would turn first onto Tompkins Avenue. Straining under the weight of many green-striped melons, the horse chewed on its leather bit and heaved the wagon forward slowly, each step an effort. The straw hat it wore shaded its sad brown eyes. Its skin, a dirty brown and white, rippled with the stress of animal work like waves slapping some muddy shore. Patched leather straps that served as reins ran over its hide and flicked at lazy green flies; the insects buzzed in the air or hovered over the shining sample of melon, its pits winking in the sun like a thousand brown eyes. The driver and his friends too were unforgettable. The hands that held the reins were calloused and coarse, yet these overly large hands with square dirty nails held the reins with an almost regal gesture. The veins and muscles in the hands and arms of this kingly watermelon man looked like the ropes on an old homemade swing. He wore a dirty vest, a torn undershirt, and melon-splattered jeans, emblems of his trade. Suddenly, his sons and nephews in the back of the wagon laughed and grinned and started the chant, "Melon, melon, watermelon." The watermelon man, his grey hair moist with sweat, his wide mouth showing a perfect set of teeth, now took up the melody. Red bandanas and gaudy handkerchiefs waving in slight breezes, these fine men sang and hummed the chant. Finally, a transaction began. A woman from a brownstone window across the street called, "Hey, them melons fresh?"

"Yes, ma'am," cried the figures in the wagon.

"Well bring me up one," she snapped from above. "No, not you ugly. You, yeah, the cute one."

"Anything else you wants 'sides a melon, honey?" replied the "cute" one, winking at his companions in the wagon who heckled and howled at this.

"Just a melon!" screamed the hoarse voice of a man from the same window above.

I, standing in front of Jack's Candy Store on the corner of Madison Street, must have snapped that scene firmly in my mind, for I still can hear the cry of the watermelon man as it struts and dances in my ears: "Melon, melon, watermelon. Git de fresh watermelon. Melon. Melon."

—Twyla Boardley

Step 2. Point of View. In any good description—whether in a poem, a story, or an essay—we are often aware of the narrator's *point of view*. Point of view is the particular angle or perspective from which the story is told. Point of view is influenced by the teller's personality, background, perception, and relationship to the thing or event being described. A successful writer will be able to change point of view to suit a particular piece of writing. Often point of view is expressed by subtle choices on the writer's part: what is noted about the weather, the landscape, the colors of things around; how much is described and what is left out from the description; whether the story is told in the *first person* (where the story is told directly by one of the characters using the pronoun "I") or whether it is told in the *third person* (where the teller is not a participant in the story at all). Try your hand at creating a strong sense of point of view in description. Imagine a small park. Then, in short poems or paragraphs of description, describe the scene from two completely different points of view. First, write from the point of view of a man who has just learned that his son has died in a war. Second, describe the exact same scene (same time of day, weather, place) from the point of view of a person newly in love.

You may want to use either first person or third person, but in either case pay special attention to *what* the narrator describes and how he describes it. Does a grieving father see things any differently from a person who is filled with joy? Will their perceptions change according to their feelings? Try to answer these questions for yourself as you write the descriptions.

For a real challenge, in the first paragraph try not to mention death, the son, or the war; in the second, try not to mention love or the other person. By doing this, you'll find you must really determine point of view by carefully choosing things for description that are most appropriate to the message or mood you are trying to create.

Step 3. Study the picture on page 247, and using what you observe, write an essay that explores the meaning you find in the photograph. Use your best sensory language to portray the scene as you see it: use color, sound, smell, and action.

Step 4. With a camera prepare an essay in snapshots about some place near your home that you can observe often and at different times. Take at least fifteen to twenty pictures, and, selecting five or six of the best, arrange them in some order. Mount them one on a page. For each photograph write first a title (see pages 109–110) and then one sentence that you see as the major point of the picture: try to use in that sentence concrete images to create a scene that matches the photograph itself.

Step 5. The following essay contains thirteen sentence fragments and nine run-on sentences. Correct all the errors directly on this page. Study the run-on and fragment review charts on pages 27–29, 69, and 115.

The Key to Comfort

Rooms often portray a person's character and personality your character is displayed in the way you keep your room in order. Whether it's neat or disorganized. To me my room is the most important room in the house, the way it's kept shows the kind of atmosphere I want it helps me seclude myself when the going gets too rough at home.

The atmosphere I try to have in my room is one of solitude. I think that comes because of the way my room is decorated. Soft walls in an off-white color. Nothing but my mirror hanging on the walls. A high dark brown dresser. The desk in the far corner is walnut on the top books stand in piles. Which I keep very neat and orderly. The stereo set and my collection of albums and tapes are in the far corner. Next to my amorphous black leather reclining chair. My room is the only room in the house that is so relaxing.

Because the surroundings are so restful. I found that it served as an important place one February evening last year. When my house was filled with guests from a card party my mother was having. I had my final examination in history the next day, I knew if I did not find a quiet place to study I would fail. I excused myself from the incessant noise of my mother's guests and determined to get peace and quiet. Marched upstairs to my room. Upon opening the door to my room. I had almost given up hope. There was still so much noise. Loud roars of laughter. People chattering. Dimes and nickels clinking on the table. I quickly slammed the door with me inside the room suddenly the noise was outside, I was trapped in a welcome silence. Because of the solitude in my room I was able to study, I passed the final examination.

Rooms help people relax and find quiet. And the appearance of a room sets the scene for relaxation. If more people would set aside a certain amount of time each day to solve their problems in a serene room of their choice. The mental pressures that many Americans suffer might disappear. Most people try to relax in an atmosphere that is more distracting than peaceful, to me, the quiet well-decorated, well-kept room is the key to comfort.

Step 6. A Collage on a Place. Make a collage to characterize some important feeling or impression that you have about some place you know well. Afterward, see if the people in your class can determine (without knowing in advance) what place you are portraying and what your impression of the place is.

CHAPTER 7

AN ESSAY ON PROCESS:
You the Expert

INTRODUCTION TO PROCESS ANALYSIS

One of the major reasons for writing is to explain something. And perhaps no explanations are more demanding in terms of clear, precise language than those that give directions.

Of course, each of us has a well of skills and talents that we can draw on to perform tasks knowledgeably and with our own special knack. Chores around the house, activities you do for fun in your spare time, part-time employment (or the full-time work)—all these give you skill in how to perform some process. You may know how to clean the garage quickly, how to make sandwiches at a crowded lunch counter, how to run a busy gas station when the boss leaves early. Even if you have never worked in your life, you still have some special interest or ability that someone else could learn from you. Or maybe you would like to *learn* how to do something or how something works so that you can show someone else how to do it.

This theme assignment asks you for a *process analysis*. When you analyze something, you break it down into parts. When you analyze a process, you explain the various steps required to carry it out successfully. Even though the process you want to explain is one you know pretty well, *writing* about it is a special challenge. Activities on the following pages will help you meet that challenge.

VOCABULARY

Step 1. Words for Explaining Processes. The words below may be helpful as you write an essay that explains a process. In the blank spaces, and using a dictionary if you need one, write definitions for these words:

1. sequential _____
2. routine _____
3. prior _____
4. outcome _____
5. subsequent _____
6. cyclical _____
7. adjacent _____
8. approximate _____
9. apparatus _____
10. synthesize _____

Step 2.   Applying Definitions. In the blank spaces below, write from the above list the word that best suits each meaning.

1. coming before _____
2. consequence _____
3. combine separate elements to produce something _____
4. almost exactly _____
5. lying next to _____
6. coming afterward in time or order _____
7. equipment used to perform a task _____
8. following an orderly arrangement _____
9. a repeated way of doing something _____
10. happening at regularly repeated time intervals _____

BUILDING COMPOSITION SKILLS

Step 1.   What Do You Know? Each of us has enough knowledge about (or enough interest in to find out about) procedures that we can explain to others. On this list of items put a check (✔) next to those you know well enough by firsthand experience to give instructions that someone else could follow. Put an X next to any process you might be interested enough in to investigate so that you could understand it sufficiently to explain to others. Discuss your choices with the class.

_____ 1. how to lose weight
_____ 2. how nuclear power works
_____ 3. how to groom a horse
_____ 4. how to roll a cigarette
_____ 5. how windmills produce electrical current
_____ 6. how to make a grilled cheese sandwich
_____ 7. how to write a complaint letter
_____ 8. how to meet a woman (or man) you like but don't know
_____ 9. how to adopt a child in your city
_____ 10. how to clean a fish

Step 2.   Giving and Following Directions: An Experiment. To understand some of the conditions required for explaining a process that someone else should be able to reproduce, ask someone in the class to give aloud directions he or she thinks someone can follow easily. Ask another person to follow directions as the first person explains. The person giving directions should bring to class any necessary equipment.

   To make this experiment work, whoever explains the process should face one of the side walls or the back wall as the other volunteer, unseen by the first but visible to the rest of the class, follows instructions. The person following directions must do so *exactly* without taking any steps whatsoever unless specifically instructed to.

Here are some possible processes volunteers might like to explain or to follow:

1. how to cover a book
2. how to make a paper airplane
3. how to file your nails
4. how to make a peanut-butter sandwich
5. how to relax your neck muscles

As the people in the class watch the joint performance, they should be prepared to evaluate the situation they are observing. Step 3 below will focus on that evaluation.

Step 3. Explaining Processes: Seeing the Problems. If your class is like most others, you have just observed (if you have followed Step 1 according to directions) an exercise in frustration. Even with the simplest of procedures, because there is so much room for misunderstanding, steps must be simply and clearly explained. How would you evaluate the two volunteers? What successes could you point to? When things went wrong, *why* did they go wrong? Use the checklist below by circling your answer to judge the scene you witnessed. (On the checklist, the *instructor* is the person who explained the process; the *performer* is the person who tried to duplicate it.) Discuss your responses with the class.

1. The instructor did not give enough informa-   *yes*   *no*   *unsure*
   tion.
2. The instructor's language was too complicat-   *yes*   *no*   *unsure*
   ed.
3. The instructor assumed that the performer   *yes*   *no*   *unsure*
   knew more about the process than he or she
   actually did.
4. The instructor did not have all the materials   *yes*   *no*   *unsure*
   that were needed to explain the process
   clearly.
5. The instructor either did not explain steps in   *yes*   *no*   *unsure*
   the right sequence or did not give all the
   steps in the sequence.

Including and Arranging Details

In order to write about a process clearly—whether you are giving directions someone can follow or you are giving information about how to do or to make something—you have to include all the important details someone would need to understand what you are trying to explain.

Details in a process essay include, first, the major steps in the procedure you are writing about. People who wanted to follow your directions themselves would need to have every step included. On the other hand, you would not have to offer information with such completeness if you were simply explaining a process readers do not intend to carry out. An essay on how to make an omelet would demand full explanations; an essay on how eggs are produced and gathered could, for most readers, rely more upon general outlines and less upon absolutely complete detail.

Not only must you include all the appropriate steps in the process, but also you must mention any materials involved and any descriptive information that will instruct your readers and will hold their interest. Concrete sensory language (see pages 5–7) can add life to what otherwise might be a boring series of "do this," "do that" instructions. Also, telling readers *why* to perform a certain step keeps their attention with valuable information.

You will discover once you decide which steps to include that arranging details presents no real problems. Usually, a process paper demands a *chronological* arrangement of materials (see pages 58–60). Readers have to know what to do first in time, what to do next, and what to do after that. However, you sometimes have other options.

In explaining how to care for puppies, for example, you might offer the elements of the process in their order of *importance* (pages 94–96)—least important element first, most important element last. Or, similarly, you might first discuss the simplest element to consider in caring for puppies; and you could build to the most difficult element. Finally, you might want to tell the details of the process in order of location—that is from one point in space to another. You could tell how to care first for the puppies' eyes, then the ears, then the mouth, the digestion, the coat, the limbs and feet. Such an order is called *spatial*.

For the most part, though, a simple ordering of steps and details by chronology works best.

Read the paragraph below in which a student gives directions on how to perform a process he expects people to duplicate. Think about the steps he includes and the kinds of details he offers in order to hold the readers' interest.

An Egg Cream Delight

Anyone who has worked as a soda jerk in a New York fountain shop knows that making and drinking an egg cream take special skill. To begin select a tall, clear glass; let no colors or fancy designs hide the delicious drink that will soon fill the container. Press down three or four times on the silver squirter marked *chocolate* so that dark, sticky syrup slips down the sides of the glass to the bottom. This leaves a layer of brown about an inch and a half thick (about two heaping teaspoonfuls for the egg cream maker at home). Be careful not to do anything else until any chocolate clinging to the sides of the glass oozes its way down. Once that happens, carefully add an amount of cold milk that is twice as much as the chocolate. Now the heavy band of brown sits comfortably under a layer of white, and by taking a breath at this point, the person awaiting the drink knows how close joy really is! After this comes the most difficult stage: adding the carbonated water. Only a tiny trickle of soda water should fizz into the glass at a time so that just a small, quiet hiss sounds at the counter. (You people at home, unless you have seltzer water in dark green bottles with siphons, will have to suffer with a second-rate egg cream; popular brands of club sodas do not do the job right.) Now stir the three liquids very gently with a metal spoon that has a long handle. As the stirring continues slowly, a foamy white layer rises to the top with the thickness of cream or beaten egg whites. That is probably the reason for the name *egg cream*, even though no eggs or cream are in the drink. Beneath this snowy top sits a well-mixed liquid the color of cocoa. Now remove the silver spoon and lick it to see if the drink is too sweet: a bit more soda water always fits in the glass. But do not add any more syrup or milk or the whole drink is ruined. The last step is to raise the glass to the lips and drink so that an equal amount of foam and liquid fills the mouth at the same time. Too much foam at the bottom after the drink disappears means the drinker has failed. But what a wonderful failure. Who will stop him from trying another time?

—*Martin Berglund*

Step 1.   Seeing Steps in the Process. Answer the questions below about "An Egg Cream Delight." Use separate paper.

1. Name the various steps in the process. Why has Martin Berglund given such complete directions?
2. What are the materials required to follow these directions? Has the writer left any out?
3. What sensory details do you find most clear and vivid? What effect do the details have in holding your interest?
4. What order does the writer choose in which to present his information? Why has he chosen that method of organization?

Step 2.   An Inventory of Materials. In explanations of processes writers must be careful to name all the materials that may be demanded for the task. Below each of the following processes, list all the equipment or material someone who wanted to duplicate the process would need.

1. repotting a houseplant

_____

_____

_____

_____

2. making scrambled eggs

_____

_____

_____

_____

_____

3. cleaning a window

_____

_____

_____

_____

4. making a gin and tonic

_____

_____

_____

_____

Step 3.   Listing Steps. For any *one* of the following processes, list on the blank lines below all the steps you think it would be important to mention in an essay that attempted to explain the process.

1. how to baby-sit
2. how to prepare dinner in twenty minutes
3. how to register for courses
4. how to change a tire
5. how to read a poem
6. how to pick strawberries
7. how to plan a wedding
8. how to hunt deer
9. how to fail a test
10. how to survive rush hour

Process: _____

_____

_____

_____

_____

_____

_____

_____

Step 4. Deciding on an Order. Which method of arrangement would you use to explain the following processes? Tell in a brief sentence the reasons for your choice.

1. how to get from your house to the nearest grocery store _____

_____

_____

2. how to eat with chopsticks _____

_____

3. how to form your own band _____

_____

4. how the pollution problem grew out of hand in your town _____

_____

5. how to avoid being caught for not having an assignment _____

_____

6. how to make zucchini bread _____

_____

7. how to have a good complexion _____

_____

8. how it is possible to eat for a whole day on $1 _____

_____

Step 5. Checking a Process through Research. In order to explain a process carefully, you may need to rely on sources outside your own experiences. For the following topics—with the help of card catalogs, the *Reader's Guide* (see pages 491–492), and your school librarian—write the names of three books or magazine articles that you could use in order to check the steps in the processes named below.

1. how a robot works

   a. _____

b. _____

c. _____

2. how Freud used hypnosis

a. _____

b. _____

c. _____

3. how to improve your reading speed

a. _____

b. _____

c. _____

4. how bridges are designed

a. _____

b. _____

c. _____

5. how to grow vegetables organically

a. _____

b. _____

c. _____

Audience

Whenever you speak to people—whether they are friends, acquaintances, teachers, fellow workers—you adjust your comments and your language to the situation in which you find yourself. What you sense about the people you are talking to tells you, first, just what topics will interest them. It also tells you how much you must say to be understood, what kinds of words to use, how strongly to make your points. Discussing rock music with your friends who know and love it demands one kind of vocabulary, one kind of talking style; discussing rock music with a neighbor or a teacher who knows little about it demands quite another.

So when you speak, you rely on an already keen sense of audience—the people reacting to your ideas.

Good writers, too, need to have a strong sense of audience. Of course, most of your writing at school is specifically for your instructors or for other people in the class. But it's not a good idea to write expressly and exclusively for them. You want to aim for a more general audience, for a wider range of readers. These would be people smart enough to understand what you are writing about without having to be specialists in your topic. All writers ask themselves as part of their prewriting activity, "Who do I want to read this? Who am I writing this for?" The clearer the answer to those questions, the easier it is for a writer to pitch language to readers so that they come away with exactly what the writer wants them to have.

Although a sense of audience is important in any written work, an essay on process demands from writers a very precise idea of whom they are writing for. Just to take one obvious example, you would use completely different approaches if you wrote to explain how to make a chocolate cake to a class of newlyweds or to a group of master bakers.

Knowing your audience is critical. The box below suggests questions to ask yourself in order to identify the precise audience you are writing for in your process paper.

IDENTIFYING AUDIENCE: QUESTIONS TO ASK FOR THE PROCESS THEME

1. Who am I trying to explain the process to?
2. Will my readers know the technical vocabulary I may have to use? Or, will I have to define new or difficult terms?
3. Do I expect my readers to be able to perform the process I am writing about? If so, what steps can I assume that they already know? (Be careful. It's easy to assume that readers know more than they actually do. Without talking down to your audience, it's always best—when in doubt—to think of your readers as having almost *no* knowledge of your subject.)
4. What purpose do my readers have in reading my essay? Do they want only to be informed, or do they expect also to be amused or inspired or moved to action?

Step 1. Seeing Different Audiences. For each of the following processes, name two or three different kinds of audiences that might be interested in reading about the process. Discuss your responses with the class. What demands would each type of audience place upon the writer? Look at the example.

Process

1. how to fix flat tires on bicycles

2. how to tell funny jokes

Kinds of Audiences

a. *young teenagers* _____

b. *bicycle repair shop owners* _____

c. *people who sell tires to bicycle*

   manufacturers _____

_____

_____

_____

3. how to keep roses healthy   _____
                                    _____
                                    _____
                                    _____

4. how to save a drowning person   _____
                                    _____
                                    _____
                                    _____

5. how to use a power saw   _____
                                    _____
                                    _____
                                    _____

6. how to write an essay   _____
                                    _____
                                    _____
                                    _____

Step 2.   Assessing Vocabulary. Column I below names a process. Column II names the readers the writer is aiming for. Column III offers several technical words required in the explanation. Considering the process and its intended audience, check only those terms you think the writer would have to define in his or her essay (or would have to replace with simpler words). Defend your choices. Look at the example.

I *Process*	*II* *Intended Audience*	*III* *Vocabulary*
1. how to stir-fry Chinese vegetables	beginning cooks	✔bok choy ✔wok ✔soy sauce tablespoon ✔peanut oil
2. how to prevent nuclear accidents	nuclear power plant managers	reactor fission geiger counter radioactivity

3. how to relax through yoga	an out-of-shape business executive	meditation tension lotus position complete breath
4. how to light a wood stove	a ski-resort vacationer from the city	seasoned hardwood flue chimney kindling asbestos mitt
5. how to register for classes in college	entering college students	prerequisites program bursar registrar baccalaureate
6. how to paint a room	new homeowner	roller brush latex spackle scraper

Essay Transitions

Using transitions effectively in an essay helps you connect your paragraphs smoothly. The following essay transition signboards suggest key places for transitions. Before you examine the charts, review pages 253–258 on the parts of the essay.

Review Hints: Remembering the Proposal Sentence

1. It must tell the reader the purpose of the essay.
2. It should allow you to discuss two aspects of your topic. It can state both aspects quite specifically, or it can merely suggest what these aspects are.
3. It is conveniently placed as the last sentence of the introduction.

Hint
See pages 258–261 for more about proposal sentences.

ESSAY TRANSITION SIGNBOARD I: FIRST SENTENCE OF PARAGRAPH 2

What to Do	*Why*

1. Tell what part of the proposal you want to discuss in paragraph 2 by
   a. repeating one of the two points you want to write about if you have mentioned them clearly in your proposal

   OR

   b. stating (for the first time) the point you want to write about, a point based upon the suggestion made in the proposal.

> These steps help show your reader that you are moving logically from your proposal sentence to the first part of your topic.

2. Use transition words (pages 14–15, pages 96–100, pages 137–139) to help you connect the opening sentence of this paragraph with the proposal.

> This makes the move from the proposal to the next paragraph smooth and not too sudden.

Step 1. Analyzing Transitions in Paragraph 2. Column I states a proposal. Decide whether or not you think the sentence in Column II would be effective as the opening sentence of the second paragraph, and tell why in Column III. Base your ideas on Essay Transition Signboard I.

I	*II*	*III*
1. Clipping the wings of a pet parakeet requires great caution.	You must first spend time in calming the bird so it feels relaxed.	_____ _____ _____ _____
2. Fall foliage season in Vermont is extremely important to the state's economy.	From the top of Mount Equinox, you can see five states.	_____ _____ _____
3. Taking photographs can increase one's visual awareness.	The rodeo in Cheyenne is an amazing sight!	_____ _____ _____ _____

| 4. My father has always been a friend to me. | As a boy my main love was for sports, especially baseball, and my father helped me learn the game. | _____
_____
_____
_____ |

Step 2. More on Paragraph 2 Transitions. Comment on the opening sentence of paragraph 2 in the student essays on pages 292–296.

Step 3. Your Own Opener for Paragraph 2. For any three proposals in Step 1, pages 259–260, write your own opening sentence for the second paragraph of an essay.

ESSAY TRANSITION SIGNBOARD II: FIRST SENTENCE OF PARAGRAPH 3

What to Do

1. Refer to the main idea of the previous paragraph (paragraph 2)

    OR

    refer to the last event, instance, or proof you discussed in paragraph 2.
2. Tell what part of the proposal you intend to discuss in the paragraph by
    a. repeating the second aspect if you have mentioned it in the proposal, or
    b. stating for the first time—based upon the suggestion you made in the proposal—the part of the topic you want to discuss in paragraph 3.

Why

to show that paragraph 3 grows logically from paragraph 2

    OR

to tie together the two body paragraphs, both of which develop your proposal

to remind the reader of the whole topic of the essay

to let the reader know exactly what paragraph 3 will contain

to remind you, the writer, to stick to the topic that you stated in the proposal

> *Hint* 1. Coordination (pages 19–20) and subordination (pages 100–109) are especially effective in opening sentences of paragraph 3.
> 2. Use transitional expressions (pages 14–15, pages 96–100, and pages 137–139) as needed.

Step 4. Openers for Paragraph 3. Read the opening sentence of paragraph 3 in each of the essays on pages 292–296. Which part of the sentence refers to the previous paragraph? Which part announces the topic of the paragraph to follow?

Step 5. Opening Sentences for Paragraphs 2 and 3. Each of the following sentences is a proposal sentence for an essay. In the spaces below, write for paragraphs 2 and 3 opening sentences that would develop logically from the proposal.

1. Retirement does not need to be a boring or purposeless time of life.

   paragraph 2: _____

   paragraph 3: _____

2. While refinishing furniture, Debbie learned how to relax after a hard day's work.

   paragraph 2: _____

   paragraph 3: _____

3. My friend Joyce really knows how to prepare an elaborate dinner without too much work.

   paragraph 2: _____

   paragraph 3: _____

4. Needless to say, I will never visit Topeka again!

   paragraph 2: _____

   paragraph 3: _____

ESSAY TRANSITION SIGNBOARD III: FIRST SENTENCE OF THE CONCLUSION

What to Do	*Why*
1. Make some reference to the main idea of the previous paragraph (paragraph 3), or refer back to the last event, instance, or proof you discussed in paragraph 3.	to show that paragraph 4 grows logically from paragraph 3 to tie paragraph 3 more closely to the conclusion you will start to develop
2. Refer to something you wrote in the introduction (see pages 261–266).	to remind the reader about how your whole idea started
a. Pick up the idea of the proposal.	
b. Pick up a point from the background material you may have given.	to help you begin writing the conclusion, which may be based upon one of the suggestions you made in the introduction
c. Repeat why you felt your subject was important.	
d. Refer to any questions you may have asked.	
e. Refer to any quotation you may have used.	to help you make sure that the introduction is an important part of your essay
f. Pick up the idea of the story you may have told in the introduction.	
g. Refer to your title.	

Step 6. **First Sentence in Conclusion.** Read and discuss the opening sentence of the conclusion in each of the essays named below.

1. "The Gloom Room" pages 256–257
2. "Practice in the High School Gym," page 294
3. "Memories of the Australian Bush," pages 259–296

Expanding Sentences and Changing Word Order

The words in the chart below all help show relationships between ideas and objects in sentences. Each word can introduce a word group that tells where, when, or how things happen.

WORDS THAT SHOW WHERE, WHEN, AND HOW (PREPOSITIONS)			
about	except	within	between
by	under	beside	below
beneath	onto	since	upon
inside	at	as to	by means of
above	across	toward	through
for	on	at	along with
over	near	beyond	because of
outside	into	up	by way of
along	after	before	on account of
among	to	like	in spite of
of	with	below	in front of

In this sentence:

An old man hobbled away.

notice how the word groups in italics expand its meaning.

A

An old man hobbled away *down the street.* The words *down the street* show *where* the old man hobbled.

An old man hobbled away *on shaking legs.* The words *on shaking legs* tell *how* he hobbled.

An old man hobbled away *before noon.* The words *before noon* tell *when* he hobbled.

Using word groups that tell *where, when,* or *how* in various sentence positions helps you vary your sentences. You can shift the word group from the end to the beginning of the sentence.

B

Down the street an old man hobbled away.

On shaking legs an old man hobbled away.

Before noon an old man hobbled away.

You can also use the word group *within* the sentence.

C

An old man *down the street* hobbled away.

An old man *on shaking legs* hobbled away.

An old man *before noon* hobbled away.

You can use two or more word groups to expand meaning even further.

D

Down the street an old man hobbled away *on shaking legs.*

Before noon an old man *on shaking legs* hobbled away *down the street.*

Of course, you cannot simply insert the word group anywhere you'd like to in the sentence. It might not make sense, or it might not sound right to you. Also, by shifting a word group you might be changing even very slightly the meaning you had intended. For example, the first sentence in A, above, says that the man hobbled down the street. In C, the first sentence says that the man was already down the street when he hobbled away. In B, you could argue that either of those two meanings worked in the first sentence. The differences are minor, certainly; but there are differences.

Step 1. Expanding Sentences. Select word groups from among the following, and use them to expand the sentences below sensibly. Use the word groups in sentence positions that you think work best for the intended meaning. Look at the example.

behind the mountain tops	in great pain
in the restaurant	at once
along the highway	with a bright smile
with great passion	by five o'clock
in a sad voice	by means of courage

1. The sky glowed brilliant reds, oranges, and purples.
   By five o'clock the sky glowed brilliant reds, oranges, and purples behind the mountaintops.

2. Two actors caused a noisy commotion.

   _____

3. Suddenly he spoke.

   _____

4. She leaped overboard and saved the crying infant.

_____

5. Gabriela strained the last hundred yards of the marathon.

_____

6. A frightening boom echoed.

_____

7. Rumbling noisily, a long black train raced away.

_____

Step 2. Changing Word Order. Using the expanded sentences you wrote in Step 1 above, rewrite them so that you shift the word group that tells *where, when,* or *how* to different sentence positions. Try for at least two new sentences for each. Look at the example. Use your own paper.

Behind the mountaintops the sky glowed brilliant reds, oranges, and purples by five o'clock.

By five o'clock behind the mountaintops the sky glowed brilliant reds, oranges, and purples.

SOLVING PROBLEMS IN WRITING

Showing Possession

a. It is the *car of the man.*
b. It is the *car belonging to the man.*
c. It is the *man's car.*

In sentence *a,* the car belongs to the man. Ownership is shown with the words *of the man.* The car is owned. The man owns it.

In sentence *b,* the car belongs to the man. Ownership is shown with the words *belonging to the man.* The car is owned. The man owns it.

In sentence *c,* the car belongs to the man. Ownership is shown by using an apostrophe *s ('s)* after the word that tells who owns the thing. The car is still being owned. The man still owns it. But in this sentence the owner is named *before* the thing that he owns. And the only way we know the owner is through the apostrophe *s.*

[owner]

It is the man's car.

[thing owned]

Sentence *a* sounds clumsy and unnatural. You would rarely say or write such a sentence. Sentence *b* is more natural, but it is wordy.

Sentence *c* is the most convenient and most usual way of indicating ownership. When we speak of *possession,* it is usually this form of showing ownership that we mean. And, because of the misunderstood apostrophe, this method often causes many difficulties.

As you practice with possession, keep in mind that ownership involves two separate ideas.

1. Somebody or something is the owner. That word will contain an apostrophe.
2. Somebody or something is being owned. That word usually comes soon after the word with the apostrophe.

Step 1. Owner and Owned. In each sentence below, circle the word that indicates who or what owns or possesses something. Put an X over the word that shows what (or who) is being owned.

Example

         X   X

The (child's) toy fell into (Mother's) waiting arms.

1. Aunt Linda's chair collapsed in front of a neighbor's eyes.
2. Dr. Asher's patients asked whether the nurse was a friend's sister.
3. Fortunately, Amy's Pinto ran out of gas just a few hundred yards from a relative's store.
4. Suzanne's only birthday wish was that Jorge's mother would leave them alone.
5. She knew that Warren's patience had worn thin when he started screaming at the child's dog.

HOW NOT TO USE APOSTROPHES

Do not use apostrophes to show plurals. Form plurals by adding *-s* or *-es*, or by any one of the special methods explained on pages 118–121.

For example, a familiar error is one like this:

The store sells pencil's and paper's.

If an apostrophe *s* is used at the end of a word, it means that the word owns something. What, according to the sentence, do the pencil and the paper possess? Nothing belongs to either of the two words written with apostrophes. The student who wrote the sentence wants only to indicate more than one pencil and more than one paper, so the sentence should be:

The store sells pencils and papers.

There is a minor exception, one case in which you do use an apostrophe to show plural. When you write numbers, letters, or symbols and you need to pluralize them, you use an apostrophe. (For example: "The word *membership* has two *m's.*") However, this use is rare enough for you not to worry about but to remember instead that apostrophes do *not* usually indicate plurals.

Step 2. Spotting Wrong Possession. Correct any incorrect use of possession in each of these sentences by changing the word to its proper plural form.

1. It cost's too much to buy doll's at toy store's these day's.
2. The morning's dampness reminded Barbara of the soggy vacation's she had spent at Joe's cottage in the Oregon hill's.
3. The guitarist's instrument's had not arrived although there were thousand's of fan's screaming for the band's first number.
4. In order to make Judy's vegetarian recipe's, it is best to buy your food fresh at a farmer's roadside stand.
5. The heroe's of the movie had children's view's of life's problems'.
6. Her mother's friend liked the two film's about a child's love for water sports'.

HOW TO FORM POSSESSIVES: TWO SIMPLE REMINDERS

REMINDER I FOR POSSESSION
If the word that names the owner *does not* end in *s*, add an apostrophe *s* (*'s*)

girl   The girl's dress ripped.

[apostrophe *s*   [This is owned by the *girl*.]
added to
girl]

senator The senator's campaign failed.

[apostrophe *s*   [This is owned by the senator.]
added to *senator*]

   Hint for Reminder I: It does not matter if the word is plural or singular. If the word does not end in *s*, add an apostrophe *s*.

[This word is plural, ——→ *women* The women's cars crashed.
even though it does
not end in *s*]   [apostrophe *s*   [These are owned
added to women] by the women.]

Step 3. Possession Reminder I in Sentences. Change the words below so that they indicate ownership. Then write your own brief sentence to use the word correctly.

Example
city   *city's*   *The city's roads are crowded on weekend mornings.*

1. Mr. Chan ———————— ————————————————————

2. medium ———————— ————————————————————

3. man ———————— ————————————————————

4. media ———————— ————————————————————

5. men ———————— ————————————————————

REMINDER II FOR POSSESSION

If the word that names the owner *does* end in *s*, add only an apostrophe (').

boys   The boys' bicycles broke.

[an apostrophe   [These are owned
added to *boys*]   by the boys.]

governors   The governors' meeting ended when the leader fainted.

[an apostrophe'   [This is owned by
added to   the *governors*.]
governors]

Hint for Reminder II: It does not matter if the word is plural or singular. If the word ends in *s*, add only an apostrophe.

[This word is singular: ——→*Doris*   Doris' trip was canceled.
it ends in *s*]

[apostrophe   [This is owned
added to   by Doris.]
Doris]

See page 278 for an alternate method of showing possession for *names* that end in *s*.

Step 4.   Possession Reminder II in Sentences. Add apostrophes to the words below so that they indicate ownership. Then write your own brief sentence to use the word correctly.

Example
nurses   *nurses'*   *The nurses' caps blew off.*

1. mosquitoes   _____   _____

2. Mrs. Bernas   _____   _____

3. animals   _____   _____

4. Nikos   _____   _____

5. cities   _____   _____

FOUR SPECIAL CASES WITH POSSESSION

I. Compound Words or Word Combinations: Only the last word shows possession.

brother-in-law   My brother-in-law's cat sleeps all day.

[apostrophe *s* to show possession]

A compound word is a combination of words that name one thing.

(continued on next page)

FOUR SPECIAL CASES WITH POSSESSION (continued)

secretary of state   A secretary of state's position is important.

[apostrophe *s* to
show possession]

II. *Time and Money Words:* Words that indicate time values, in certain uses, are said to show ownership.

hour   One hour's rest is too much.

[apostrophe *s* added
to *hour* (Reminder I)]

[This word is thought of as
"possessing" the rest.]

minutes   Five minutes' rest is all you need.

[apostrophe added
to *minutes* (Reminder II)]

Words that indicate money value, in certain uses, are said to show ownership.

[apostrophe *s* added
to *quarter* (Reminder I)]

quarter   A quarter's worth of apples will not feed many children.

[This word is thought of as
"possessing" the worth.]———

dollars   He bought three dollars' worth of chocolate.

[apostrophe added to
dollars (Reminder II)]

III. *Two People as Owners:* When both people are thought to be equal owners of the same thing, only the last word shows possession.

McGraw-Hill's textbooks
Standard & Poor's Index

If two people own things individually, show possession for both words.

Harry's and Jerome's cars crashed.

IV. *Pronouns and Ownership:* Pronouns never have apostrophes to show possession.

his book	NOT	*his'* book
That is *hers.*	NOT	*hers'* or *her's*
The pen is *yours.*	NOT	*yours'* or *your's*
Those are *ours.*	NOT	*ours'* or *our's*
Is it *theirs?*	NOT	*theirs'* or *their's*
The cat hurt *its* paw.	NOT	*it's* or *its'*

Hint: Look at the mirror words, pages 23–27.

Step 5. Practice with Special Possessives. Underline the correct words in the parentheses.

1. In an (hour's, hours') time, (Carlos' and Maria's, Carlos and Maria's) house will be up for sale, but (their's, theirs) is not an attractive place.
2. The (editor in chief, editor in chiefs, editor in chief's) comment was, "In three (days, day's, days') time this office will no longer be (mine, mines, mine's)."
3. Generally the (Grand Union's, Grand Union) dairy prices are slightly higher than (its, it's) competitors.
4. When I was a child, we used to go to (Anna and Pop's, Anna's and Pop's) store to buy three (cent's, cents) worth of candy.
5. Not two (months, month's, months') time had elapsed, and the public was demanding the (secretary of interior's, secretary of interiors') resignation.
6. When (Nora and Aldo, Nora's and Aldo's, Nora and Aldo's) car slowed, they put in two (dollars, dollar's, dollars') worth of gasoline.

IF YOU THINK A WORD NEEDS AN APOSTROPHE BECAUSE IT SHOWS POSSESSION

1. See if you can figure out what is being owned.
2. See if the word in which you want to use an apostrophe is the owner of something. Usually, the thing owned appears in the sentence soon after the owner.

   Exceptions
   It is David's.
   We ate at Carl's.

   Here the thing owned is not specifically mentioned, but understood.
   David's (book)
   Carl's (house)
3. Sometimes the owner is more than one. Make sure the word shows plural with the right ending.
   a. If the word does not end in *s,* add an apostrophe *s.*
   b. If the word does end in *s,* add only an apostrophe.

   Examples
   a. You want to show that a boy owns books. The word *boy* does not end in *s.* The possessive is shown this way:

   the *boy's* books
         [Add apostrophe *s.*]
   b. You want to show that many boys are the owners of books. The word *boys* ends in *s.* The possessive is shown this way:

   the boys' books
           [Add apostrophe after *s.*]

Step 6. Adding Possessive Endings. In the blanks at the ends of the words below, add *s,* *'s,* or simply an apostrophe (') so that the sentence is correct. For some words you need to add nothing.

1. Two women_____ stood on the bridge as a man_____ bicycle swerved into a post, denting it_____ surface.
2. The typewriters_____ in Richard Yee_____ office are much newer than your_____.
3. Shirley_____ and Jesus_____ children brought toy_____ to school; mine_____ brought only a book and two pen_____.
4. Because the electric company_____ rate_____ are increasing, many elderly people will not be able to heat their_____ homes this winter.
5. It is neither Carlos_____ or Antoinette_____ fault that their_____ parents_____ are getting divorced.
6. Rodney Dangerfield_____ comedy routine is largely based on joke_____ made at his_____ wife_____ expense.

Step 7. Possession Review. Add apostrophes wherever needed in the sentences below. Numbers in parentheses tell how many apostrophes to use.

1. Its wise to buy a dollars worth of doughnuts. (2)
2. The boss new secretary wanted two weeks pay in advance for Christmas shopping. (2)
3. "The childs books and pens are not expensive, but no one is interested in buying yours," he said. (1)
4. Charlie and Muriels daughters wedding was a big hit with all the relatives. (2)
5. If its yours take it in a minutes time. (2)
6. My sister-in-laws father works at Davis and Hargoods Department Store. (2)
7. Yeats poems excited even the students who claimed their interests were only in computers. (1)
8. Our neighbors houses were all damaged by the winds of the last storm. (1)
9. Phyllis cat lost its bell so if youre able to get her another, her mother will pay you five dollars. (2)
10. Three hours work a week is no womans idea of full employment. (2)
11. Mothers-in-laws advice often makes their sons wives best intentions seem selfish. (3)

WRITING THE PROCESS ESSAY

ASSIGNMENT: Select some process that you can command, and explain it in a clear essay that takes into account the principles you have been exploring in this chapter.

Learning from Other Students

Step 1. Two "How-to" Essays. Read the following samples by students, and answer the questions that follow their essays.

Ironing for Food

I have never doubted the usefulness of an iron. It presses crisp pleats into my jeans and eliminates networks of tiny wrinkles in blouses I have jammed into my closet. Since coming to Penn State, however, I found that an iron is not only useful as a piece of laundry equipment but also as a fantastic cooking appliance for a dormitory room. University regulations prohibit the use of hot plates, ovens, or grills. So, when one of my cravings aroused me, I decided to experiment with my iron. Since that time I have become an expert at "iron cooking," my specialty being toasted cheese sandwiches.

When the urge for one of them strikes me, I convert my dorm room into a kitchen. I dig through the shoes and boxes at the bottom of my closet and resurrect my iron. Since I do not own a portable ironing board, I improvise. I drag my footlocker out from under my bed and place it in the center of the floor. My white bath towel serves as the cover. At the bathroom sink I fill the steam chamber of the iron with water. Examining the battered cord for exposed wires, I plug it into the outlet closest to my makeshift ironing board and turn the small black dial on the handle to the wool setting. Laying the iron down on the towel to heat, I gather ingredients for my sandwich. From our refrigerator I collect the cheese slices, bread, and pats of butter that my roommate and I smuggled out of Redifer Dining Hall. I grab a knife and a roll of aluminum foil out of my bolster cupboard and spread the supplies out on my desk.

Preliminary preparations over, I concoct my special toasted cheese sandwich. I select two slices of bread, and butter both sides of them lightly, careful not to tear holes in the bread with the knife. Melted cheese drips out of any holes in the finished sandwich and makes a gooey mess. Once I butter the bread, I tear off about one foot from the roll of foil and place it shiny side down on the top of my desk. On the foil I lay one slice of buttered bread, then two slices of cheese on it, topping these with the second piece of bread. Then, I wrap the sandwich in the foil. Crimping its edges tightly, I tear off another piece of foil and cover my sandwich with it. Secured between two shields of armor, my creation awaits the iron. I put the sandwich gently on my ironing board, and with one smooth motion I pick up the iron and touch it to the foil. Steam pours out and hisses angrily as I move the iron back and forth without pressure. (Too much pressure crushes the bread.) It takes only three minutes to grill one side; afterwards I remove the iron and wait for the steam to clear. With a washcloth potholder I flip the sandwich over and iron the other side. When the foil cools slightly, I peel it away, always burning my fingers despite my potholder. The aroma of melted cheese and warm bread pours into the room. Beneath the crisp toast, melted cheese peeks out. For me, heaven is seconds away.

Using my iron, I can prepare delicious sandwiches in fewer than ten minutes, and I can satisfy my late night cravings or can escape dining hall meals with my simple technique. But, more important, here in the midst of my college education where my teachers are cramming acres of information into my brain, I have learned a little something on my own to meet my needs at the moment. I do not expect to make a career of "iron cooking"; and I am sure that my knowledge and skill will have no long-range benefits for humanity. Still, learning takes place in unexpected ways. A professor's formal lectures, as important as they are, can never replace good old necessity as the best teacher.

—*Stacy Kissinger*

Picking Pears

The day starts when I rise at four in the morning. Dawn has not yet broken over Kibbutz Ein Zurim. Still, the members of this Israeli commune are beginning their tasks for the day. Today, the picking of pears awaits me; inexperienced, I am both excited and worried about the job.

Preparing for it takes some time. I fumble in the darkness, finding my closet. The door creaks as I open it, and I grab my yellow T-shirt, my gray socks and slacks, and my blue sunhat. Sitting back on my bed, I dress expectantly. As I slide open the front door to go outside, the hall light stings my eyes. Then into the chill morning I stroll, ready to meet my companions and to start the day's work. I pass the bungalows of other workers as crickets murmur their sounds. Two lizards chase each other while the sun makes its way over the desert sky. As I hop onto the old bus hooked up to a tractor, its mustiness makes me cough. Around me my companions slump on the hard leather seats, resting weary heads on the window sills in last minute efforts at sleep. But the sudden, grinding sound of the tractor ends the morning's silence as we make our way down bumpy dirt roads to the pear field and our coming chores.

By the time we reach it, everyone is fully awake. We leave the bus and each of us receives a sturdy plastic bucket with a steel hook on the handle, a steel or a wooden ladder, and a small wooden square with a circle cut out in the middle. Our leader Danny instructs the group in Hebrew on which pear trees to pick. "We are to pick the fifth row of pears and when we are finished to go on to the sixth," Renee repeats in English. I follow the group to the fifth row and directly against a tree I place my ladder so its legs hit the dirt sturdily. I climb up among the massive trees with my bucket and square. Pulling one of the leafy branches downward, I hang the bucket on it with the hook. With my left hand I grab another branch full of pears and pull it closer to me. Raising my right hand, I try to slip a pear through the hole in the wooden square. The pear does not fit; that means it is big enough for picking, I give this test to each pear. If it is ripe enough, I grasp it by the bottom, lift it upward, and give it a sharp snap. If I do not do it this way, the pear might break at the bottom of the stem, and that would make the fruit unsalable. To avoid bruises further, I do not drop it into the bucket; instead, I place the pear down very carefully. When my bucket fills up, I remove it from the branch and step down the ladder. A few feet away I tenderly place the pears in a huge wooden crate. When I return to my ladder, I see that all the pears on my tree have been picked. I grasp the ladder on both sides, tilt it horizontally, lift it, and lean it on my shoulder. Not far away, another tree needs picking, and I dig the legs of my ladder into the dirt close to the trunk. Once again I climb up to repeat the procedure.

For Kibbutz life in Israel everyone works equally. Both regular commune members and volunteers like me plant the fields and harvest the crops. Even the leaders work with us, the sun beating down on all our backs together. This group effort helps us tolerate our job. We join in songs, or we talk to our neighbors on nearby ladders. At breaks, given every two hours, we rest together on crates as we joke, gulp down water, brush off the dust on our clothing. I have a wonderful feeling of pride in this work, a feeling that comes from my playing a part in a large and important task. Too often we look at the work we do as single efforts involving ourselves alone, but I am learning that when there is a strong spirit among people, it is easy to accomplish even the most unpleasant chores.

—*Myra Grossman*

1. What, according to the proposal sentences, does each essay intend to show?
2. One of these essays explains a process that someone could easily duplicate; the other essay is more an explanation of how something is done, an effort to show a procedure without expecting the reader to try to do it. Which is which?
3. In each essay which words in the opening sentence of paragraph 2 help make a transition from paragraph 1? Which words in the opening sentence of paragraph 3 help connect it to paragraph 2?
4. Which details in the essays do you find most original and most clear? Find appeals to the sense of sight (color and action), sound, touch, and smell.
5. Myra Grossman's theme is a personal narrative that serves to show how a process is performed. Is her approach successful? Why?
6. For what kind of audience does each writer intend her process? How can you tell?
7. Discuss the conclusions in both essays. Do they summarize the main point of the essay? In which sentences do you find summaries? What else do the conclusions achieve here?

Some Topics to Think About

You might find these possible topic ideas helpful as you consider various processes and how to approach them during your prewriting. More suggested topics appear on pages 307–308.

1. how to enjoy a movie
2. how to tune an engine
3. how to shovel a walk
4. how to milk a cow
5. how to take notes in Professor _____'s class
6. how to make ice cream
7. how to ride a horse
8. how your governor was elected
9. how a steam engine works
10. how to pick up a girl (boy)
11. how drug addiction works in the body
12. how a computer works
13. how to do the backstroke
14. how to read a novel
15. how to avoid being mugged
16. how to wait on tables
17. how to play stickball
18. how to hunt with a bow and arrow
19. how to make chili con carne
20. how to stop poverty
21. how to eat healthful foods
22. how bees make honey
23. how to ready soil for planting
24. how to camp out
25. how to choose a good wine

Prewriting

Because completeness and sequence of steps are so important in a process paper, a helpful prewriting activity calls for making a list. Simply write down all the possible steps you can think of, steps required in the process you want to write about. Don't worry about whether you are repeating yourself or whether or not you have put in things that don't belong or have left out things that do belong.

Just keep writing and letting thoughts develop. The point here is to get down on paper, before you attempt a draft, as much raw material as possible. And don't worry about spelling or other errors in mechanics. At this stage they are unimportant.

Once you have your list, look it over. If you've left lots of space between entries, you'll have room to add any steps or details you may have left out. You might want to rearrange some steps or to group some together logically. Little by little, the shape of your essay will suggest itself. Certain steps you'll describe in the first body paragraph because they fit together there sensibly. Other steps you will develop in the second body paragraph. Using your list and the changes you've made with it, you can then move on to your rough draft.

Look at the list below, prepared for an essay on growing roses.

Topic: planting a rose garden

1. *piece of earth 15' x 5'*
2. *turn soil and rake it (tell them to watch out for rocks)*
3. *have 8-10 different rose bushes (point about variety)*
4. *treat soil with peat or compost or manure — lime too*
5. *work soil to depth of 2'*
6. *dig hole 1-1/2 times as big as root ball (watch out for bud and root joint: DEFINE!)*
7. *cover roots with soil and water right away*
8. *pine bark mulch keeps weeds away*
9. *prevent diseases with early treatment for aphids and black spot*
10. *spray or dust weekly during growing season*
11. *feed every four weeks*
12. *stop feeding in mid-August*
13. *to protect plants against cold weather let rose flowers mature into hips*
14. *mulch base of plant heavily in fall*
15. *prune only in early spring — not fall*

— Lee Bowen

Step 1.   Understanding the List. Discuss the answers to these questions about Lee Bowen's list. Or, write your responses on separate paper as your instructor suggests.

1. The announced topic is "planting a rose garden," but all the points Lee Bowen has written on his list suggest a more expanded topic. How might you restate his topic so that it allows him to deal with most of the steps he states on his list? What thesis sentence might you write as a result of that topic? On the other hand, if the writer wanted to stay with his announced topic, "planting a rose garden," what steps would you suggest he leave out?

2. Notice the little note the writer made for himself in item 2 on the list. How will the note help him expand details? What other messages has he written to himself?

3. In item 6 the writer reminds himself to define "bud and root joint." Why does Lee Bowen want to define this term? How does his wish to define it suggest the audience he wants to write for? What other words do you think he should define for that audience?

4. The items on the rough list suggest one possible grouping of steps into three categories: readying the soil, planting the bushes, caring for the new plants. If you were rewriting this list before you did your first draft, which points would you group in each of these categories? How could the grouping help you plan the body paragraphs of the essay?

Step 2.   Prewriting: Making Your Own Rough List. Select a topic you think you could develop into an essay that explains a process. Then, using Lee Bowen's list as an example, on separate paper prepare your own rough list of steps the process suggests. At first, list everything that comes to mind. Skip lines between items. Later, go back to add steps or to take them away. You might want to group steps together in broad categories, as question 4 in Step 1 above suggests.

Progress Reminders: A Checklist of Questions

As you prepare your list and do other prewriting, as you do your first and later drafts, and before you write your final copy, use this checklist so that you follow as many of the suggestions as possible. After you prepare your manuscript to hand in to your instructor, fill in the checklist and submit it with your theme.

1. Did I spend time considering the topic? Did I follow some   _____
   prewriting activity that works well for me? (See page
   39.)

2. Did I make a list of the steps in the process and then change   _____
   and regroup the steps in the list?

3. Did I write a rough draft and any other needed drafts   _____
   before making my final copy? Did I make changes in my
   rough drafts so that I expressed thoughts clearly and
   smoothly?

4. Did I write a proposal sentence that defines my topic clearly   _____
   and that allows me to develop two aspects of it, one in each
   of my body paragraphs? (See pages 258–261.)

5. Does my introduction provide a strong beginning for my   _____
   essay? Does my conclusion close off my point successfully?

6. Did I use transitions to tie together paragraphs one and   _____
   two? two and three? three and four?

7. Did I use adequate detail? If I wrote from personal experi-   _____
   ence, did I use images of color, sound, action, smell, and

touch? Or, did I use statistics, cases, quotations, or paraphrases as supporting detail?

8. Did I experiment with sentence structure? Did I try for one   _____
   or two sentences that changed word order like those explained in this chapter? (See pages 320–322.)

9. Did I define my audience as clearly and as precisely as I   _____
   could? The audience I intend this essay for is

   _____

10. Did I try to use words from the new vocabulary on pages   _____
    306–307?

11. Did I take care to include all the steps my audience needs to   _____
    understand the process? Did I leave out any unnecessary
    steps? Did I pay special attention to the sequence of steps,
    making sure that I discussed them in the right order?

12. After making changes in my drafts for clarity and smooth-   _____
    ness, did I check my draft over by proofreading for my
    usual mistakes? Did I check especially for errors in word
    placement and in the use of apostrophes?

13. Did I use a dictionary for any words whose spelling troubled   _____
    me?

14. Did I write a strong title?   _____

15. Did I read the sample themes on pages 330–331 to help me   _____
    see how other students explained processes clearly?

16. Am I convinced that if I read my essay I could perform this   _____
    process with little or no difficulties?

GETTING READER RESPONSE

It is most important in a "how-to" paper that you include *all* the steps of the
process. Team up with four other students and pass your papers down the line
so that everyone has a chance to read the others' process paper. As you get each
paper, note on a separate sheet where you think instructions may have been
omitted that would make it difficult for you to perform the task. Such responses
from four other readers will help you revise your draft so that you explain the
process fully.

THE PROFESSIONALS SPEAK

Among the more popular articles currently found in magazines and journals are
the "how-to" pieces, essays by professionals who tell you how to accomplish
everything from improving your life-style to flattening your stomach. Two such

pieces appear below. First, from *Blair & Ketchum's Country Journal,* a specialist in how to grow and care for plants explains the steps in making a terrarium—a closed, see-through container in which small plants are grown. Next, from a popular text, *How to Read a Book,* two teachers explain how to make a book your own. As you read, notice how the selections reflect some of the principles you've explored in this chapter.

SOME WORDS TO KNOW BEFORE YOU READ

devotee: an enthusiast; supporter
lichens: small plants made up of an alga and a fungus
transparent: clear enough to see through
brandy snifter: a pear-shaped goblet
tamper: something that packs down materials
drainage: a system for water to run off through
waterlogging: excessively filling up with water
sterilized: made free from germs
topography: the form and features of a place
romantische Landschaft: German for *romantic landscape*
ecosystem: a self-contained environment functioning in nature

How to Make a Terrarium

If you need an excuse for a walk in the woods, make a terrarium. Gathering terrarium ingredients sharpens one's appreciation of the rich variety of life at boot level. Terrarium makers see the world in fine. No detail escapes their attention. A confirmed devotee could probably wander in a redwood grove with gaze fixed on the ground—looking for moss of just the right texture, tiny seedling trees, interesting bark chips. After I made my first terrarium, I found myself gathering tiny plants, lichens, and pebbles on every walk—and mentally collecting when I was not walking our own land.

Woodland plants are perfect for the terrarium. Most things that grow on the forest floor thrive in cool, moist, partly shady situations, which are easy to provide under glass. Many house plants adapt equally well to life in a terrarium. You can even grow exotics like the Venus flytrap, which requires warmth and moisture and gets along on soil nutrients when no flies happen by.

Whether you gather the makings of your miniature landscape on the trail, in a greenhouse, or from among your houseplants, the procedure for assembling the terrarium is the same. First, you need a container. Any kind of transparent, waterproof, easily covered container may be used to house a terrarium. Some of the more popular enclosures for these self-contained gardens include brandy snifters, apothecary jars, fish bowls, rectangular aquarium cases, and large glass carboys. Wine jugs, large test tubes, butter jars, mason jars, gallon mayonnaise jars (from restaurants), and even baby-food jars may also be used. Jean Hersey, the authority on wildflowers, once constructed a terrarium in the globe of a 150-watt light bulb with the threaded end broken off.

Wide-mouthed containers are easiest to plant by hand; those with narrow necks are tricky but by no means impossible. You need a few tools—a planter made of a length of wire coat hanger straightened out, with a loop on one end to hold the plant;

a tamper, which could be a dowel stuck into a cork, or whatever you can improvise from materials at hand; a digger, a long-handled spoon, or any kind of long, thin poker capable of making a hole in loose soil. A long-handled tweezers is also useful. Use a rolled-up newspaper as a funnel to direct the soil to the bottom of the jug.

Begin by putting down a base composed of several layers, as follows, remembering that each layer serves a purpose. First, put down a mat of moss to absorb moisture and form an attractive lining. Then pour a layer of sand or fine gravel over the moss to promote drainage and prevent waterlogging. Next scatter a handful of charcoal pieces over the gravel to prevent souring of the soil.

Now add the final layer—soil. Bagged sterilized soil is fine, but if you want to mix your own, aim for the following proportions:

2 parts topsoil
1 part sand
1 part leafmold or compost

Put in a thin layer, just covering the charcoal. Then set the plants in place and firm the remainder of the soil around their roots. Much of this soil will later settle lower around the roots.

Arranging the topography of the terrarium is a matter of taste. You might keep in mind that a variety of leaf textures is usually pleasing, and that plants of different heights and shapes—pyramidal, tall and spiky, short and shrubby, trailing—make the scenery interesting. If your container is large enough you can even make a small hill or a path within its bounded wildness. Color may be provided by including partridge berries, mushrooms, lichens, and stones. No well-made terrarium needs a plastic deer or a china bird, but the woods are full of props that can add local color to your small scene: mossy twigs, weathered pieces of wood, scraps of textured bark, squirrel-gnawed nutshells. A weird craggy stone may be just the boulder you need for a classic gothic scene—a *romantische Landschaft* in miniature.

The pleasure of terrarium building, though, has more to do with the freedom to improvise, collect, seed, play with your materials, arrange a world as *you* would have it, than with conformity to a form. Do with it what you wish. Arrange and rearrange the plants until you are happy with the way they look.

When all the plants are in place, water the soil lightly, using less water than you think you'll need. You can always add more but you can't remove it. Overwatering encourages rot, mold, and fungus.

Covering the terrarium makes it a self-contained system, with its own weather: water vapor condenses on the walls and returns to the soil. Use the cover provided with the vessel or simply place a circle of glass over the top. (Plastic wrap is a more temporary but nonetheless practical cover.) Since each terrarium is a different ecosystem with its own water balance, it is impossible to formulate definite schedules for watering. Observation is the key. If the glass is misty, or if you notice mold anywhere within it, or water pooling on the bottom, the terrarium needs to be ventilated. Uncover it for about a day. Some people ventilate their terrariums routinely once a week.

When should you add water? Seldom, if at all. If the terrarium is too dry, the soil will be lighter in color and the whole thing will feel lighter than normal when you pick it up. Use an eye dropper to add water—you'll be less likely to overwater.

Terrarium plants need some light, but direct sun will cook them. Indirect light on a table or light from a north window should suit most plant populations. If leaves turn brown, the terrarium is probably too hot. Try putting it in a cooler place.

Those of us accustomed to fertilizing houseplants may tend to include the terrarium in that routine, but it is best to keep terrarium soil on the lean side, lest the plants outgrow the container. Choice of plants influences the length of their stay too, of course. Our first house—a mid-nineteenth-century Philadelphia weaver's cottage —is now guarded by a pine that spent its first two years in a terrarium. When its top hit the cover we planted it in front of the loom shed. Now, twenty years later, it towers over the house. The loom shed is gone, but pine needles fall around its foundation. Everything lasts, we think as we drive by—just in a different form, sometimes.

—Nancy Bubel
Blair & Ketchum's Country Journal

1. What is Bubel's purpose in writing the essay? Why do you think that she does not state that purpose in a proposal (or a thesis) sentence?
2. Make a list of the general steps to follow in making a terrarium.
3. What details does the writer provide to help readers understand the process? Which words in paragraph 8 paint especially clear pictures that rely on sensory detail?
4. What audience do you think Bubel is aiming for? How do her language and sentence structure serve that audience?
5. What order does the writer use in explaining the process? What transitions are used to connect ideas within paragraphs and to connect one paragraph with another?
6. How does the introduction serve to involve the reader? In what way does the last sentence in the closing paragraph establish a new frame of reference?

SOME WORDS TO KNOW BEFORE YOU READ

theoretically: presumably
efficient: productive; competent
prelude: an introductory event
fruitfully: productively; profitably
doodad: a scribble
recollection: memory
inveterate: firmly established by habit

How to Make a Book Your Own

If you have the habit of asking a book questions as you read, you are a better reader than if you do not. But, as we have indicated, merely asking questions is not enough. You have to try to answer them. And although that could be done, theoretically, in your mind only, it is much easier to do it with a pencil in your hand. The pencil then becomes the sign of your alertness while you read.

It is an old saying that you have to "read between the lines" to get the most out of anything. The rules of reading are a formal way of saying this. But we want to persuade you to "write between the lines," too. Unless you do, you are not likely to do the most efficient kind of reading.

When you buy a book, you establish a property right in it, just as you do in clothes or furniture when you buy and pay for them. But the act of purchase is actually only the prelude to possession in the case of a book. Full ownership of a book only comes when you have made it a part of yourself, and the best way to make yourself a part of it—which comes to the same thing—is by writing in it.

Why is marking a book indispensable to reading it? First, it keeps you awake—not merely conscious, but wide awake. Second, reading, if it is active, is thinking and thinking tends to express itself in words spoken or written. The person who says he knows what he thinks but cannot express it usually does not know what he thinks. Third, writing your reactions down helps you to remember the thoughts of the author.

Reading a book should be a conversation between you and the author. Presumably he knows more about the subject than you do; if not, you probably should not be bothering with his book. But understanding is a two-way operation; the learner has to question himself and question the teacher. He even has to be willing to argue with the teacher, once he understands what the teacher is saying. Marking a book is literally an expression of your differences or your agreements with the author. It is the highest respect you can pay him.

There are all kinds of devices for marking a book intelligently and fruitfully. Here are some devices that can be used:

1. Underlining—of major points; of important or forceful statements.
2. Vertical lines at the margin—to emphasize a statement already underlined or to point to a passage too long to be underlined.
3. Star, asterisk, or other doodad at the margin—to be used sparingly, to emphasize the ten or dozen most important statements or passages in the book. You may want to fold a corner of each page on which you make such marks or place a slip of paper between the pages. In either case, you will be able to take the book off the shelf at any time and, by opening it to the indicated page, refresh your recollection.
4. Numbers in the margin—to indicate a sequence of points made by the author in developing an argument.
5. Numbers of other pages in the margin—to indicate where else in the book the author makes the same points, or points relevant to or in contradiction of those here marked; to tie up the ideas in a book, which, though they may be separated by many pages, belong together. Many readers use the symbol "Cf" to indicate the other page numbers; it means "compare" or "refer to."
6. Circling of key words or phrases—This serves much the same function as underlining.
7. Writing in the margin, or at the top or bottom of the page—to record questions (and perhaps answers) which a passage raises in your mind; to reduce a complicated discussion to a simple statement; to record the sequence of major points right through the book. The endpapers at the back of the book can be used to make a personal index of the author's points in the order of their appearance.

To inveterate book-markers, the front endpapers are often the most important. Some people reserve them for a fancy bookplate. But that expresses only their financial ownership of the book. The front endpapers are better reserved for a record of your thinking. After finishing the book and making your personal index on the back endpapers, turn to the front and try to outline the book, not page by page or point by point (you have already done that at the back), but as an integrated structure, with a basic outline and an order of parts. That outline will be the measure of your understanding of the work; unlike a bookplate, it will express your intellectual ownership of the book.

—Mortimer J. Adler
and Charles Van Doren
How to Read a Book

1. What is the stated purpose of this essay? Explain it in your own words.
2. What sort of audience are the authors addressing? How do you know?
3. What materials are suggested for the process described? Are any more needed? Why?
4. According to Adler and Van Doren, why is it important to have a pencil in hand while reading a book?
5. According to the authors, does "full ownership" of a book occur at time of purchase? If not, when and how does such ownership come about?
6. For what three reasons is writing in a book important? What does it show about the relationship between the reader and the author?
7. Name and briefly describe the types of book markings suggested. What purposes are served by writing in the margins of pages?
8. The authors mention two uses of the front endpapers of a book. What are they? Which do the authors prefer? Why?
9. What arrangement do Adler and Van Doren use in their essay? Why?

REACHING HIGHER

Step 1. Different People, Same Process. Select a process you know how to perform well, and outline the steps you use. Then interview three people, and write down their methods for performing the same task. (You should select something simple, such as a recipe or changing a tire.) Write a paragraph in which you compare or contrast the variations on the process. Evaluate whether or not those variations affect the final product. For hints on interviewing techniques, see pages 380–381.

Step 2. A Process in Visual Terms. Take pictures of someone performing some process that interests you. You'll need to take quite a few shots. After you have the pictures developed, select the important ones, those that could serve to illustrate the major steps in the process. Arrange the steps in an appropriate order. Mount the photographs on heavy paper and write a sentence to accompany each.

Step 3.   Adapting to Audiences. After your instructor returns your process essay, and after you have had a chance to correct it fully, consider how your essay would look if you were writing for a completely different audience from the one you aimed at originally. Decide on some other group who might enjoy or benefit from instruction in the process you are teaching. With that group clearly in mind, rewrite your introductory paragraph. How does it compare with your original?

CHAPTER 8

A SHORT RESEARCH ESSAY:
The World of the Child

INTRODUCTION TO THE SHORT RESEARCH THEME

How do children learn? What forces are most crucial in shaping their lives: the family? the schools? the street? the playground? How can we understand children's needs, their fears, their inner voices, their magical worlds? How should we teach them, discipline them, love them?

This theme assignment asks you to investigate some aspect of child development that interests you. In Chapter 5, you practiced writing from expert testimony that you drew from data provided to you. You'll have to use expert testimony again, only this time around you'll have to research materials on your own. That is, you'll have to explore and limit a topic that you yourself identify about children, you'll have to find and record books and periodicals that deal with your topic, and you'll have to take notes on what you read. From your research, you'll develop a four-paragraph essay. The essay will provide to your readers concrete detail that you've chosen from reliable sources, detail that supports a proposal you make about the child's world.

VOCABULARY

Step 1.   Words for Growth. These words appear frequently in a discussion of child development. Write definitions next to words you already know. For any words whose meanings you do not remember, check a dictionary or see Appendix A for some help.

1. phase _____

2. retarded _____

3. verbal _____

4. socialization _____

5. cognitive _____

Step 2.   Words for a Child's World. The words in italics below will help you as you write about children. Determine the meaning of the word from the way it is used in the sentence. Circle the letter next to the best definition. Then check the correct definitions in Appendix A.

1. The child was *naive* enough to believe that the Cookie Monster on *Sesame Street* was a real animal.
   a. stupid   *b.* unsophisticated   *c.* unaware   *d.* foreign
2. Young children are especially *vulnerable* to measles, mumps, and chicken pox.
   a. susceptible to injury   *b.* valuable   *c.* protected   *d.* delicate

3. It is important to *nurture* children carefully so that they will achieve their full potential.
   a. watch   *b.* nature   *c.* nourish   *d.* mature
4. When Tommy barked like a dog and crawled on the floor, Ms. Rivera scolded his *immature* actions.
   a. pretty   *b.* funny   *c.* childish   *d.* imaginative
5. Children are sometimes influenced more by their friends and *peers* than by their parents.
   a. equals   *b.* teachers   *c.* television shows   *d.* brothers

Step 3.   Writing Sentences with New Words. Write a sentence using the words listed below.

1. socialization _____

2. phase _____

3. immature _____

4. vulnerable _____

5. cognitive _____

6. nurture _____

7. peers _____

8. retarded _____

9. verbal _____

10. naive _____

BUILDING COMPOSITION SKILLS

Step 1.   Sharing Ideas. Here are several statements about different aspects of child development. Pick out one or two remarks with which you strongly agree or disagree and discuss your opinions briefly, giving reasons to support your point of view.

1. Children in low socioeconomic groups do not learn as easily as children in higher socioeconomic groups.
2. Women teachers are best for young children.
3. The mentally retarded can be educated within degrees.
4. Boys do not learn as quickly as girls.
5. Many children in American schools get poor instruction in reading.
6. Child abuse is a serious problem in American families.
7. Most children are not fed properly.

8. There is not enough disciplining of children in our society.
9. Busing has a harmful effect on children.
10. State governments should spend more money to support day-care centers.
11. Public schools do not stimulate the creativity of our children.
12. The youngest child in a family usually has the most difficult problems.
13. Television has a negative effect on a child's learning and development.
14. The public schools are not doing enough for the physically handicapped student.
15. The number of students who drop out of high school is increasing each year.
16. Adopted children are generally happy with their adoptive parents.
17. Public school children should receive sex education.
18. Most parents do not understand the emotional needs of their children.

Prewriting

For research-based assignments that require a number of activities before you can produce a rough draft, you will find it useful to plan a deadlines schedule in advance. In that way, you can set a realistic program of deadlines for yourself based upon the date that your final manuscript is due. Without such a plan, you can easily postpone some of the steps required to produce your paper and, as a result, you can discover suddenly that not enough time remains to complete your work successfully. If your instructor plans to examine work you do at various stages, you'll need to build your schedule around the due dates announced to the class. Instructors who collect materials you produce will return them in time for you to move to the next stage.

The form below may help you to produce your own plan. On the following pages, you will explore the various steps listed on the plan.

Research Essay: Schedule of Dates

Activity	*To Be Completed By*
1. Browsing to identify topic	_____
2. Development of limited topic and discussion (or submission) for evaluation by instructor or classmates.	_____
3. Preparation and discussion (or submission) of bibliography cards.	_____
4. Preparation and discussion (or submission) of note cards on two readings.	_____
5. Preparation and discussion (or submission) of remaining note cards.	_____
6. Preparation and discussion (or submission) of written proposal sentence for the essay.	_____

7. Preparation and discussion (or submission) of note-card   _____
   summary guide.

8. Preparation and discussion (or submission) of outline.   _____

9. Preparation and discussion (or submission) of tentative   _____
   introductory paragraph with revised proposal.

10. Preparation and discussion (or submission) of rough draft.   _____

11. Preparation and submission of final draft.   _____

Step 1.   Planning a Schedule. Using the form above or a form developed with your instructor's guidance, write out a plan for your research-based theme.

Starting Research: Browsing

Any of the statements you discussed in Step 1 on pages 344–345 might help you identify an interest that you have in children. But your topic might not yet be clearly formed in your mind; and you don't really know yet whether or not there is adequate material for you to research. You'll want to do some preliminary browsing in the library, therefore. When you *browse,* you inspect, informally, books and articles in your general area of interest. Your purpose in reading materials at this stage is not research. Instead, you're trying to limit your topic and to think about ways of developing it and ways to organize your research.

These pointers will help you browse about the library as you explore a topic idea:

- Look in the library reference section at encyclopedias, almanacs, and other reference books for an overview of your area of interest.
- Check the card catalog under the subject that interests you. (See pages 493–495). The card catalog helps you to see some possible subtopics under a large topic that you are exploring (*children,* for example, or *education*); it also helps you see the range of books written about your topic. Simply by examining titles of books, you can see many possibilities for topics to write about.
- Using the call numbers for books named in the card catalog, go to the shelves that contain several of the titles you've identified. Examine them and other books on those shelves. Because library classification systems group, near each other, all books on similar topics, you have at your fingertips many approaches to your topic. Flip through the books; look at the table of contents, the index, the glossary or appendixes. Read the preface or the introduction. Read the first paragraph of a chapter or two. Practices like these can give you excellent ideas for shaping a topic.
- Examine indexes to periodicals. A *periodical index* is an alphabetical listing (usually annual) of authors, titles, and subjects of articles in magazines, journals, or newspapers. An index like the *Readers' Guide to Periodical Literature* (see pages 491–492) has entries for popular magazines like *Time, Newsweek,* and *The Atlantic. The New York Times Index* lists articles and stories that appeared in

The New York Times. There are many other indexes, some highly specialized, about particular subjects or writers.

Like the card catalog, an index shows you at a glance the kinds of subtopics current writers have addressed as parts of larger topics. Reading over the titles of current articles, you can see a variety of approaches to a topic that interests you.

• Talk to the librarians. Often they can direct you to appropriate reference materials that can help you develop a topic.

Step 1. Browsing in the Library. For any topic under the broad heading of *children, child development,* or *education,* or for some topic you've already limited somewhat, browse in the library by following the pointers above. Then answer these questions:

1. Which encyclopedias or other reference tools did you use?

   _____

   _____

   _____

   On which pages did you find information that may help you develop

   your topic? _____

2. From the card catalog, list three book titles (and their authors) that you feel may help you with your topic.

   _____

   _____

   _____

   _____

3. Remove from the library shelf any book you listed in 2, or any other book nearby that deals with your general topic. Look through the index, and write down the names of three or four entries you find there that might help you with your topic.

   _____

   _____

   _____

   _____

   _____

4. Check under a subject heading in last year's or this year's *Reader's Guide to Periodical Literature* (see pages 491–492). Name two or three articles that you might want to examine for information on your topic. Also, name the authors

   and the magazine in which the article appears. _____

_____

_____

_____

_____

Limiting the Topic

One of the most important goals in doing research is limiting the topic. Especially when you face a topic as broad as *child development,* you must consider carefully how to narrow the subject down so that you are not overwhelmed with reading. Even when you think that you have selected some reasonable area within a large topic idea, you can no doubt shave the subject down even more. The chart below shows how to narrow down a topic in a series of steps.

Too General	*Still Broad*	*Less Broad*	*Narrow Enough*
teaching	teaching number concepts	teaching number concepts to children	teaching number concepts at home to children under five
child behavior	how children play together	how girls play together	patterns of play among four- and five-year-old girls
childhood diseases	fighting polio	vaccination in the fight against polio	the government's role in vaccination against polio
children	disciplining children	disciplining adolescents	disciplining adolescents by the methods of Haim G. Ginott

Step 1.   Limiting the Topic. How would you narrow the following topics down into reasonable areas for research?

1. busing _____

2. education and the courts _____

3. foods for children _____

4. children and computers _____

5. television and children _____

6. juvenile delinquency _____

7. child abuse _____

    After your first effort to limit your topic as a result of browsing and of some preliminary thinking, you should expect to limit your topic even further. Later on, as you read and think about what you've read, you'll discover new ways of looking at your subject.

Step 2. Limiting Your Own Topic. After you browse about the library and after you select some topic that interests you, limit it using methods similar to those explained above.

Step 3. Getting Feedback. Read your chosen topic aloud as other students evaluate it, using the criteria established on page 348. Or, your instructor may ask you to write your tentative topic down and to submit it so that he or she can offer comments about it.

Bibliography Cards

Once you've limited your topic, you'll have to return to books and periodicals that deal with the specific subject you have chosen.

    Because you'll be reading information from more than one source, you'll want to keep track of the sources you use. Most students use *bibliography cards,* 3 × 5 inch index cards on which the researcher copies basic bibliographic information about books or articles consulted in research.

Sample Bibliography Card (a Book)

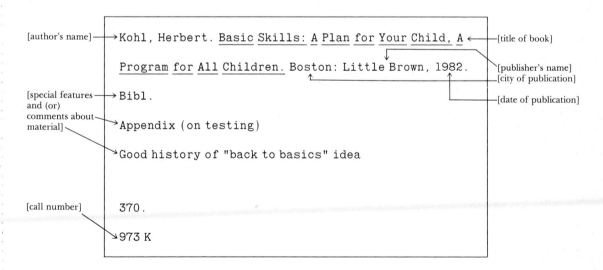

Sample Bibliography Card (a Magazine)

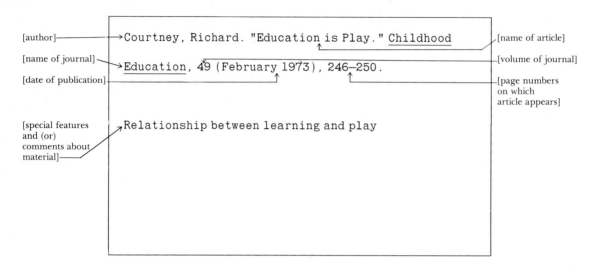

Bibliography cards are useful because

- You have an accurate record of all the sources you consulted with all the critical information about them.
- If you are required to do so, you can prepare a bibliography (see pages 495–497) from the data on the bibliography cards.
- Since all bibliographies are alphabetical, you can arrange the cards in alphabetical order by moving them about easily.
- Notations to yourself about your first impressions of the materials help you decide later whether to return to the source for closer study.

Although your first sources of information for your bibliography cards are the card catalog (see pages 493–495) and periodical indexes like the *Readers' Guide to Periodical Literature* (see pages 491–492), you must check all information against the books and articles themselves.

Preparing accurate bibliography cards saves you time later on. For example, with the call number of the book written on your card, you do not have to waste time returning to the card catalog each time that you must consult your book. With magazine titles and page numbers written down for articles, you can go directly to the periodical without having to check in the index again.

Step 1. Preparing Your Bibliography Cards. For the topic you have limited, prepare at least six bibliography cards for books and periodical articles related to your topic. Of the six, at least two should be from magazines or newspapers.

Note Cards

Most researchers find it useful to take notes on 4 × 6 inch cards (see also pages 506 and 509). As you read about your topic in books or periodicals, you have to record important information that you can use to write your essay later on. Because a good research essay relies upon exact quotes drawn from other writers, you should record whatever information you select accurately.

On your note cards, copy, word for word, any passages of importance to your topic. (Use an *ellipsis,* three unspaced dots, to indicate words you decide to leave out. See page 203.) Copy only one piece of information on a card; this will help you organize your thoughts later on. In order to keep track of your resources, record, on each card, the last name of the author, the name of the book or article, and the page number you've copied from.

1. Sample Note Card: Exact Quote

```
"In his first years, before he gets to school, the
child lives his life, as he should, all in one piece.
His work, his play, and his learning are not separated
from each other. What is even more important,they are
not separated from him . . . But in school . . . the
child is taught to think that his work, his play, and
his learning are separate from each other, and all
separate from him . . . ."
                              —Holt, Freedom and
                                Beyond, p. 254.
```

From a note card like the one above, you could choose words, phrases, or sentences from *Freedom and Beyond* to use in your own essay. Also, you might decide to paraphrase some of this material, that is, to put it into your own words (see pages 203–205), but you would have at your fingertips the writer's exact comments from which to work.

However, copying only exact quotes on everything you read can be exhausting and time-consuming. Therefore, many researchers paraphrase rather than quote information directly on their note cards. Or they will combine quotations and paraphrases in taking notes. Paraphrasing compels you to think carefully about what you read so that you can express it in your own words.

The risk in preparing note cards of paraphrase is that when you write your own essay from such cards, you no longer have the writer's exact words. Should you later decide that a quote rather than a paraphrase would better suit your point, you will have to return to the source. With note cards that combine quotations and paraphrases, you must be certain that you can tell your own words from the words of the writer whose idea you are recording.

2. Sample Note Card: Paraphrase

```
In early years, child lives "all in one piece." Work,

play, and learning are connected to each other. In

school, however, child believes that all those are

separate and that all are apart from himself. *Check

against Holt's How Children Learn. Use in intro?*

                              —Holt, Freedom and

                                Beyond, p. 254.
```

In the note card directly above, the student paraphrases information from the book. The words "all in one piece" are quoted exactly as a reminder to enclose them in quotations if the student decides to use them in the paper. Notice, too, how an asterisk (*) comes before and after the student's own thoughts. Asterisks (or some such symbols) can help you separate the words and ideas of your source from any ideas of your own that your reading stimulates.

Sometimes you write a note card merely to remind you of the content of pages you have read. This kind of card is especially useful when you have the book physically available to work from as you draft your essay. Thus, you can return to the text if you need to select a quote. (Unfortunately, much research is done from resources that must remain in the library, and fuller note cards like 1 and 2 above are more the rule.)

3. Sample Note Card: Reminder Card

Good discussion of how children's attitudes toward
learning (reading especially) change for the worse
because of values set by the schools (Holt, <u>Freedom</u>
<u>and Beyond</u>, pp. 254–256). Compare with <u>How Children</u>
<u>Learn</u>, (Holt) and <u>Hooked on Books</u> (Fader). Use in
intro?

The note card above signals the student to return to selected pages in the book *Freedom and Beyond* and, possibly, to use a quotation from those pages in the introduction of the student's research essay.

When you are preparing a draft of your essay and you do select data or quotes from your note cards, you must be sure to cite your sources according to your instructor's directions. You can review internal citations and footnotes as possible formats for such citations on pages 203–205 and 497–499.

Step 1. Making Note Cards. For whatever readings you have singled out as pertinent to your topic—a chapter (or a few pages) from a book, an article in a magazine, or a newspaper—prepare note cards. Remember that if you quote or paraphrase you should put *only one* piece of information on each card.

If your instructor requests it, submit a set of note cards on one or more of your readings for comments and suggestions.

Developing a Proposal

As you read material on your topic, you should start developing ideas for a proposal (or thesis). Your proposal, as you remember from Chapter 6, makes some assertion about your subject. That is, the proposal states a limited topic and gives your opinion about it. The proposal also allows you to discuss at least two specific aspects of the essay, one in each body paragraph. (Be sure to reread pages 258–261 to review guidelines for good proposals.)

But don't think of your proposal as anything fixed or permanent at this stage. As your research continues, you'll want to change your proposal, modifying it to address new ideas you learn as you read. The student who developed the limited topic below read books and articles that helped her formulate the proposal on the right.

Topic	*Proposal*
teaching number concepts at home to children under five	Parents can teach important number concepts to five-year-olds at home.

The student's research convinced her that parents do play a role in helping children learn about numbers at home; and so, after some initial reading, she formulated the proposal you read above. As she examined more and more books and periodicals, she changed her proposal a few times until she produced the following, which she finally used in her essay.

Using simple techniques and easy-to-find materials in the home, preschool children can have fun exploring number concepts with a parent's guidance.

The new proposal does change the writer's focus. Now the essay will deal essentially with what the *child* can do; the first proposal stressed the parent. There is also more specific attention to the actual techniques than can be used. Next, the writer injected an opinion, "fun," and the readers' interest is newly heightened as we expect details to support the notion of enjoyment. Any techniques explained in the essay will have to demonstrate the element of fun in this kind of home learning.

You should be ready to revise your proposal as often as necessary both during your research and during your writing of early drafts.

Step 1.   Writing Proposals. For each topic in the box on page 348, write a draft of a proposal sentence.

Step 2.   Your Own Proposal. Write a proposal sentence based upon the research you have done up to this point. Submit your proposal for your instructor's comments, or discuss your proposal in small groups in class.

Organizing Notes

By the time you finish reading, no doubt you'll have quite a stack of note cards. You'll want to organize them so that you can write your essay using the cards to provide data.

First, collect all your cards, and number them consecutively. Next, reread them carefully, looking for similar subject groups related to your proposal. Several of your readings will undoubtedly address the same issues, and you will find it useful to identify easily all the cards that pertain to the same subtopics. If you prepare a summary of your note cards by listing the major issues you noticed as you read over your cards, you can then write the number of the pertinent note card alongside the issues you've listed. Look at the following example:

Issue	*Card Number*
mathematics toys and games for pre-schoolers	6, 12, 13, 14, 15, 16, 28, 52, 53
child's attitudes toward numbers	1, 2, 3, 19, 20, 26, 30, 31, 54
counting objects at home	4, 5, 7, 8, 9, 11, 24, 29, 33
writing numbers	10, 17, 18, 21, 22, 23
drawing and pasting for number concepts	25, 27, 36, 37, 38, 39, 40

A summary like the one above allows you to arrange your cards in groups according to general headings. Since each card is numbered and contains the name of the author and the title of the book or article, you won't confuse your sources. With this method of organization, you can try different grouping patterns, and you can shift around the order of the issues you may address in your essay before you actually write about them. Also, if your instructor requires a formal outline (see pages 515–516), you can prepare one by using the card summary as a guide.

Step 1. Summarizing Your Note Cards. Gather together your note cards, and number them consecutively. Read them over, looking for subtopics related to the proposal you developed in Step 2, page 354. Now, prepare a guide like the one above.

Transforming Sentences: Active-Voice Verbs for Strong Meanings

Many verbs can express the same thought in two different ways. Which of these sentences do you find more satisfactory?

1. *The tired employee locked the office door.*
2. *The office door was locked by the tired employee.*

If you selected sentence 1, you probably realized, correctly, that the extra words needed to make sentence 2 really added nothing of importance to the sentence. Why take more words to say exactly what you could say with fewer words?

Notice further that in sentence 1, the subject (*the tired employee*) performs the action of the verb. (It is he who *locked the office door.*)

But in sentence 2, the subject (*the office door*) does not do anything. In fact, something happens to it (it *was locked by the tired employee*).

Because the subject of sentence 1 actively performs the action of the verb, we say the verb is in the *active voice*.

Because the subject of sentence 2 is acted upon by the verb, we say the verb is in the *passive voice*.

Hint

In most cases, choose the active voice over the passive.

It is easy to transform passive-voice sentences to active ones. Just remember these pointers:

1. Passive-voice sentences always use some form of *to be* in combination with the verb. Look for word groups like *is seen, will be observed, can be cleaned, was done, should have been bought, would have been eaten.* You will have to remove the *to be* part to write an active-voice sentence.
2. Decide who performs the action of the verb. Usually the performer appears after the word *by.* Make that word the subject.

Passive

The pencil was sharpened *by* Harriet.

[This is a clue to who performs the action.]

[This is who performs the action of the verb *sharpen.*]

Active ⎾[*was* is removed.]

Harriet sharpened the pencil.

[The person who performs the action is now the subject of the verb.]

Step 1. Passive into Active. In the spaces provided, change the passive-voice sentences into active-voice ones.

Hint

Sometimes the person who performs the action is not mentioned in the passive-voice sentence. You will have to determine the performer of the action before you write the active-voice sentence. Study the example.

Example

The two employees were quickly brought before the manager.

(Here we do not know who actually brought them to the manager. Decide who you think performs the action and then rewrite.)

The guards quickly brought the two employees before the manager.

_____

1. The rose bushes were planted in the garden by my sister Consuela.

_____

2. A new Chevrolet was purchased by my wife and me.

_____

3. A college diploma is expected by many employers.

   _____

4. The iceberg was rammed by the ship.

   _____

5. The issue of funding for mass transit is raised in the article.

   _____

6. We were given as much help as we needed at Center Hardware Store.

   _____

7. The blazing Montana sunset can be seen from Len Anderson's ranch.

   _____

8. At Glacier National Park, we were visited by mountain goats at our campsite.

   _____

9. The better-paying jobs cannot be obtained by less-skilled workers.

   _____

10. Roses were delivered to Susan Wo Tan at five o'clock in the afternoon.

   _____

SOLVING PROBLEMS IN WRITING

Degrees of Comparison

When we use describing words, we can often compare one thing with another merely by changing the ending of a word.

Example
One boy is tall. Another boy is tall*er*. Parker is the tall*est* boy at the party.

   You have to be careful, however, to use the correct ending.

Use *-er* at the end of a word if you want to compare only two items.

Use *-est* at the end of a word if you want to compare three or more items.

One person or thing is	Of two people or things, one is	Among three or more people or things, one is
short	shorter	shortest
smart	smarter	smartest
silly	sillier	silliest

If the word you are using to compare has *three or more* syllables:

Use *more* in front of the word if you want to compare only two items.

Use *most* in front of the word if you want to compare three or more items.

Hint
If you are not sure how to make the correct form of the word, use your dictionary.

One person or thing is	Of two people or things, one is	Among three or more people or things, one is
beautiful	more beautiful	most beautiful
enormous	more enormous	most enormous

Some words do not form comparisons in the usual way; these you have to memorize because they are irregular.

One person or thing is	Of two people or things, one is	Among three or more people or things, one is
bad	worse	worst
done badly	done worse	done worst
good	better	best
done well	done better	done best
little	less	least
many	more	most
much	more	most

Some words may not be compared at all because their meanings do not allow for degrees in comparison.

unique   empty
perfect   full

Step 1. Correct Comparison. Fill in the spaces in the three columns below. The word you write must make sense in the blank line that appears in the sentence on top of the column. Look at the example.

Hint
For some words you have the choice of either adding an ending (-*er* or -*est*) or of using *more* or *most. But remember, use one or the other—not both.*
Wrong: She is more thriftier than her friend.

Right: She is more thrifty than her friend.
OR
        She is thriftier than her friend.

The teacher is _____.	Between Professor Merryl and Professor Grace, Professor Grace is ___*more*___.	Of all the teachers I have had, Professor Grace is *the most attractive* .
1. attractive	*attractive*	_____
2. witty	_____	_____
3. informative	_____	_____
4. busy	_____	_____
5. messy	_____	_____
6. funny	_____	_____

Hint

Check spelling rule 2 on page 476.

Step 2.   Changing Wrong Comparisons. Each of the following sentences uses a comparison incorrectly. Draw a line through the wrong word, and write in the blank space at the right the word or words that you would use to make the sentence correct.

Example

He runs the ~~most~~ fastest on the team.   *fastest* _____

1. Of the two boys Juan and David, David is more wiser.   _____

2. Heather is the talentedest of all the poets.   _____

3. Mr. Chin is the most smartest teacher I ever had.   _____

4. Don is the more creative of all the writers.   _____

5. Deborah is the most cutest of all the women I know.   _____

Step 3.   Your Own Comparisons. Use correctly, in a sentence of your own, each of the following words or word groups. Use separate paper.

1. most
2. better
3. more slowly

4. best
5. nastiest

Parallelism

> **WHAT IS PARALLELISM?**
>
> Parts of a sentence with the same function generally need the same form. When you place sentence elements in a series or when you use certain types of connectors in pairs, you must use parallel form. *Parallelism* is a quality of correct sentence structure that balances connected parts by using the same form for ideas joined equally.

Balancing Connected Parts: Keeping the Same Form

Words or word groups in a series must match in form.

> **Hint**
> You can often recognize a series by commas and the words *and, but, or, nor.*

The homemaker liked to bake, to sew, and to cook.
[all infinitives]
NOT
The homemaker liked to bake, to sew, and *cooking.*

We prefer dancing and singing.
[both *-ing* words]
NOT
We prefer dancing and *to sing.*

[verb]   [verb]
We heard that the President spoke to his advisers, contacted reporters, and then made his announcement to the public.
[verb]

NOT

We heard that the President spoke to his advisers, contacted reporters, and *of his announcement to the public.*

Step 1.   Making the Parts Fit. Add a word group that completes the series with a balanced part.

1. The horse refused to eat or _____.

2. José likes swimming, diving, and _____.

3. The speaker praised the candidate, shook her hand, and _____

_____.

4. On Tuesday, Mrs. Kuo worked at the lab, cooked dinner, and _____

_____.

5. Rather than go home, Marie offered to drive us to Pennsylvania or _____

_____ .

6. In his shop, Alfonse cut hair, sold flowers, and _____

_____ .

Balancing Connected Parts: Repeating the Series Opener

Often you need to repeat, for each part of the series, the first word in the opening item of the series. The sentences on the right are clearer because they repeat the opening word.

Not	*But*
They approved his plan because it was logical and it promised to succeed.	They approved his plan *because* it was logical and *because* it promised to succeed.
He spoke out for the party, for its leaders, but not its principles.	He spoke out *for* the party, *for* its leaders, but not *for* its principles.

SOME SERIES OPENERS THAT OFTEN NEED REPEATING

because, for, of, by, to, at, that, so that, a (an), who, which, could

---

Step 2. Balance through Repetition. Rewrite the incorrect underlined portion in each sentence so that it balances with the rest of the series.

1. The coach announced that athletes need special diets, that sweets add needless fat and calories, and <u>we should avoid chocolates at all costs.</u>

   that we should avoid chocolates at all costs.
   _____

2. For this course you need a textbook, <u>lab manual,</u> and <u>dissecting kit.</u>

   _____

3. He chose to withdraw his money from the bank, <u>place</u> it in a steel box, and <u>hide</u> the box under his bed._____

   _____

4. Don drove all night because he was wide awake and mainly <u>he was excited to</u> <u>see Debbie.</u> _____

   _____

5. Mr. Dunbar's new wonder feed could be used for cattle, for pigs, and <u>chickens.</u> _____

   _____

6. Martin chose his dancing clothes so he would feel comfortable and <u>he would attract girls.</u> _____

_____

7. It is a long journey which is made by steps forward and <u>falls downward.</u>

_____

Balancing Connected Parts: Paired Words and Matching Forms

A special effect of balance in sentences comes about through certain connectors that work in pairs. These paired connectors must be followed by words that have the same form. In the sentences below, connectors are in boldface. *X*'s appear over words that do not match in form. Underlined words show matching forms.

The registrar is **either** <u>working</u> at his desk **or** <u>visiting</u> the dean

NOT

xxxxxxxxxxxxxxxxxxxxxx

The registrar is **either** working at his desk **or** on a visit with the dean.

I wondered **whether** <u>to make</u> the telephone call **or** <u>to see</u> her in person

NOT

xxxxxxxxxxx

I wondered **whether** I should make the telephone call **or** to see her in person.

Words that Work in Pairs

either . . . or	whether . . . or
neither . . . nor	not only . . . but also
both . . . and	if . . . or

Step 3.   Paired Words and Forms That Match. Add a word group to each sentence below, making sure that what you add matches the underlined segment.

Example

1. We saw not only <u>all the movies he directed,</u>
   but also the television commercials he wrote. _____

2. Fran couldn't decide whether to date Steve or

_____

3. We have neither enough money nor

_____

4. Geoff wondered if he should make stew for dinner or

_____

5. You either <u>should use the pliers</u> or

_____

6. The wind is both <u>howling through the trees</u> and

_____

Step 4.   Balanced Sentence Ideas: More Practice. The sentences below contain errors in parallelism like those explained in the previous pages. On separate paper, rewrite the sentences so that they are correct.

1. Titian is a painter of great skill and who uses color in dramatic ways.
2. She not only works every weekday but also is working nights.
3. During vacations we like to drive through the Rockies or we camp in the valley.
4. Sunday is a good day for sleeping late, eating a big breakfast, and to spend hours reading the newspaper.
5. He enjoyed the movie for its ideas on modern life but not the photography; most, he liked the scene between a business executive and elevator operator.
6. There are clothes to wash, formulas to make, diapers to change, and just the general playtime also.
7. There are three aspects of my life which I recognized as signs of the end of my childhood: my treatment of my parents, my relationships with my friends, and school.
8. The advantages are as follows: fairly cheap, easily available, and easy to use.
9. The three articles agree that the aftermath of rape can be traumatizing, humiliating, and to scar the victim mentally.

Misplaced Modifiers

Words or word groups must stand as closely as possible to whatever they aim to describe. Words like *only, just, even, almost, hardly*—depending upon where they are placed in the sentence—affect the meaning that the writer wishes. Look at the word *just* in five different places in the same sentence below and examine the explanation of the meanings.

Just he suggested that we leave early.
(This means he was the only one who spoke.)
He *just* suggested that we leave early.
(This means that he merely told of one idea. It also means that he made the suggestion a short while ago.)
He suggested *just* that we leave early.
(This means that he made no other suggestion.)
He suggested that *just* we leave early.
(This means that he meant nobody else should leave early.)

He suggested that we *just* leave early.
(This means that he felt we should do nothing else but leave early.)

Words placed too far from the words they describe *(modify)* often create confusing sentences. *Misplaced modifiers* are words or word groups that, because of faulty placement, do not describe the words they intend to describe. (See also pages 213–215.)

Our neighbor sold dresses to my sister without buttons.
(The *sister* has no buttons?)
At the age of five the doctor administered a smallpox vaccination to me.
(The *doctor* was five years old?)
I watched as an old car was pulled down the street that had a flat tire.
(The *street* had a flat tire?)

Here are the sentences with the describing words in the proper places.

[This word group describes *dresses:* put it close to what it describes.]

1. Our neighbor sold dresses *without buttons* to my sister.

[This word group describes *me:* put it close to what it describes.]

2. The doctor administered a smallpox vaccination to me *at the age of five.*

3. I watched as an old car *that had a flat tire* was pulled down the street.
[This word group describes *car:* put it close to what it describes.]

Step 1.   Explaining Placement. Discuss the meanings created by the italicized words in the sentences below.

1. Over the vacation we *only* had our memories to share.
2. Over the vacation *only* we had our memories to share.
3. Over the vacation we had *only* our memories to share.
4. Over the vacation we had our memories *only* to share.
5. Over the vacation *only,* we had our memories to share.

Step 2.   In the Right Places. Add the italicized word group in the right place in the sentence so that it expresses a logical and clear idea. Rewrite the sentences in the space provided. You may want to rearrange words.

1. *with a loud cry*
   A blue jay stood in the backyard oak. _____

   _____

2. *while I could still drive*
   I decided to go home even though I was sick. _____

3. *last year*
   In history class I did not see why the settlers struggled westward in covered

   wagons to cross the desert. _____

   _____

4. *in hot water*
   Elvin washed the laundry for his neighbor. _____

   _____

5. *that it had begun to snow*
   A cold chill ran up my spine and sent a message to my brain. _____

Step 3. Changing Faulty Placement In the sentences below, words or word groups do not appear close enough to the words they describe. On your own paper, rewrite each sentence by putting the words in their proper places. If the sentence is correct, mark it *C*.

1. They only sleep late on Sundays.
2. In the past ten years, heating bills for the elderly have become unbearable.
3. Mr. Jones is a handsome man; he has a wide forehead, a straight nose, and long brown hair with glasses.
4. We hung wallpaper in the room that was easy to apply.
5. I agree that a college diploma these days is only worth the paper on which it is written to a certain degree.
6. The functioning of the heart and respiratory system in our society has traditionally been the basis for proclaiming death.
7. Today's children are becoming violence-oriented on Saturday mornings.
8. After that incident, I was aware of manhood more than ever.
9. The high-calorie, high-fat, high-sugar, low-fiber American diet is typical in most households.
10. We saw a giraffe in the San Diego Zoo that had a long neck with sad eyes.

WRITING THE BRIEF RESEARCH ESSAY

ASSIGNMENT: Write an essay in which you present research on some vital issue concerning the growth and (or) education of children. In order to support your ideas, draw upon statistics, cases, and quoted material you have chosen from your readings. Your readings should include a minimum of four sources, at least two of these from periodicals.

Learning from Other Students

Read the following essays, written by students who investigated specific areas of child development.

Reading Skills for Preschool Children

Television programs like *Sesame Street* and *Electric Company* have helped countless children to learn the basics of reading. Watching these programs with lively images and humorous characters acting out words and teaching the names and the sounds of letters, children can practice their alphabet and can improve their sight vocabulary. But educators have developed other methods that rely more upon live interaction between the child and someone who teaches him. Both formal structured methods and informal unstructured approaches certainly can help children acquire the ability to read before they enter grade school.

To help bring about this goal, Glen Doman in *How to Teach Your Child to Read* advocates one system for preschool reading instruction that calls upon scientifically designed materials. The child examines large red lower-case letters printed on cards. These cards progress in difficulty to normal-sized black upper-and lower case letters as the "visual pathway" matures. Systematically, the child learns to differentiate between simple words such as "mommy" and "daddy." Later the child assimilates "self" and "home" vocabulary. In the first group are words that reflect the child's individual needs; in the second are words for objects in the child's immediate world of the household. Following "self" and "home" words, "sentence structure vocabu-lary" develops in the context of "structural phrases and sentences." Because the alphabet is such an abstract concept, it is taught last. Another systematic approach to preschool reading is outlined by John J. DeBoer and Martha Dollman in *The Teaching of Reading.* They cite teaching three- and four-year-old children to read at the Whitby School in Whitby, Connecticut. Instructional aids include vowel shapes cut from light-colored sandpaper mounted on dark cards, and consonants and groups of letters cut out of black sandpaper mounted on white cards. The children learn to select words, and eventually phrases and sentences, from baskets. Enthusiastically, they translate the words into sounds and carry out the actions that they read.

Aside from these highly structured programs, educators now advise parents to help their children learn to read at home in more informal settings. Nancy Larrick stresses the point in an article called "No More Hands Off to Parents, We Need You." Parents, with their infants, are enrolling in "home-based projects" that lead directly to success in reading. Mothers and fathers learn how to read aloud and how to hold a book so that the child can see and participate. The parents also learn how to follow reading with casual conversation, how to question the child, and how to stimulate the child's interest. Certainly these are personal techniques that no television program can replace. Carol Vukelich, in her May, 1978, article in *Education Digest,* "Parents Are Teachers," recognizes how important the child's preschool years are to later reading success, and she urges active participation by parents in a preschooler's learning program. Vukelich discusses the Preschool Readiness Outreach Program (PROP) in which parents construct educational games to develop their children's talking, listening, and seeing skills. She states that "children whose parents participated actively in the program achieved significantly greater gains than those whose parents participated minimally." Her conclusion can convince any reader that parents must take part and must work with teachers in developing children's reading abilities.

Clearly, preschoolers can learn a good deal about reading before they enter grade school. A literacy survey by the National Reading Center disclosed that at least 18 million Americans aged sixteen and over were not functionally literate, and nearly one out of every six adult Americans is handicapped with reading problems. Those unfortunate statistics urge as much help for children as they can possibly get. Yet many people believe that nursery schools should deemphasize formal learning and should concentrate instead on motor skills and on values. These people also believe that parents should not teach their children because tensions can develop easily between a child and a mother or a father who insists on teaching the child skills better taught by trained teachers in the schools. When parent and child become teacher and pupil something of the original relationship may, in fact, disappear forever. However, a child's literacy is one of his most basic rights, and a parent who refuses to assume a strong role in teaching the child seriously violates those rights.

—*Muriel Guba*

Step 1.   Reviewing the Essay. Discuss your answers to these questions about Muriel Guba's essay.

1. Identify the proposal sentence and comment upon it. Does it introduce the main point of the essay?
2. Does the introduction engage your interest? How has Muriel Guba achieved this?
3. What quotations and paraphrases does the writer offer to support her points? Are her citations clear and complete? How would you improve them?
4. What generalization does the conclusion develop? Does the writer convince you of her position?
5. Comment on the first sentences of paragraphs 2 and 3. How does each serve as a transition in the essay?

The Advantages of Attending Kindergarten

The Digest of Education Statistics shows that 3,024,398 American children attended kindergarten in the spring of 1970. This may appear to be a large number of children, but, in reality, it is not. James Hymes states in *Teaching the Child Under Six* that "only about 60% of our five-year-olds go to any kind of kindergarten: public, private, or church-sponsored. About 40% go to no school at all." Hymes also gives one of the main reasons for the low rate of attendance: "Only 29 states provide state aid for kindergartens, 21 do not. And most of the 29 provide only half aid. . . ." These are discouraging figures because kindergarten is one of the essential educational experiences for children.

It improves the child's long-range learning skills. In *The Guide to an Effective Kindergarten Program* David Mindess states that "children who have attended kindergarten show less tendency to reverse and confuse letters, have more positive work habits, do more accurate work," and are "able to work independently as well as in groups." Mindess reports on a four-year study by researcher Loretta McHugh. Involving 709 kindergarten and 620 non-kindergarten children, the study concludes "that the verbal abilities, quantitative reasoning and phonetic abilities of the kindergarten children were superior to those of the non-kindergarten group. In the third grade the kindergarten group's total achievement was markedly superior and had more satisfactory school adjustment over the non-kindergarten groups." And, reporting in *Elementary English* (April, 1966) on a reading readiness program in Glenview, Illinois, Robert L. Hillerich says that "children who had the readiness program in kindergarten began reading sooner in first grade and also read many more library books during the year."

As the Mindess study suggests, the kindergartner develops not only learning skills but also social skills. Kindergarten stresses play, allowing the child freedom of expression during a large part of the school day with classmates. According to "Education is Play," an article in the February 1973 issue of *Childhood Education,* "Play is the . . . way the small child discovers how to use the world for his own purposes, to manipulate it. He does so by imagining in his head . . . and then externalizing those imaginings in his play." Kindergarten is also the child's first opportunity to learn from television with the aid of a teacher, and this, too, is part of an important socializing process. *"Sesame Street:* Shaping Broadcast Television to the Needs of the Preschoolers," an article in *Educational Technology,* makes the following observations about two classes: "One class gave the program its entire attention. Down the hall a class of children the same age was only partially attentive. . . . The explanation seems to be found in the different attitudes of the two teachers. One teacher is indifferent. . . . Her colleague down the hall socializes the attitude in the opposite direction. When the program hour draws near, she enthusiastically announces, 'It is *Sesame Street* time.'" She then gets the children's attention and encourages a positive attitude toward the program. Improved perception and social awareness are achievements of kindergarten programs that provide a fruitful learning experience for a child.

That is what kindergarten really is, a fruitful learning experience. Public education officials in many states are robbing five- and six-year-olds of opportunities for knowledge by not supporting large-scale kindergarten programs. Although high costs for education are a problem everywhere, we can take advantage of unpaid volunteers who might be interested in helping children. Senior citizens who are retired or who are out of work, for example, could help many states expand limited educational programs. With some simple training, volunteers could assist in providing important skills for school-age children throughout the country. And, such a program would help bring meaning to the lives of many old people who have little to do but waste time. Early learning experiences are essential for children, and to assure a strong society we must provide the means for educating kindergartners in social and intellectual skills.

—*April Wynn*

Step 2. Understanding the Essay.
1. How does April Wynn's introduction set the stage for her proposal?
2. What two basic features of kindergarten does she support in her essay?

3. What statistics or cases do you find most impressive? Which quotation is most dramatic in supporting the writer's point?
4. What new context does the writer set in her conclusion? Has she made a convincing point? Explain your reasons.

Some Topics for Child Development Essays

You might want to choose one of these suggested topics to develop in an essay that relies upon research. Some of the topics are quite specific; others require narrowing before they can lead to productive essays. (Review pages 345–355.)

open classrooms in England

the "new math"

computers and learning to read

black schools in a southern city

teaching children about drug abuse

sibling rivalries

student dropouts

adopted children

teaching Chinese students English

the effects of busing

the value of *Sesame Street*

John Dewey's basic views

the gifted child

teaching the mentally retarded

the effects of television commercials on young children

training the early-childhood teacher

learning rate: boys' and girls'

diet and hyperactive children

day-care centers and the learning process

economics and education

teaching the slow learner to read

developing oral language for the deaf

early-childhood sex education

driver-education programs

the emotional needs of children

role models for children

children's books

juvenile delinquency

education in foreign countries

teaching independence to children

speech disorders and the young child

GETTING READER RESPONSE

After you write a draft of your introduction and first body paragraph, divide the class into groups of three. Let each person read his or her paper aloud while the other group members take notes. After each paper is read, answer the following questions:

1. Does the proposal sentence inform the reader of the writer's main purpose in the essay?
2. Does the introduction capture and hold the reader's interest?
3. Does the writer make a smooth transition from the introduction to the next paragraph?
4. Are there sufficient details drawn from reliable sources?
5. Are there citations? Are the citations named correctly?

Progress Reminders: A Checklist of Questions

As you plan and write your various drafts, use these questions to check on your progress in preparing your research essay. Fill in responses to the questions and submit this checklist with your essay.

1. Did I think carefully about the topic, using whatever pre-   _____
   writing techniques work for me? Did I plan a realistic work   _____
   schedule?
2. Did I check several library resources, including books and   _____
   periodicals?
3. Did I limit my topic sufficiently?   _____

4. Did I prepare bibliography cards and note cards?   _____

5. Did I write a proposal sentence that asserts the topic clearly and allows me to develop two aspects of it, one in each of my body paragraphs? (See pages 258–261.) Did I revise the proposal sentence, if necessary, to reflect changes in my thinking as my research and writing progressed? _____ _____

6. Did I organize my research notes with a note-card summary or some such plan? Did I write an outline if my teacher required one? (See pages 515–516.) _____ _____

7. Did I write a rough draft and subsequent drafts changing language and sentence structure for clarity and correctness? Does my final draft follow correct manuscript form? _____ _____

8. Did I use adequate detail—statistics, cases, quotations, concrete sensory images, or a combination of these? Did I write quotations and paraphrases correctly, and did I cite my sources according to the instructions on pages 201–205 or 497–499? _____ _____

9. Did I read the student themes on pages 366–368 as models for my essay? _____

10. Did I use transitions to connect ideas smoothly and logically, both within paragraphs and from one paragraph to another? _____

11. Did I write an introduction that stimulates the reader's interest? (See pages 261–266.) _____

12. Does my conclusion bring to a successful closing the points I make in the essay? _____

13. Did I use a variety of sentence types? Did I open sentences with subordinators (pages 100–109); -ing words, infinitives, and other verb parts (pages 208–213); and one or two -ly words (page 60). _____

14. Did I proofread my paper carefully both before and after I prepared my final draft? Did I check my Theme Progress Sheet (page 523) in advance so that I could look especially for my own usual errors? _____ _____

15. Did I write a title for my essay? _____

THE PROFESSIONALS SPEAK

Read the selection below and answer the questions that come after it.

SOME WORDS TO KNOW BEFORE YOU READ

concede: acknowledge as true
debilitating: weakening

determinism: a theory in which causes and effects are linked together
insubordination: not giving in to authority
facilitated: made easier
analogous: similar

Why Some Schools Succeed

What makes a child learn? What keeps him from it? Is it the school building or the pupil-teacher ratio? The mood of the classroom? The way the lessons are taught? Or, in the long run, do things like that really not matter much, and is a child's academic fate determined instead by such factors as his race, his family's social class and the condition of his neighborhood?

That traditional debate has been joined by a group of British experts in an important new book that disputes some well-established theories about elementary education.

After a four-year study of 12 schools in poor neighborhoods of London, they found that the way a school is run can make a huge difference in how much a child learns and how he behaves.

Their findings, backed up with impressive statistics, fly in the face of a popular American theory that holds that if a student body has too many social disadvantages, there is not much that can be done for it educationally.

"Our study should give hope to anyone who had despaired of improving the quality of education in inner cities," said Dr. Janet Ouston, one of the four co-authors of the book, which is called *Fifteen Thousand Hours* (a reference to the total amount of time that a child spends at school). "Simply put, we found that there really are ways that the schools can be improved to make them more effective."

What matters most, the researchers found, is what they called the *ethos* of a school—the general tone of the place—which seemed to have more effect on pupil performance than such factors as the age of the physical plant or how strictly the children were disciplined.

The finding that schools do make a difference may seem obvious; as the book concedes, it "will come as no surprise to parents, who often go to a good deal of trouble to get their children into schools of their choice."

But regardless of what parents have thought, a good many professionals on both sides of the Atlantic have been greatly influenced over the past decade by Dr. James Coleman and Christopher Jencks, two American educators whose writings led many to the conclusion that schools in the poorest neighborhoods are unlikely to do much for their pupils until the neighborhoods are improved.

"Variations in what children learn at school," Mr. Jencks wrote in 1972, "depend largely on variations in what they bring to school, not on variations in what schools offer them," and the result achieved by a school "depends largely on a single input—the characteristics of the entering children."

That theory, and what some see as the debilitating determinism that it encourages, are disputed by the London study.

"The findings showed that school differences were not just a reflection of intake patterns, and that much of the effects of schools were linked with their features as social organizations," the authors declare, and then set out to prove it, showing how similar schools only a few miles apart can produce radically different results.

If the Jencks theory is correct, two inner-city schools that take in the same proportion of boys with behavior problems should turn out about the same proportion of boys with behavior problems. But that is not at all what happened in the schools studied here.

Fifteen Thousand Hours describes what it calls *School A* and *School B*, in each of which one-third of the incoming 10-year-olds had exhibited behavior problems, such as truancy, vandalism or insubordination. Four years later, fewer than 10 percent of the boys at School A had behavior problems, whereas the proportion at School B had risen to 48 percent.

"Clearly, one school was doing the right thing and the other was not," Dr. Ouston said. "In other words, the school did make a difference."

The research team, which was headed by Michael Rutter, a professor of child psychiatry at the University of London, came to the same sort of conclusion in regard to academic achievement. Although the schools studied tended to have pupils of about the same intellectual range, as measured by independent tests at the age of 10, there was marked variation in how the children did a few years later.

In one of its most startling findings, the University of London team reported that children in the bottom aptitude rank of the best school did as well, in final examination scores, as the children in the top rank of the worst school. In other words, a dull child entering one of the better schools had statistically the same chance to make good grades as a bright child entering one of the worst ones.

Moreover, a school that was good in one area tended to be good in others as well, reinforcing the theory that how the school is run makes a difference.

The book did not try to comprehensively assess exactly what it is that makes good schools good, leaving that to future research. But Dr. Rutter's team tentatively concluded that a major factor in making schools good was what it called "their characteristics as social institutions," including the degree of academic emphasis, the degree to which teachers got involved in lessons, the availability of rewards for students, and the extent to which children were given responsibility.

Children tended to do better, for example, in schools where the classes began on time, where teachers gave immediate and frequent praise, and where the pupils were made to feel that success was expected of them.

Naturally, good teaching was of great importance. But the study found, in comparing the schools, that "it was very much easier to be a good teacher in some schools than others."

For example, it concluded that results were better in the schools in which the disciplinary policy and the curriculum were discussed and worked out together by the teachers, rather than being dictated from above.

"It was not just that this facilitated continuities in teaching—although it did—but also that group planning provided opportunities for teachers to encourage and support one another," the book concluded.

In the best schools, though overall standards were higher, inequalities persisted. In the schools in which children of ordinary ability did better than usual, the able children also tended to do better. And it continues to be a built-in advantage to have well-educated parents.

The comparison is analogous, the book explains, to changes in body height: over the last 50 years, the height of the average British school child has increased by 9 centimeters (about 3½ inches), presumably because of better nutrition. But that does not mean, of course, that all children are now the same height. There have been "major changes in level, without any reduction in inequality."

The same thing can be done, *Fifteen Thousand Hours* maintains, with academic performance; schools can be improved to the benefit of everyone's performance.

It is not argued that schools are the most important influence on children's progress," the book concludes. "Education cannot compensate for the inequalities of society. Nevertheless, we do suggest that schools constitute one major area of influence, and one which is susceptible to change."

—William Borders
The New York Times

1. What is the writer's main source of information? Why might you believe it to be a reliable source?
2. What statistics does the writer cite? Underline them in the passage.
3. Where has the writer quoted directly from someone else's work? Where does he paraphrase someone else's findings? How has he avoided plagiarism?
4. What cases does the writer use? Underline them.

REACHING HIGHER

Step 1. More Topics to Research. Here are several other areas in which statistical information might provide astonishing conclusions. Select one and prepare a well-written essay using the skills you have learned in this chapter.

poverty in your home state
ghetto health conditions
nuclear-bomb production
dishonesty in politics
prison conditions in your city
violence in the schools
coal mines and working conditions
mental illness in America
automobile safety
illegal adoption services
saving oil
the effects of jogging on physical well-being

Step 2. The Perfect Child. Prepare a list of features that you think would characterize the perfect child. Include information on appearance, behavior, personality, philosophy, and any other qualities you think are important. Then, using the most outstanding features on your list, write a paragraph in which you explore the idea of a "perfect" child.

CHAPTER 9

ARGUMENTATION:
Women in the World of Men

INTRODUCTION TO THE USE OF ARGUMENT

Since Susan B. Anthony led the fight for reform in women's rights in the 1800s, the position of the female in American society has changed dramatically. Though there are still those who would deny a woman's right to equal opportunity, the gains are clear and strong. The twentieth-century woman is moving—for some, too quickly, for others, not quickly enough—into a world once thought exclusively for men. Women doctors step through hospital corridors in greater numbers than ever before; the idea of a woman as a top business executive or a college president is now accepted, even approved, by most people. And females make up 30 to 40% of America's job force. A survey of graduates with B.B.A.'s at the University of Texas revealed in 1975 that starting salaries for female graduates were higher than those for male graduates. In 1965, the average starting salary for a woman graduate in business was 75% lower than that of a male graduate; ten years later the female's salary was 4% higher. During the recession of 1979–1982 women over twenty years old grew in the labor force by over three million, an increase of 8%. Adult males during the same time rose as workers by only a meager one-half of 1%. But other studies show that as men and women advance in their jobs, men usually earn more than women doing the same work. Economist Frances Hutner says, "In 1939 women earned 58 percent of what men earned. Twenty years later, in 1959, women earned 59 percent of what men earned. And in 1977, women still earned only 59 percent of what men earned."

Where do you stand on the issue of women's rights? Do you think that men and women are exactly alike and deserve complete equality? Do you think women are different from men and as a result require special treatment? Do you think women are pretty much ignored for the top jobs in our society? Do you think women *should* be ignored for top positions in business and government? This theme assignment asks you to look at your own attitudes toward women in society and their changing position in the twentieth century.

But you will have to be able to support your attitudes in some way as you write your essays. The true test of an opinion is the way in which the writer makes it convincing and believable. Anyone can scream a point of view angrily, but most educated people require solid reasons before accepting opinions. You can convince someone reasonably about your impressions by illustrating those impressions through dramatic experiences in your own personal life. Or you can try to support your opinions with information that you gather from other sources. If you choose that path, you will have to learn how to avoid the faults in reasoning beginners often show when they write essays to persuade people to change their beliefs.

In this chapter you will also learn more about tying together the parts of an essay more closely. You will examine some of the vocabulary of liberation, and you will practice with problems in writing that cause a number of difficulties: the uses of verbs to indicate time correctly.

VOCABULARY

Step 1. Familiar Words in the Women's Struggle. Much of the language of women's liberation includes words like the following. Using your dictionary, write definitions for them (Appendix A will help you too).

_____   1. feminist

_____   2. suffragist   [These words identify people who are either for or against the

_____   3. chauvinist   women's liberation movement.]

_____   4. hormonal

_____   5. femininity   [These words name biological ideas related to discussions on

_____   6. mortality   women's equality]

_____   7. inferiority

_____   8. stereotype   [Women active in the battle for equality try to fight these condi-

_____   9. degradation   tions.]

_____   10. prejudice

Step 2. Matching Meanings. From the list of words in Step 1, write on the blank line the word whose meaning appears alongside.

_____   1. a person with blind enthusiasm for a cause

_____   2. the quality or nature of the female sex

_____   3. fixed ideas based upon oversimplified opinions about people

_____   4. indicating something poor in quality

_____   5. condition that lowers dignity or quality

_____   6. based upon substances given off by the glands in the body

_____   7. one who believes in the extension of women's activities in social and political life

_____   8. an unfavorable opinion formed in advance without considering the facts

_____   9. women who fought for the right to vote in the early 1900s

_____   10. the stage of human development in which the person becomes sexually mature

Step 3.   More Words in the Struggle for Equality. Write definitions for the following words. Use a dictionary, if necessary, to write your own clear meanings (Appendix A will help you too).

1. pornography _____

2. downtrodden _____

3. inequity _____

4. emancipation _____

5. activist _____

Step 4.   Using Words in Freedom's Fight. From the vocabulary above, write a word that

1. means the state of freedom _____
2. describes someone who works hard for a cause _____
3. names the presentation of erotic behavior to cause sexual excitement
   _____
4. describes people who are kept from advancing and who are ruled over severely, people who are "trampled upon" _____
5. describes an instance of unjustness or unfairness _____

Step 5.   Words in Your Own Sentences. On separate paper, write sentences using any ten words you have learned in this chapter.

BUILDING COMPOSITION SKILLS

Step 1.   A Questionnaire on Women. The statements below examine your attitudes on women in our society.

   If you agree with the statement completely, put the number 1 in the blank space.

   If you agree with the statement to some degree, put the number 2 in the blank space.

   If you completely disagree with the statement, put the number 3 in the blank space.

   If you have no idea or feeling at all about the statement, put the number 4 in the blank space.

_____   1. Women should not hold a position of great responsibility because they are much more emotional than men.

_____   2. Unmarried women are not as happy as married women.

_____ 3. A woman's greatest fulfillment is giving birth and being a mother.

_____ 4. Women are by nature more artistic than men.

_____ 5. Housework does not have to be dull; a woman can find her job in the house creative and rewarding.

_____ 6. The right of abortion is one that all women should be able to use if they want to.

_____ 7. Certain jobs are "women" jobs; certain jobs are "men" jobs.

_____ 8. Women enjoy being treated like little girls and being taken care of by the men who love them.

_____ 9. A woman should no longer be forced to take her husband's last name when they get married. It is an outdated and sexist tradition.

_____ 10. If the choice for a job is between a woman whose husband works and a man who must support his family, the job should go to the man.

Step 2. Illustrating Opinions. Select any statement from the above questionnaire for which you have written a 1 or a 3 in the margin. Discuss your reasons for believing what you do by giving an illustration from your own experience.

Step 3. Woman Talk. These famous statements on women come from people in our time and in the past. Discuss with the class the one that you think most appropriate in today's world.

1. To be born a woman has been to be born, within an allotted and confined space, into the keeping of men. The social presence of women has developed as a result of the ingenuity in living under such tutelage within such a limited space.
—*John Berger*

2. . . . the Black movement is primarily concerned with the liberation of Blacks as a class and does not promote women's liberation as a priority. . . . The feminist movement, on the other hand, is concerned with the oppression of women as a class, but is almost totally composed of white females. Thus the Black woman finds herself on the outside of both political entities, in spite of the fact that she is the object of both forms of oppression.
—*Kay Lindsey*

3. The great question that has never been answered, and which I have not yet been able to answer despite my thirty years of research into the feminine soul, is: What does a woman want?
—*Sigmund Freud*

4. A girl should not be too intelligent or too good or too highly differentiated in any direction. Like a ready-made garment she should be designed to fit the average man.
—*Emily James Putnam*

5. Man's best possession is a loving wife.
—*Robert Burton*

6. Women in our society complain of the lack of stimulation, of the loneliness, of the dullness of staying at home.

—*Margaret Mead*

Interview Techniques

For a current topic like women's rights, a topic that interests a wide range of people, you can gather ideas and details by interviewing. An interview gives you firsthand experience in collecting and comparing data; by talking to several people, you broaden your sense of the issue. Further, if you have taken notes carefully, you have lots of raw material upon which to draw as you plan and write your essay.

THE INTERVIEW: TIPS FOR GOOD TECHNIQUES

1. Write down questions about the general idea you are investigating. If you choose to interview people about whether or not women should serve in high political offices, you might prepare a list like this one:
   a. Should women get preferred treatment in political offices?
   b. What special qualities, if any, can women bring to high-pressure jobs?
   c. Would a woman make a good president of the United States?
   d. What women in politics do you admire? dislike?
   e. Are there any sex-related qualities that make men or women better suited for certain political jobs? What are those qualities?
2. Good questioning is a real skill. Try to make your questions draw out the answers you want to know.
3. Listen carefully to what people say. Take notes as they speak, eliminating any information that is not important. Be careful to get as much important material as you can as accurately as you can. If someone says "sometimes" or "maybe," make sure that you do not change those remarks into "always" or "definitely."
4. Ask everyone the same questions. That gives you a basis for comparing any differences of opinion.
5. Identify the people who agree to give information to you. Be specific so that in your essay you are able to quote somebody's exact words accurately. Say "Charles Davidson, a freshman at Fairleigh Dickinson, said '. . . .'" If you want to present your interviewing results statistically in your essay, you do not need to identify every person you interview. You can say, "Seven out of the ten people I spoke to agreed that . . . . "
6. Write down exact quotations where you can. This requires very careful listening and quick writing. But often the interviewee says something so unusual or so important that you want it down exactly as it is said; then when you write up your findings in an essay, the quote can add liveliness and interest to your own work.
7. If the person you are interviewing is important, take down some details of his or her character and appearance to spark your own presentation of the person's ideas.

Step 1.   Practice Interviewing. Select some aspect of women's rights that interests you, and conduct at least five interviews with people in your school or home community. Your instructor may suggest that the class break down into groups so that students can ask each other questions. Follow the tips for good techniques in the chart above.

Logical Arguments

When you relate from your personal experience some moment about a given topic or subject, you are not attempting to *prove* your idea. You merely demonstrate your point in that way. When you seek to argue a point by giving *proofs,* however, you often need more than just a single instance from your life. To try to prove that women are competent as doctors by basing your argument upon one experience you had with one good woman doctor would be unconvincing. For readers to agree with your point of view, you need material that is solid and plentiful, evidence that is believable, reasoning that is not faulty.

The fifteen types of poor reasoning below show some of the more familiar kinds of incorrect evidence students frequently use in essays. Each logic trap is followed by an example and an explanation alongside.

FIFTEEN FAULTS TO FAIL THE ARGUMENT

1. *Don't* give too few instances to prove a point.

Example
Women cannot be trusted to make decisions when the pressure gets rough. My wife cries as soon as some high-pressure situation arises.

How could one instance support the point?

2. *Don't* use famous people's names as the sole proof of your point.

Example
Whitney Lewis, the actor, advertises that camera, so I'm sure it's good.

How does the mentioning of the name prove that the product is good?

3. *Don't* praise or blame the *people* who state a proof you cite—and then ignore the idea.

Example
She's such a brilliant scholar that any candidate she supports has to be good.

Praising the woman's intelligence does not prove that the candidate is a good one.

He's an atheist. As a candidate, therefore, he has to be weak.

Attacking the man's religious beliefs does not prove that the candidate is a poor one.

4. *Don't* try to prove something by showing that people always believed in a certain thing.

Example
Women have never been allowed to compete with men in professional sports. Why should we allow it now?

People may have believed one thing a long time ago. But they can change their minds.

5. *Don't* try to prove something by showing that everyone is doing it.

Example

Young people all over the world are using marijuana without harm. And many middle-aged people too are joining the drug culture. How harmful can marijuana be?	So what if everyone does it? How does that prove it is not harmful?

6. *Don't* try to prove something by saying the point over and over again.

Example

Women ought to have the same rights as men. Women's rights are just as important as men's rights, and women should receive the same treatment as men. After all, women have rights, too.	There is no proof here at all, just the same point made again and again.

7. *Don't* use a source to back up an idea unless the source is reliable and an authority.

Examples

My brother Jerry says politicians are liars and cheats, and I have always trusted his judgment.	What makes Jerry an authority on politicians?
The president of Apco, a leading oil company, believes that lead in automobile gasoline is really not a polluting agent.	An oil company that has to remove lead from its fuel may have to spend large sums of money. It might be expected to try to disprove lead as a polluter.

8. *Don't* make a comparison that is weak or not true.

Example

I know I can drive a motorcycle. I can ride a bicycle, can't I?	The writer fails to realize that there are many differences between bicycles and motorcycles.

9. *Don't* appeal to a person's prejudices or unreasonable emotions.

Examples

Foreign-born people should not be allowed to work at all kinds of jobs. If they are, Americans will be squeezed out of work, and you and I will be out of employment.	This writer tries to arouse the reader by appealing to personal involvement. Where is the proof that readers will lose their jobs to others?
Anyone who opposes Governor Badley's re-election is anti-American!	This writer uses a word intended to fire up emotions unreasonably. Instead of real proof, he uses a name that is designed to arouse feelings.

10. *Don't* draw conclusions that do not follow from previous information.

Examples

When Astor was president of the union we really made progress. Now that Alterman has taken over, men are losing jobs and getting less and less overtime.	The writer doesn't take into account other factors. There is no proof here that the loss of jobs has anything to do with the new president.

| When I went to college, I got all A's and B's. Anyone who wants to can get good grades. | The second sentence doesn't follow from the first because the writer does not take into account individual learning abilities. |

11. *Don't* try to prove that someone or something is good or bad only because of associations with other "good" or "bad" things.

Examples

| How could he be a criminal? He goes to work in the morning, has dinner out with his family on Sundays, and is best friends with the mayor and the principal of our high school. | This proof of innocence is built by trying to associate a person with good and solid qualities of citizenship. But it does not prove the man is no criminal. If he deals in drugs, what would his friendship with the mayor prove? |
| Since the dean was found guilty of robbing city funds, surely the president himself must have some illegal dealings too. | This is "guilt by association": The president is not guilty of crimes because one associate is guilty. |

12. *Don't* generalize—that is, don't make one fact the source of a broad conclusion. *Don't* state the proof so strongly as to admit no possibilities of exceptions; always leave room for a margin of error.

Example

| Women drivers are the worst drivers on the road. | It may be true that some women—like some men—are poor drivers, but this certainly is not true of all of them. |

13. *Don't* try to show that if something happened *after* an event, that thing is necessarily a *result* of the event.

Example

| Five convicted killers said that when they were younger, they enjoyed watching programs of violence on television. This proves that watching violent actions on the screen can lead to murder. | Did the killers murder *because* they watched violence on television? This might be a contributing factor, but as a proof alone, it is not very solid. |

14. *Don't* state your proof in *either-or* terms.

Example

| It is no wonder that he failed so many courses. College students go to school or they work; they certainly cannot do both. | What about the people who work only an hour a day, or those who work weekends or summers? This writer suggests that there are only two alternatives when there are many |

15. *Don't* ignore information that contradicts the point you wish to make.

Example

| A large number of investigations suggests that legalizing heroin would be a positive step toward controlling drug abuse. | On such a controversial issue, the writer should mention studies that disagree with the statement. Much material is available on the failure of parts of the British system in which drugs have been legalized. |

Step 1.   Finding Foggy Thinking. Each statement below contains some error in argument such as the ones described above. Discuss the errors the writers make. Then tell how you would correct the statement.

1. Samuel Taylor Coleridge and Edgar Allan Poe both used drugs and still created great works of art. Writers should use some drug if they need stimulation for their work.
2. You're kidding! You're twenty-three years old and you don't drink?
3. The whole mood of the country is changing. Just last week, the school board forbade us to teach Kurt Vonnegut in literature classes anymore.
4. Most minorities live in such wretched conditions. Why don't they get off welfare, get jobs, and clean up their neighborhoods?
5. How could anyone who keeps his hair so long and who wears dungarees and sandals all the time know anything about politics?
6. A recent study by WKLO-TV shows no connection between actual violence and violence performed on television programs.
7. That family does not go to church on Sundays. They must all be atheists.
8. If we don't stop the Russians in El Salvador, they'll be at our doorstep soon enough.
9. Those boys left the party right after the diamond ring was stolen. They must have taken it!
10. That actor played the role of Fidel Castro so convincingly, he must believe that Castro is a good man.

Step 2.   Straight Thinking, Strong Proofs. How would you go about proving or disproving each statement below? Discuss your answers, making sure to avoid the faults in argument you just learned.

1. Women's rights expanded markedly in the 1970s.
2. A father who raises children without the help of a wife does a less efficient job than a mother who raises children without the help of a husband.
3. Women executives in business are more efficient than men executives.
4. The attitude of single young women toward sex has not changed in the last ten years.
5. A woman competing with a man in a high-pressure political job would never stand a chance of success.
6. Most feminists are too aggressive; therefore, they alienate more people than they convert.
7. In the 1980s, more and more women have come to accept their natural roles as wives and mothers.
8. A major problem for women who want to get ahead in business is not men but other women.

Step 3.   Proof for Attitudes on Women. Return to the questionnaire in Step 1, pages 378–379. Select any item for which you have written the number 1 or 3, and in the blank lines below show how you would attempt to prove your opinion.

Hint

This time do not use personal experience as proof. Plan on using other kinds of details. See crucial questions 2 to 4 on page 401.

_____

_____

_____

_____

Using Opposing Arguments

If you are trying to support an idea that you know not everybody agrees on, you can defend your point of view with details of personal experience, statistics, or quotations. But you should not ignore the issues raised on the other side of the argument. What the opposition (those who disagree with you) believes can give you the content of a solid paragraph.

WHY TO MENTION OPPOSITE OPINIONS

1. Your reference to opposite opinions shows that you know what others are saying.
2. It shows that you are not purposely overlooking points in order to make your own ideas look stronger.
3. It shows that you are fair and that you do not see things in black and white only, that you are willing to consider ideas and points that do not agree with yours.
4. It gives you more to write about: you can go on to attack the ideas others have, if you wish.

   Hint: The introduction is a very good place in any essay to mention the points of view that oppose yours: as you discuss those ideas that do not go along with your own, you build up to your own proposal that states what you believe and what you will try to prove.

Step 1. Seeking the Opposition. Assume that the proposal in Column I is one that you would try to support in an essay. Write in Column II three *opposing* arguments that others might raise against your point of view.

I   *II*

Example
A. A woman's place is at home with her family.

1. *Women are efficient workers.*
2. *Women are creative on the job.*
3. *Some women are psychologically unfit for the dullness of housework.*

_____

B. A woman who rises to the top of a corporation leads a life of excitement and challenge.

1. _____

2. _____

3. _____

C. There are few differences between the
way men and women perform as teachers.

1. _____

2. _____

3. _____

D. Women are not as practical as men.

1. _____

2. _____

3. _____

E. In every profession, a woman should receive equal pay for doing the same work
as a man.

1. _____

2. _____

3. _____

Opposing Arguments: Where to Place Them

The introduction is a good place in an essay to mention the points of view that
oppose yours. Using the ideas that do not go along with your own, you can build
up to a proposal sentence that states what you believe in and what you will try to
prove.

In the introduction below notice how the writer discusses opposing arguments. The effect here comes, of course, when the reader finally reaches the
proposal sentence. It is apparent only there that the writer's position is opposite
to all the points made so far.

The jogging craze is sweeping the country. Before dawn, at noon, after dusk, men
and women everywhere take to the trails and to the streets; in fancy jogging suits or
in simple jeans and T-shirts these people are running to improve their health and
fitness. Jogging tones the muscles, helps the heart work more efficiently, takes off
unwanted poundage. Psychologically runners boast a relaxed life-style, a sense of
peace with themselves. But this exercise is probably the worst form of self-torture any
human being can inflict upon mind and body.

There are other places in the essay where you can explore your opposition.

If you know sound arguments that are raised in opposition to your
proposal, you can build one body paragraph around those opposing arguments.
Paragraph 2 of your essay can mention a few of the points made by people who
disagree with you, and you might show with solid details the evidence these
people give for believing what they do. Another possibility, if there are many
arguments on the opposition's side, is to state in the second paragraph of your

essay as many of the most effective arguments against your position as you possibly can. Then you can write paragraph 3 in one of two ways.

1. Try to disprove the arguments of the opposition. Give details to convince your reader that you are right and that "they" are wrong.
2. Say that the points the opposition raises are good, but that you believe differently. Give details to convince the reader that your points are just as good as the points made by those who oppose you.

On pages 406–409 you can see how opposing arguments serve in a body paragraph.

Step 2. Paragraph Practice: The Opposition in Introductions. Select any proposal and opposing ideas from Step 1 on pages 385–386. Write a brief introduction that mentions the opposition's points as it builds to the proposal statement. You may change the proposal somewhat. Use separate paper.

Hint

Transitional expressions like *however, but, on the other hand* will help you introduce the proposal.

Step 3. Paragraph Practice: The Opposition in a Body Paragraph. Select any proposal from Step 1 on pages 385–386 as the proposal of any essay, and write a brief first body paragraph in which you show what arguments could be used against your proposal. Develop just a few arguments with specific details, or mention a number of arguments that are frequently used against the proposal. Use your own paper.

Hint

In this paragraph do not try to prove that the opposition is wrong.

Sentence Combining: Changing Verb Forms to Expand Sentences

You remember from exercises in another chapter how verb parts as sentence openers help you vary your style. You can use verb parts in other positions, too, to connect logically elements in one sentence to another nearby. In some cases, eliminating all or part of a verb helps you unite thoughts. Looking over your early drafts, then, you can tighten sentence structure by manipulating verbs.

Look at this group of sentences:

(A) Charlene slumped in the driver's seat. (B) She gripped the wheel tightly. (C) Her neck was tense. (D) Her eyes were red. (E) She stared angrily through the windshield.

1. You could combine sentences A and B by changing one of the underlined verbs into an *-ing* form and by using it to open a new sentence:

Slumping in the driver's seat, Charlene gripped the wheel tightly.

or

Gripping the wheel tightly, Charlene slumped in the driver's seat.

2. In another kind of combination you could keep the verb in its *-ed* form and combine A and B in this way:

Slumped in the driver's seat, Charlene gripped the wheel tightly.

3. Sometimes you can drop the verb or part of it and can join what's left of the sentence to a sentence nearby. If you took out the verb *was* from sentence C look at how the rest of it combines with B or A or E:

Her neck tense, she gripped the wheel tightly.
Her neck tense, Charlene slumped in the driver's seat.
She stared angrily through the windshield, her neck tense.

The steps numbered 1, 2, and 3 are especially helpful in allowing you to transform—transform means to change into something else—a series of complete thoughts into one sentence that combines the ideas of the several sentences. Of course, you have to decide which ideas you want to stress so that your new sentence structure emphasizes them. The kind of transformation you do depends upon the meaning you are aiming for. But transforming sentences is valuable because it means, first, that a writer can often use fewer words than otherwise necessary to make a point and, next, that a writer has more options for varying sentence structure.

By using the techniques explained in 1, 2, and 3 to combine a whole series of sentences connected in meaning like those in sentences A through E above, look at just two of the possibilities you have for expanded sentences:

Slumping in the driver's seat (A) and staring angrily through the windshield (E), Charlene gripped the wheel tightly (B), her neck tense (C), her eyes red (D).

Her neck tense (C), her eyes red (D), slumped in the driver's seat (A) and gripping the wheel tightly (B), Charlene stared angrily through the windshield (E).

In each case, before you combine you need to decide which sentence in the group you think is most important, which sentence you want to emphasize. Keep that as the base sentence and use the other sentences, which you change by transforming their verbs, to expand and to modify it.

Hint

Be sure that the verb part you use stands close enough to the word it modifies so that you avoid illogical sentences. Instructions about verb-part *openers* on pages 208–213 go for verb parts used in any sentence positions.

Step 1. Combining Sentences by Transforming Verbs. Create one complete sentence by combining the sentences in each group. Transform the verb into another form as you saw in the previous examples. You may have to change a noun subject into a pronoun, or vice versa.

> *Hint*
>
> Decide which sentence will be your base sentence; transform the verbs in the surrounding sentences only.

1. A crow sat on the branch of an oak tree. He cawed at the wind. He hopped from branch to branch. His feathers were black as tar. His eyes were small and beady.

   _____

   _____

   _____

2. My husband worked hard in the kitchen. He was sweating. His face was red and hot. He lifted the turkey. He turned it over. He pushed it back into the oven.

   _____

   _____

   _____

3. The actor proclaimed himself a feminist. He spoke passionately at a rally. His voice trembled. He looked nothing like his usually calm character. He thrilled the crowd listening to him.

   _____

   _____

   _____

4. Night crept up on us. It came with no warning. It completely enveloped us. It made it nearly impossible to find our way back to camp. It worried us greatly.

   _____

   _____

   _____

5. Feminism works for all people. It encourages equality among the sexes. It is an important political philosophy for today. It brings people together on the strength of their abilities.

   _____

   _____

   _____

SOLVING PROBLEMS IN WRITING

Verb Tense

Every verb has three main forms, called *principal parts,* and from these all the different tenses are made. The present tense, the past, and the future you usually have little trouble using; but other tenses are not so simple. Look for a moment at the verb *to laugh* and its three main parts. Underneath, you will find an explanation of the tense that is made from each part.

TO LAUGH

I	*II*	*III*
laugh *The Present Tense*	laughed *The Past Tense*	laughed *Tenses That Show Continuing Action*
They *laugh* too loudly. She *laughs* softly.	I *laughed also.* They *laughed* aloud.	He *has laughed without stopping.* *(This action began in the past, but may go on into the present.)* She *had laughed* before they arrived. *(This action began in the past but was over before another action in the past.)* Before next week she *will have laughed* at all the dull jokes in the book. *(This action will be finished before some definite time in the future.)*
The Future Tense They *will laugh* tomorrow. I *shall laugh* too.		

    Hint: How to Form Tenses That Show Continuing Action:
1. Always use the third main part of the verb. (You will see later the main parts of many other verbs. These parts are always arranged in the same order as those above.)
2. Always use a helping verb:
   has   had   will have
   have   shall have

(continued on next page)

TO LAUGH *(continued)*

For *most* verbs (like *to laugh),* the principal parts are easy. All you need to know is the infinitive. If you take away the word *to,* you have the first main part of the verb (and you can form the present and future tense). If you add *-d* or *-ed* to the first main part, you have *both* the second and third main parts, and you can form the past tense and all the tenses that show actions that continue. Here are two other examples:

	I	*II*	*III*
		(add *-ed*)	(add *-ed*)
to talk	talk	talked	talked
	They talk. She talks. We will talk. I shall talk.	I talked. They talked.	She has talked. They have talked. She had talked. They will have talked.
		(add *-d*)	(add *-d*)
to dance	dance	danced	danced
	They dance. She dances. We will dance. I shall dance.	I danced. They danced.	She has danced. They have danced. She had danced. They will have danced.

Step 1. Writing Main Parts of Verbs. From each infinitive below, make the three main parts in the same way as in the examples *to talk* and *to dance.* Write the verb parts in the columns listed.

	I	*II*	*III*
to kiss	_____	_____	_____
to clean	_____	_____	_____
to whisper	_____	_____	_____
to skate	_____	_____	_____
to inquire	_____	_____	_____

Troublesome Verb Parts

Unfortunately, a number of verbs do not form their parts as easily as the ones above. These verbs—called *irregular* because they are different from the usual—also happen to be among those we use most often, so it is not surprising to hear and to see a number of mistakes with them in spoken and written

English. Although the list below does not include *all* the irregular verbs, it tries to indicate those most frequently used incorrectly. The starred verb is not irregular, but it still confuses many writers.

Thirty-Three Headaches: Irregular Verb Parts You Need to Know

I	II	III
Today I	Yesterday I	Frequently I have
am	was	been
begin	began	begun
break	broke	broken
bring	brought	brought
burst	burst	burst
choose	chose	chosen
come	came	come
do	did	done
drink	drank	drunk
*drown	drowned	drowned
eat	ate	eaten
fly	flew	flown
freeze	froze	frozen
give	gave	given
go	went	gone
know	knew	known
lend	lent	lent
ring	rang	rung
rise	rose	risen
run	ran	run
see	saw	seen
sing	sang	sung
sit	sat	sat
speak	spoke	spoken
steal	stole	stolen
swim	swam	swum
take	took	taken
teach	taught	taught
tear	tore	torn
think	thought	thought
throw	threw	thrown
wear	wore	worn
write	wrote	written

SOME ADVICE IN MAKING TENSES

   1. If you can say *now, today, at present* before the verb, select the form from Column 1.

   Example
   Now I *take* French.
   Now they will *write* a letter.
   At present she *swims* well.

   2. If you can say *yesterday* before the verb, select the form from Column II.

   Example
   Yesterday I *wore* a black tie.
   Yesterday they *swam* at sea.

   3. If you can say *frequently* or *often* and one of the helpers *(has, have, had, shall have, will have)* before the verb, select the form from Column III.

   Example
   Often I *have done* good work.
   Frequently they *have stolen* bicycles.

Step 1.   Saying Aloud Correct Verb Parts. Many people do not use verb parts correctly in their writing because the correct forms sound incorrect to the ear. Speak aloud each sentence below so that you learn the sound of the correct verb—no matter how strange it sounds to you.

1. The telephone *has rung* fifteen times. Why don't you answer it?
2. A cat *drowned* in Hyat's Creek yesterday.
3. I *lent* Elyssa my copy of Tillie Olsen's book.
4. They *have* already *drunk* a case of cola.
5. After the boy *had swum* across the lake, he rested.

Step 2.   Correcting Students' Errors. Cross out any incorrect verb part in the sentences below, which have been spoken or written by college students. Put the correct verb part in the blank space on the left.

_____ 1. I seen him running away.

_____ 2. I wish I had took an English class instead of a computer math course.

_____ 3. Was I surprised when he brung those flowers!

_____ 4. Everyone in the courtroom had rose by the time the judge entered.

_____ 5. Don't look at me—they done it.

_____ 6. Mary has chose the wallpaper with pretty yellow daisies.

_____ 7. The bubble busted when I saw her with another man.

_____ 8. Frequently I have ate at the sidewalk cafe.

_____ 9. Nobody could have sang "Summertime" as well as Billie Holiday did.

Using *Has* or *Have* with Verbs

You use *has* or *have* with a verb form from Column III if you want to show an action that started sometime in the past but is still continuing.

She *has laughed* for five minutes.
↖ [She began in the past but is still laughing now.]

If the action began in the past and ended in the past, use the past tense (Column-II verb form).

She *laughed* for five minutes.
↖ [She began in the past, but ended before now.]

Step 3.   Verbs with *Has* or *Have*. For each infinitive in parentheses, write the correct form of the verb in the blank space on the left.

> *Hint*
> If *has, have, had, will have,* or *shall have* appears before the verb, pick the form from Column III on page 392.

_____ 1. The children have (to ring) the doorbell.

_____ 2. By this afternoon I will have (to eat) four dozen clams.

_____   and Jim will have (to drink) ten cans of cola.

_____ 3. Rosalita has (to choose) to attend the University of Nebraska.

_____ 4. Charles has (to speak) of you many times.

_____ 5. Because Esteban has (to give) his time to repairing the windows, we will all be comfortable this winter.

_____ 6. For the past three years a child has nearly (to drown) in the ocean each summer.

_____ 7. The class has (to come) to an agreement about the final exam.

_____ 8. It is so cold that the lock has (to freeze) solid and the pipes have (to

_____ burst).

_____ 9. Where have you (to go)?

Had as Verb Helper

If a sentence expresses two actions in the past and one of the actions came before the other, the verb that names the earlier action needs *had* as a helper.

The man thought that he *had seen* a ghost.

    [This is one   [This past action came
    past action.]   before the man had the
                              thought.]

Step 4. Using *Had* Correctly as Verb Helper. Complete each sentence below by using *had* with the correct form of the verb in parentheses and any other words you need to complete the thought. Study the example.

(to come) 1. Yesterday we heard that you *had come late to class.* _____

(to steal) 2. Fortunately we visited the museum before thieves _____.

(to take) 3. We found out too late that Carmen _____

_____.

(to know) 4. Before he moved into the neighborhood, I_____.

(to tear) 5. I arrived too late; she already_____

_____.

(to drink) 6. We saw the sparrow after it_____

_____.

(to rise) 7. Before the rooster crowed, an orange sun _____

_____.

(to teach) 8. He left his faculty position in 1981; before that he _____.

(to write) 9. Sonia was thrilled because the magazine accepted the story

she_____.

Will Have, Shall Have with Verbs

Use *will have* or *shall have* with a verb part if you want to show that an action will be finished before some definite time in the future.

By tonight, I *will have made* twelve telephone calls.

    Hint
In formal writing, *shall* is used only with *I* and *we. Will* is used with any subject.

Step 5.   Your Sentences with *Will Have* or *Shall Have*. Use each of these word groups in a sentence of your own. Use separate paper.

shall have spoken	will have taken
will have written	shall have seen
will have swum	

Example
By tomorrow I shall have seen your employer.

Shifting Tenses

When you write, be careful not to switch back and forth unnecessarily from present to past tense. If you are telling about an event that occurred in the past, use the past tense. Look at this sentence:

    I saw my friend Thomas and he asks me, "Where are you going?"

Saw is a past-tense verb.

Asks is a present-tense verb and should be replaced by *asked,* a past-tense verb.

Are is not incorrect, even though it is in the present tense, because the writer is quoting someone's exact words.

    The correct sentence would be

    I saw my friend Thomas and he asked [*not asks*] me, "Where are you going?"

Step 1.   Tense Shifts. Correct the tense shifts in each sentence below. Write the verbs correctly in the spaces on the left. Write *C* if the sentence is correct.

_____   1. When I noticed him he looks the other way and runs off.

_____   2. I wanted a small pizza, but she carries out a large one and hands it to
_____   me. I decided to keep it.

_____   3. I feel the softness of the tulip petals as they brushed the back of my
_____   hand.

_____   4. My life was pretty easy until I graduate from high school.

_____   5. I told him the bench was wet, but he sits down without listening and

_____   then gives a loud yell of anger.

_____   6. After he awakens, he prepares breakfast before he showers and

_____   dresses for work.

_____   7. Rose waited hours for her brother to come home.

_____   8. Men fear changes because they brought up feelings of being domi-

_____   nated by women.

_____   9. Years ago, people went to college because they want to educate

___ _____   themselves.

Some Confusing Verbs: *Lie* and *Lay*

The words *lie* and *lay* are two different verbs.

To lie means "to rest or to recline."

To lay means "to put or to place something."

Here are the three main parts of *to lie* and the tenses that are made from them.

lie	*lay*	*lain*
I lie in bed.	He lay down for a nap.	The cat has lain in the
The book lies there	She lay there quietly.	driveway for hours.
unnoticed.		She had lain in bed for
Tomorrow we will lie in the		hours before the doctor
grass.		arrived.

Hint
The past tense of *to lie* is the same as the present tense of *to lay*. That is the source of much of the confusion Also, *to lie* means "to tell an untruth." The principal parts of this verb are *lie, lied, lying*.

The *-ing* form of *to lie* is *lying*.

The flowers *are lying* on the table.
A cat *is lying* in the yard.

Here are the three main parts of *to lay* and the tenses that are made from them.

lay	*laid*	*laid*
I lay the pencil on the desk. The child usually lays his head on a small pillow.	The cowboy laid his gun on the bar.	She should have laid the carpet on the hallway floor. After Lynn had laid out the map, directions were easier to follow.

> **Hint**
>
> There must always appear after the word *lay* or any of its forms the thing that is being put somewhere. Also, if you can use the word *put* or *place* for the verb you want, select a form of the word *lay*.

The *-ing* form of *to lay* is *laying*.

He was laying out his clothes on the bed.

Step 1. Using *Lie* and *Lay*. Follow directions. Use your own paper.

1. Write a sentence using the words *he lies* to mean "he rests."
2. Write a sentence in which you use *lay* to mean "put" or "place."
3. Use *has lain* correctly in a sentence.
4. Use in a sentence the word *lay* so that it means "rested" or "reclined."
5. Use the word *laid* in a sentence so that it means "put" or "placed."
6. Use the words *has laid* correctly in a sentence.
7. Use in a sentence the word *lying* to mean "resting."
8. Write a sentence in which you use the word *laying* correctly.

Some Confusing Verbs: *Raise* and *Rise*

Raise means "lift up."

Rise means "get up" or "go up."

> **Hint**
>
> There must always appear after the word *raise* or any of its forms the thing that is actually being raised.

Here are the main parts and the tenses of *to raise*.

raise	*raised*	*raised*
[thing being raised] He raises his hand. I raise the flag at dawn.	She raised our scores. [thing being raised]	He has raised enough money to start a business. [thing being raised]

-ing form: raising

The farmer was raising beans.

Here are the main parts and some of the tenses of *to rise.*

rise	**rose**	**risen**
Everyone rises when the judge enters. I will rise when he speaks.	He rose to shake our hands.	The sun has risen earlier than usual.

-ing form: rising

We were just *rising* to leave.

Step 2.   *Raise* and *Rise:* **Which Is Right?** Pick out the correct word in the parentheses and write it in the blank space.

_____   1. After the sound of a trumpet an old soldier had (risen, raised) the American flag.

_____   2. An eagle (rose, raised) its wings against the pale sky.

_____   3. The students had (risen, raised) before the instructor rushed into the room.

_____   4. There is a famous picture of Marilyn Monroe in which her skirt is (risen, raised) by steam from the subway.

_____   5. Stephen's temperature (rose, raised) to 103°F in the past two hours.

_____   6. The feminist movement has (raised, risen) the consciousness of men and women alike.

Some Confusing Verbs: *Sit* and *Set*

Sit means "to take a seat."

sit	**sat**	**sat**
I sit in the last row. She sits quietly.	They sat in the office.	The dog has sat there without moving. She had sat down before they asked her to.

Set means "to place" or "to put."

Hint

There must always appear after the word *set* the thing that is being put somewhere.

set	*set*	*set*

[thing being put somewhere]

I set my dictionary where I can reach it easily.

Yesterday she set her coat in the closet.

[thing being put somewhere]   [thing being put somewhere]

By the time he had set the pot on the stove, we were not hungry anymore.

Step 3.   Completing Sentences with *Sit* or *Set*. Write the correct form of *sit* or *set* in the blank spaces below.

1. After I had _____ down, the telephone rang.
2. After I had _____ the glass down, Stella arrived.
3. You are the first person to _____ in that chair since I refinished it.
4. I would rather she had _____ her glass on a napkin.
5. Let me _____ awhile before I leave.

Some Confusing Verbs: *Leave, Let; Stay, Stand; Can, May*

To let means "to allow."

To leave means "to go away from."

Let me speak to you.   We want *to leave* early.
       NOT
Leave me speak to you.

To stay means "to remain."

To stand means "to be in a straight up-and-down position."

I stayed in bed with a cold.
       NOT
I *stood* in bed with a cold.
I should have *stayed* home.
       NOT
I should have *stood* home.

Can asks whether or not you are able to do something.

May asks whether or not you will get permission to do something.

Can I drive the car?
(This question means: Do I have the ability to drive the car?)

May I drive the car?
(This question means: Will you give me permission to drive the car?)

Step 4. *Leave, Let; Stay, Stand; Can, May.* Circle the correct words in the parentheses.

1. (May, Can) you ever forgive me for acting so foolishly?
2. If you (let, leave) that dog alone, it will (stand, stay) in its house and not bite you.
3. If you (leave, let) me go early, I will visit my aunt in the hospital.
4. I (stood, stayed) in the house waiting for your call.
5. (Can, May) I (leave, let) my car on this side of the street?
6. She (stood, stayed) in bed with a cold for a week.
7. (May, Can) you (let, leave) me speak to the manager?

WRITING THE ESSAY OF ARGUMENT

ASSIGNMENT: Write an essay in which you explain and defend a strong opinion you have about the women's movement. As you write your various drafts, be sure that you have avoided faults that will fail your argument (see pages 381–383) and that you have successfully dealt with the opposition (see pages 384–387).

Think about some point of view that you hold about the trends in women's liberation—perhaps something suggested in the early pages of this chapter or in the list of suggested topics on page 410. Use some prewriting techniques (see page 39) that work successfully for you. You might try the *subject tree,* explained in this chapter on pages 410–412.

Once you think you know what topic you want to write about, and once you can prepare a proposal that states what your essay will discuss, your concern is then with details: how can you illustrate your point to the reader? If you ask yourself these questions before you begin the essay, you will know before you write just what source of supporting details to use.

ON THE HUNT FOR DETAILS: FOUR CRUCIAL QUESTIONS TO ASK YOURSELF

1. What moments have I experienced in my own life that can help me illustrate my reasons for believing what I do about the topic?
2. What have I read recently in books, newspapers, or magazines—or what can I read quickly and easily before I write—that can help me support my reasons for believing what I do about the topic?
3. What have I learned from the television, the movies, or the radio that can help me support my reasons for believing what I do about the topic?
4. What have I learned from reliable friends, parents, relatives, teachers that can help me support my reasons for believing what I do about the topic?

Suppose, for example, that you believe that as drivers of automobiles, women are very competent. And you can remember two specific moments in your life that will illustrate to readers why you feel the way you do, moments that might even persuade them to believe what you believe. After you write an introduction (see pages 261–266), you might show in each body paragraph one of those moments expanded with concrete sensory details. You will not have *proved* that women are excellent drivers or that they are better drivers than men; but you will have *illustrated* to the readers how your own experiences explain the opinion you hold. That is a very effective way to build an essay.

But you may want to use several reasons to back up your opinion. Make a list. Eliminate any ideas you think would be hard to illustrate or prove. Then perhaps your list will look something like this:

1. Women think very quickly in times of danger.
2. Women are very cautious on the road.
3. Women are courteous drivers.
4. Women are particularly familiar with safety regulations.
5. Women rarely drink before they drive, so they have fewer fatal accidents than men.
6. Women have fewer accidents, in general, than men.

Consult now the Four Crucial Questions on page 401. Did you live through incidents that could illustrate any of these reasons? Did you, on the other hand, see important statistics about women drivers and their safety record? Did you read an article about women drivers (and could you quote or paraphrase accurately from this article)? Did you hear on one of the radio or television talk shows an interview in which you learned about the driving patterns of women and the effects of these patterns on insurance rates? Of course, you will have to decide how to arrange the details effectively.

Whatever points you decide to develop, your essay should have some kind of support. If you feel that you have a great deal of support to offer for *two* of the reasons above, fine. Forget about the other four. Discuss one of the two points in the first body paragraph (paragraph 2 of the essay), using support you think convincing. Discuss the other point in the next paragraph. There too, you need to use as many details as you think will convince the reader that you are right.

But perhaps you want to discuss in your essay *all* the reasons listed above. Fine. First try to pick out the reason for which you have the most solid and convincing support. Save that one until later! In the paragraph that comes after the introduction, discuss all the *other* reasons, giving brief support for each that you mention. In the third paragraph, discuss the one most important reason you have. By saving the most important reason for last and for treatment in its own paragraph, you impress the reader with your most striking evidence.

Perhaps you want to show in the paragraph after the introduction the arguments many people give when they say women are *not* good drivers (see pages 385–387). In paragraph 3, then, you can go about trying to show why all those reasons are, in your opinion, wrong. You would support the points you made with some strong details. Or you can say at the beginning of paragraph 3 that you think there is some truth in what others say; and then go on to develop your own reasons for believing what you do about women drivers.

These are only suggestions: *you* decide what you want to include in each paragraph, how many points you want to discuss, whether you want to stress certain ideas more than others. You will need to think about the various ways of developing paragraphs (explained in Part I of this book) so that you can figure out which method will be best for your essay. As one of your options you might consider writing a definition of a key word in a body paragraph or in the introduction. You might want to define a word such as *woman, freedom,* or *masculinity*. But you must have answers to one or more of those crucial questions on page 401 so that you will know just what details to use before you write, and so that you will not run out of things to say. Everyone has opinions (you have hundreds of your own about the status of women), but the details that illustrate your opinions are what will convince readers that you know what you are talking about.

HANDY PAGES FOR REVIEWING DETAILS

1. Imagery and Sensory Language   pages 5–7, 248–249, 464–465
2. Using Statistics and Cases   pages 190–199
3. How to Paraphrase   pages 200–205
4. How to Use Quotations   pages 200–205, 499–500

Step 1. Practice Planning for the Essay. Read the proposal sentences below. Consult the list of Four Crucial Questions. Then tell briefly what you might discuss in each body paragraph and what kinds of details you would use. Study the example.

	Body Paragraph 1	*Body Paragraph 2*
1. Even in the field of hard physical labor, women should not be overlooked.	*Discussion of women laborers in Russia. Statistics from New York Times Almanac.*	*American women overlooked for jobs of hard physical labor. Paraphrase of TV interviews with Women's Liberation leader. More statistics from Labor Department.*

2. Women excel in professional competitive sports.

_____ _____
_____ _____
_____ _____
_____ _____
_____ _____
_____ _____
_____ _____

3. Women need not take sole responsibility in childraising; in fact, attention from both parents will aid a child's emotional growth.

_____ _____
_____ _____
_____ _____
_____ _____
_____ _____

4. Because of past discrimination, women should be allowed special privileges for jobs and education.

_____ _____
_____ _____
_____ _____
_____ _____
_____ _____

5. Women are underrepresented in politics.

_____ _____
_____ _____
_____ _____
_____ _____
_____ _____

Learning from Other Students

Step 1.   Arguing from Personal Experience. Although the theme below offers no *proof* for its main arguments, dramatic illustrations serve to explain to the reader just why the writer holds the opinions she does. Read "Deprived Children" and discuss the questions after the essay.

Deprived Children

An untrained observer watching a group of children at play may see no real difference between them. The child sitting in the sand pile looks similar to the one squealing happily down the sliding pond. Yet a closer look might reveal many differences. Each child has her own physical appearance; each has her own mental abilities; each has a home life that may not resemble the others'. A few people do notice, however, that some children appear insecure and unhappy; I believe that these are frequently the children of working mothers.

Children of working mothers are deprived of the security of a healthy and loving environment. As a young child with a working mother, I felt her absence deeply. On my first day in third grade, for example, a violent storm shook the streets of Brooklyn. Happy at the idea of a new teacher and new friends, the class grew even more excited by the trees whipping back and forth across from our first floor windows and the sound of September rain pounding against the glass. However, this happiness soon wore off when streets flooded and winds of sixty miles an hour soaked the sidewalks. All the classes moved to the basement, and the principal, Mr. Greenwalder, announced that only children whose parents came for them could go home. Nervously hugging my new notebook to my thin jacket, I prayed somehow my mother would get to me. A slow line of mothers holding yellow raincoats and black umbrellas and boots trudged in to pick up their nervous children while I stared at a speck on the floor. The hours unfolded gradually, and soon I stood in the midst of the huge gray basement, alone except for my faithful teacher, Mrs. Timmins. The fear of a trip home in the hurricane disappeared in the pain and shame I felt that day by not having a mother at home like everyone else. As a child of a working mother I often felt that sense of loss and shame.

The results of such feelings in the children of a working mother can be very serious as the example of my brother Richie clearly illustrates. My older brother, younger sister, and I grew up in the care of indifferent housekeepers. At eleven years old, Richie often left the house for hours at a time with no excuses or explanations of his absences. No one really knew his friends, and my mother's own daily battle with tiredness after work kept her from questioning Richie's activities. As we grew older, Mother's continued absence became an accepted part of our family life, and neither my sister nor I could detect the gradual change in our brother. Richie grew into a sullen, moody, overweight teen-ager. He failed miserably in school, finally dropping out. He rarely spoke to anyone in the house. Although these signs all pointed to tragedy, I was too busy with my own problems to pay any attention—and Mother just was not around. One night a call from a far off hospital told us that Richie's condition was fair after a drug overdose. My mother's eyes looked confused as if to say, "How did it happen?" when we sped to the hospital, but through the shock I *knew* the cause. Richie survived and is now in the midst of costly psychiatric care. But in my opinion, this whole tragedy might have been avoided through the presence and guidance of a mother. My mother was never there.

In many cases, then, a working mother's child is under great stress. She must become independent early in life and must learn to accept the loss of a parent. She can easily fall under bad influences and must be strong enough to resist if she wants to stay out of trouble. At a very young age she must learn the difference between right and wrong and must often face the difficult chore of choosing alone. These tasks present a challenge to the child of a working mother, and one can only hope that she will succeed in mastering them.

—Phyllis Gold

1. What, according to the proposal sentence, does the essay try to illustrate? How does the purpose of paragraph 2 differ from the purpose of paragraph 3?
2. Has the writer convinced you that what she believes is true? If she has, what kinds of details has she used to do so? Which images do you find most appealing?
3. Do you find any examples of the kinds of poor reasoning described on pages 381–383?

Step 2.   Themes that Meet the Opposition. The student samples below use arguments made against their own proposals. Read the essays and answer the questions that appear below.

Job Discrimination for Women?

Several years ago, Betty Friedan, author of *The Feminine Mystique* and activist in the Women's Liberation Movement, stated, "Women are not being brought into the mainstream of American society in equal partnership with men. The oppression of females is especially noticeable in our economic structure." Are women really the object of discrimination and exploitation by employers?

In recent years, the Women's Liberation Movement screamed out "Yes!" as it challenged discriminating practices against women. For instance, airlines forced stewardesses to retire at the age of thirty-five when no such requirement existed for males. Further, a study by Professor James White, author of *Women in the Law,* showed how of all women law school graduates in the years 1959 to 1968, approximately half have been objects of discrimination by employers. For example, the average income differed sharply based on sex. After eight years, male law graduates earned an average of $18,000 while female law graduates earned only $10,000. Women have also argued about discriminatory practices against them when both female and male applicants show equal qualifications for jobs. Employers usually hire males because males do not leave jobs to have babies and raise families. Like Robin Morgan, editor of *Sisterhood Is Powerful,* many argue that "women are an oppressed class. They are exploited as domestic servants and cheap labor" and "men have controlled all political, economic and cultural institutions. They have used their power to keep women in an inferior position."

In spite of the cries of the Women's Liberation Movement, women make up a substantial part of the work force in the United States, so what are they crying about! Today, nearly half the women in the United States work; that amounts to more than 33 million women, representing 40 per cent of the work force. Obviously, a woman's place is no longer in the home, and any real effort to discriminate against women would have dropped that total considerably. Dr. David Gilbert, chief economist for the First Pennsylvania Corporation, described the changing female role in *Nation's*

Business Magazine. He stated, "Over 63 per cent of the female labor force participants are married. From 1948 to 1970, the labor force participation rates of married women rose from 22 per cent to 40 per cent." Significantly, the greatest percentage increase in married female job holders over this period occurred among women with children. Working women today also tend to be better educated than females years ago. In the period 1952 to 1970, a Federal survey shows that the median number of years of education in the women's labor force had risen from 12.0 to 12.4. Historically, women selected clerical work as a major occupational area. However, with more education, more women today assume professional and technical positions of importance. I believe that with the increasing number of women completing college and obtaining higher degrees, this trend should continue. Even in jobs thought only for males, women have advanced. A recent article in the *New York Daily News* showed that the female policewoman is equal to her male counterpart. Just as the males on the police force serve in every area, the females too work all types of beats and receive the same pay as men. It is not so strange on a New York City street to see a female in a blue uniform while she drives a police patrol car, her partner, a male, sitting and chattering away next to her.

Although some complaints about discrimination may be true, I believe current evidence shows great strides for women in the job world. What then are women crying about? Why instead of stressing the advances do they scream about the continued failures? I think this is really a question about human nature, one that has nothing to do with sex. Men and women seem rarely to be happy with what they have. People earning $20,000 a year wish for $40,000. Single men long for marriage; married men dream of being single. Women with children feel crushed by the burdens of responsibilities; single women hope for marriage and children. Children pray to be older; older people wish they had back their youth. In the winter we complain of the cold and wish for summer; in the summer we moan about the heat and wish for winter. It seems to me that dissatisfaction is just another of the traits that make human beings what they are.

—*Richard Tomasuolo*

Working Mothers

"Toward the end of World War II," reports economist Dr. Eli Ginzberg, "large numbers of wives and mothers entered the labor force, but the experts were sure that when peace came, the mothers would return to their traditional ways, leaving the work force to devote themselves exclusively to child-rearing, homemaking, and volunteer activities." Time proved the experts wrong. The percentage of working wives and mothers kept on accelerating through the 50's, 60's, and 70's. "Today," he says, "about two out of every five women with a child under six is working at an outside job." Those are strong figures. Millions of mothers are pushing their way into the job market, and are dealing successfully with responsibilities as parents, workers, and homemakers.

It is easy, however, to understand the feelings of many mothers who refuse to work, mothers who quit their jobs to stay at home and devote their full time to raising children. In a special issue on working mothers by *Parents' Magazine* (April, 1977) Ellie Brock explained that it is her sole responsibility as wife and mother to take care of her three-year-old daughter Lauren, her husband Richard, and their home in Arlington, Virginia. An attorney, Richard is busy all week and unable to help. No paid housekeeper or sitter, Ellie is convinced, could devote more time and energy than she herself could. No longer teaching high school students, she is less tired and, therefore, she feels, more interesting to her husband. Many working women like the freedom being at home offers. They can do things they had no time for when they worked, reading for an hour on a living room chair, taking courses in yoga or tennis or dance at the neighborhood health club, tinkering around the kitchen with a chocolate cream pie or a Caesar's salad. My own mother, a "floor lady" in a pocketbook factory for thirteen years, quit her job twenty years ago for the coming birth of her first child, my older brother Salvatore. Three more babies came in the next seven years, and Mom feels that her staying at home all this time kept the family strong.

Although many women choose to stay home and care for their families, increasing numbers of working mothers have made new lives for themselves outside the home. In the same issue of *Parents' Magazine* Eleanor Seale, mother of three-year-old Archie, tells of a life filled with active, money-making work. During the day she is secretary to Justices Thomas Dickens and Clifford A. Scott of the New York State Supreme Court. Between eight and ten at night, she keeps the books, does ordering and inventory work, and serves customers at the Seale's new, family-owned store. "We weren't born with silver spoons in our mouths," she says. "We want certain things for our family and we have to struggle to achieve them." Women like Eleanor feel that their jobs make them more attractive and more interesting to their husbands. With the money earned by a working mother the family enjoys things they otherwise could not: a shiny new sedan, perhaps, a summer vacation on the West Coast, an assured college education for the children. These mothers believe that carefully selected day-care centers, nursery schools or at-home sitters enrich the child's life with experiences no parents alone can offer. Perhaps children have much less time with a working mother than they do with a mother close by all day long; but the quality of the time is what is important. In a single hour a thoughtful working mother can give to her child as much love and attention as a mother at home all the time can give to her child in a full day.

Because of the attention to women's rights, many mothers who in the past might have felt trapped in their homes have seized opportunities to use their energy and potential in stimulating careers. Yet there are women at home who see their work there as more important than anything. The point in all this, as I see it, is that the society must be made to tolerate choices so that no one is locked into a hateful life simply because someone expects him or her to behave in a required way. People must be free to choose the lives they believe are best for themselves and must have enough opportunities to change their minds if they make mistakes.

—*Carmelyn Martini*

Women: Fragile Flowers?

Whenever people discuss the idea of women in the world of men, a male voice always cries out that women are biologically different from men, even in the animal kingdom. Such was the case last Tuesday when a hot discussion on "women's lib" filled our freshman English class. With an air of authority George Kerman rattled off biological "facts" to back up his statements on how women are "different." Although I felt that I wanted to contradict him, I knew better. I had no biological statistics to back up my beliefs, just a bit of pride that hurt when he compared women to female peacocks. But now I can stand my own ground well assured of my resources. Women are not the weaker sex.

Many like George would paint a pretty picture of womankind as a fragile flower easily bent. The argument that women are biologically different from men always hints that women are *inferior* to men, inferior in terms of stamina, stability, and thinking. A number of scientists argue that males are sturdier and able to withstand stress more admirably than females. Dr. Edgar Berman, a former surgeon and one-time State Department consultant on Latin American health problems, agrees with George. "Women should be excluded," Dr. Berman says, "from high executive positions because of their monthly raging hormonal imbalances." People like Dr. Berman point out that women cry while men keep a stiff upper lip, meaning that women have poor responses to life's problems. There are also statements on record that women usually have lower I.Q.'s than men do, and that this accounts for the low percentage of women in professional jobs. All these remarks certainly do seem to point a finger at women as delicate butterflies, needing protection and care and not needing positions of responsibility in the world today.

But the finger is pointing in the wrong direction because *men* lack all the important biological features. The term "biologically different" used against women tries to be impartial but it still is an expression of a male's prejudice. In fact, men are the weaker sex. The female of almost any species is sturdier than the male. Dr. James Hamilton, an endocrinologist, shows that from worms to humans the male is less able to tolerate life's everyday stresses. "There can be little doubt that the male has a higher mortality rate in almost all forms of animal life studied." Even during the first week of life, the death rate for infant males is 32% greater than that of females. Later on in life the society puts strain on the man to compete, produce, and succeed; this also affects the survival rate. Another part of the problem of male mortality is the male hormone testosterone, which brings about a higher metabolic rate in most tissues, wearing them out faster. But there is no proof that the woman's monthly "hormonal imbalance" is a sign of inferiority. True, many women do experience some discomfort each month; some even are quite ill for a day or two. But most women do not suffer with any reactions. Federal surveys in every job category show that women take off the same amount of time from work as men. Although crying is often another "proof" of woman's difference from man, United States Public Health data show that females have a much lower suicide rate—less than half that of males. Isn't it better to cry? And there are no sex differences in regard to I.Q. On all forms of intelligence tests the female's I.Q. is not significantly different from the male's. Women are, in my opinion, biologically superior to men.

Woman has not been able to prove she is not the weaker sex because the society has assigned her to an inferior position. Few brilliant women have tried to develop their talents, simply because there has been a small market for brilliant women in this country. The few who have bothered to develop their creative talents find that the world views them as "odd balls." The stereotype of a brilliant woman is that of a horsefaced, flat-chested female in support shoes, one who has hidden all her sexual instincts in her search for a career. It may be fun being treated like a fragile flower by a boyfriend or a date, but there's a time and place for everything. It is time society stopped giving out positions based on stereotypes. We women must develop and make use of our wasted female brain power.

—*Stella Tesoriero*

1. Richard Tomasuolo states his proposal as a question. Do you think that is an effective technique? If you were to change his proposal to a statement, what would it be?
2. What kinds of evidence does he offer to show that women have been discriminated against? How does he then support the idea that women have *not* suffered discrimination in jobs? Which do you find most convincing, paragraph 2 or paragraph 3?
3. What, according to the proposal in "Women: Fragile Flowers?" is Stella Tesoriero's purpose in writing her essay? What details in paragraph 2 does she use to show why people think women *are* the weaker sex?
4. Where does Carmelyn Martini argue against her own proposal?
5. What kinds of details does each of the writers use to support points in the body paragraphs? Which writer uses the highest degree of sensory language? Which writer might have used more sharply visual language?
6. Comment on the transitions each writer uses to connect the second paragraph to the first, the third to the second, the fourth to the third.

Some Topics to Think About

In case you have trouble finding a topic, here are some possibilities for topics for this theme assignment.

1. child custody: always with the mother?
2. alimony: reverse discrimination?
3. the Chinese woman versus the American woman
4. I don't want to be liberated.
5. my experience with a woman doctor (lawyer, salesperson, dean, insurance agent)
6. my mother's expectations compared to mine
7. the image of women in advertising
8. women politicians
9. women as artists
10. women drivers
11. men cannot accept a truly liberated woman.
12. women football players? men baby nurses? how far will it go?
13. women in the work force
14. pornography: degrading the modern woman
15. women in the military

You may wish to challenge one of the statements in Step 3 on pages 379–380. You may wish to write about a topic suggested in the questionnaire on pages 378–379.

Prewriting: Making a Subject Tree

As with free association (see pages 125–127), the subject tree is a prewriting technique that helps you move from one level of thought to another as your mind considers the topic. In this way you follow your thoughts as they develop into higher and higher levels of specificity. The final product looks like a tree with branches reaching out toward possibilities for focused writing. After you consider what your tree includes, any one branch can serve as a starting point for the development of other ideas, for expanding and grouping details, and, ultimately for writing a first draft. Look at the following example. The general topic, "Women in the Work Force," appears at the bottom of the page.

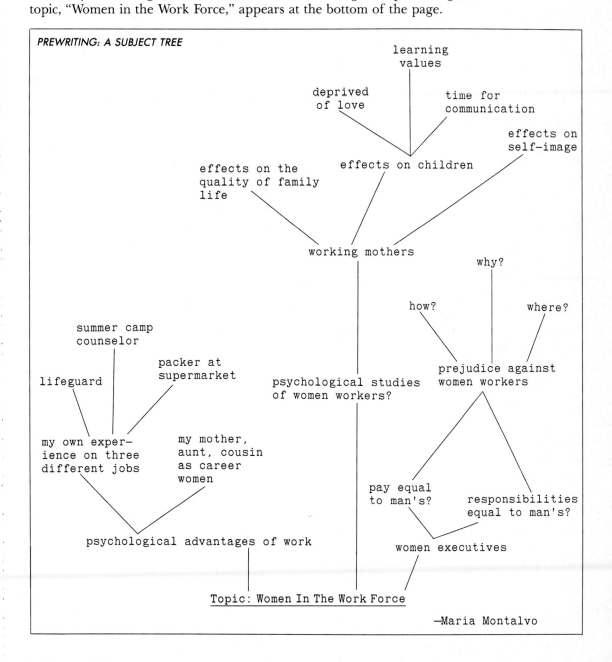

PREWRITING: A SUBJECT TREE

Step 1.   Examining a Subject Tree.

1. What are the three general topic ideas Maria Montalvo uses to start branching into specific areas?
2. If she chose to write about the psychological advantages of work, according to her subject tree, what kinds of details might she use? How do you know? If she chose to deal with working mothers, what kinds of details might she use?
3. Select any one of the topic ideas on her subject tree. What proposal sentence could you develop for it? How might some people argue against that topic? What points could you make in each of the body paragraphs?

Step 2.   Your Own Subject Tree. Using a topic from the list on page 410 or one of your own, develop a subject tree in which you explore by branching a number of different possibilities for your basic idea.

Progress Reminders: A Checklist of Questions

As you prepare a subject tree or do other prewriting for your essay, as you do your first and later drafts, and before you write your final copy, use this checklist so that you can follow as many of the suggestions as possible. After you prepare your manuscript to hand in, fill in the checklist and submit it with your theme.

1. Did I consider the topic carefully before writing anything? _____
   Did I use some prewriting activities that work particularly well for me?
2. Did I write a rough draft and any other needed drafts _____
   before making my final copy? Did I make changes in my rough drafts so that I expressed thoughts clearly and smoothly?
3. Is my proposal clearly stated? _____
4. Did I use smooth transitions as explained in the Essay _____
   Transition Signboards I, II, and III on pages 316–320?
5. Did I avoid the traps in logic and clear reasoning by _____
   studying the Fifteen Faults to Fail the Argument on pages 381–383?
6. Did I sufficiently consider the opposition's arguments and _____
   include some of them in my essay? (See pages 385–387.)
7. Did I consider carefully the types of details I want to use in _____
   my essay by asking myself the Four Crucial Questions explained on page 401? Do I know the difference between *illustrating* my opinion and *proving* my opinion is correct?
8. Did I use a variety of sentence patterns: coordination and _____
   subordination, sentences with verb-part openers, sentences joined by transforming verbs?
9. Did I try to use strong verbs, clear expressions, and images _____
   that appeal to the senses?

10. If I used statistics, cases, or opinions expressed by others,   _____
    have I mentioned the source of my information? Have I
    used reliable sources?

11. Did I read carefully the themes on pages 405–409 to help   _____
    me see how other students presented their ideas on women's
    rights?

12. After making changes in my drafts for clarity and smooth-   _____
    ness, did I reread my essay, looking for errors, especially in
    the use of possession and in the kinds of mistakes I usually
    make? Did I examine my own Progress Sheet?

13. Did I try to use some of the new vocabulary listed in this   _____
    chapter?
    Here, from my theme, is a sentence that uses one of those
    words: _____

    _____

14. Did I write a convincing conclusion to my essay?   _____

15. Did I use a title that will attract the reader's attention?   _____

16. Did I ask others to read my drafts and to tell me if they were   _____
    convinced by my argument?

GETTING READER RESPONSE

Pair up with just one other person and carefully read through a draft of each
other's essays. Read through one time just to get the main idea of the essay.
Then, as you read a second time, write questions in the margins about points
that still need to be explained, arguments that are not yet convincing, reasoning
that seems to be faulty, and so on. Also, note where you feel the other writer has
dealt with the opposition.
    A sample marginal notation might read

Why exactly do you think the woman in a male-female police team might let her
partner down sometimes?
Do you have any evidence to support this claim?

    After you have finished writing your questions, discuss them with each
other.

THE PROFESSIONALS SPEAK

In the first of the following selections, Anita Shreve discusses the dilemma of
motherhood for the working woman. Shreve bases her points on firsthand
interviews with successful women workers. In the second selection, you will read

about how many textbooks for children consistently present males and females in sex stereotypes. Answer the questions after each selection.

SOME WORDS TO KNOW BEFORE YOU READ

leave of absence: a period of time off from a job.
stress: pressure; emotional strain
surrogate: substitute
reconcile: come to an agreement
antithetical: directly contrasting in ideas
nurture: care for
pivotal: causal; critical

The Lure of Motherhood

Marcie Schorr Hirsch, the director of career planning at Brandeis University, has reassessed her priorities. Having juggled the four roles of mother, wife, career woman and graduate student with varying degrees of success and stress, Mrs. Schoor Hirsch, 32, has had it with being Superwoman. Currently on a year's leave of absence from her job, she has chosen, for the time being, to stay home with her second child, a son born last April.

To be sure, Mrs. Schorr Hirsch has not stopped working: She is seeing private clients for career counseling at home, co-writing a book and completing her graduate work at the Harvard University Graduate School of Education. But her hours are flexible and thus more accommodating to an infant than those of one full-time job. And she has more time for the rest of her family as well. "I'm concerned about the quality of my existence as well as that of my family," she says. "I think it's time to attend, to some extent, to that need. It's not that I'm not willing to work hard anymore. But I don't want to work hard at everything all the time."

Like Mrs. Schorr Hirsch, many women are discovering the difficulties of trying to negotiate the demands of a full-time career and motherhood. They fear and suspect that the sacrifices such a juggling act entails are costly to their careers, to their children and to their marriages. They are beginning to re-evaluate their goals and to question their ability to "do it all."

In the absence of clear solutions to the career-mothering dilemma, some women are abandoning their careers—at least temporarily. More frequently, they are modifying their work schedules, either by negotiating part-time positions where they work or by looking for flexible hours elsewhere. The San Francisco law firm of Heller, Ehrman, White & McAuliffe, for instance, had no written part-time policy before 1978. Today, more than 20 percent of the female attorneys on staff are working part time, and some of them were already mothers when they were hired. Some employers are deciding that they can no longer ignore the needs of working mothers, and a few are actually beginning to do something about it.

Most companies, however, have not formulated a policy to deal with the problems of working mothers. Many have yet to acknowledge that such problems exist, and others do not think that there are enough working mothers in their employ to warrant any action on their part. Some corporations believe it is not their responsibility to provide such assistance, and others say that it is not feasible in the current, troubled economic climate.

Nevertheless, a large number of established career women in their early to middle 30's have decided to embark on child rearing—before it's too late. The number of women between the ages of 30 and 34 who gave birth for the first time doubled between 1970 and 1979. By March 1982, almost 49 percent of married women with preschool children were employed (in 1960, that figure was only 19 percent); 45.3 percent of married women with children *under* 3 were employed. Also as of March 1982, almost 54 percent of unmarried women with preschool children were working. The high divorce rate and the troubled economy are forcing some mothers into the work force who might, in more prosperous times, have preferred to stay home.

What is now emerging is the extent of the stress these women and their families experience as a result of this societal shift. In the absence of adequate day care (there are twice as many children whose parents are seeking day care as there are slots available nationwide), good role models, accommodating employers or experienced professionals from whom to seek advice, many women feel like pioneers in an uncharted landscape. "Am I doing the right thing?" is the question of the hour as they confront a number of thorny issues.

Some women successfully combine work and family life, and others have no choice but to work full time—single mothers and those whose husbands do not earn enough to support their families. But many women who have the luxury to choose wonder if the rewards of a career are worth the necessary 8- to 14-hour-a-day separation from their babies.

They worry, as they steal time for their family, that they are putting their careers in jeopardy. They try to come to terms with the concept of being merely "a support player" in the lives of their children—and they are concerned about whether it is harmful to leave them in the care of surrogate parents—with a nanny or at a day-care center. Finally, they struggle to reconcile the antithetical skills and emotions needed to nurture and appreciate an infant on the one hand and to succeed in a corporate environment on the other. Half mother, half careerist, such a woman often feels inadequate and unfulfilled in either role. And some women are beginning to suspect that, in the end, the great tragedy is not that their children or their careers will suffer, but that they themselves cannot fully enjoy either.

It is difficult to assess the toll such stress is exacting from half an entire generation of women, but the social cost may be high. For many of these women are in high-level positions in the private and public sectors and are pivotal members of today's nuclear families. If the stress on these women becomes too great, both family life and economic productivity could be seriously affected.

—*Anita Shreve*
The New York Times

1. What is the major point of Shreve's article? Is it stated outright, or is it implied?
2. What do you think Anita Shreve means when she uses the word *Superwoman* to refer to Marcie Schorr Hirsch in paragraph 1? Why did Mrs. Schorr Hirsch quit her job? How does her case support Shreve's argument?
3. Where does Shreve use statistics to support her argument?
4. What reasons does Shreve offer for increased stress on working mothers?
5. Of mothers who have a choice to work or not, why are more and more questioning whether they want to continue to combine work and a family life? What alternatives are there to the career-mother dilemma?

6. What does Shreve suggest might be the effects of continued stress on mothers to try to balance high-level jobs and family life? on society in general? How does this analysis serve as a conclusion to Shreve's essay?

SOME WORDS TO KNOW BEFORE YOU READ

overwhelmingly: to an overpowering degree
predominate: be the stronger, controlling element
implication: suggestion
depicted: portrayed; shown
constrained: held back
domain: area under control
epitome: high point
prototype: model
deprecate: express disapproval of
perpetuate: carry on and on

Sex Bias in Textbooks

Textbooks have always been a cornerstone of our education system. Although the main function of textbooks is to convey specific information, textbooks also provide the child with ethical and moral values. Thus, at the same time that a child is learning history or math, he or she is also learning what is good, desirable, just.

This second type of information—which sociologists refer to as the "latent content" of textbooks—provides standards for how men, women, boys, and girls should act. This latent content was the focus of research we carried on for the last three years. During that time, we have analyzed the latent content of the most widely used textbook series in the United States in each of five subject areas: science, arithmetic, reading, spelling, and social studies. (A grant from the Rockefeller Family Fund supported the research.) Through computer analysis, we obtained data on the sex, age, racial distribution, and activities of the textbook characters by grade level and subject area.

This article will summarize the ways in which the two sexes are portrayed and the type of behavior encouraged for each.

Sex Distribution. Since women comprise 51 percent of the U.S. population, one might expect half the people in textbook illustrations to be females. However, males overwhelmingly predominate in all series: Females are only 31 percent of the total, while males are 69 percent. Of over 8,000 pictures analyzed, more than 5,500 are of males. Girl students using these books are likely to feel excluded.

Sex Differences by Grade Level. The percentage of females varies by grade level. In all series combined, females comprise a third of the illustrations at the second grade level, but only a fifth of the total on the sixth grade level. In other words, by the sixth grade, there are four pictures of males for every picture of a female. This contrast is vividly illustrated in the accompanying figure. Thus, as the textbooks increase in sophistication, women become less numerous and, by implication, less significant as role models.

This decline in female role models makes it harder for a girl student to identify with the textbook characters and thus may make it harder for her to assimilate the lesson. Covertly, she is being told that she, a female, is less important as the textbook world shifts to the world of adults—to the world of men.

This declining representation of females is particularly striking in some of the series. For example, in the second grade spelling series, 43 percent of the illustrations are of females, but in the sixth grade series, the percentage has declined to a mere 15 percent.

Sex Distribution of Text Illustrations by Grade Level

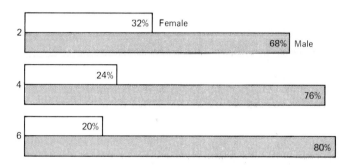

Sex Differences in Activities. The pictures of children show three striking differences between the boys and girls. First, boys are portrayed as active, skillful, and adventuresome; girls are typically shown as passive—as watching and waiting for boys.

Second, while boys are depicted as intelligent and as mastering work-related skills, girls are shown engaging in domestic activities or in grooming themselves, trying on clothes, and shopping. Third, girls are depicted as affectionate, nurturing, and emotional, but boys almost never embrace or cry. Thus, the young boy is taught that to be manly he must control his emotions. In the same way that girls are constrained by images which stereotype them as pretty and passive, boys are constrained by images which stereotype them as strong and unemotional. The textbooks thereby encourage both sexes to limit their development.

Adult men and women in textbooks are even more sex-stereotyped. While only a few women are shown outside the home, men are portrayed in over 150 occupational roles. A young boy is told he can be anything from a laborer to a doctor. He is encouraged to imagine himself in a wide variety of roles and both to dream about and plan his occupational future.

In contrast, the future for young girls seems preordained: Almost all adult women in textbooks are housewives. In reality, however, 9 out of 10 women in our society will work at some point in their lives. By ignoring women workers, the textbooks fail to provide the necessary occupational role models for girls and thus unnecessarily restrict future horizons.

Sex Differences in Subject Areas. There are systematic differences in the treatment that girls and women receive in different subject areas. The percentage of females in illustrations varies from a high of 33 percent in social studies to a low of 26 percent in science. These subject differences are important in understanding why children like certain subjects and want to major in them—or why, in contrast, they feel unwelcome because of the covert messages they receive.

In science, the most male-oriented series, 74 percent of the pictures are of males. The science texts seem to imply that the world of science is a masculine domain. When boys are shown, they are actively involved in experiment—looking through microscopes and pouring chemicals. In contrast, when girls are shown, they observe the boys' experiments. The epitome of the male prototype in science is the astronaut. But only boys are pictured as astronauts and, in the text, only boys are told to imagine that they can explore the moon.

In mathematics textbooks, many problems are based on sex-stereotyped roles, with men earning money and women dividing pies. Further, despite the Equal Pay Act of 1963, we found math problems in which girls were paid less than boys for the same work. (It would be hard to imagine a textbook publisher allowing an example in which a black child is paid less than a white child.)

In the reading series, story titles provide a good indicator of the relative importance of males and females. Boys predominate in every grade. The series examined had 102 stories about boys and only 35 about girls.

Even the female heroines reinforce traditional female roles. For example, Kirsten, the heroine of a third grade story, wins over the girls who have rejected her by making Danish cookies and having the most popular booth at the school fair. The moral in this story is that girls can succeed by cooking and serving. But Kirsten slights herself and the very skill that had earned her favor when she says, "It's easy; even I can do it, and you know how stupid I am." Thus, even when girls succeed, they tend to deprecate themselves. In contrast, boys show a great deal of confidence and pride.

Both the reading and spelling series demonstrate a surprising amount of antagonism and hostility toward females. In the spelling series, female characters are yelled at and pushed around. In the reading series, they are shown as stupid and clumsy three times as frequently as males.

In social studies, the best series studied, women were often skillful and important. Here, mothers play a crucial role in passing on their cultural tradition to their daughters. Although we applaud these positive pictures of women, it should be noted that mothers in the series teach only their daughters, not their sons. Similarly, fathers teach only sons. Thus, traditional sex roles are perpetuated. Today, boys need to learn to manage in the home and to be parents, and girls need to learn about vocations and the outdoors. Textbooks could expand rather than contract children's potential.

Although this series has the largest percentage of females in pictures, still 2 out of 3 are pictures of males. Women are in the section on the home but are absent from the sections on history, government, and society.

After studying these textbooks for three years, one cannot help but conclude that children are being warped by the latent messages in them. We urge teachers to examine the textbooks they use and to check the ways in which sex roles are stereotyped. Only teachers can change the impact that these books will have on our young people and on the next generation of adults. Teachers can tell their girl students about the world and the real options they have in it. Teachers can encourage them to dream and can help them plan.

What is sorely lacking in textbooks and thus desperately needed in the classroom is a new image of adult women and a wide range of adult role models for young girls. Girls—and boys too—should learn about the history of women in this country, about suffrage and the current women's liberation movement, and about female heroines of our country and the world. What a difference it would make if young girls could point to adult women with pride and feel that they themselves have an exciting life ahead.

   While we must all create pressure to change the textbooks, in the meantime, it is up to teachers to counteract the latent messages in them and to create positive images of adult women in the minds of students.

—Lenore J. Weitzman and Diane Rizzo
Today's Education

1. What is *latent content* in regard to textbooks?
2. What are some of the latent messages the authors see in textbooks? How do the numbers of males shown in textbook pictures compare with the numbers of females? How are the activities of boys shown to differ from the activities of girls? How does the story of Kirsten effectively show how girls deprecate themselves even when they succeed?
3. Although they praise the social studies texts they have examined, the writers find some fault there. What is it? Do you agree that sex roles are perpetuated by such presentations?
4. What evidence do the authors give to support the idea that children are being hurt (*warped,* the writers say) by the latent sex messages in textbooks? What evidence might you give?
5. Do you agree that teachers can counteract latent messages in textbooks and can create positive images of adult women in the minds of students? How can this be done?
6. This piece appeared in the mid-1970s in *Today's Education.* Are the points made here still valid today? Is there still sex bias in textbooks schoolchildren use? What evidence can you offer to support your point of view?
7. The authors have used subheadings (in italics) to divide their work into smaller parts. None of the subheadings is a complete sentence. Rewrite each of them so that it
   a. is a complete sentence
   b. provides an effective transition from the previous section
   c. states clearly the purpose of the section that follows it
8. Is the essay a good example of argumentation? Why or why not?

REACHING HIGHER

Step 1. An Essay in Pictures and Words. Using a camera you can easily operate, take a number of pictures (on or near the college campus) that show either the advances made by women in a man's world or the way in which women are kept down in a man's world. Take pictures of women (a relative, a friend, a stranger) at work, women at leisure, women on their way to their jobs or at the supermarket or in their homes. Select the ten best pictures, and for each write one sentence that summarizes the main point of the snapshot.

Step 2.   More Topics on Liberation. The struggle for freedom and equality over the centuries knows no sex or nationality. Using any effective kinds of details, develop one of these liberation ideas in a four-paragraph essay:

the black people's struggle in South Africa today
the Jew and equality in large cities
a slave revolt in the South
the Italians' charge of prejudice today
Palestinian rights
machismo—myth or reality
busing in Boston for racial equality in schools
the American Indian and equal opportunity
the Irish immigrant in the New York City of 1900
unfair treatment of Mexican-Americans
freedoms in the Republic of China

Step 3.   What Others Think. Choose, from page 410, one of the three topics about which you have strong feelings. Write a paragraph or two discussing your opinions; then, devise a questionnaire (see pages 378–379) to measure other people's attitudes toward the same topic. Ask ten men and ten women to fill out your questionnaire. Then, write a short essay in which you analyze the differences in responses according to sex.

Step 4.   A Collage to Present a Point. Using old magazines, newspapers, paint, ink, pieces of advertisements for captions, and any other materials, develop a theme in a collage that presents an argument. You may want to focus on an idea such as women's rights, ecology, overpopulation, violence, or some other pressing problem in the world today. You might want to answer a question in your collage. In any case, what you should try to do is to persuade someone to agree with your point. Use colors and visual images of action carefully to help make your point.

CHAPTER 10

AN EXTENDED DEFINITION:
Life's Moments for Meanings

INTRODUCTION

The dictionary is a valuable tool for defining words whose meanings we do not know. Yet, when it attempts to explain certain words, it is often inadequate. If you have ever looked up *hate* or *patriotism, fear* or *loneliness,* for example, you know that your own ideas of those words are not really the same as the definitions the dictionary gives. Your own definitions are much more specific. You might not define fear as "a painful feeling of coming danger or trouble," but if you ever wander down a dark street late at night and hear the gasp of the wind in alleys, in hallways, through ghostly trees—you have a personal and very real sense of the meaning of fear.

As a human being—moving, learning, confronting—you constantly re-define vocabulary based upon the experiences you meet. When Carl Sandburg said

Hope is a tattered flag and a dream out of time. . .
The shimmer of northern lights across a bitter winter night,
The blue hills beyond the smoke of the steel works

he built his definition of hope from the moments in his daily life. But more than personal experiences inform your concepts of words. You read about new applications for vocabulary all the time. In your textbooks, in newspaper and magazine articles, in the novels and stories you read for pleasure, you develop new insights into word meanings. Perhaps a television talk show or a new film or a popular song helps you understand a word in a way you never understood it before.

For this theme assignment, you will write an extended definition of a word that has special meanings for you. You can draw upon personal experience or upon any other sources of detail—such as books, magazines, and films—that allow you to enrich your definition with detail. And as you plan your paper, you'll want to review the various techniques you've learned so far for organizing ideas in paragraphs and essays. The definition theme can draw upon many of those techniques, depending, of course, upon your topic. Thus if you chose to define a word like *love,* for example, you might describe it in visual terms; you might narrate an incident; you might illustrate your definition by drawing upon two or three examples; you might contrast love to hate, or you might compare two kinds of love; or you might explain the process of falling in love.

VOCABULARY

Important Prefixes and Suffixes

A *prefix* is a letter or group of letters placed at the *beginning* of a word to contribute to its meaning.

A *suffix* is a letter or group of letters placed at the *end* of a word to contribute to its meaning.

If you know some of the prefixes and suffixes used most frequently, it is often possible to determine the definition of a word, or at least to get an idea of the kind of word being used, without using the dictionary.

For example, if you saw the word *apolitical*, and you knew that the letter *a* placed at the beginning of a word means *not*, you could figure out easily that *apolitical* means "*not political.*"

If you saw the word *heroism*, and you knew that *-ism* added to a word means "*the quality of*," you could conclude easily that *heroism* means "*the quality of being a hero.*" And suppose, in your reading, you saw a sentence like

The doctor prescribed an *antirheumatic* medicine.

If you knew that the prefix *anti-* means "*against*," you could figure out that *antirheumatic means "against* some rheumatic disease."

Below are some common prefixes and suffixes and their meanings, along with examples of words that use these prefixes or suffixes.

Prefixes that say no:

a-: not (asocial)

an-: not (anarchy)

un-: not (unattractive)

im-: not (impossible)

in-: not (insecure)

non-: not (nonviolent)

mis-: wrongly (mistreated)

ir-: without, not (irresponsible)

il-: not (illegible)

mal-: bad or wrongful (maladjustment)

anti-: against (antimissile)

contra-: against (contradict)

Prefixes that show placement:

ab-: from or away from (abstain)

circum-: around (circumference)

com-: with, together (commission)

trans-: across (transport)

dis-: away (displace)

sub-: under (submarine)

inter-: among or between (interlocking)

intra-: within, inwardly (intramurals, introvert)

in-: in or on (invest)

de-: down from (deflect)

Prefixes that tell time:

ante-: before (antedate)

pre-: before (predict)

post-: after (postdate)

ex-: former or out of (exconvict)

re-: again, back (repeat)

Prefixes that tell degree:

hyper-: too much (hypertension)

super-: above or highest (superman)

poly-: many (polyangular)

pro-: in favor (proponent)

semi-: half (semicircle)

extra-: beyond, outside (extracurricular)

Prefixes that mean "one":

uni-: single, one (uniform)

homo-: same (homogenize)

self-: one's own person (self-propelled)

mono-: one (monologue)

auto-: self, same (autograph)

Step 1. Making Words with Prefixes. From the lists above, select the correct prefix that has the meaning in parentheses, and use it before the word or word part that appears. On your own paper, write the new word and a definition. Check your dictionary to make sure that the word you have written is correct.

1. (many) + -*gamy*
2. (under) + way
3. (not)   + social

4. (again) + educate
5. (against) + -*biotic*
6. (one)   + lateral

7. (within) + state
8. (among) + state
9. (the same) + -nym
10. (before) + -bellum
11. (out of) + -hale

12. (across) + Canadian
13. (together, with) + mingle
14. (one) + biography
15. (not) + probable

Suffixes to Signal Meanings

Relating to or Pertaining to

-al (formal)

-ic (sonic)

-ance (performance)

-ence (permanence)

Able to Be

-ible (terrible)

-able (capable)

State or Quality of

-ship (statesmanship)

-ment (management)

-ion (tension)

-ness (happiness)

-ism (terrorism)

-hood (manhood)

-tude (aptitude)

Someone Who

-er (speaker)

-or (debtor)

-ist (florist)

Filled with

-ous (joyous)

-y (juicy)

-ful (sorrowful)

Without

-less (mindless)

Step 2. Suffixes for Correct Words. Change the words in italics in the sentences below to the proper form by adding a correct suffix. You may have to change the final letters of the starting word before you add an ending. Write at *a* the new word and at *b* the meaning of the suffix you added. Check the dictionary for spelling. Study the example.

Example
1. On *chill* days we run home quickly.

1. *a.* _chilly_____
   b. _filled with_____

2. The *sense* slaughter of seals by *greed fur* is an *outrage* activity.

2. *a.* _____
   b. _____

a. _____

b. _____

a. _____

b. _____

a. _____

b. _____

3. The *neighbor* grew old and shabby as more and more buildings fell to ruin; the sight was *awe*.

3. *a.* _____

   b. _____

   a. _____

   b. _____

4. The *jewel* showed us a *shine, flaw* diamond.

4. *a.* _____

   b. _____

   a. _____

   b. _____

   a. _____

   b. _____

5. Jim was the most *rely acupunture* we knew.

5. *a.* _____

   b. _____

   a. _____

   b. _____

6. It seemed *inconceive* that such a *nerve* person could display such *hero*.

6. *a.* _____

   b. _____

   a. _____

   b. _____

   a. _____

   b. _____

7. *Adult* is not necessarily measured by age, but by *achieve* and *intellect mature*.

7. *a.* _____

   b. _____

   a. _____

   b. _____

a. _____

b. _____

a. _____

b. _____

Ten Roots for Word Meanings

Roots—or *stems*—are those parts of words to which pieces may be added at the beginning or end. Several roots, coming from Greek, Latin, or other languages, appear frequently in English words; therefore, to know a select number of roots is to improve your skill with word recognition. The following ten roots play an important part in our vocabulary:

Roots of the Senses		*Example*
spect, spic	means "look"	*spect*ator
loqu, locut	means "speak"	e*loqu*ent
tang, tact	means "touch"	*tang*ent
vid, vis	means "see"	*vis*ion
voc, vok	means "call"	*voc*al
Roots of Action		
vers, vert	means "turn"	di*vert*
pos	means "place"	*pos*ition
port	means "carry"	*port*er
mor, mort	means "die"	*mor*atorium
mit, mis	means "send" or "put"	ad*mit*

Step 3.   Roots for Definitions.   Underline the root in each word in italics below. In *a* write a meaning of the word based upon your knowledge of the root. In *b* write the definition given by the dictionary. (Appendix A will help you too). How close do the two come in meaning?

1. There sounded a *moribund* howl, then silence.

1. a. *dying* _____

   b. *on the verge of death* _____

2. One hundred clowns marching down
   Main Street created quite a *spectacle.*

2. a. _____

   b. _____

3. My Aunt Sally is quite *loquacious*.   3. *a.* _____

    b. _____

4. The typewriter was easily *portable*.   4. *a.* _____

    b. _____

5. The child *reverted* to bad behavior.   5. *a.* _____

    b. _____

Step 4. Prefix, Root, and Suffix in Combination. Each word below is made from prefix, root, and suffix. Write below the word the meaning of each part, and then write a suitable definition of the entire word in Column I. Use a dictionary if you need to. (Appendix A will help you too). Look at the example.

Example   **I**

   1. submitter   *someone who gives in to someone else*
     under put one who   _____

   2. circumlocution   _____

                                _____

   3. irrevocable   _____

                                _____

   4. intermission   _____

                                _____

   5. comportment   _____

                                _____

   6. intangible   _____

                                _____

   7. homogeneous   _____

                                _____

   8. visionary   _____

                                _____

   9. commercial   _____

                                _____

10. introspection   _____

                                _____

BUILDING COMPOSITION SKILLS

Judging a Dictionary

Although a dictionary is your main aid in finding definitions, very often the meanings given for abstract words—words that stand for ideas more than for physical things—are not adequate. Frequently a word is so familiar to us that people who use it may have different ideas of its meaning. With such words, it is important for you to add to the dictionary definition exactly what you mean when you use the word.

Step 1. Dictionary Meanings. Look up the following words, and write in the blank lines a definition based upon what the dictionary says. Then, check yes or no to show whether or not you think the dictionary meaning is complete, effective, and accurate. Tell the class the reason for your choice by adding information to the definition in order to make it reflect what you mean when you use the word.

	Yes	_No_
1. democracy _____	_____	_____
2. ghetto _____	_____	_____
3. maturity _____	_____	_____
4. religion _____	_____	_____
5. happiness _____	_____	_____
6. truth _____	_____	_____
7. pride _____	_____	_____
8. beauty _____	_____	_____

Step 2. Talking About Meanings. Because our thoughts and experiences help to shape the meanings of words, especially abstract words, it's useful to discuss those meanings and to compare definitions with other people in the class. Think of some specific moment in your life in which the meaning of an abstract word (like those in Step 1 above) became clear to you because of some experience you had. Then describe and explain that experience as Carl Stearns has in the following:

Ghetto

I learned what _ghetto_ meant after my first drive down Washington Street one December morning. A dozen empty buildings in one side of the street had broken windows and large black smears from a fire. I saw boarded-up doors, overturned garbage pails, and clumps of newspapers along the sidewalk. Three children without coats played with the stuffing of an abandoned couch on an empty lot. A scraggly mutt stretched out on the corner. Everything looked so old and depressing and worn out. No dictionary ever gives that idea in its definition.

—Carl Stearns

Step 3. Personal Meanings. Choose a word from the following list (or choose a word of your own) and, in a talk of a minute or two with the class, describe a personal experience that taught you the true meaning of the word.

1. fear
2. loneliness
3. joy
4. success
5. relief

6. nervousness
7. courage
8. friend
9. teacher
10. violence

A One-Sentence Definition

Writing a clear one-sentence definition is important for many of your courses. In science, business, and humanities programs, you meet new terms all the time, and you have to develop concise meanings for those terms so that you can share a common language with other people in the class and so that you can show that you know the important basic vocabulary of the subject. Also, in writing an essay of extended definition, often one sentence crystallizes the meaning of the word you're trying to define.

In order to write a logical one-sentence definition that is clear and easy to understand, write your sentence in the following four parts:

1. Name the term to be defined.
2. Use the word *is*.
3. Name the general group of things to which the term belongs.
4. Name some specific characteristic that distinguishes the term from the rest of the group.

You will have to use your dictionary or encyclopedia as a starting point in the preparation of accurate and precise meanings.

Examples

[term] ["is"] [general group to which term belongs] [specific characteristic: shows the special use of the plot of ground]

A garden is a plot of ground for cultivating plants.

[term] ["is"] [general group to which term belongs] [special characteristic: shows how this pardon is different from any other kind]

Amnesty is a pardon for offenses against a government.

[term] ["is"] [general group to which term belongs]

A church is a building for public Christian worship.

[specific characteristic: shows the special nature of the building]

TOWARD ACCURATE ONE-SENTENCE DEFINITIONS

Don't use *where* or *when* after *is*.

Wrong: A closet is *where* you store clothing, food, or tools.
Right: A closet is an enclosure for storing clothing, food, or tools.

Don't use in your definitions either the word you are attempting to define or one of its forms.

Wrong: Anger is the act of being angry.
Right: Anger is a feeling directed at someone who performs a real or imagined wrong action.

Don't use negatives in your definition.

Wrong: Sadness is *not* being happy.
Right: Sadness is a feeling characterized by sorrow or depression.

Exception: Sometimes negative qualities are the specific characteristics of words. In those cases, negatives are acceptable parts of definitions.

Example: An orphan is a person *without* parents.

[negative]

Step 1. A Definition in a Sentence. Fill in the following blanks to create logical one-sentence definitions. Use your dictionary. Study the examples in the chart and the example below.

The Term	*Is*	*General Group*	*Specific Characteristic*
1. A *silkworm*	is	a caterpillar	that spins a fine thread to make a cocoon.
2. A *ruby*			

3. *Fascism* _____ _____ _____
_____
_____

4. *Seniority* _____ _____ _____
_____
_____

5. An *engineer* _____ _____ _____
_____
_____

6. An *aside* _____ _____ _____
_____
_____

7. *Anorexia* _____ _____ _____
_____
_____

8. *Fennel* _____ _____ _____
_____
_____

9. A *sanction* _____ _____ _____
_____
_____

10. A *bill of lading* _____ _____ _____
_____
_____

11. *Fortran* _____ _____ _____
_____
_____

A Paragraph Definition

In an extended definition, you might want to expand a single sentence into a
paragraph so that readers can understand and identify the term that the rest of

your essay will develop. Your paragraph should begin with the one-sentence definition, adding significant features in five or six more sentences.

Some questions you should try to answer as you expand your definition are

1. What are the physical features of the object: size, shape, color?
2. What may the object remind readers of? Does the object look like any other object?
3. What materials contribute to the object?
4. What is the object used for?

Look at the following sample:

What is Rayon?

Rayon is a fiber produced from cellulose and used to weave fabrics. Chemicals dissolve the cellulose (wood pulp or short cotton fibers), which machines then force through tiny holes. The dissolved material, hardened in warm air or liquid, forms filaments that either may be twisted into threads or cut and spun. Spun filaments of rayon may look like wool, linen or cotton. Because yarns with new features are developed all the time, rayon now has a variety of uses: it appears in automobile tires, in grease-proof cellophane sheets, in sponge rubber as a substitute for cellulose, and in special glass that cannot be shattered.

—*Caroline Narby*

Step 1.   Writing a Definition Paragraph. On separate paper, write a paragraph to define any one of the following words or a word of your own choosing. Use a dictionary, an encyclopedia, or some other reference text to help you build a definition in your own words.

1. impressionism
2. intelligence
3. narcissism
4. maturity
5. grudge
6. utopia
7. sonnet
8. astrolabe
9. metaphor
10. martini

Writing Conclusions

The concluding paragraph of an essay is very much like the closing sentence of a paragraph. It should do all the things you learned about closing sentences in Chapter 5. A good conclusion, therefore, should

• tell the reader that your essay is coming to a close
• give the reader a feeling that you have accomplished what you set out to do.

But a closing paragraph permits the writer to develop some larger application for the topic. A good conclusion applies the topic of the essay to a broader issue. In a conclusion you can illustrate that the subject you have written about has importance beyond the ideas developed in your body paragraphs. You show that you have used what you have written to help you think about other ideas. This is not an easy chore. You run the risk of sounding too "important," too philosophical, too much like a show-off. As a result, the concluding paragraph needs especially careful thought and must often progress through several rewritings, but the finished product is well worth it: it helps the reader see that the narrow topic you developed has relevance in other critical areas. It gives you an opportunity to develop an idea that has an important relationship to your topic, but is new in the frame of the essay itself.

Let us examine the conclusion of an essay you read earlier and the relationship of the conclusion to the rest of the theme. Stella Tesoriero wrote in "Women: Fragile Flowers?" (pages 408-409) this proposal sentence:

Women are not the weaker sex.

In her second paragraph, she tried to show how others would argue against her proposal. (She brings up the arguments of women's inferiority in stamina, stability, and thinking.) The third paragraph answers these arguments by presenting proof that they are incorrect and that women have a biological superiority to men. Here is Stella Tesoriero's conclusion:

Woman has not been able to prove she is not the weaker sex because the society has assigned her to an inferior position. Few brilliant women have tried to develop their talents simply because there has been a small market for brilliant women in this country. The few who have bothered to develop their creative talents find that the world views them as "odd balls." The stereotype of a brilliant woman is that of a horsefaced, flat-chested female in support shoes, one who has hidden all her sexual instincts in her search for a career. It may be fun being treated like a fragile flower by a boyfriend or a date, but there is a time and place for everything. It is time society stopped giving out positions based on stereotypes. We women must develop and make use of our wasted female brain power.

The conclusion shows why women have not advanced in society. That is *not* an idea that is clearly part of the writer's proposal sentence:

Women are not the weaker sex.

Yet, by bringing in the related idea of stereotyping and the reasons for woman's inferior position in today's world, the writer offers a new significance for the topic. From the topic idea of woman's superiority to man, Stella Tesoriero moves into a larger application: the reason women have for so long been kept down in society. She is showing the reader how the ideas she developed in paragraphs 2 and 3 (the superiority of man or woman) suggest a broader, more general application for the topic (the reasons why women do not show their superiority).

Her new application works effectively in the essay, but it is not the only possibility that she could have chosen. The conclusion—based upon the proposal and the supporting body paragraphs—might have treated any one of these broader issues:

- women in the future replacing men in high-pressure jobs
- women as top political leaders
- the failure of male scientists to treat women fairly in experimental data
- a world in which men stay home to raise children and do housework

This list is not complete, but any of these points, developed with sufficient supporting details, might nicely suggest a wider and more general truth for the ideas proposed in the rest of the essay.

Notice, furthermore, that the first sentence of Stella Tesoriero's conclusion refers back to the ideas developed in previous paragraphs by mentioning the topic that the writer set out to develop. Look at the two sentences side by side:

Proposal	*First Sentence of Conclusion*
Women are not the weaker sex.	Woman has not been able to prove she *is not the weaker sex* because the society has assigned her to an inferior position.

The italicized words in the first sentence of the conclusion act as a transition because they bridge the conclusion to the topic as stated in the proposal. In addition, these words help summarize the topic for the reader who has read two full paragraphs since last seeing the proposal. This device of summary is excellent early in the conclusion because it reminds readers of what the essay set out to do, and permits them to evaluate the writer's success in developing the proposal.

For dramatic conclusions, follow these steps (see also pages 205–208):

1. Remind the reader that you have achieved what you set out to do and that your essay is drawing to an end.
2. Strive to establish a new, a larger, a more general application for your topic.
3. Summarize briefly the main point of your essay.
4. Make the conclusion an important part of the essay, not an afterthought you glued on to add more words.
5. Do not
   a. start a whole new topic
   b. contradict your entire point
   c. make obvious or overused statements
   d. apologize for your lack of knowledge
   e. end suddenly with a one-sentence conclusion such as "That's all I have to say."

    f. draw conclusions that are absolute or too general (make sure that you allow for possibilities or exceptions)

    g. talk about other parts of your own essay by mentioning words like "my introduction," "so my conclusion is," "my proposal sentence said."

Step 1. Essay Conclusions. Examine the following essays, paying special attention to the concluding paragraphs. Write in the blank lines below the title the writer's proposal (you may have to restate it in your own words so it is clear when you remove it from the essay). Then, in the blank space alongside, write the broader issue that the writer tries to develop in the conclusion. Study the example.

                               *Larger Application
(Broader Issue) in
Conclusion*

1. "Deprived Children," pages 405–406.

    Proposal: *children of working mothers are*   *what children left on their own must*
    frequently insecure and unhappy.   *learn.*

    _____   _____

2. "Practice in the High School Gym," page 294.

    Proposal: _____   _____

    _____   _____

3. "Ironing for Food," page 330.

    Proposal: _____   _____

    _____   _____

    _____   _____

4. "Uncle Del's Barn," pages 292–293.

    Proposal: _____   _____

    _____   _____

    _____   _____

5. "The Advantages of Attending Kindergarten," pages 367–368.

Proposal: _____   _____

_____   _____

_____   _____

_____   _____

6. "Memories of the Australian Bush," pages
   295–296.

   Proposal: _____   _____

   _____   _____

   _____   _____

   _____   _____

Step 2.   Finding New Areas of Relevance. For each essay you have reread in connection with Step 1 above, suggest some *other* area of importance the writer could have developed in the conclusion. Base your suggestions on the proposal sentence and on the two body paragraphs. Use separate paper.

Imitating Sentence Patterns

You can add variety to your sentences by consciously imitating an impressive pattern used by another writer. Benjamin Franklin writes in his autobiography about how he developed his writing skills by copying the style of contemporary essayists he admired. When you imitate someone else's sentence pattern, you use your own words and ideas in the same structure that you are copying.

In the following model sentences, the words in italics illustrate a particular structure that you should try to copy as you write a sentence on any topic of your own choosing. Later, when you write your essay, try to use the new structure within one of your paragraphs. Look at the example from Conrad and at the sentence written by Maurey Chase, who tried to copy the structure of Conrad's sentence. This is an example of two coordinated sentences each beginning with an *-ing* group, the second sentence ending in a simile (see pages 19–20).

Streaming with perspiration, we swarmed up the rope, and, *coming into the blast of cold wind*, gasped *like men plunged into icy water.*

—*Joseph Conrad*

Racing down the hot street my brother reached the house, and standing briefly in the shadow of our oak tree, leaped suddenly up the steps like a bird chased by a cat.

—*Maurey Chase*

Notice how Maurey Chase copied the structure of the sentence by the novelist Joseph Conrad. To start each coordinated element in his sentence, Mr.

Chase uses an *-ing* structure: *racing down the hot street* and *standing briefly in the shadow of our oak tree*. His sentence, like Conrad's, ends in a simile: *like a bird chased by a cat.*

Step 1. In the space below, write an original sentence in which you copy the structure of Conrad's sentence. Read your sentence aloud as the class listens and compare the two.

_____

_____

_____

_____

_____

_____

Step 2.   Imitating Patterns by the Masters. Read the following sentences, taken from professional writers, and the explanations of the particular structures you should copy. Also, note the italics, which point out those structures. Discuss the sentences with your instructor and the class. Then, in the space provided, write your own sentence in which you imitate the pattern of the original. Use language rich in sensory detail wherever you can.

1. Three word groups that show relationships (prepositional phrases: see page 446) at the beginning of a sentence:

In the street, in the cars, in the subways, I was always seeking, ceaselessly seeking for eyes, a face, the flash of a smile that would be light in my darkness
                                                                    —*Anna Yezierska*

_____

_____

_____

_____

_____

2. Descriptive words after the noun:

A half-moon, *dusky-gold*, was sinking behind the black sycamore tree.
                                                                    —*D.H. Lawrence*

_____

_____

_____

_____

_____

3. An infinitive (to + verb) as the subject of a sentence:

To see Kean act <u>was</u> like reading Shakespeare by flashes of lightning.
                                        —*Samuel Taylor Coleridge.*

_____

_____

_____

_____

_____

4. Two -*ing* word groups at the end of a sentence:

Swallows were going to and fro overhead, *dashing against the eaves* and *dropping their faint twitterings.*
                                        —*L.B. Gilkes*

_____

_____

_____

_____

5. A series of verbs (three or more) with the same subject:

He *threw* his affectation of detachment to the winds, *moved* his shoulders slightly, very slightly, *made* a step nearer to the couch, and *looked* down on her with an expression of amused courtesy.
                                        —*Joseph Conrad*

_____

_____

_____

_____

SOLVING PROBLEMS IN WRITING
PRONOUN PRACTICE

Pronouns as Subjects

PRONOUN CHART I: SUBJECT PRONOUNS		
Singular Pronoun Subjects		*Plural Pronoun Subjects*
I	it	we you
he	you	they
she	who	

You remember from your work in subject-verb agreement that the pronouns that appear above may be used as subjects of verbs.

_____ *run(s).*

Any of the pronouns you see in the chart could be used in the blank space in the sentence above.

Example
I run.
He runs.
They run.

Although you would never say or write *Me run* or *Him runs,* when you use two subjects (one of which is a pronoun) for the same verb, you can forget to use the subject pronouns from this chart. The following sentences from student papers fail to use pronouns correctly. Alongside the incorrect sentence you will see the sentence written with the right subject pronoun.

Incorrect

1. My father and *me* never got along.
2. *Him* and *me* watched fireworks from across the bay.

Correct

1. My father and *I* never got along.
2. *He* and *I* watched fireworks from across the bay.

HINTS FOR CORRECT PRONOUNS WHEN YOU USE TWO SUBJECTS
FOR THE SAME VERB

1. Always pick a pronoun you want to use as a subject from Pronoun Chart I on page 440.

2. Test each subject *alone* before you decide which pronoun to use. For example, suppose you do not know whether to use *her* or *she* in the blank space in this sentence:

Her mother and _____ rushed into the house.

First say
a. *Her mother* rushed into the house.
    Then say
b. *Her* rushed into the house.
    That does not sound right. Then say
c. *She* rushed into the house.
    That is correct. Now combine the two subjects from *a* and *c.*

Her mother and *she* rushed into the house.

Step 1.   Speaking About Two Subjects. Combine any one of the subject pronouns (*he, I, she, it, we, they, you, who*) with the name of someone you know to tell about a place you recently visited. Speak your answers aloud.

Example
Suzette and he bought a house in Seattle.
My father and I drove into Waco last night.

Step 2.   Filling in Pronoun Subjects. Fill the blank spaces with any pronoun subjects that make sense to you. Use different pronouns in each sentence.

1. Mrs. Chandler and _____ fixed the flat tire.
2. Charlotte and _____ dance well together.
3. _____ and her aunt own a health food store.
4. Before _____ and their friends entertain, they always notify the neighbors.
5. His father and _____ share all the cooking.
6. _____ and the children would rather stay in a motel than camp out.
7. Wilma and _____ listened to a Chopin concert at Tanglewood last night.
8. You and _____ else saw the Rolling Stones last November?

PRONOUNS AFTER TO BE

                                 [part of *to be*]

a. Everyone thought it was her.

b. Everyone thought it was she.

      If you had to choose between *a* and *b*, you would probably select *a* as the sentence that you hear more frequently. However, sentence *b* is correct, and in writing, you want to remember this suggestion:

      After a form of the verb to be *use a subject pronoun.*

      The verb *to be* has many forms, a number of which appear below.

am	has been	should have been
is	have been	should be
are	had been	could be
was	will be	may be
were	must have been	could have been

      Hint: The expression "It's me" (It is me) is not correct formal English: "It is I" is what formal writing requires. However, "It's me" is used in conversation and is acceptable.

Step 3. Pronouns after *to Be*. Complete each sentence below by writing a correct *pronoun* after the verb. Circle the pronoun you use. You may add any other information you like.

Example

1. It was (he) *who sang* _____ .

2. We know it is _____ .

3. The leader may have been _____ .

4. It could have been _____ .

5. It will be _____ .

6. That should be _____ .

Step 4. Selecting Pronouns. Choose *subject pronouns* in the parentheses below to make the sentences correct.

1. Nancy and (she, her) gave me a collection of poetry for my birthday.
2. The other actors and (he, him) didn't want to do the play.
3. Although it was (he, him) who was absent often from class, the instructor still gave him an A for the course.

4. (He, Him) and (me, I) went to the restaurant together.
5. Both (him, he) and his brother believed it should have been (they, them) who received the jobs.
6. Not only (he, him) but his entire family believed it was (they, them) who were discriminated against.
7. It must have been (her, she) who asked Jaime to help move furniture.
8. Dr. Wells and (we, us) are convinced that classical music or soft jazz will soothe the babies.

Pronouns as Objects

PRONOUN CHART II: NONSUBJECT PRONOUNS (OBJECTS)	
Singular	*Plural*
me	us
him	them
her	whom
whom	

Hint: The words *it* and *you* may be used as subject or nonsubject pronouns.

The pronouns above are not subject pronouns and do not appear as subjects in sentences. Yet these words are usually found in two important sentence positions.

1. *Pronouns after Verbs*

[verb] [pronoun]
Give **me** the book.

[verb] [pronoun]
Bonnie selected **him** as her dancing partner.

[pronoun]
You *told* **whom** about the riot?
[verb]

Although you would never write

Give *I* the book

OR

Bonnie selected *he* as her partner

whenever you use *two* words after the verb (one of which is a pronoun), you probably have some difficulty selecting the correct pronoun. Look at these sentences; is *a* or *b* correct?

[verb]

a. The instructor praised Harriet and *I* for our creativity.

[verb]

b. The instructor praised Harriet and *me* for our creativity.

You remember that *I* can be used only as a subject. In sentence *a*, the subject is *instructor* (for the verb *praised*). Since the pronoun you need comes *after* the verb *praised,* select the pronoun from the chart above. Since *me* appears in the chart, sentence *b* is correct.

HINTS FOR CORRECT PRONOUNS AFTER VERBS

1. Select the pronoun from Pronoun Chart II, page 443.
2. If two words must come after the verb, test each word alone before you decide which pronoun to use. Suppose you do not know whether to use *he* or *him* in the blank in this sentence.

The teacher praised his brother and _____ for their cooperation.

First say
a. The teacher praised *his brother.*
Then say
b. The teacher praised *he.* (That wouldn't sound right.)
Then say
c. The teacher praised *him.*
That is correct. Now combine the words after the verb in *a* and *c.*

The teacher praised *his brother* and *him* for their cooperation.

Step 1. Writing Pronouns after Verbs. On separate paper, write sentences for any ten of the following verbs. Use *two* words after each verb, one a noun and the other a correct pronoun. Write about things that really happened, and use as many different pronouns as possible. Look at the example beneath the list of verbs.

saw	wanted	resisted
hurried	begged	threw
needed	replaced	forgave

allowed   annoyed   frightened

questioned   forced   chased

Example

The movie left my sister and me with an unpleasant feeling. _____

_____

Step 2. Choosing Pronouns after Verbs. Select the pronoun in parentheses that correctly completes each sentence.

1. Nancy asked Cristina and (I, me) to prepare the room for painting.
2. You invited David and (who, whom) else to your graduation?
3. The judge accused Roberto and (they, them) of disrupting the peace at a political rally.
4. I never noticed you and (she, her) until last Monday.
5. The editorial insulted you and (us, we) terribly.

  2. *Pronouns after Connecting Words That Show Relationship*

      Aside from their use after verbs, the pronouns in Chart II are used after certain connecting words, called prepositions, that relate one word or word group in the sentence to some other sentence part. First, look at some of the connecting words that show relationship.

  a. We read a *book* **about** *teenagers.*

The word *about* relates the words *book* and *teenagers* to each other by showing the kind of book.

  b. Charlene *ran* **toward** *David.*

The word *toward* related *ran* and *David* by showing where the action was performed. Now, if you wanted to use a pronoun instead of *teenagers* and instead of *David,* you would need a word from Pronoun Chart II (page 443):

We read a book **about** *them.*

Charlene ran **toward** *him.*

Connecting words that show relationships like *about* and *toward* are called *prepositions.* You've already seen many of these in the exercise on expanding sentences and changing word order (page 320).

SOME CONNECTORS THAT SHOW RELATIONSHIP (PREPOSITIONS)

about	except	within	between
by	under	beside	below
beneath	onto	since	next to
inside	at	as to	by means of
above	across	toward	through
for	on	at	along with
over	upon	beyond	because of
outside	into	up	by way of
along	after	before	on account of
among	to	like	in spite of
of	with	below	in front of

Step 3. Remembering Connectors. Study the connectors above. Then, after covering the chart, write from memory as many as you can in the blank space below.

_____

_____

_____

_____

_____

    You probably would not have trouble writing *one* correct pronoun after the connector words mentioned above. No one would write

Give the book to *I*.

       OR

The boy ran toward *he*.

    But as soon as *two* words are used after the connector, students can have difficulties.

    Give the book **to** Mary and (I, me).
    The boy ran **toward** the child and (he, him).

    Since the pronoun you need comes after a connecting word that shows relationship (*to* and *toward*), you must select a pronoun from Pronoun Chart II. The words *I* and *he* are not correct because they are subject pronouns (Pronoun Chart I) and must be used as subjects of verbs. Correctly written, the sentences above become

Give the book to Mary and *me*.

The boy ran toward the child and *him*.

HINTS FOR PRONOUNS AFTER CONNECTORS THAT SHOW RELATIONSHIP

1. Select the pronoun from Pronoun Chart II, page 443.
2. If *two* words come after the word that shows relationship, test the words one at a time before you decide which pronoun to use. If you don't know whether to use *I* or *me* in this sentence:

   The dean spoke about Joe and _____.

   First say

   a. The dean spoke about *Joe*.

   Then say

   b. The dean spoke about *I*.

   That doesn't sound right.
      Then say

   c. The dean spoke about *me*.

   This is obviously correct.
      Now combine the results in *a* and *c* above.

   The dean spoke about *Joe* and *me*.

Step 4.   Pronouns for You to Choose. Fill in both blanks in each of the following items. Use a pronoun in at least one of the blanks. You can use a noun *or* another pronoun in the other blank. Look at the example.

1. toward ___*him*___ and ___*me*___

2. above _____ and _____

3. beyond _____ or _____

4. except _____ and _____

5. from _____ and _____

6. in front of _____ and _____

7. because of _____ and _____

8. in spite of _____ and _____

9. as to _____ and _____

10. between _____ and _____

Step 5.   Writing Sentences with Connectors That Show Relationship. Use five of the subject-verb combinations below in sentences of your own. After each

subject-verb combination, use correctly one of the completed word groups from
Step 4 above.

you speak	an eagle soared
he played	the child cried
they drove	he watched
they included	everyone bowed
a motorcycle roared	

Example

1. _They drove toward him and me._____.

2. _____.

3. _____.

4. _____.

5. _____.

6. _____.

A Special Problem

Some of the words listed as connectors that show relationship may also act as
coordinators or subordinators. You remember that coordinators and subordinators (see pages 19–20 and 100–109) introduce subject-verb groups that are
connected to complete sentences. So, it *is* possible to find a subject pronoun after
one of the words listed as connectors that show relationship. But notice how
differently the word is used in each of these sentences:

A

My brother ran <u>before</u> me.

B

<u>Before</u> I <u>ran</u> away, my brother left home.

In *A*, the word *before* is a connector that relates the word *ran* and *me* by
showing where the action took place.

In *B*, the word *before* is a connector that subordinates the subject-verb word
group *I ran away* to the complete thought *my brother left home.*

Step 6. Connectors in Two Ways. Fill in each blank after the connector with
the correct pronoun from either Pronoun Chart I or Pronoun Chart II.

Hint

1. If the pronoun is the subject of a verb, use Pronoun Chart I.
2. Study the hints on pages 441, 444, and 447.

1. They brought the tools for my girl friend and_____.
2. The civic agency distributed the food equally among
   _____ and _____.
3. Inez gently placed the blanket over _____.
4. Since Blanche and _____ couldn't climb any higher, they threw the rope toward Carlos and _____.
5. We were very thirsty, for my brother and _____ ate hot sauce.
6. After Delores and _____ cooked the frankfurters, they raced to the lake.
7. A lonely dog followed Charles and _____.
8. The operator finally connected Edwina and _____.

Pronoun Agreement

a. The girl kissed <u>her</u> mother.
b. The boys brought <u>their</u> gloves.

In these two sentences, the underlined word is a pronoun that takes the place of the noun to which the arrow is drawn. In sentence *a*, the word *girl* is singular and the pronoun that refers back to it must be singular (*her*). In sentence *b*, the word *boys* is plural and the pronoun that refers back to it must be plural (*their*). It is easy to see that *boys* is plural and *girl* is singular.

c. She kissed <u>her</u> mother.
d. They brought <u>their</u> gloves.

In sentence *c* and *d*, the underlined pronoun takes the place of another pronoun. *Her* takes the place of *she;* since *she* is singular, *her* must be singular. *Their* takes the place of *they:* since *they* is plural, *their* must be plural too. But with words like *boys, girl, they,* and *she,* it is easy to decide whether the word is singular or plural. Several pronouns—although they may look plural—are always singular. If another pronoun later on in the sentence refers back to one of these special singular pronouns, that pronoun must be singular too.

SPECIAL SINGULAR PRONOUNS

anyone	everyone	someone	one
anybody	everybody	somebody	neither
each	either	no one	none
			nobody

Hint

If a pronoun refers to one of these words, the pronoun must be singular.

Everyone	should bring	*his* own assignment.
Each	of them packed	*his* own bag.
Anybody	may raise	*his* own hand.
Either	of the boys can drive	*his* own car.
Anyone	can love	*his* own country.
One	of them sold	*his* own camera
None	of them helped	*his* own country.

[This pronoun refers to one of the special singular pronouns.]

HIS OR HER?

His is used as a pronoun even when the group contains men and women. *Her* is used when the group is clearly all women.

> Everyone of them drove *her* own car.
> Either of them can make *her* own clothes.

Many writers who are sensitive to sex stereotyping try to avoid using *his* to refer to mixed groups that contain men and women. Sometimes plural forms help avoid choosing *his*.

Examples

Singular	**Plural**
Everyone should bring his own assignment.	*All* the students should bring their assignments.
Each of them packed his own bag.	*They* all packed their own bags.

Some writers use the form *s/he* to refer to mixed groups, but it has not won wide popular approval.

Step 7. Selecting the Right Pronoun. Write in the blank spaces the correct word in the parentheses. Or, rewrite the sentences so that they use plural forms.

Example
Everyone sharpened _____*his*_____ pencil (his, their).

1. Women have begun to feel independent by earning _____ own money (her, their).
2. We asked each student about _____ political preferences (their, his, her).
3. Each of them should have driven _____ car more safely (her, their).
4. Everybody likes taking pictures of _____ vacation trips (their, his).
5. All the drivers started _____ engines at the same time (their, his).
6. Residents of the canal area were forced to abandon _____ homes (their, his, her).

Pronouns That Point Out: Demonstrative Pronouns

This book is mine.
These papers ripped.
That girl fell.
Those cars sped along the highway.

Only *this, these, that, those* point out. Don't use *them* to point out.

NOT   *Them* windows look dirty
BUT   *Those* windows look dirty.

Since *this* and *that* are singular, the words that they point out must be singular.
Since *these* and *those* are plural, the words that they point out must be plural.

[singular] [singular]
This kind of book is stimulating.
               NOT
[plural] [singular]
These kind of books is stimulating.

[plural] [plural]
These kinds of cars save money on gasoline.

Step 8. Pointing Out with Pronouns. Fill in the blanks with *this, that, these, those,* or *them.*

1. Never eat _____ kind of sandwich.
2. _____ faucet always leaks.
3. With _____ sort of friends, you never need enemies.

4. _____ kinds of people buy many books but never read
_____ .

5. _____ kind of movie annoys me.

REVIEW

PRONOUN CHART I	PRONOUN CHART II
Subjects	**After Verbs and After Connectors That Show Relationship**

PRONOUN CHART I

Subjects

I   we

he

she   they

it

you   you

who

After *to be*, use subject pronouns.
Use *this, that, these, those* to point out. Don't use *them*!

these boys

  NOT

them boys

  Hint

Use a singular pronoun to refer to a special singular pronoun like *anyone, everyone, anybody, someone, no one, neither, either, each.*

PRONOUN CHART II

After Verbs and After Connectors That Show Relationship

me   us

him

her   them

it

you

whom

If you need a pronoun as one of two words, try one word at a time.

He asked Barry and (I, me).

He asked *I*. [wrong]
He asked *me*. [right]

Then: He asked Barry and me.

The Use of the Pronoun *You*

In informal writing, where the writer is actually addressing the reader, the pronoun *you* works nicely. However, it sometimes creates problems in style when *you* includes the reader unintentionally. In the second of the two sentences below, the writer addresses the reader as if the reader were present.

My room is a restful place. When you look out the window you can see tall pines against the gray sky.

The use of *you* in the second sentence is too informal and, hence, not appropriate to essay writing. The *you* assumes that the reader can join the writer in the actual experience.

One way to avoid the informal *you* is to use *I* (or *we*, if it works), a more accurate pronoun under the circumstances.

My room is a restful place. When *I* look out the window, *I* can see tall pines against the gray sky.

Although American writers (as opposed to British, say) do not always feel comfortable with the pronoun *one*, *one* can serve well for more formal effects than *I*.

My room is a restful place. When *one* looks out the window, *one* can see tall pines against the gray sky.

Another solution is to use a word like *person* or some other noun that works in the sentence.

My room is a restful place. When a *person* looks out the window, *he* can see tall pines against the gray sky.

Finally, a writer could combine sentences to eliminate the pronouns for a smoother, fuller, more descriptive sentence.

My room is a restful place; beyond the window tall pines nestle against the gray sky.

Step 9.   Avoiding *You* in Sentences. Rewrite the sentences below for formal papers by removing the pronoun *you*.

   Hint

If you use *one*, make sure that your new sentence does not sound too formal or too strained.

1. The car is only one year old. You wouldn't know it by looking at it though. _____

_____

2. In Rose of Lima Church you can see the stained glass windows just above your pew if you look to your left. _____

_____

3. An old brown chair stands near the door. If you're tired you can sit down and rest your feet. _____

_____

4. When you open the classroom door, you see the desks and chairs lined up in neat rows. _____

_____

5. If you have worked in a factory, you know what it is to come home tired.

_____

For the steps below, use the review chart on page 452. Make sure that you know the connectors listed on page 446.

Step 10.   Pronouns in Your Sentences. On separate paper, use the following word groups correctly in sentences.

1. my roommates and me
2. the girl and I
3. the author and us
4. we and they
5. Sandy and me

6. those kinds
7. Maria and who
8. Greg and me
9. him and me
10. he and I

Step 11.   Reviewing Pronoun Usage. Write on the blank line in the margin the correct pronouns you select from parentheses. Look at the example.

Is College Worth It?

1. ___*I*___   Sometimes I wonder if college and (me, I) were meant for each
                   other. These days, many people say that a college diploma is worth
2. _____   only the paper it is written on. (Them, Those) people may be right. My
3. _____   father tells me that all his friends and (he, him) have done just fine
4. _____   without college degrees. In many ways he and (them, they) are very
5. _____   successful. To anyone who measures (their, his) success by big cars,
6. _____   large houses, and fancy clothes, a college degree may not be worth
7. _____   (his, their) time. However, for my friends and (I, me) success means
8. _____   something else. Every one of us wants more for (his, their) life than
9. _____   just material things. Sure, (them, those) symbols of status are very
10. _____   nice and comfortable, but against (it, them) we'll compare even one
11. _____   finely tuned mind. So, although we may never have Cadillacs and
12. _____   diamonds, the people whom I respect and (me, I) will always have
13. _____   our knowledge. (You, One) can lose (your, one's) riches, but knowl-
14. _____   edge always remains.

Step 12.   Pronouns in Review. Circle the correct pronouns in the parentheses.

1. Each of the photographers brought (her, his, their) cameras.
2. The Forché family wanted very much to invite Carolyn and (I, me) for Thanksgiving dinner.
3. Was it really (her, she)?
4. George gave (them, those) tickets to Anna and (I, me).
5. Maria and (I, me) loved to sketch people in the park.
6. The doctor and (he, him) agreed on the diagnosis.
7. Between (he, him) and (I, me), there was never a loss for words.
8. (Those, Them) tomato plants wilted in the sudden freeze.
9. Ellen and (she, her) said it was (they, them) who sent the card.
10. Someone left (his, their) briefcase full of money in the taxi.

WRITING THE DEFINITION ESSAY

> ASSIGNMENT: Write an essay in which you offer an extended definition of some word or term that has special meanings for you.

For this theme, select some abstract word and, in a four-paragraph essay, write a definition of that word. Write a proposal sentence that makes very clear the word you have singled out for definition and the approach you will take with that word. The proposal must allow you to discuss two aspects of your definition—one in each body paragraph. Write an introduction, following any of the suggestions on pages 261–266.

In the body paragraphs you have to choose, as usual, from several kinds of illustrative details. You can use sensory details, statistics, statements from books, comments made on television or radio, actual cases that you know: any of these will add lively support to your paragraph topics. The methods of paragraph development that appear in Part I of this book can suggest the ways you can put details together successfully in your paragraphs.

But the most fruitful definition is one that starts in your own experience. For that reason, you might consider relating a moment or two in your life, a moment when you learned an important feature of the definition of the word you have chosen. What you will produce in this kind of essay, therefore, is a personalized definition, one that gives the reader a background of your experience through which to understand your application of language. The student themes you will examine later develop definitions in this manner, illustrating moments (expanded with concrete sensory language) in which the writers learned the meaning of some abstract term.

Your conclusion requires special attention in this essay. As you learned on pages 433–437, your concluding paragraph will attempt to develop a broader issue that is related to your proposal, an issue that illustrates the importance of your topic beyond the limited application you have made in your essay.

Prewriting for Your Definition Theme

In writing a definition theme, you will find it useful as a first step to read what dictionaries say about the words you are considering as subjects for your essay. (To review the various features of a dictionary entry, see pages 482–483.) As you recall, a dictionary offers essentially the *denotative* meanings of words, and the contrast between how a dictionary defines a word and what you and others mean to suggest by it can help you develop a lively, interesting paper. Checking more than one dictionary, if you like, you can make a comparative list with dictionary definitions (in your own words) to one side of the page. On the other side, you can write either your own meanings or any questions raised by dictionary definitions or your comments and criticisms about the meanings supplied by your dictionary.

Prewriting for Definition Theme
Word: teacher

Dictionary meanings	My meanings
1. one who teaches, especially a person hired by a school to teach	Not just anyone who teaches is a teacher; real teacher is a special person. All the qualities of "teacher" are missing from the dictionary definition: patience, warmth, concern, intelligence, firmness, flexibility.
2. one whose occupation is to instruct	Person who is a teacher does not have to teach as an occupation. My mother taught me to play the piano—she's no teacher. Everyone who has special personality traits and who really wants to impart knowledge can be a teacher —role of religion in teaching? issue of morals or values but religious instruction prohibited in public school classroom.
3. a religious instructor or preacher not regularly ordained in a congregational church	

—Simon Blakey

Step 1. Dictionary Meanings in Review. Following the example above, record dictionary definitions for one or more of the words you think you'd like to define in an essay. Alongside or below the meanings you copy, write

• your own meanings, that is, what *you* mean by the word
• any questions that the dictionary meanings stimulate
• any comments or criticisms stimulated by the dictionary meanings

Use separate paper.

Examining Student Themes

Read the essay below, which defines anger for the reader. As you read, consider how the writer has personalized the definition and how the concrete detail holds the reader's attention throughout.

"You Must Be Crazy!"

If sibling rivalry, as Freud suggests, was supposed to dominate the relationship between two brothers, the way Matt and I got along was no example. We had our harmless arguments, certainly, but for the most part, little friction kept us apart. We often played together, whether swatting softballs in John Burns Park or sledding down the hill at Mill Road on winter mornings. At sixteen, two years younger than I am, Matt is a good companion. It is all the more surprising to me, therefore, that I could explode so dangerously at him. I became aware of the ugly features of anger in my personality when I faced my brother at his bedroom door one March afternoon last year.

I stood there holding the tan sweater Matt had borrowed and then had returned to my drawer in a crumpled heap. Grease stains were all over the sleeve and near the collar. "How did this happen?" I grumbled, pointing to a large black spot. On the floor, near his bed in a circle of lamplight, he looked up casually from his *Sports Illustrated.* "Oh," he said. "I was fooling around with the Chevy. Oil dripped on everything." I could not believe my ears. "You wore my good sweater to work on your stupid car? I don't believe you!" My neck tightened and my hands grew wet and cold. I felt my eyelid twitch. Indifferently, Matt rubbed the arch of his left foot covered in a white cotton sock. Then he shrugged his shoulders as he looked up from his magazine. "Those are the breaks," he said, dropping his eyes to the page again.

It was probably that lack of concern that drove me wild. Lunging at him, I pushed him down against the brown rug, stiff and rough. The more I pushed against him, the angrier I felt. Some strange power had overtaken me. I was almost a mindless animal on the attack, not much better than a shark or a tiger. Luckily Matt's face suddenly registered in my mind. When I saw how pale he looked and when I heard him choking, I realized that I had my elbow pressed against his throat. What was I doing? I jumped up: Matt lay sputtering beside the bed. "You must be crazy!" he gasped in a voice I could barely hear. His small blue eyes stared at me in amazement. "You could have killed me." I remember looking at my hands and then back at Matt. He was right. I was crazy with anger. If rage could turn me into such a monster with my own brother, imagine what it could do under other conditions. "I'm sorry," I said, my face hot with embarrassment. "I'm really sorry."

At that moment I realized the full meaning of anger. In *Introduction to Psychology* Clifford T. Morgan, Richard A. King, and Nancy M. Robinson (New York, McGraw Hill, 1979) say that "Most adults have learned to contain their anger . . . so that we seldom observe outright displays of it" (p. 250). Perhaps I am not adult enough, but I do not think that containing anger is as easy as Morgan, King, and Robinson suggest. Anger is a strong and dangerous emotion that can easily overpower a person. Knowing the possible results of anger in each individual's life might help bring the emotion under some control, and many adults have to work hard to regulate their tempers. But if one brother can turn upon another with such violence, I do not think checking anger is easy. Street fights, homicides, battle combat—these are all extensions of a person unable to deal with passionate feelings and of the angry eruptions one human being directs against another. In the story of Cain and Abel is the story of anger that can grow into war.

—*Thomas Healey*

Step 1. Evaluating the Essay. Discuss the following questions and comments about the student essay you just read.

1. Put a check next to the proposal sentence. What two aspects of the topic does Mr. Healey's proposal suggest?
2. What method of development appears in the body paragraphs?
3. Which details are clearest to visualize—which sensory images are most outstanding?
4. Comment on the transitions used in the first sentence of paragraph 2.
5. Which part of the first sentence in paragraph 3 reminds the reader of the

subject of the previous paragraph? Which part of the sentence suggests the content of paragraph 3 itself?

6. What generalization appears in the conclusion? How is the generalization related to the proposal sentence?

Some Titles for the Definition Essay

Here are some suggestions for titles of your essay on the definition of a word you have learned through personal experience.

My Definition of Fear

When I Learned the Meaning of Love

Two Moments of Anger

How I Learned What Prejudice Means

My Experience with Loneliness

What Is Hope?

What Is Pain?

What Is Joy?

What Is Sadness?

Learning the Meaning of Injustice

I Learn to Hate

Brotherhood in Action: Two Moments in Definition

The Meaning of Pride

The Meaning of Poverty

My Definition of City

Excitement: Two Moments in Definition

My Meaning of Unselfishness

My Definition of Education

Teacher: Two Moments in Definition

My Definition of Fun

A Definition Checklist: Evaluating Your Own Essay

After you write the first draft of your essay and *before* you write the final copy, study this checklist, making any changes you may need to improve the quality of your paper. If you cannot check *excellent* or *good* for most of the questions, you need to revise your essay carefully. Then, after you are satisfied with your final copy, fill out the checklist by putting an *X* on the blanks that best describe (in your opinion) the way you followed the directions. Submit the checklist with your essay.

	Excellent	*Good*	*Fair*	*Does Not Appear*
1. I did prewriting for my essay and produced drafts, which I revised before doing a final copy.	_____	_____	_____	_____
2. My proposal sentence explains the intention of my essay and allows me to discuss *two* aspects of my topic, one in each body paragraph. My proposal comes as the last sentence of paragraph 1.	_____	_____	_____	_____
3. My first sentence of paragraph 2 tells what aspect of the topic I will discuss and makes a transition to the proposal sentence.	_____	_____	_____	_____
4. My first sentence of paragraph 3 refers back to paragraph 2 *and* states the topic that will appear in paragraph 3.	_____	_____	_____	_____
5. Each of my body paragraphs provides adequate detail that helps define the word clearly for my reader.	_____	_____	_____	_____
6. There are several examples of concrete sensory images in my paper. My essay contains several words that show colors and actions, name sounds and smells, state sensations of touch. I have used simile, metaphor, and personification (pages 134–135) to improve	_____	_____	_____	_____

the visual qualities of my paper.

7. Before I prepared my final copy, I studied my own list of misspelled words and my own Theme Progress Sheet. I was careful to look over my paper for my usual errors. I proofread my essay very slowly according to directions on pages 42–43.

8. I have chosen for my topic some word that has deep and important meanings for me.

9. I have used a number of sentence types in order to achieve variety in writing. I have employed

a. subordination (pages 100–109)

b. coordination (pages 19–20)

c. -*ing* openers (pages 208–212)

d. -*ed* openers (pages 212–213)

e. one or more sentence patterns provided in this chapter (pages 437–439)

f. openers with word groups that show relationship (pages 320–322).

10. I have checked my paper for pronoun errors of the type explained in this chapter.

11. I have written a conclusion that applies my topic to some other issue or idea that may be viewed in the light of the subject I have developed (pages 433–437).

GETTING READER RESPONSE

After each person in the class has done a rough draft, divide the class into groups of three. Take about five minutes to identify the questions people in each group would like to have answered about their drafts before going on to the next draft. One person in each group should report back to the class on those questions as the class prepares a master list on the chalkboard.

Using the master list, read your definition essays aloud in your groups as people listening take notes in an effort to answer the questions on the board. Then, discuss each paper, making suggestions to the writer about how to revise the paper in the next draft.

THE PROFESSIONALS SPEAK

In the following selection, the writer defines *happiness* in modern, urban terms. Notice how she draws upon her own experiences to expand the various meanings of the word. Read the selection and answer the questions that come after it.

SOME WORDS TO KNOW BEFORE YOU READ

Buddha: Indian philosopher at the center of a large religious cult
Rev. Mr. Moon: contemporary religious leader with wide following
esthetically (also aesthetically): in a manner pertaining to the sense of beauty or taste
distraction: something that draws attention away from one's original focus
exhilarates: makes invigorated, cheerful, stimulated
putrid: rotten; foul smelling; vile

Happiness

Happiness is still new to me, so I still notice things about it. Mainly I notice what it is and what it isn't. For example, it isn't cheeriness. I know that because, although I am cheery now, when I was miserable I was even (albeit defensively) cheerier. Nor is happiness having everything you want. If you have that you're probably dead. Same goes for the other notion about happiness: it does not mean that bad things stop happening to you. If bad things stopped happening to you, you'd probably be dead, too.

Nor is happiness particularly quiet. That surprises me because people are always talking about it in terms of peace. So I guess I thought when I got happy I'd lie down more. But I run around as much as I ever did—often as foolishly. So it seems happiness does not alter one's rhythm. At least it hasn't altered mine. Perhaps it's different when happiness comes via Buddha or the Rev. Mr. Moon.

What happiness is occurred to me the other day when I got off a bus at the corner nearest to where I live. I think everyone experiences a certain pleasure—however small or unconscious—in getting off the bus at the corner nearest to where one lives.

Maybe you've screwed up everything else that day, but you've gotten off at the right stop. And even if home is a dump and you hate it, there's still something nice about turning the key in the lock and hearing the cylinder roll over.

Well that, I think, multiplied many times over, is what happiness is: a sense of having gotten off at the right stop and rolled over the right cylinder; that among all the stops you might have chosen, you have picked—or fallen into—the one that is uniquely, marvelously, morally, esthetically and astonishingly (astonishment is a big part of this because it shows you've noticed) right for you.

Sometimes when I notice happiness, it's with an eye toward what's missing. Loneliness is missing. Paradoxically though, ever since I stopped being lonely I don't mind being alone. Sometimes I even like it. I suppose the reason is that before, being alone reminded me that I was lonely. Now, being alone reminds me that I'm not.

I cry on an average of, say, two or three times a year (not counting movies). I used to cry that many times a week. And quantity isn't the only thing that has changed. In the old days I'd weep from the soles of my feet up. Sobs, when they came, were like typhoons. They'd go through every bone, artery and capillary. Now when I cry it's strictly a local affair. It stays around the eyes. Then sniff sniff, blow blow, and it's over. And afterward—unless I've been crying about someone other than myself—I don't feel rotten. I feel silly.

Those old Sundays aren't there anymore, either. Sundays used to hurt. By Sunday the distractions of the week—and of the weekend—were over. Which made Sunday a day of contemplation and reflection. Well if your life is lousy, the last thing you want to do is contemplate and reflect. On Sundays I even had a hard time acting cheerful.

Happiness, as everyone knows, has nothing to do with money. Except everyone is wrong. Money alone won't do it; but money is one of life's great garnishes. There's nothing like having it on the side. I'm not exactly rich myself, but I'm a lot richer than I used to be, so I feel rich. It's an incredibly pleasant way to feel. Money soothes, sweetens and occasionally ("I'll take four!") exhilarates. I also happen to be a tightwad, which makes it all the kinkier. As delightful as it is to spend money when you have it, *not* spending money when you have it has a special charm.

Happiness has its down side, and I find myself noticing that, too. I'm continually nervous, for example, that it will stop. When you're unhappy you expect—or at least you hope—your life will change. When your life is good, however, you are terrified it will change. Moreover, you are sure it *will*, whereas when you're unhappy you are sure it won't.

So I worry about that. And further I worry if, when life takes a plunge, will all of my old coping skills come back? E.g., avoidance, self-deception, positive thinking, exercise, loud music, novels, cocktail parties: I remember what the techniques are, but is it like riding a bicycle? Will I be able to *do* it all again? I also wonder, when it gets bad, how bad will it get? And when will it happen? Will it be gradual or Pow! . . . I'm most afraid of Pow. Sometimes when I start thinking this way I get angry at myself. You're happy, for God's sake! I shout at the person inside my head. You should be *happy!!*

Happiness, I've noticed, can cause work to slide. When my life was putrid I worked like mad to compensate. Now that I don't need to compensate, the motive to work has become more pure. It has also become more scarce. Instead of working all the time, I find myself—I guess the word is lingering. I stand at windows and look out even when there's nothing much to see. Or I sit on the swivel chair in my living room and swivel.

I think I'm more boring now. Not only because I stare and swivel, but because—I can't help it—I talk about being happy. Or even if I don't talk about it, it probably shows. Which not only bores people; it also depresses them. Unless, of course, they're happy too. But then they want equal time. . . . By the way, it's amazing how many happy people there are. When I was in that other state I thought everyone else was, too. It would have been too awful to think they weren't. I've even met some people who are happily *married*. I don't think anyone knows about them, but they're everywhere! Even in New York! And I'm not talking about couples who have "worked out their problems" or who have learned to "communicate" or any of that other stuff. I mean people who really like each other! They get along! Some of them from the start!

I like these people. This surprises me, too. When I was young I thought happy people were boring. They are, but I like them anyway. They're nice. They're kind. They make good friends. The funny thing is a lot of them don't have any more going for them than anyone else. The difference is they think they do.

Since happiness hit, I think I'm not as funny as I used to be. I hadn't realized, until I got less funny, to what extent humor is rooted in despair, rage, misfortune. I've been accused of having been funny about cancer. But of course! That was easy! Now ask me to say something funny and I'll give you one of my new glassy stares.

I guess I haven't made happiness sound all that great. Well, that's wrong; it is great. It's just that everything has a price.

And I guess I haven't mentioned what I'm happy about. Probably I'm a little embarrassed because (Freud was right) it's the same old thing: love and work.

—*Betty Rollin*
The New York Times

1. What are some of the personal experiences Rollin draws upon to build her definition of happiness?
2. The writer says that happiness "multiplied many times over" is "a sense of having gotten off at the right stop and rolled over the right cylinder." What does she mean by that statement? Why should getting off a bus at the right place or putting a key in the right lock lead to happiness?
3. For many people who do not live in cities, buses are infrequent modes of transportation and door locks are unnecessary. How can Betty Rollin's definition apply to such people? What general principle might she be suggesting with this definition in the third and fourth paragraphs?
4. Explain the part of her definition that includes what happiness is not. What does Rollin mean when she says that happiness has its "down side"?
5. Where does the author use comparison and contrast strategies in this essay?
6. What is the meaning of the last paragraph?

REACHING HIGHER

Step 1. Image as Definition. Look at the photograph on page 421. Write a paragraph that names and explains the word you think the photographer is defining in the picture.

Step 2.   A Photo Essay as Definition. Select any *five* abstract terms and, from magazines and newspapers, cut out and mount a face, a scene of action, or a place that you think illustrates each abstraction. Or, you might wish to take your own photographs of scenes or people, photographs that would show in concrete terms what you mean by some abstract word like *fear, love, happiness, hatred,* or *sorrow.*

On the back of each mounted picture, write a sentence that names the word you are defining and explains why you represented it by the picture you selected.

Definitions through Images

An effective way to define difficult words—especially abstract ones—is by means of imagery (see pages 5–7). The dictionary defines *love,* for example, as "the attraction, desire, or affection felt for a person who arouses delight or admiration." Although this is surely an adequate definition, anyone who has experienced love knows how incomplete the dictionary meaning is. A great number of words in the language suggest through our own experiences a number of definitions that go beyond what the dictionary says. This is what is meant by the *connotation* of words: the ability to suggest or hint at meanings that are not part of what the word actually points out. The actual dictionary definition of a word (like the definition given above of the word *love*) is called *denotation.* (See page 455.)

Step 3. In a paragraph of definition, define any word you wish through a series of strong images based upon your own observations. Select a word that stimulates images for you, a word that calls up a string of pictures of happiness, tension, delight, or pain. Use sensory details to make each picture sharp and clear.

Read the student sample below as an example.

Old: A Spider's Web, An Attic Trunk

Old: a lump of coal in a dark, moist corner of my basement, an abandoned spider's web still clinging to its gritty surface; the metallic smell of a coin, its date rubbed silvery smooth; that gray-brown chunk of oak in my backyard, its bark as cold as stone on my fingers; the scent of photographs when I open the brown shoe box, and the slick, glossy feel of the yellowing snapshots inside; the squeal of the attic trunk as with dust-covered hands my brother Al and I push back the lid to eye Mom's rotting silks and satins; the musty aroma of a book from my childhood, *Peter Pan,* whose brown-stained pages crackle as I turn them; that brown mahogany chair Aunt Polly once owned, the one with the grinning face carved into it, the one with the cold wooden tongue that licks at my spine whenever I lean back; the craggy folds surrounding grandma's smile as she carefully knits pink yarn into a blanket for her first great-grandchild, my brother's new baby; the breath of my dog, Pepper, who looked up at me with milky eyes as I stroked his fur for the last time.

—Karl Joreid

Follow these steps as you write your definition through images:

1. Select a word that suggests many definitions for you, a word that calls pictures into your mind. *Your success in the paragraph depends on the selections of a word that has important meanings to you.*
2. Write at least ten images that you associate with the word. Make your images rich in color, sound, smell, and touch.
3. Mention the names of specific places and people.
4. Vary the length of the images. Make some images long; write one or two brief images of strong visual quality.
5. Use a colon after the word that you are attempting to define.
6. Use a semicolon after each image.

Hint
Each image is a fragment, not a complete sentence. Notice that the verb used in most of the images is an *-ing* or an *-ed* verb part. Some of the images contain no verb part at all. But the *-ing* adds a certain liveliness to your picture, so try to use it often in the imagery.

7. Make up a title that uses both the word you are defining and a piece of your favorite image or two. What images do the words after the colon in Mr. Joreid's title come from?

Step 4. Words for Image Definitions. Here are some words that might suggest a series of sharp pictures to you. You can use one of these, if you wish, in your paragraph definition.

1. love
2. blue (or any color)
3. old
4. May (or any month)
5. Saturday (or any day)
6. dream
7. autumn (or any season)
8. ocean
9. maturity
10. breakfast
11. pleasure
12. ecstasy

PART III

A MINIBOOK OF EIGHTEEN SPECIAL SKILLS

1. Improving Spelling
2. Learning Vocabulary
3. Reading a Dictionary Entry
4. Using a Thesaurus
5. Confusing Words: A Glossary
6. Using the *Reader's Guide*
7. Using the Card Catalog
8. Preparing a Bibliography
9. Writing Simple Footnotes
10. Quoting from Books and Articles
11. Format of a Business Letter
12. Applying for a Job You Want
13. Filling Out Applications
14. Taking Notes
15. Writing a Summary
16. Writing about Literature: Some Approaches to Consider
17. Answering Essay Examination Questions
18. Making a Formal Outline

1. IMPROVING SPELLING

HOW TO BE A BETTER SPELLER

1. Keep a list of the words you usually have trouble with: write the word correctly spelled; underline the troublesome letters; and make up some way of remembering the word. Start your list on page 481 after you examine the sample.
2. Write troublesome words several times, saying the letters aloud.
3. Trace the letters with your fingers after you think you know the spelling.
4. Use a dictionary to find correct spelling. Note the syllables.
5. If you cannot find the word in a dictionary, don't assume that the dictionary left out the word you are looking for. Try as many possible letter combinations as you can. For example, let us imagine that you had real trouble spelling *conscious.* You look first under the letter *k* (it often makes the same sound as *c* at the beginning of a word), but when you find no *kon* combination, you have to look for another possibility: *con* starts many words. If you had trouble with letters after *con,* you might look next at *sh* (it makes the same sound as *sci* here). But when you find no *consh,* you need to think of other possibilities: maybe even *consch.* If you follow these suggestions, you will often locate the correct spelling. When you find the spelling that looks right to you, *read the definition* to make sure that the spelling offered is the correct one for the word you want.
6. Learn the spelling demons, words most frequently misspelled by many people. One hundred and fifty appear below.
7. Learn spelling rules for the most difficult problems.

Spelling Demons: Group A

1. *abundance* Have a bun; then dance.
2. *accommodate* two c's, two m's
3. *achievement* i before e
4. *adolescence* -scence
5. *allowed* Look for all.
6. *analyze* -yze
7. *apparent* double p; -ent
8. *appreciate* double p; iate
9. *arrangement* Don't drop the e.
10. *attendance* two t's; end in dance
11. *available* Ail is in this word.
12. *becoming* Drop the e in become; one m only.
13. *benefited* Look for the fit after bene.
14. *business* The bus is in so add -ess.
15. *category* an e between cat and gory
16. *cigarette* two t's surrounded by e's
17. *competition* Make the last e in compete an i; add -tion.
18. *conscious* sc + ious

19. *cruel*   u + e
20. *dependent*   -ent ending
21. *dilemma*   Emma has a dilemma.
22. *discipline*   -sci
23. *eliminate*   e + lim + i + nate
24. *environment*   nm combination
25. *exaggerate*   two g's
26. *existence*   exist + ence
27. *familiar*   The word liar is in familiar.
28. *grammar*   **Hint:** ram and mar are the same letters reversed.
29. *guiding*   Drop the e in guide.
30. *hoping*   only one p in hope
31. *independence*   -ence at the end
32. *jealousy*   Jealousy is lousy!

33. *loneliness*   lonel~~y~~i + ness
34. *management*   Add ment to manage.
35. *mischief*   The Indian chief does mischief.
36. *organization*   drop the e in organize; add -ation.
37. *particular*   i c u are particular.
38. *persuade*   Add -suade to per.
39. *precede*   pre + cede
40. *presence*   If you are present make your presence known.
41. *proceed*   The church needs the proceeds.
42. *receive*   i before e except after c
43. *rhythm*   rhy + thm
44. *satisfied*   -fied
45. *separate*   Separate means part.
46. *sincerely*   Keep the last -e.
47. *succeed*   two c's, two e's
48. *thorough*   a rough word to spell
49. *thought*   -ought
50. *unnessary*   two n's, two s's

Step 1. Practice with Group A Words. Fill in the blanks with correct letters to complete the words below.

1. We must all pro_____d to el_____m_____te the
   un_____c_____ary pollution of the env_____n_____nt if we are
   ever tho_____r_____ly to ap_____c_____te our
   ex_____st_____ce.
2. Because he a_____ow_____d it to continue, Mr. Powell did not seem
   con_____i_____s of how cr_____l his son's m_____ch_____f
   was, or else he would have th_____t twice about it.
3. Jazz often consists of se_____ate r_____t_____ms combined in a
   p_____rti_____lar ar_____g_____ment.

4. A f_____l_____r dil_____ma of adoles_____n_____e is a choice
between the need for ach_____v_____t and ind_____p_____ce on
the one hand and for dis_____pline and
comp_____t_____t_____n on the other hand.
5. We rec_____ve complaints annually about ci_____ar_____tes from
those trying to p_____rs_____de us to stop smoking in public places.

Spelling Demons: Group B

1. *acceptance*   accept + ance
2. *accompanied*   two c's + -ied
3. *acquaintance*   ac + quaint + ance
4. *advertisement*   tise
5. *all right*   two words like "all wrong"
6. *annually*   double n
7. *appearance*   An ear is part of your appearance.
8. *approach*   a double p before the roach
9. *article*   -le ending
10. *attitude*   double t
11. *basis*   ends in is
12. *behavior*   Don't forget the i.
13. *breathe*   We breathe to take a breath.
14. *career*   two e's
15. *certainly*   cer-tain-ly
16. *coming*   Drop the e in come.
17. *condemn*   Don't forget the silent n.
18. *convenience*   con + ven + ience
19. *deceive*   i before e except after c
20. *description*   des
21. *disappoint*   dis + appoint
22. *discussion*   discuss + ion
23. *embarrass*   two r's, two s's
24. *equipment*   Look for the *quip.*
25. *excitable*   Drop the e in excite; add -able.
26. *experience*   -ence at the end
27. *fascinating*   sc after the a and before the i
28. *guaranteed*   guar as in guard; two e's at the end
29. *height*   -ei in the middle
30. *hungrily*   Make the y in *hungry* an i; add -ly.
31. *intelligence*   Can you tell he has intelligence?
32. *knowledge*   Did you know the ledge was there?
33. *losing*   Drop the e in lose.
34. *marriage*   marry + age
35. *morale*   Ale will lift a soldier's morale.
36. *parallel*   Are all lines parallel.

37. *peculiar*   A liar is peculiar.
38. *pleasant*   Drop the e in please and add an ant.
39. *preferred*   Start with pre; double -r at the end.
40. *principle*   A principle is a rule.
41. *psychology*   psy to open
42. *recommend*   one c, two m's
43. *ridicule*   rid + i + cule
44. *schedule*   s + ch
45. *significance*   -ance
46. *studying*   study + ing
47. *surprise*   no z in this word
48. *tragedy*   no d before the g
49. *valuable*   Drop the e in value; add able.
50. *weather*   I can't bear the weather.

Step 2.   Practice with Group B Words. Unscramble the following list of jumbled letters in order to spell the words correctly.

Hint

The first letter of each word is in boldface; the second letter is underlined.

1. c e m e r d m o n _____
2. a n n i e s c i f i g c _____
3. l u n i y h g r _____
4. l l e l a r p a _____
5. a p e r u l i c _____
6. e e e v c i d _____
7. h o y g l s p y c o _____
8. l e e d u c h s _____
9. o a r l e m _____
10. n l e t i l i e g c n e _____

Step 3.   More Group B Practice: Looking for Smaller Words. In the Group B words, there are many words that contain another word of five letters or more. Write nine of these words below and underline the smaller word contained in each.

Example

1. *discussion* _____
2. _____
3. _____
4. _____
5. _____
6. _____
7. _____
8. _____
9. _____
10. _____

Spelling Demons: Group C

1. *accidentally*   two c's, two l's
2. *accustom*   double c
3. *admittance*   two t's
4. *aggravate*   two g's
5. *amateur*   e u r
6. *apologized*   Look for the log; add i z e d
7. *applying*   two p's. Don't drop the y at the end!
8. *argument*   Drop the e in argue.
9. *athlete*   Don't forget the e in "let." No e after h.
10. *audience*   At such a bad show the audience almost died.
11. *beautiful*   y in beauty changes to i
12. *believe*   Don't believe a lie.
13. *brilliance*   two l's + iance
14. *carried*   double r.
15. *changeable*   Leave the e in change.
16. *committee*   two m's, two t's, two e's
17. *conscientious*   A scientist is conscientious.
18. *criticize*   -cize
19. *definitely*   Look for the finite.
20. *difference*   two f's; ence
21. *disastrous*   no e between the t and r
22. *efficient*   -ient after c
23. *emphasize*   Does it emphasize your size?
24. *especially*   This word has something special: double l.
25. *exercise*   no -z here!
26. *extremely*   The m stands between two e's.
27. *genius*   -ius not ious
28. *guidance*   Put gui before dance.
29. *heroes*   Add es to hero.
30. *ignorance*   He ran in ignorance.
31. *interest*   in + ter + est
32. *leisure*   -ei + sure

33. *magnificent*   magnify + -cent
34. *miniature*   mini + a + ture
35. *noticeable*   Was not ice able to freeze the lock?
36. *paralyze*   -yze
37. *performance*   -ance after perform
38. *possession*   two double s's
39. *prejudice*   Look for the dice.
40. *privilege*   Privilege is vile.
41. *pursue*   two u's
42. *relieve*   Lie down to relieve your pain.
43. *sacrifice*   sacrifice

44. *seize*   The -e comes before the -i.
45. *similar*   ilar
46. *sufficient*   double f; -cient
47. *transferred*   two r's
48. *unusually*   three u's all in one word
49. *villain*   The villain had lain on the street.
50. *writing*   Drop the e in write.

Step 4.   Group C Practice. In each of the following sets of words, one is misspelled. Write that word, correctly spelled, in the space provided at the left.

_____	1. beautyful	amateur	criticize	heroes
_____	2. pursue	admittance	writting	seize
_____	3. especially	efficeint	athlete	possession
_____	4. privilege	villain	argument	paralize
_____	5. performance	carried	definately	exercise
_____	6. ignorence	unusually	genius	leisure
_____	7. transferred	noticeable	aggravate	disasterous
_____	8. brilliance	beleive	conscientious	accustom
_____	9. apologized	committee	similar	intrest
_____	10. magnificent	miniature	sufficient	changable

Step 5.   Mastering Spelling Demons. Fill in the blanks to complete the words (taken from Groups A, B, and C) in the following phrases.

1. not_____ble jazz r_____t_____m
2. the sig_____fi_____ of the ar_____ment
3. it was a_____l r_____t to ap_____ch
4. an amat_____ ath_____te
5. a successful b_____iness car_____r
6. appl_____ng the princip_____
7. a be_____t_____ful des_____iption
8. con_____us of his j_____lo_____y
9. to exa_____erate the d_____le_____a
10. a d_____ast_____us exper_____nce
11. e_____ci_____ly high mo_____le
12. the p_____chology of human behav_____
13. to s_____ze val_____ble gems
14. her ap_____r_____t ability
15. a cr_____l ex_____t_____nce
16. a fa_____inating per_____m_____nce
17. we conde_____ pre_____dice
18. her magn_____cent appe_____nce
19. must have suff_____ent exer_____e
20. an eff_____ent sch_____d_____le
21. he was be_____m_____g too ex_____t_____le
22. un_____ally th_____r_____gh job
23. pl_____sant w_____ther
24. a di_____us_____ion about their her_____s
25. the e_____pment is gu_____ant_____ed.
26. to emb_____a_____s him ac_____dent_____y
27. to be_____ve the th_____g_____t
28. to p_____sue knowl_____e
29. con_____entious stud_____ing
30. a cigar_____te advert_____ement
31. to rec_____ve their indep_____nd_____nce

32. the lon____l____ness of
    adol____c____nce
33. his par____c____lar in____est
34. an ext____mely good
    env____ro____ent
35. hop____ng to suc____d
36. to sac____f____ce his
    pos____e____ion

37. They are def____nit____ly
    sim____l____r.
38. a chang____ble a____itude
39. the bri____nce of a ge____s
40. to pers____de sin____ly
41. sat____sf____d with his
    wri____ng

SOME SPELLING RULES FOR DIFFICULT PROBLEMS

Rule 1.   Solving -ie Headaches

1. *i* usually comes before *e*.

   Examples
   field   yield   achievement   relieve

2. If the letter immediately before the -ie combination is *c*, the *e* usually comes before the *i*.

   Examples
   deceive   receive   conceive

3. The *e* also comes before the *i* if the combination of letters sounds like the *a* in *say* or *clay*.

   Examples
   neighborhood   weight   eight
   _____ [this sounds like *a* in *say*, so the *e* comes before the *i*.]

EXCEPTIONS FOR YOU TO MEMORIZE	
either	leisure
foreign	science
seize	height
neither	efficient

The following jingle will help you to remember the rule:

i before *e* except after *c*,
or when sounded like *a*
as in *neighbor* and *weigh*.

Step 1.   Using -ie Correctly. Fill in *ie* or *ei* in the following words:

1. dec_____ve
2. rec_____pt
3. s_____ve
4. l_____surely
5. w_____rd
6. w_____ght
7. sl_____gh
8. s_____zure
9. rec_____ve
10. misch_____vous

11. coeffic_____nt
12. r_____gn
13. y_____ld
14. rel_____f
15. n_____ther
16. p_____ce
17. for_____gn
18. sc_____ntific
19. f_____ld
20. conc_____ved

Rule 2.   Changing *y* to *i*

1. If a word ends in *y* and the *y* is directly preceded by a consonant (any letter other than *a, e, i, o,* and *u*), the *y* is changed to *i* before an ending (*suffix*) is added.

Examples

[This is the new ending.]

fly + es = flies   carry + ed = carried

[The *y* is preceded by the consonant *l*.]

2. However, when the ending begins with *i* as in *-ing*, the *y* is *not* changed.

Examples

study + *ing* = studying   try + *ing* = trying

```
EXCEPTIONS FOR YOU TO MEMORIZE

lay + ed = laid     say + ed = said     pay + ed = paid
```

Step 2.   Adding to Words that end in y. Using the above rule, add the suffixes indicated to the following words.

	-ed	-ing	-(e)s
1. apply	_____	_____	_____
2. marry	_____	_____	_____
3. play	_____	_____	_____
4. fry	_____	_____	_____
5. annoy	_____	_____	_____

Step 3. More Practice. Add the indicated endings to the following words.

1. carry + *ed* _____
2. destroy + *ed* _____
3. tally + *ing* _____
4. lonely + *ness* _____
5. category + *s* _____

6. fancy + *ful* _____
7. mislay + *ed* _____
8. portray + *ed* _____
9. bury + *ing* _____
10. deny + *al* _____

Rule 3. Words that Drop the Final *e*

1. Words ending in silent *e* usually drop the *e* before a suffix beginning with a vowel.

Examples

use + -*ing* = using   use + *able* = usable

2. However, the silent -*e* usually remains before a suffix beginning with a consonant.

Examples

use + ful = useful   care + less = careless

EXCEPTIONS: FOR YOU TO MEMORIZE

argue + *ment* = argument

judge + *ment* = judgment

true + *ly* = truly

notice + *able* = noticeable

change + *able* = changeable

courage + *ous* = courageous

canoe + *ing* = canoeing

mile + *age* = mileage

Step 4. Working with the Final *e*. Using the above rule, add the suffixes indicated to the following words:

	-ing	*-ment*	*-able*
1. arrange	_____	_____	_____
2. achieve	_____	_____	_____
3. state	_____	_____	_____

4. refine   _____ _____ _____

5. advertise   _____ _____ _____

Step 5. More Practice. Add the indicated suffixes to the following words:

1. babble + *ing* _____
2. love + *ly* _____
3. debate + *able* _____
4. home + *less* _____
5. survive + *al* _____

6. bereave + *ment* _____
7. chase + *ing* _____
8. outrage + *ous* _____
9. write + *ing* _____
10. safe + *ty* _____

Rule 4. Doubling the Final Consonant

When you add a suffix to a word, the final consonant of that word is doubled if the following are true:

1. The suffix begins with a vowel.

Example
let + -*ing* = letting

2. The word is one syllable *or* is accented on the last syllable.

Examples
sit + -*ing* = sitting
(This word is one syllable.)
control (con-trol) + ed = controlled
(The accent is on the last syllable.)
suffer (suf-fer) + ed = suffered
(The accent is *not* on the last syllable, and so the final consonant is *not* doubled.)

Step 6. Doubling Practice. Add the indicated suffixes to the following words:

1. drop + *ing* = _____
2. prefer + *ed* = _____
3. happen + *ed* = _____
4. begin + *ing* = _____
5. depend + *ence* = _____
6. forget + *ful* = _____

7. benefit + *ing* = _____
8. big + *est* = _____
9. swim + *able* = _____
10. lessen + *ing* = _____
11. plan + *ing* = _____
12. benefit + *ed* = _____

13. admit + *ing* = _____   17. hug + *ed* = _____

14. whip + *ed* = _____   18. visit + *ing* = _____

15. stop + *ed* = _____   19. travel + *ing* = _____

16. commit + *ed* = _____   20. forbid + *en* = _____

Step 7.   Mastering the Spelling Rules. Test your mastery of the preceding spelling rules by adding the indicated suffixes to the following words. The numbers in parentheses refer to the spelling rule that applies to that word.

1. study + *ing* _____ (2)   21. delay + *ed* _____ (2)

2. judge + *ment* _____ (3)   22. offer + *ed* _____ (4)

3. deprive + *ing* _____ (3)   23. beauty + *ful* _____ (2)

4. manage + *ing* _____ (3)   24. profit + *able* _____ (4)

5. differ + *ence* _____ (4)   25. dismay + *ed* _____ (2)

6. accompany + *ed* _____ (2)   26. transfer + *ed* _____ (4)

7. inhibit + *ed* _____ (4)   27. entire + *ly* _____ (3)

8. lonely + *ness* _____ (2)   28. arrange + *ment* _____ (3)

9. unwit + *ing* _____ (4)   29. quarrel + *ed* _____ (4)

10. knowledge + *able* _____ (3)   30. receive + *ing* _____ (3)

11. annoy + *ed* _____ (2)   31. pay + *ed* _____ (2)

12. argue + *ment* _____ (3)   32. write + *ing* _____ (3)

13. forbid + *en* _____ (4)   33. cut + *ing* _____ (4)

14. deny + *al* _____ (2)   34. true + *ly* _____ (3)

15. revenge + *ful* _____ (3)   35. forget + *ful* _____ (4)

16. slip + *ed* _____ (4)   36. apply + *ing* _____ (2)

17. petrify + *ing* _____ (2)   37. deplore + *able* _____ (3)

18. concur + *ed* _____ (4)   38. ship + *ment* _____ (4)

19. canoe + *ing* _____ (3)   39. admire + *ing* _____ (3)

20. spy + *es* _____ (2)   40. bury + *ed* _____ (2)

Fill in *ie* or *ei* in the words below. To check your spelling, refer back to rule 1.

1. f_____ld   3. n_____ghbor

2. aud_____nce   4. l_____sure

5. gr_____ve   8. rel_____ve
6. conc_____ve   9. s_____ze
7. sl_____gh   10. f_____gn

YOUR OWN DEMON LIST: WORDS YOU MISTAKE

Fill in the columns on page 481, as indicated, with your own troublesome spelling words. Study the examples. Continue your list, if necessary, on your own paper.

2. LEARNING VOCABULARY

HOW TO LEARN NEW WORDS

The following steps will help you build your vocabulary:

1. Look up new words in a reliable dictionary.
2. Read definitions carefully. Pick only definitions that explain words as you want to use them or as they are used in what you have read.
3. Write each word on a small index card. Put definitions on the other side.
4. Categorize study words in related groups: *size* words, *liberation* words, *space-age* words, and so on.
5. Study words briefly on many occasions rather than for long periods on few occasions.
6. Say words and meanings aloud.
7. Write sentences using the words.
8. Add new words to your speaking vocabulary.
9. Use new words in writing sentences.
10. In reading, if you see an unfamiliar word, try to figure out its meaning from

   the way it is used in a sentence
   the prefix, root, or suffix that you see
   the words that may be put together to make up the new word
   a smaller word you recognize within the new word

Step 1. Predicting Meanings. Try to determine the meanings of the words below in any way that you can. Write definitions in the blank spaces.

1. underestimate _____

2. inconclusive _____

3. keepsake _____

4. paramedical _____

Word Correctly Spelled	Confusing Letters Underlined	A Way to Remember
You're	You're	You're = you + are
accommodate	accommodate	double c, double m

5. heartfelt _____

6. warmonger _____

7. irrevocable _____

8. spittoon _____

9. For that <u>laudable</u> plan, you deserve all the praise and thanks that the

    committee can give. _____

10. He was so thrilled by her political ideas that he overcame his usual <u>apathy</u>

    and promised, "I'll join the campaign right now!" _____

3. READING A DICTIONARY ENTRY

Most instructors encourage you to use dictionaries to check meanings and spellings even when you write a test or an essay in class. Although pocket dictionaries give simplified entries for words, you still need to understand the several parts of each entry. Here are samples from the *New Merriam-Webster Pocket Dictionary:*

[The word is a noun. Other abbreviations and symbols of parts of speech (vb., adj., adv., etc.) are explained in dictionary.]

[History of the form of the word. "OF" means Old French. Check key in front or back of book for abbreviations.]

[Pronunciation: all symbols explained in front of dictionary or on bottom of pages]

[This stands for same form of word as main entry.]

[Main entry]

[Period between syllables shows where to break word at end of a line]

→¹**forge** \'fōrj\ *n* [OF, fr. L *fabrica*, fr. *faber* smith] **:** SMITHY
→²**forge** *vb* **1 :** to form (metal) by heating and hammering **2 :** FASHION, SHAPE ⟨~ an agreement⟩ **3 :** to make or imitate falsely esp. with intent to defraud ⟨~ a signature⟩ — **forg·er** *n* — **forg·ery** *n*
→³**forge** *vb* **:** to move ahead steadily but gradually
→**for·get** \fər-'get\ *vb* -**got**; -**got·ten** *or* -**got**; -**get·ting 1 :** to be unable to think of or recall **2 :** to fail to become mindful of at the proper time **3 :** NEGLECT, DISREGARD ⟨*forgot* his old friends⟩ — **for·get·ful** *adj* — **for·get·ful·ness** *n*

[Past forms of verb: only irregular forms appear]

[Words that come from main word]

Step 1. Understanding Dictionary Entries. Using the *New Merriam-Webster Pocket Dictionary* or some other handy pocket dictionary, look up the word *essay*. Write the answers to the following questions:

1. What languages did the word come from? _____

    _____

2. What syllables make up the word? _____

    _____

3. What part of speech is the word? _____

_____

4. How is the word pronounced? _____

_____

5. What is an alternate pronunciation? _____

_____

6. How many definitions appear? _____

_____

7. What suffix can combine with it? What new word is created? _____

_____

8. Which definition is new to you? Write it here. _____

_____

4. USING A THESAURUS

A *thesaurus* is a dictionary of synonyms. You can look up a word like *humorist* (given below), for example, and find fifteen or twenty words, which are in some way related in meaning to that word.

WHEN TO USE THE THESAURUS

when you repeat the same word too often

when a word does not sound right in your sentence

when you write slang or nonstandard expressions and you want more formal language

when you learn new words and you want to see other words used in a similar way.

Two Hints for Thesaurus Use

1. Different methods of organization are used in preparing a thesaurus. One thesaurus groups synonyms according to ideas or subject categories. There, you look up words in the back of the book, find the section numbers in which the word you want appears, and then turn to a specific section, which gives the synonyms that interest you. Other thesauruses are alphabetically arranged, like dictionaries.
2. Not all synonyms listed for any word have the same meaning. And the thesaurus rarely tells the difference in shades of meaning among the synonyms offered. Therefore, know definitions of any words you select. Don't pick words just because they are unusual, impressive in length, or new to you. Use a dictionary to check out differences in meanings.

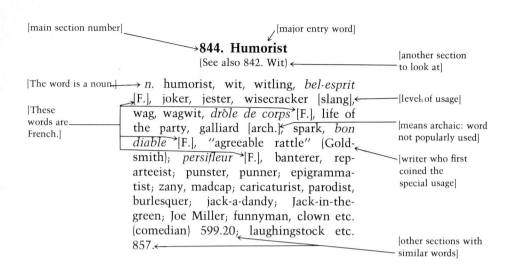

[main section number]   [major entry word]

→ **844. Humorist**
(See also 842. Wit) ←——————— [another section
                                      to look at]

[The word is a noun.] —→ *n.* humorist, wit, witling, *bel-esprit*
[F.], joker, jester, wisecracker [slang], ←—— [level of usage]

[These words are French.] wag, wagwit, *drôle de corps* [F.], life of
the party, galliard [arch.], spark, *bon* ←—— [means archaic: word
                                              not popularly used]
diable [F.], "agreeable rattle" (Gold-
smith); *persifleur* [F.], banterer, rep- ←—— [writer who first
                                              coined the
arteeist; punster, punner; epigramma-   special usage]
tist; zany, madcap; caricaturist, parodist,
burlesquer; jack-a-dandy; Jack-in-the-
green; Joe Miller; funnyman, clown etc.
(comedian) 599.20; laughingstock etc. ←—— [other sections with
857. ←——————————————————   similar words]

Step 1.   Thesaurus for Synonyms. Use a thesaurus to look up the following
words. For each word, select and write down three synonyms whose meanings
you do not know. Then, using a dictionary, write definitions of the three new
words. Look at the example. Use your own paper.

Example

Word

happy

Synonyms

1. *opportune*
2. *auspicious*

3. *joyous*

Definitions

1. *coming at the right time*
2. *favorable; suggesting
   success*

3. *full of delight*

1. compulsion
2. to observe
3. obedient
4. pleasant
5. gesture

5. CONFUSING WORDS: A GLOSSARY

accept, except

accept—means to *receive,* to *welcome,* to *say yes.*

We *accept* your offer of help.

except—means *leaving out, excluding.*

Everyone *except* Barry ate together.

affect, effect
affect means 1. to *assume* or *pretend.*

He *affected* a smile of agreement.

2. to *influence* or *act on.*

Good study habits *affect* learning speed.

Hint
Think of the **a** in *affect* as a signal to **a**ct.

effect means 1. to *bring about.*

His disposition *effected* a change in our mood.

2. *result* or *outcome.*

Hint
Think of the **e** in *effect* as a signal for r**e**sult.

The *effect* of her speech cannot be measured.

Hint
If *the* or *an* comes before the word, you must choose *effect.*

all ready, already
all ready—means *fully prepared.*

The team was *all ready* to play.

already—means *by this time* or *before a set time.*

When you arrived, I had *already* eaten.

among. See **between.**
amount, number
amount—refers to things in large masses, things that cannot be counted.

A large *amount* of water filled the tub.

number—refers to countable things.

He received a *number* of parking tickets.

bad, badly. See **good, well.**
barely. See **hardly.**
being that—avoid this expression. Use *since* or *because.*

Because (not "being that") I felt tired, I went to sleep.

between, among
    between—used to name relationships between *two* people or things.

Between you and me the book is dull.

    among—used to name relationships referring to *three* or more people or things.

Among the students only Carol answered.

could have, could've, could of
    could have—correct for all forms of written or spoken expression.

We *could have* studied more carefully.

    could've—a contraction, good for informal writing or speaking.

"You could've been more careful," Sandra replied.

    could of—incorrect! *Could've* sounds like *could of* but this last form is not correct
        in writing. Also, for the following words,
            use *should have*   *not* should of
                would have   *not* would of
                might have   *not* might of
If you need a contraction, use *should've* for *should have,*
                might've for *might have,* and
                would've for *would have.*
But remember, contractions appear most of the time in informal writing only.
different from, different than
    different from—the preferred form, although *different than* is sometimes used
        when a subject and verb follow it.

That pen is *different from* mine.

effect. See **affect.**
except. See **accept.**

fewer, less

fewer—used for things that can actually be counted.

He has *fewer* books than I have.

less—shows worth, quantity, or degree.

The cigarette has *less* tar than yours.
His car costs *less* than hers.

former, latter

former—between two objects, *former* refers to the first thing named.
latter—between two objects, *latter* refers to the second of two things named.

Neither the car nor the motorcycle would start; the *former* because of a bad carburetor, the *latter* because of faulty ignition.

Hint

If three objects are involved, do not use *former* and *latter; use first, second* (or *next*), and *last.*

A dog, a cat, and a horse appeared in the cartoon; the *first* did a tap dance while the *last* played a guitar.

good, well; bad, badly

good, bad—describe things or people.

A *good* movie is hard to find.
What a *bad* idea!

well or *badly*—describe actions named by most verbs.

She reads *well.*
She dances *badly.*

NOT

She reads *good.*
She dances *bad.*

Hint

After one of these verbs use *good* or *bad: is, am, are, were, have been, look, remain, appear, taste, smell, feel.*

She looks *bad.*

The soup tastes *good.*

The news was *bad* this morning.

If you want to indicate someone's health, use *well* or *bad* with one of the above verbs.

I feel *well* today.

hanged, hung
> *hanged*—shows someone's life was taken by execution.

> The mob *hanged* the criminal without a trial.

> *hung*—refers to things, not to people.

> We *hung* the mirror on the wall.

hardly, scarcely, barely
> Since these words are already negative, do not use them with *never, not,* or with verb contractions ending in *n't.*

> I *could hardly* breathe.

> > NOT

> I *couldn't hardly* breathe.

hung. See **hanged.**
in, into
> *in*—movement within one place.

> He ran *in* the room. (This means he was already inside the room when the action began.)

> *into*—movement from one place to a position within.

> He ran *into* the room. (This means he was not already within the room when the action began.)

irregardless Avoid! See **regardless.**
latter. See **former.**
learn, teach
> *learn*—means *gain information or knowledge.*
> *teach*—means *give information so that someone else learns.*

> He *taught* me right from wrong.

> > NOT

> He *learned* me right from wrong.

less. See **fewer.**
might have, might've. See **could have.**
myself

> Use *myself* to stress the word *I* in a sentence or to show that the subject and the receiver of the action are the same.

> I *myself* will judge.
> I shaved *myself* this morning.

> Avoid using *myself* as a substitute for *I* or *me.*

> It was Larry and *I.*

>> NOT

> It was Larry and *myself.*
> She took Beverly and *me* to the Dean.

>> NOT

> She took Beverly and *myself* to the Dean.

number. See **amount.**
regardless, irregardless

> Use *regardless* only; *irregardless* is incorrect.

> *Regardless* of our suggestions, he voted in his own way.

scarcely. See **hardly.**
should have, should've. See **could have.**
somewhere, somewheres

> Do not use an *s* at the end of any of the compound direction or time words. Use

somewhere	NOT	somewheres
anywhere	NOT	anywheres
nowhere	NOT	nowheres

teach. See **learn.**
well. See **good.**
would have, would've. See **could have.**

Step 1.   The Right Words in Your Sentences. Write a brief sentence of your own that uses correctly each word or word group.

1. different from
2. among
3. could hardly

4. fewer
5. hanged
6. myself

7. almost   9. already
8. affect   10. except

Step 2.   Correcting Sentences. Several sentences below contain errors. Underline each mistake, and write a correct word or word group to replace it. If the sentence is correct, mark it *C*. Use separate paper.

1. For a child she plays the piano very good.
2. Johnny Cash's last record is much different than his earlier ones.
3. He learned his son how to chop wood.
4. Irregardless of what you say to me, I will never except your apology.
5. The bank robbers divided the loot between the four of them.
6. "I could of been a contender!" is a line spoken by Marlon Brando in the movie *On the Waterfront*.
7. I might of won the dance contest if my partner didn't tango so bad.
8. Bruce had nowheres to go after the landlord evicted him being that he was too noisy.
9. The temperature on Thursday was anywheres from 70 to 85 degrees.
10. That suit looks well on you.

Step 3.   Making the Words Work. Follow instructions.

1. Tell in a sentence what happens to your own personality when you get very little sleep at night. Use the words *the effect* in your sentence.

   _____

   _____

2. Tell in a sentence what kind of music you dislike. Use *accept* or *except* correctly. _____

   _____

   _____

3. Use *scarcely* in a sentence to describe a test you recently passed. _____

   _____

   _____

4. Use *myself* in your own sentence. _____

   _____

   _____

5. Write a sentence about planting seeds for vegetable gardens. Use *in* or *into* correctly. _____

_____

_____

6. Use *affected* to mean *pretended* in a sentence. _____

_____

_____

_____

7. Use *affect* or *effect* in a sentence that tells how a friend's decision about something led to a certain unexpected result. _____

_____

_____

_____

8. Write a sentence about sharing household responsibilities with your family, friends, or spouse. Use *between* or *among* correctly. _____

_____

_____

9. Correct this sentence: *He had to return his tickets for the high school reunion game being that his mother was sick.* _____

_____

_____

10. Write a sentence about the long-range effects of chocolate on the teeth. Use *amount* or *number* correctly in your sentence. _____

_____

_____

6. USING THE READER'S GUIDE TO PERIODICAL LITERATURE

The *Reader's Guide to Periodical Literature* is a semimonthly report giving the names of authors and the titles of articles in many important magazines like *Time*, the *Atlantic, Saturday Review, Harper's,* and *The New Yorker*. The reports are bound together in volumes each year.

HOW TO USE THE READER'S GUIDE TO PERIODICAL LITERATURE

1. To find articles on any given subject, look up the subject in the index. Several authors, titles, and names of the magazines in which they appear are listed.
2. To find an article written by an author whose name you know, look up the author's last name in the index.

Sample Subject Entry

ATOMIC WEAPONS
↖[the subject of the article]

[article has illustrations]

A question of survival.   M. E. Thompson.   il↙
[title of article]   [author's name]

USA Today   111:48–50   S' 82← [date of issue]
[name of   [volume   [pages on which
periodical]   number]   article appears]

Sample Author Entry

↙[author's name]
NILSON, Lisbet

[title of article]   [illustrations]
How will museums survive in tomorrow's world?   il↙

[volume]   [page number]
Art News   81:78 +   Summ '82←   [date]
[name of   [article continued on later pages]
periodical]

Hint

All abbreviations appear in a key at the beginning of the *Reader's Guide*. Look up any abbreviations you do not understand.

Step 1. Looking for Articles and Essays. For each subject below, check the latest volume or issue of the *Reader's Guide* and copy from it one magazine reference on the line provided. Be prepared to explain the abbreviations in your entries.

1. terrorism in Central America _____

2. horror films _____

3. energy _____

4. television advertising _____

5. poverty _____

7. USING THE CARD CATALOG

The basic means for finding books in most libraries is the card catalog. It is usually a set of drawers with cards that index all the books found in that library. (In order to save space many libraries now have photographed these cards and make them available on microfilm.) In the card catalog you can find at least three cards for each book: an *author card* (indexed alphabetically by the author's last name); a *title card* (indexed alphabetically by the first word of the title, excluding *a* or *the*); and a *subject card* (indexed alphabetically according to what the book is about). Card-catalog entries will not only tell you where in the library the book is located, but also will give you useful subheadings and cross-references to lead you to other helpful sources of information. You will probably also want to consult various periodical indexes and the microfilm or microfiche catalogs to complete your research.

Below are sample author, title, and subject cards for Herbert R. Kohl's book *Basic Skills*.

Title Card

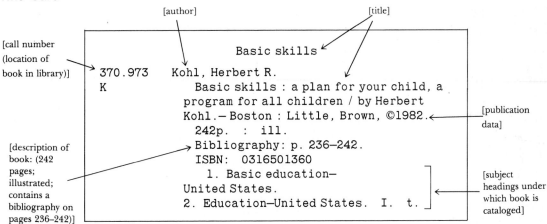

[author]   [title]

[call number
(location of
book in library)]

[description of
book: (242
pages;
illustrated;
contains a
bibliography on
pages 236–242)]

```
                        Basic skills

370.973    Kohl, Herbert R.
    K            Basic skills : a plan for your child, a
          program for all children / by Herbert
          Kohl.— Boston : Little, Brown, ©1982.
          242p.  :  ill.
          Bibliography: p. 236–242.
          ISBN:  0316501360
             1. Basic education—
          United States.
             2. Education—United States.  I.  t.
```

[publication
data]

[subject
headings under
which book is
cataloged]

Author Card

[author]

```
370.973    Kohl, Herbert R.
K              Basic skills : a plan for your child, a
           program for all children / by Herbert
           Kohl.—Boston : Little, Brown, ©1982.
              242p.  :  ill.
              Bibliography: p. 236—
              242.
              ISBN: 0316501360

              1. Basic education—
           United States.
           2. Education—United
           States.  I.  t.
```

Two Subject Cards

[subject headings] ⟶ BASIC EDUCATION—UNITED STATES.

```
370.973    Kohl, Herbert R.
K              Basic skills : a plan for your child, a
           program for all children / by Herbert
           Kohl.—Boston : Little, Brown, ©1982.
              242p.  :  ill.
              Bibliography: p. 236—
              242.
              ISBN: 0316501360
              1. Basic education—
           United States.
           2. Education—United
           States.  I.  t.
```

Two Subject Cards (continued)

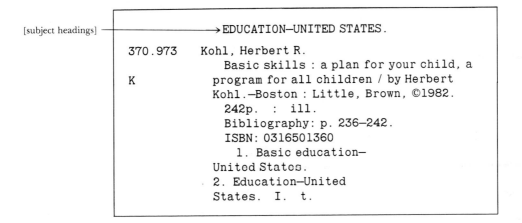

[subject headings]

EDUCATION—UNITED STATES.

370.973   Kohl, Herbert R.
                Basic skills : a plan for your child, a
K   program for all children / by Herbert
             Kohl.—Boston : Little, Brown, ©1982.
                242p. : ill.
                Bibliography: p. 236–242.
                ISBN: 0316501360
                  1. Basic education—
             United States.
               2. Education—United
             States. I. t.

8. *PREPARING A BIBLIOGRAPHY*

Whenever you do a paper based upon research, readers expect to find a *bibliography,* an alphabetical list of the sources you have consulted or quoted from in your paper. When you prepare a bibliography, keep in mind these guidelines:

1. The bibliography appears on a separate page at the end of the paper.
2. Items are *not* numbered but are listed alphabetically according to author's last name.
3. Write author's last name first, then first and middle name.
4. List alphabetically according to title other works by the same author, directly under the first entry for the author's name.
5. For works by more than one author, list the entry under last name of first author, giving other writers' names in regular order (first name, middle, last).
6. List works with no authors alphabetically according to the first important word in the title.
7. Do not give pages for books. Do give pages on which essays and articles in periodicals, encyclopedias, and newspapers appear.
8. The first line of each bibliography entry starts at the left-hand margin. Indent all other lines.
9. Double-space all entries but separate one entry from another by triple-spacing.

NAME _____ CLASS _____ DATE _____

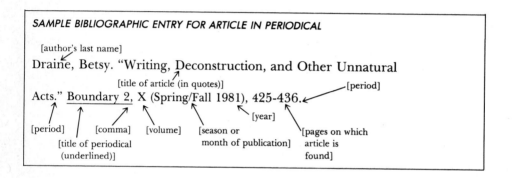

Here is the bibliography April Wynn prepared for her theme, "The Advantages of Attending Kindergarten" on pages 367–369.

Bibliography

Courtney, Richard. "Education Is Play." <u>Childhood Educa-</u>

<u>tion,</u> 49 (February 1973), 246–250.

Grant, Vance W. <u>Digest of Education Statistics.</u> Washington

D.C.: U.S. Government Printing Office, 1975.

Hymes, James L. Jr. <u>Teaching the Child Under Six.</u> Colum-

bus, Ohio: Charles E. Merrill Publishing Company, 1968.

Kohl, Herbert R. <u>Basic Skills.</u> Boston: Little, Brown, 1982.

Mindess, David. <u>Guide to an Effective Kindergarten Program.</u>

    New York: Parker Publishing Company, Inc., 1972.

Palmer, Edward L. "Sesame Street: Shaping Broadcast Tele-

    vision to the Needs of the Pre-schooler." <u>Educational</u>

    <u>Technology,"</u> 11 (February 1971), 18-22.

"Play." <u>World Book Encyclopedia,</u> 1969.

Step 1. A Bibliography Exercise. Using the resources of your college library, prepare on a separate sheet of paper a bibliography of *five* entries for one of the topics below. Make sure that at least one of your entries is for a periodical.

1. exercise
2. anti nuclear-power protests
3. white-collar crime
4. Haitian immigration
5. teenage alcoholism

9. WRITING SIMPLE FOOTNOTES

Sometimes you need to tell in footnotes the source for a statement you are quoting from someone else's work. Each quotation or paraphrase in an essay with such requirements, then, should be consecutively numbered slightly above the line and at the end of the statement you are borrowing from someone else's writing. At the bottom of the page or at the end of the essay, give the information about your source for each numbered quotation.

    Compare these footnote entries with bibliographic entries for the same book and periodical by looking at page 496.

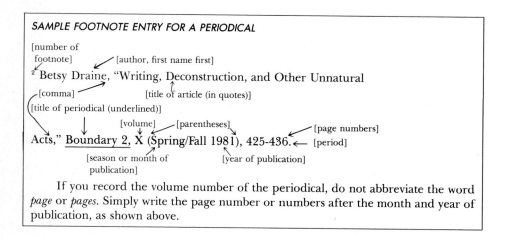

SAMPLE FOOTNOTE ENTRY FOR A BOOK

[author's name,
first name first]   [title of book underlined]

¹Raymond Carver, What We Talk About When We Talk About

[number of   [comma]
footnote]

                                    [means "page"]
        [parentheses]   [period after abbreviation]
Love (New York, 1981), p. 32. ← [period at end]

[city of   [date of   [comma]   [page number]
publication]   publication]

SAMPLE FOOTNOTE ENTRY FOR A PERIODICAL

[number of
footnote]   [author, first name first]

² Betsy Draine, "Writing, Deconstruction, and Other Unnatural

[comma]   [title of article (in quotes)]

[title of periodical (underlined)]

        [volume]   [parentheses]   [page numbers]

Acts," Boundary 2, X (Spring/Fall 1981), 425-436. ← [period]

        [season or month of   [year of publication]
        publication]

   If you record the volume number of the periodical, do not abbreviate the word
page or *pages*. Simply write the page number or numbers after the month and year of
publication, as shown above.

   If you quote from a book or an article and the very next quotation you use
in your paragraph comes from the same book or article, do this:

[capital letter]   [This means *pages*.]

[period]   [the page numbers]

²Ibid., pp. 29–30. ←   [period at end]

    [comma]   [period]

[This is an abbreviation for the Latin *ibidem*,
meaning *in the same place*.]

   If you quote again from a writer's book or article that you have described in
an earlier footnote but not in the immediately preceding footnote, do this:

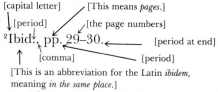

[This means *pages*.]

        [period]

⁴Carver, pp. 58–59.   [page numbers]

            [comma]

[author's
last
name]

Step 1.   Understanding footnotes. Look at the footnotes at the bottom of the paragraph on page 500. Explain the reasons for each of the entries.

10. QUOTING FROM BOOKS AND ARTICLES

1. If the passage you select to quote has fewer than one hundred words, work the quotation smoothly into your own sentences. Use a colon or a comma before the quotation. Use quotation marks at the beginning and at the end of the statement you are quoting (example *a* below).
2. If you quote a longer passage (three or more typed lines or more than one hundred words), block the quotation off from the rest of the text by leaving several spaces from the margin on each side. If you type, this longer quotation should be single-spaced (the rest of the paragraph or essay is double-spaced). Do not use quotation marks when you set off this longer passage (example *b* below).
3. If you want to leave out any words of a sentence in the selection you are quoting, use three dots (. . .). If a complete sentence precedes the omission, use four dots (. . . .).

Here is part of a student's paragraph on understanding reading problems. Note the correct use of quotations.

Every teacher and psychologist knows that emotional fac-

tors play an important part in the way a child reads; but

specialists are still unsure of how emotional problems re-

ally affect reading skills. No one knows whether or not

the problems are there to prevent the child from reading

properly or come after the child sees that he cannot learn

the way others do. One teacher of reading says, "Some   [quotation mark]

writers have gathered evidence to support the view that   [comma]

emotional upsets are perhaps caused by reading

[quotation mark]

failure."[1] Failure affects the way we all regard ourselves,

and reading failure would have an emotional effect on a

a.

student.[2] Even if this is true, however, there does not

seem to be any pattern in how personality affects reading

competence. Analyzing the findings in some recent studies,

a leading specialist concludes:

[colon]

[no quotation mark]

[single-spaced]

    If one hopes for consistent grade-to-grade findings in
these results one is bound to be disappointed. However
. . . if one takes a developmental approach, one discovers that relationships between reading and
personality . . . found at the primary level become
inconsistent at the intermediate and junior high
school grades, and so far as the evidence is concerned, seem completely to disappear at the high
school and college levels. Of course, there may be
many possible explanations, such as the increased se-
lectivity of students, the unreliability and use of
different types of tests, etc.[3]

b.

[no quotation mark]

But no matter how these factors work in the reading pro-

cess, no one can disagree that "Students who are . . .

disturbed by major fears and anxieties should be referred

to persons qualified to help them. . . ."[4]

c.

—Steve Lederman

[footnotes
to show
sources;
see pages
497–498]

     [1]Robert Karlin, *Teaching Reading in High School*
(Indianapolis, 1964), p. 29.
     [2]*Ibid.*, pp. 22–30.
     [3]Jack A. Holmes, "Personalty Characteristics of
the Disabled Reader," *Journal of Developmental
Reading,* 4 (Winter, 1961), 1961, 112.
     [4]Karlin, p. 29.

11. FORMAT OF A BUSINESS LETTER

An important on-the-job demand, once you graduate from college, is the writing
of clear business letters. When you write, you need to observe several principles
agreed upon by the business community. In this letter requesting information
(page 504 presents a letter of job application), the parts of the letter and some
suggestions appear in the margin.

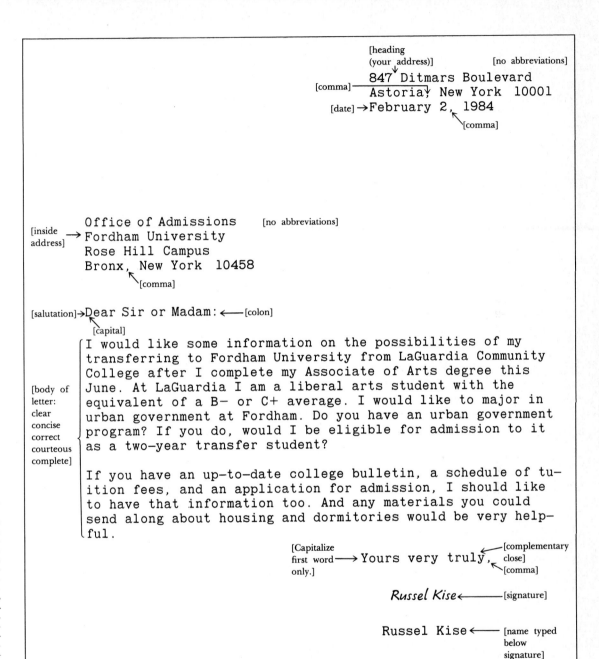

[heading
(your address)]   [no abbreviations]
                              847 Ditmars Boulevard
[comma] —————————————— Astoria, New York 10001
        [date] → February 2, 1984
                                        [comma]

[inside
address] → Office of Admissions   [no abbreviations]
           Fordham University
           Rose Hill Campus
           Bronx, New York 10458
                    [comma]

[salutation] → Dear Sir or Madam: ← [colon]
              [capital]

[body of letter: clear concise correct courteous complete]

I would like some information on the possibilities of my transferring to Fordham University from LaGuardia Community College after I complete my Associate of Arts degree this June. At LaGuardia I am a liberal arts student with the equivalent of a B− or C+ average. I would like to major in urban government at Fordham. Do you have an urban government program? If you do, would I be eligible for admission to it as a two-year transfer student?

If you have an up-to-date college bulletin, a schedule of tuition fees, and an application for admission, I should like to have that information too. And any materials you could send along about housing and dormitories would be very helpful.

[Capitalize first word only.] → Yours very truly, [complementary close]
                                              [comma]

                    Russel Kise ← [signature]

                    Russel Kise ← [name typed below signature]

Step 1. Letter Writing. Follow the suggestions below to write a letter requesting information. Use separate paper.

1. Write to a college out of the state for a copy of the college bulletin or for copies of other campus publications.

2. Write to a local newspaper requesting a back issue that deals with drugs or pollution in your neighborhood.
3. Write to the U.S. Department of Interior asking for information about the standard of living for American Indians.
4. Write to the chamber of commerce of a city or state you want to visit. Ask for information about hotels, amusements, places of interest.
5. Write to your state board of education for material on special programs in education for minority-group students or students in poverty areas.

12. APPLY FOR A JOB YOU WANT

Preparing a Résumé

When an advertisement for some good job appears in a local paper, the employer often receives hundreds of responses. If you are one of those interested in such a position, you will want to make sure that your response attracts the employer's interest. Your answer should be brief but to the point; and your qualifications should be clearly stated. A convenient method of presenting your qualifications is through a *résumé,* a statement of your particular accomplishments in summary form. In a résumé, a prospective employer can see at a glance just why you feel he or she should select you for the job opening.

Notice in the résumé on page 503 how the writer groups information together for easy reference to show clearly her qualifications as an accountant's assistant.

HOW TO WRITE YOUR RÉSUMÉ

1. Include your name, address, and telephone number.
2. Sometimes an office will advertise several available positions, so make sure to indicate the job for which you are applying.
3. If you have a specific salary in mind, include it in the résumé.
4. Include honors or awards that show your qualifications for the job you want. Otherwise leave out this part.
5. Include all your job experience. Any job can give you skills that may be helpful in the position you are seeking.
6. Extracurricular activities show your interest in voluntary service and often reflect skills that might be handy on the job. Susan Davis' membership in the Business Honor Society suggests that her skills are advanced.
7. Show whatever specific training you have had that makes you eligible for the job.
8. List two or three references—their names and addresses—so that information about your character and abilities is easy to obtain. Make sure that you include people who know you well enough to give a fair evaluation of your character. It is a good idea to ask someone's permission before giving that person as a reference.
9. *Type* your résumé on sturdy typing paper. Avoid errors and erasures.

RÉSUMÉ

Personal Data

Susan E. Davis
18–25 Deegan Road
Elmhurst, New York 11373
Telephone: (212) 481–9998

Age: 18
Height: 5 ft., 1 in.
Weight: 100 lbs.
Marital Status: Single

Career Objective: Junior Accountant

Educational Background: Long Island City High School
(Commercial Diploma: June, 1981). LaGuardia Community
College
(Major: Accounting; A.A.S. Degree expected June, 1983).

Major Courses: Accounting, data processing, statistics,
insurance, business organization and management, writing
for business, bookkeeping, business law, economics,
stenography, typing.

Special Skills: Typing (65 W.P.M.); stenography (40 W.P.M.);
machine experience: IBM electric typewriter, IBM 029
and 129 Keypunch.

Honors and Awards: Perfect attendance award (1979–1980);
certificate for highest yearly average in bookkeeping
(1980); outstanding service award (1979).

Extracurricular activities: Business Honor Society (1977–
1978); Program Committee (1977–1978).

Experience

Pantry Pride Supermarket
82–86 Broadway
Elmhurst, New York 11373
Manager: Mr. Micelli

August 1976 to present
Cashier and Office Worker
Duties: Recording sales in
the ledger book.

F. W. Woolworth Company
976 Third Avenue
New York, New York 10002
Manager: Mr. Pastore

April 1976 to August 1976
Part–time Cashier
Duties: Pricing merchandise
and filling shelves.

Abraham & Straus
Fulton Street and East Broadway
New York, New York 11201
Section Manager: Mr. Murray

November 1975 to January
1976
Sales Clerk
Duties: Recording cash and
charge sales and displaying
merchandise.

References

Mr. John Micelli, Manager
82–86 Broadway
Elmhurst, New York 11373

Mr. John Weigel, Asst. Professor/Coordinator
Division of Cooperative Education
Fiorello H. LaGuardia Community College
31–10 Thomson Avenue
Long Island City, New York 11101

108 East 93 Street
Brooklyn, New York 11212
October 5, 1982

Mr. Harry Koster
Chief of Division of Receipts
Comptroller's Office of the City of New York
New York, New York 10007

Dear Mr. Koster:

Your advertisement in the New York Chief yesterday called
for a part-time accountant's assistant to help in the processing
of city income tax forms. Because of my interest in accounting
and city government, I think I am well qualified to apply for
the job you are advertising.

You will see from my résumé that I have had both training
and experience in the field of accounting. My course of study at
college is designed to qualify me as an accountant after graduation. My interest and skill in mathematics contribute to my
qualifications for this job.

My schedule at college now requires me to attend classes
late in the afternoon; for this term I am available for work
from 9 a.m. to 11:30 a.m. every day but Wednesday when I can
work from 9 a.m. to 11:00 a.m.

May I please come for an interview any morning during the
week? I will telephone your office to arrange a time convenient
to you. You will find me an eager and cooperative worker.

Very truly yours,

Darrel M. Farnsworth

Darrel M. Farnsworth

Step 1.   Writing Your Résumé. Prepare a résumé about yourself on a separate sheet of paper. Assume that you want to apply for a job for which you feel well qualified. Résumés often include additional information, such as travel experience, military status, bilingualism or other language skills, hobbies, involvement in sports; many of these may be appropriate for your résumé. The kind of job always determines the range of information to be included.

A Letter of Application

The letter that you send along with your résumé should be a brief and sincere attempt to arouse the employer's interest in you. Paragraphs in a business letter (see pages 500–501 for the correct format) are often just three or four sentences long, making the letter easy to read quickly.

The first paragraph usually includes a statement about how the job came to your attention and expresses your interest in the position. The second paragraph mentions briefly the highlights of the résumé that you send along with the letter: if you are not planning to send a résumé, the second paragraph (and the third as well, if you need more space) should indicate all your special qualifications for the job.

Another paragraph can indicate any special conditions you may have to present. If you are not sending a résumé, name your references in this paragraph. Another brief paragraph should show your willingness to come for an interview—suggesting a convenient time and a day. On the facing page appears the letter that will accompany Darrel Farnsworth's résumé.

13. FILLING OUT APPLICATIONS

Whether you are interested in getting a job, a checking account, a life insurance policy, or a driver's license, you have to make out application forms that give important data about yourself. Filling out these forms correctly requires care, attention, and some preparation beforehand.

FILLING OUT AN APPLICATION: SOME GUIDELINES

1. Look the whole application over carefully before you begin writing answers.
2. Print all your answers clearly in ink. If you can, type your responses.
3. Answer all questions required of you. If you have no answer to one or more of the questions, do *not* simply leave a blank space. Put in a dash (–) or write *NA* (not applicable); such a response shows that you have read the question but that it does not pertain to you.
4. Answer all questions honestly. Leaving out required information can only hurt your chances of getting what you are applying for.
5. Some applications have special boxes or sections for office workers' notations. Those sections often say: *DO NOT WRITE IN THIS SPACE* or *FOR OFFICE USE ONLY*. Follow instructions. Leave those lines blank.
6. Try to use available space to answer questions on the form. If, however, you see that the space is too small for your answer, don't try to squeeze in information by writing in very small letters. Instead, attach a sheet of paper on which you can respond fully. Make sure that you indicate on the form that you have added a sheet; and be sure to number your answers on that sheet so that they correspond to numbered questions on the application.
7. To be prepared, try to anticipate the kind of information you might be asked for. A job application, for example, will always ask for information about your education and about other jobs you've held. Make a list at home of your graduation dates, your previous employers and their addresses, the dates you worked for them. With the list in hand as you fill out your application, you'll have all the data you need at your fingertips. What kind of information might you be asked for on an application for life insurance? for a loan?

Step 1. Filling Out a Job Application. Using the application form on pages 507–508, fill in the blanks carefully as if you were applying for a job of your choice with L. L. K., Inc., Insurance.

14. TAKING NOTES

Few people remember accurately what they read. That is why note taking is such an aid to the student who is frequently asked to read a great deal of material for exams, reports, and term papers.

TAKING NOTES ON READINGS

1. Write down the names of the author and the book, article, essay, or story you need to take notes on.
2. Take notes on one paragraph at a time.
3. Look up any words you do not know.
4. Write in your own words the main idea of the selection.
5. Write in your own words the subtopics of the selection if they are clearly stated.
6. Jot down briefly the key words, most important facts, illustrations, details, or statistics. Use the author's own words for special key ideas.

L.L.K., Inc. Insurance
Employment Application

An Equal Opportunity Employer
L.L.K., Inc., policy and federal law prohibit discrimination because of race, religion, age, marital status, sex, disability, or natural origin.

Date _____

Personal Data

Applying for position as _____ Salary required _____ Date available _____

Name: _____
           (Last)   (First)   (Middle)   (Maiden)

Present address _____
           (Street)   (City)   (State)   (Zip)   (How long at this address)

Permanent address _____
           (Street)   (City)   (State)   (Zip)   (How long at this address)

Telephone number _____ Social Security number _____
           (Area code)

Are you a U.S. citizen? ☐ Yes ☐ No   If non-citizen, give Alien Registration No. _____

Check appropirate box for age: Under 16 ☐, 16 or 17 ☐, 18 through 69 ☐, 70 or over ☐

Person to be notified in case of emergency:

Name _____ Telephone _____

Address _____

Will you consider relocation? Yes ☐ No ☐   Domestic Yes ☐ No ☐   International Yes ☐ No ☐

Educational Data

Schools	Print address for each school given	Date	Type of course or major	Graduated (yes or no)	Degree received
High School		From_____ To			////////
College		From_____ To			
Graduate School		From_____ To			
Business, Correspondence, Night, or Trade School		From_____ To			
Other		From_____ To			

Approximate scholastic average: High School _____ College _____

Activities

Do not name organizations that will reveal race, religion, age, sex, or national origin.

School and college activities _____

Special interests outside of business.
  1. _____
  2. _____
  3. _____

Indicate the amount of time devoted to each.
  1. _____
  2. _____
  3. _____

Skills

List any special skills you may have _____

What foreign languages do you: ☐ Speak _____ ☐ Speak _____ ☐ Speak _____
☐ Read _____ ☐ Read _____ ☐ Read _____
☐ Write ☐ Write ☐ Write

Business machines you can operate _____

Typing speed _____ words per minute ☐ Electric / ☐ Manual   Steno speed _____ words per minute   Method _____

References

List names, addresses, and telephone numbers of three people who can attest to your character.

	1.	2.	3.
Name			
Address			
City, State, Zip			
Phone Number			

Employment Data   Begin with most recent employer. List all full-time, part-time, temporary, or self-employment.

Company name				Employed from	Mo-Yr	To	Mo-Yr
Street address				Salary or earnings	Start		Finish
City	State	Zip code		Telephone (Area code)			
Name and title of immediate supervisor				Your title			

Description of duties

Reason for terminating or considering a change

Company name				Employed from	Mo-Yr	To	Mo-Yr
Street address				Salary or earnings	Start		Finish
City	State	Zip code		Telephone (Area code)			
Name and title of immediate supervisor				Your title			

Description of duties

Reason for terminating

I agree that after accepting employment I will complete a medical exam by a physician recommended by L.L.K., Inc. Insurance.

Date _____   Signature of Applicant _____

Personnel Interviewer _____

Do Not Write Below This Line

Interview number _____

Reference check   1. _____

2. _____

3. _____

Applicant employed as _____ Will begin work

on _____ at a salary of $ _____ per _____

Salary Code _____   Signed _____ Date _____

Title _____ Dept. _____

Additional approval _____

508

Read the paragraph "Racism in Education" on pages 200–206. Then look at the following notes, taken by a student as he read.

Notes on paragraph "Racism in Education," by Maude White Katz
Main Idea: Racist beliefs make Negro appear "subhuman or only semi-human."
Subtopics and Important Details: The Establishment, through colleges and mass media, gives racist philosophy.
Black child can be educated
  intelligence tests dishonest
  when intelligence of whites differs many reasons given as possible explanations
  when Blacks and whites differ, reason is genetic
Other instances of racism
  Blacks excluded from trade schools
  Craft union officials keep Blacks out of schools
  Sheet Metal Workers Union Local 28 in New York has 3,300 white members, no Blacks: State Commission on Human Rights finds union guilty
                                                           —Geoffrey Hunte

---

UNDERLINING

If you own the book, underlining is a very good method of note taking because it saves time. Remember these tips about underlining:

1. Underline the main points, subpoints, and the key supporting details.
2. Write notes to yourself in the margin: jot down a question; say an idea more simply than the author has, using your own words; write down an idea the author's writing makes you think about.

Step 1. Note Taking on Your Own. Reread the paragraphs by John W. Wright on pages 228–229. Take notes on your reading, using separate paper.

Step 2. Underlining. Read "Why Some Schools Succeed" on pages 372-374, underlining as you read. Follow the suggestions above.

15. WRITING A SUMMARY

Much college writing—especially brief reports and homework questions—is summary writing. A summary gives a brief idea of material you have read. It is usually a statement you write from your notes or from your underlining. Good summaries focus on main ideas, major subtopics, and only *important* details. (See also pages 351–353, "Making Note Cards.")

FOR CLEAR SUMMARIES THAT MAKE THE POINT

1. Read carefully. Take notes as explained on pages 506 and 509. Look up words you do not understand.
2. Your first sentence should state the main idea of the selection you are summarizing.
3. Use your own words in repeating details. Use the author's exact words for certain key ideas.
4. Repeat information accurately.
5. Follow the author's development in the selection you are summarizing. If information is arranged chronologically or by importance; if material is presented through comparison-contrast, narrative, several examples—your summary should reflect the author's pattern.
6. Revise your first draft so that your sentences flow smoothly. Use subordination to tighten ideas.
7. Summaries should be brief, usually not more than a third of the total number of words in the original.

Here is a summary written from Mr. Hunte's notes that appear on page 509.

Summary of "Racism in Education"

Racist beliefs make many Americans view Negroes as "subhuman or only semi-human." The Establishment (higher education and mass media) is responsible for this philosophy. Yet Blacks *are* educable, in spite of dishonest intelligence-test results. Although valid reasons appear for intelligence differences among white children, Blacks are said to differ from whites for genetic reasons. Proofs of racism in education appear in the exclusion of Blacks—through craft union officials—from trade schools. The New York State Commission on Human Rights found guilty the Sheet Metal Workers Union Local 28 because none of its 3,300 members was Black.

—*Geoffrey Hunte*

16. WRITING ABOUT LITERATURE: SOME APPROACHES TO CONSIDER

Often in your courses you will have to report on assigned reading. In your English class you may have to give your responses to a novel, perhaps, a short story, a play, or a poem. As with all writing assignments your first step as part of prewriting activity is to limit your topic. Of course, there are many possibilities for writing that each piece of literature itself suggests, but with an idea of some *possible* approaches to take, you might find it easier to prepare an essay on a literary work. Below appear some suggestions that singly or in combination may help you focus your discussion.

Approaches to Writing about Literature

1. Write about the *theme*. The theme in a poem, novel, play, or short story is its main idea, the dominant point the writer had in mind for the work. Because the writer rarely states the theme outright—it is almost always implied—you have to figure out the main idea by thinking about the people, the characters, the events in what you have read. Is the writer trying to make a point about human behavior? about social conditions? about religion or morality? about personal psychology? about humanity's place in the universe? How does the work of literature reveal one or several of those points? Once you have an idea about the theme, you will have to support that idea with specific details drawn from the work itself.

2. Write about one *character* or about several of the characters. Explain what you think their motives are; discuss their behavior and the results of it; show how characters interact; examine their personal psychologies. Are the characters realistic? Do they change through the course of the work or do they remain constant? Pages 512–513 explore in greater detail some approaches to writing about characters in books or poems.

3. Write about the *action*. Although you may need occasionally to summarize some details of the plot (the story line, the events that take place), writing a report that is almost entirely a summary is not a good idea because it reveals none of your abilities to evaluate. Therefore, in writing about action, you must avoid a simple plot summary. You might want to discuss the climax of the action, its major turning point; you might show how various incidents are connected to each other; you might show how characters are forced to behave in certain ways because of events; you might point out the elements that cause suspense; you might show how the events are rooted in historical occasions.

4. Write about the *structure* of the work. How does the writer put the pieces together? How is the work similar to or different from other examples of literature like it? If you are writing about a love poem, for example, how does the poet conform to what readers expect to find in such poems? How does a writer make a work special, however? How do the different stages (or chapters or acts or scenes) interact with each other?

5. Write about the *tone* of the work. What is the writer's attitude toward the subject? Is it serious or mocking? What attitude does the writer show toward the characters? Is it admiration or dislike or pity?

6. Write about the *language* in the work. What is the quality of the writer's use of words. Are the images particularly clear and vivid? Are figures of speech used (see pages 134–135) with any special skill? Are there any patterns that you can figure out about the images? Does the writer have special talents in

writing dialogue? Does the language portray actions clearly? Does any special strength lie in the use of details?

An Essay on a Book Character

The pages of novels and biographies are rich in unforgettable characters who make exciting topics for book reports. One approach to take to an essay on character is to select *two* dramatic moments that illustrate something significant about an important person in your book. Then, you can expand each moment in a body paragraph as you try to illustrate your proposal. Study the guidelines and the student model on the next pages before you write.

ESSAY GUIDELINES FOR BOOK CHARACTERS

1. Decide on some important personality trait of the hero in your book. Is the person *brave, mean, thoughtless, loving, pitiful?* Write a proposal sentence that indicates that personality trait.
2. Let each body paragraph relate one specific moment that illustrates from the book the impression you stated in the proposal sentence. ⋅
3. Select moments that are important in the growth and development of the hero. A moment that focuses on the hero in the midst of a crisis or a turning point (especially where some important decision must be made and acted upon) is especially emphatic for the reader.
4. Make the sounds and colors and smells of each moment alive. Show the actions of the character. What is he or she doing, thinking about, or saying?
5. Follow the suggestions on pages 261–266 for writing good introductions: be sure also to include the author's name and the title of the book in your first paragraph.
6. Make sure that you use in your essay a quotation right from the book. This may be a sentence or two that describes an action or it may be something said by one of the characters.

In the student essay below, notice how the two body paragraphs effectively support the proposal sentence.

Antonia's Strength

History books are filled with words of praise for the pioneers who settled the West. But the struggle with personal hardships by the courageous families who cleared Nebraska and Kansas come to life in Willa Cather's *My Antonia*. In the novel the heroine, Antonia Shimerda, faces familial hardships with unusual strength.

She shows it first after her father's suicide. A girl in her early teens, Antonia loved her father deeply. When Jim Burden, the narrator of the novel, arrives at the house for the burial, Antonia rushes out to him and sobs, her heart almost breaking. But at the funeral she is much more controlled. Her dead father lies in the coffin with his knees drawn up. "His body was draped in a black shawl," writes Cather, "and his head was bandaged in white muslin, like a mummy's; one of his long, shapely hands lay out on the black cloth; that was all one could see of him." Yet Antonia, in spite of that awful figure, follows her mother up to the coffin and makes the sign of the cross on the bandaged head of her dead father. When Antonia's mother, a woman with little maternal softness, pushes her youngest daughter Yulka up to the body, the child cries wildly. After a neighbor insists that the child not touch the body, it is Antonia who puts her arms around the younger girl and holds her close. I'll never forget the warmth of that scene: Antonia, herself so sad, comforting her little sister as a fine, icy Nebraska snow falls outside.

That quiet moment of courage Antonia matches later on with physical strength. On an April afternoon after Mr. Shimerda's death, Jim Burden rides out to the house; he has not seen Antonia for three months. When he spots her as the sun drops low, he watches her drive a team of horses up to the windmill. She wears her father's boots, his old fur cap, and an outgrown cotton dress with sleeves rolled up. Antonia has taken upon herself to work the fields in her father's absence. Although she cries briefly at not being able to attend the sod schoolhouse, she states in her broken English, "I ain't got time to learn. I can work like mans now. . . . School is all right for little boys. I help make this land one good farm." Jim is disappointed at her mannish ways: she yawns at the table, eats noisily like a man, and boasts often of her strength and the chores she can perform. But this is just an outgrowth of what is really strength of character. To accept the challenge of the soil as a man in her father's place is certainly an act of courage.

Antonia's courage should be a lesson for women of today. Living the soft life, I and many of my contemporaries complain about the slightest trouble. We complain when the washing machine is broken or when we have to walk to the bus. We complain if we have to wash dishes by hand or if the garbage barrels need pushing out to the street. Antonia Shimerda would look these minor inconveniences in the eye and say, "I can work like mans now."

—Phyllis Dubin

OTHER APPROACHES TO LITERATURE ESSAYS ON CHARACTER

1. Compare and contrast two characters with different traits, showing a dramatic moment to illustrate each personality.
2. Show how the hero changes by relating two different instances, one from an early part of the book and one from a later part.
3. Show how the hero responds to a moment of crisis and then show how a moment in your own life was similar to or different from the hero's. Or, show how you would have behaved in the hero's place.
4. Show how a moment in a book compares with the same moment in a movie about the book.

---

17. ANSWERING ESSAY EXAMINATION QUESTIONS

Midterm or final examinations in college courses usually ask—in addition to short-answer questions—that you answer some questions in *essay* form. Although the word *essay* in this sense is used loosely, it usually means some longer response to a question that requires extended thought and development.

Hint

If the exam asks you to answer more than two or three *essay* questions, a one-paragraph response is often adequate for each question.

If the exam asks you to answer only one or two questions, plan to write a four-paragraph essay to develop your responses.

MAKING THE GRADE: HOW TO ANSWER ESSAY QUESTIONS

1. Think about the question before you write. Take clues for the development of your paragraph or essay from the question itself.

   a. If the question says *compare and contrast,* use comparison-contrast methods of development.

   b. If the question says *how,* show how something is done or how something works. If the question says *explain, tell, illustrate, discuss,* use any method of development that uses facts, statistics, paraphrases, or quotations in order to back up your point.

   c. If the question says *define,* write a paragraph or an essay that uses substantial details to illustrate the meaning of a word, an idea, or a theory.

   d. If the question says *list,* it is often enough just to write your answer by numbering 1 through 10, for example, and by writing some fact for each number. But you can also "list" ideas in paragraph form.

   e. If the question asks *why,* make sure that you understand what conclusion the instructor wants you to reach. Then, give as many details as you can to explain the *causes* for the result you are asked to explain.

2. Repeat the main part of the question in your topic sentence (for one-paragraph answers) or in your proposal sentences (for four-paragraph essay responses).

3. If you answer in a four-paragraph essay, your introduction and conclusion may be much briefer than those urged in other parts of this book. But do not abandon other requirements of the well-constructed essay.

   a. Make sure that your proposal sentence allows you to discuss two aspects of the topic your instructor asks you to write about.

   b. Make sure that the proposal sentence comes *last* in paragraph 1.

   c. Make sure to use a clear transition in the first sentence of paragraph 2.

   d. Make sure that in the first sentence of paragraph 3 you refer back to the topic in paragraph 2 and that you introduce the new aspect of the topic of paragraph 3.

4. In your conclusion, say again your main point by summarizing the topics of paragraphs 2 and 3. Then, apply your topic to some general principles, if possible (see pages 433–437).

5. Use a number of details to illustrate or to prove whatever points you make in your paragraphs. In this book you have learned how to use the following kinds of details and illustrations:

   a single moment from your life experience
   concrete sensory details
   figurative language and imagery
   statistics
   quotations and paraphrases
   illustrative moments from fiction
   cases

Step 1. Understanding Questions. These essay-type questions all come from college textbooks. Explain on a separate sheet of paper how you would go about answering them; tell what methods you would use in developing your paragraph or essay.

1. Discuss the growth of trade unions in the 1930s in America.
2. List the basic features of the open classroom.
3. Compare *realism* and *naturalism* in literature.
4. Explain Freud's Oedipal theory.
5. Compare and contrast Marxism in Europe and Latin America.

18. MAKING A FORMAL OUTLINE

To sort out ideas on a complicated topic, we often use the sentence outline. An outline allows you to see the main ideas of each paragraph at a glance; it also shows how major details (and subtopics) relate to each main idea; and it illustrates quickly just how each body paragraph relates to the proposal sentence. Writing each outline entry in a full sentence allows you to express main thoughts fully and to avoid writing fragments in the essay itself.

> **Hint**
>
> Outlines are designed to help you write and are useful only so long as they serve that function. Even after you prepare an outline you may change your subtopic or even main-idea sentences in the essay. Outlines are especially useful *after* you write a draft of an essay; an outline can help you see how the parts of your paper fit together logically.

Here is a simple outline for the essay "Antonia's Strength" that appears on pages 512–513. You will find, in the margin, explanations of the letters and Roman numbers.

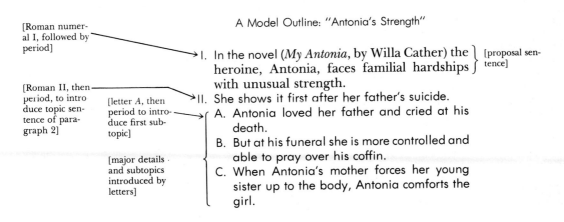

A Model Outline: "Antonia's Strength"

[Roman numeral I, followed by period]

I. In the novel (*My Antonia*, by Willa Cather) the heroine, Antonia, faces familial hardships with unusual strength. } [proposal sentence]

[Roman II, then period, to introduce topic sentence of paragraph 2]

[letter A, then period to introduce first subtopic]

[major details and subtopics introduced by letters]

II. She shows it first after her father's suicide.
A. Antonia loved her father and cried at his death.
B. But at his funeral she is more controlled and able to pray over his coffin.
C. When Antonia's mother forces her young sister up to the body, Antonia comforts the girl.

[Roman III introduces main idea of paragraph 3.] → III. That quiet moment of courage Antonia matches later on with physical strength.   } [topic sentence: paragraph 3]

[Each letter introduces a major subtopic or detail.]

- A. Jim Burden rides up to Antonia's house and sees her dressed like a man.
- B. She has taken the field work upon herself.
- C. Though she has some regrets, she is devoted to building up the farm.
- D. Jim is disappointed at her mannish ways, but this is really strength of character.
- E. To accept the challenge of the soil as a man in her father's place is courageous.

[Roman IV introduces opening statement of conclusion.] → IV. Antonia's courage should be a lesson for women of today.

[summary]

[new area of application]

HOW TO MAKE THE OUTLINE HELP

1. Check Roman numerals II and III to see if they clearly follow from the proposal you wrote for Roman numeral I.
2. Check subtopics A, B, C, etc. under each Roman numeral: make sure each subtopic relates to the topic sentence.
3. Leave out minor details.
4. Don't elaborate on the proposal or the introduction in the outline. You can do that in the essay itself.
5. Check to see if the transitions in the opening sentences of paragraphs 2 and 3 are clear and obvious.
6. Make sure that every entry you have written is a full sentence.

Step 1.   Seeing an Outline Work. Write an outline 'for "Reading Skills for Preschool Children," the essay by Muriel Guba on pages 366–367. Use separate paper.

Step 2.   Putting an Outline Together. Select a topic suggested in any chapter in this book and, on separate paper, prepare an outline following the form and suggestions given on pages 515–516.

VOCABULARY EXERCISES:
Definitions by Chapter

CHAPTER 1

A. Words to Describe Situations

1. boisterous: noisy in an active way
2. amiable: friendly
3. awesome: inspiring
4. malevolent: wishing harm to others
5. dismal: dreary; causing gloom
6. spacious: amply roomy
7. elegant: stylishly fancy
8. tranquil: peaceful
9. cluttered: piled up in a disorderly way
10. musty: moldy, stale

B. Words That Name Sounds

1. guffawed: laughed in a loud burst
2. din: a loud, confused noise
3. inaudible: incapable of being heard
4. squealed: cried out with a shrill sound
5. resonated: echoed back with vibrations

CHAPTER 2

A. Words for Actions

1. grimace: show disapproval with the face
2. stagger: move unsteadily with loss of confidence
3. hurl: fling; throw vigorously
4. swagger: walk conceitedly
5. saunter: stroll
6. plunge: enter violently
7. careen: lurch, swerve without control
8. bellow: call in a deep, loud voice
9. collapse: fall in; give way in exhaustion
10. lunge: thrust forward suddenly

B. How People Do or Say Things

1. irresponsibly: in a way that is not dependable; unreliably
2. contemptuously: scornfully
3. sullenly: gloomily
4. spontaneously: impulsively; without any thought
5. benevolently: charitably; generously
6. brazenly: loudly; shamelessly
7. precariously: dangerously
8. painstakingly: with great care
9. infrequently: seldom; occasionally
10. vehemently: forcefully; with passon

CHAPTER 3

A. Words for the Past

1. reminisce: recall and tell of past experiences
2. nostalgia: a longing for things, persons, or events no longer present

3. memorable: worth being remembered
4. evokes: calls forth memories
5. recollect: remember
6. discern: detect; perceive the distinctions

7. interlude: a period of time that comes between events
8. remembrance: something remembered
9. contemplate: consider thoughtfully
10. retrospect: a review of things in the past

B. Words for Unforgettable Personalities

1. compulsive: acting as if compelled by irresistible impulses
2. domineering: ruling like a tyrant over others

3. absurd: silly, foolish
4. gregarious: sociable
5. volatile: explosive

CHAPTER 4

A. Words for Opposite Qualities

1. *a.* dexterous: skillful in the use of the hands
   b. awkward: clumsy
2. *a.* diminutive: tiny
   b. massive: bulky; solid
3. *a.* rotund: plump
   b. slender: gracefully slim

4. *a.* conventional: following the accepted norms
   b. rebellious: resistant to authority or tradition
5. *a.* altruistic: having high regard for others
   b. egocentric: interested only in oneself

B. Words for Contrasting Moods

1. content: satisfied
2. confident: assured
3. affectionate: loving
4. pacific: calm
5. exuberant: overflowing with joy

6. irate: angry
7. apathetic: bored, uninterested
8. anxious: extremely uneasy
9. masochistic: deriving pleasure from being hurt
10. depressed: saddened

CHAPTER 5

A. Meanings from Context

1. technology: means for production
2. correspondent: one who communicates by means of letters; also, a person or a firm having regular business relations with another, especially at a distance

3. liabilities: debts
4. dynamo: an energetic individual
5. laissez-faire: economic doctrine that opposes government regulation
6. entrepreneur: one who organizes business enterprises

7. assets: financial resources
8. trends: prevailing tendencies

9. productivity: output at work
10. insolvency: bankruptcy

B. Checking Definitions

What employers look for in workers:

1. compatibility: ability to work well with others
2. initiative: self-motivation
3. assiduity: diligence; steady attentiveness

4. integrity: honesty
5. loyalty: constancy

What workers look for in employers:

1. inspiration: motivation; incentive
2. generosity: willingness to give
3. compassion: consciousness of others' concerns

4. amity: friendly relations
5. indulgence: leniency; gratification

C. Checking Meanings

1. sputtering: speaking in an explosive way
2. asserting: claiming
3. familiarizing: making acquainted with

4. lauding: praising
5. assenting: agreeing

CHAPTER 6

A. Learning Words for Shape and Size

1. vast: very great in size
2. miniscule: tiny
3. towering: noble, reaching high intensity

4. voluminous: very spacious
5. amorphous: without definite shape

B. Sharpening the Senses

1. savory: something with special flavor
2. putrid: rotten-smelling
3. musty: moldy; smelling or tasting of dampness
4. pungent: sharply stimulating
5. medicinal: relating to medicine

6. pliant: able to bend easily without breaking; flexible
7. clammy: damp, sticky, and cool
8. gossamer: thin, sheer fabric
9. rigid: stiff; not easily shaped.
10. sinewy: physically strong

CHAPTER 7

A. Words for Explaining Processes

1. sequential: characterized by an order of events or steps
2. routine: habitual performance; established routine
3. prior: occurring before
4. outcome: result; effect
5. subsequent: following in time order
6. cyclical: moving in an order in which a regular event (or a sequence of events) takes place
7. adjacent: next to; nearby
8. approximate: nearly correct
9. apparatus: materials to perform a particular procedure
10. synthesize: produce by putting together or combining elements

CHAPTER 8

A. Familiar Words in the Women's Struggle

1. feminist: one who believes a woman's activities should be extended in social and political life
2. suffragist: a woman who believes women should have the right to vote
3. chauvinist: anyone who has blind devotion to any cause
4. hormonal: relating to substances given off by certain organs in the body
5. femininity: femaleness
6. mortality: the condition of being subject to death
7. inferiority: the state of being lower in rank
8. stereotype: a fixed idea about a person or thing based upon oversimplified points of view
9. degradation: the state of being lowered in quality or estimation
10. prejudice: an unfavorable opinion formed beforehand, without knowledge

B. More Words in the Struggle for Equality

1. pornography: erotic pictures or writing designed to be sexually stimulating
2. downtrodden: trampled upon; ruled over severely
3. inequity: injustice; unfairness
4. emancipation: the act of setting free
5. activist: an especially enthusiastic worker in a political cause

CHAPTER 9

A. Words for Growth

1. phase: stage of development
2. retarded: delayed in progress
3. verbal: relating to words
4. socialization: the process of adapting to social environment
5. cognitive: knowing

B. Words for a Child's World

1. naive: lacking sophistication
2. vulnerable: unprotected from danger; easily hurt
3. nurture: promote growth and development; educate
4. imature: not fully grown or adult
5. peer: a person who has equal standing with another in age, class, or rank

CHAPTER 10

A. Roots for Definitions

1. moribund: on the verge of death
2. spectacle: public performance or display
3. loquacious: extremely talkative
4. portable: easily carried
5. reverted: returned to a former condition or belief

B. Prefix, Root, and Suffix in Combination

1. submitter: someone who gives in to someone else
2. circumlocution: a roundabout way of speaking
3. irrevocable: incapable of being revoked; unalterable
4. intermission: recess; period between acts in a performance
5. comportment: behavior; bearing
6. intangible: unable to be touched
7. homogeneous: all belonging to one grouping
8. visionary: someone who can foresee the future
9. commercial: having to do with business transaction
10. introspection: act of looking into one's self and examining one's own mental state

THEME PROGRESS SHEET

After your instructor grades and returns your themes, count up and enter the number of errors you make in each category listed on top of the chart. Before you write each following composition, study this sheet so that you know your errors and so that you can avoid them in your writing. The symbols for the errors and the page numbers on which to discover how to make specific corrections appear on the inside covers of this book.

															Date		
															Title of composition		
															RO		
															Frag		
															Agr	Grammar	
															Vb		
															Pro		
															Ms		
															Cap	Mechanics	
															It		
															Abbr		
															,		
															;		
															'		
															"		
															./		
															!/	Punctuation	
															?/		
															:/		
															–/		
															( )/		
															-/		
															Sp	Spelling and vocabulary	
															Voc		
															Us	Diction	
															Ef		
															Var		
															Ord		
															//	Strong sentences	
															mm		
															Dang		
															¶		
															¶ Det	Paragraphs and essays	
															¶ Dev		
															E		

RECORD OF TEACHER-STUDENT CONFERENCES ON COMPOSITIONS

Date	*Discussion Points*	*Follow-up Assignment*

ACKNOWLEDGMENTS

Mortimer J. Adler and Charles Van Doren, from *How to Read a Book,* pp. 48–51. Copyright 1940, 1967 by Mortimer J. Adler; copyright 1972 by Mortimer J. Adler and Charles Van Doren. Reprinted by permission of Simon & Schuster, Inc.,

JoAnne Alter, from *A Part-Time Career for a Full-Time You.* Copyright © 1982 by JoAnne Alter. Reprinted by permission of Houghton Mifflin Company.

William Borders, "Study Indicates Why Some Schools Succeed," *The New York Times,* July 24, 1979. Copyright © 1979 by the New York Times Company. Reprinted by permission.

Claude Brown from *Manchild in the Promised Land.* Copyright © 1965 by Claude Brown. Reprinted by permission of The Macmillan Company.

Nancy Bubel, "How to Make a Terrarium." Reprinted by permission from Blair & Ketchum's *Country Journal.* Copyright © December 1978 Country Journal Publishing Co., Inc.

Pearl S. Buck, from "The Frill," copyright © 1933 by Pearl S. Buck. Renewed. Reprinted by permission of Harold Ober Associates Incorporated.

Careers chart from *Money* magazine. Reprinted from the May 1980 issue of *Money* magazine by special permission; copyright © 1980, Time, Inc. All rights reserved.

James F. Fixx, *The Complete Book of Running,* pages 96–98. Copyright © 1977 by James F. Fixx. Reprinted by permission of Random House, Inc.

Langston Hughes, "Mother to Son." From *Selected Poems,* by permission of Alfred A. Knopf, Inc. Copyright © 1926 by Alfred A. Knopf, Inc., and renewed 1954 by Langston Hughes.

Maude White Katz, from "End Racism in Education: A Concerned Parent Speaks." Reprinted from *Freedomways Magazine,* vol. 8, no. 4 (fourth quarter), 1968.

Edna St. Vincent Millay, "Lament," from *Collected Poems.* Harper & Row. Copyright © 1921, 1948 by Edna St. Vincent Millay.

The New Merriam-Webster Pocket Dictionary; copyright © 1971 by G. & C. Merriam Co., publishers of the Merriam-Webster Dictionaries. Entries reprinted by permission.

George Orwell, from *Such, Such Were the Joys.* Copyright © 1953. Reprinted by permission of Harcourt Brace Jovanovich, Inc., and Mrs. Sonia Brownell Orwell.

Robert Phillips, "The Mole," *The New Yorker,* August 13, 1979, page 62. Reprinted by permission; © 1979 The New Yorker Magazine, Inc.

Bruce Porter, "It Was a Good School to Integrate," *The New York Times,* Feb. 9, 1975. Copyright © 1975 by The New York Times Company. Reprinted by permission.

Leonard Reed, "The Hokum of Comparing Pay; Why Federal Pay Levels Should Be Cut," *The Washington Monthly,* May 1980. Reprinted with permission from *The Washington Monthly.* Copyright © 1980 by The Washington Monthly Co.

John R. Regan, "My Room at the Lilac Inn," from *The Purple Testament,* ed. Don M. Wolfe. Copyright © 1946 by Don M. Wolfe. Reprinted by permission of Don M. Wolfe.

Theodore Roethke, "My Papa's Waltz." Copyright 1942 by Hearst Magazines, Inc. Reprinted from *The Collected Poems of Theodore Roethke* by permission of Doubleday & Company, Inc.

Roget's International Thesaurus. Copyright © 1946 by Thomas Y. Crowell Company. Entries under the word "humorist," #844, reprinted by permission of the publisher.

Betty Rollin, "Happiness," *The New York Times,* Sept. 16, 1982. Reprinted by permission of the William Morris Agency, Inc., on behalf of the author. Copyright © 1982 by Betty Rollin.

Berton Roueche, "A Walk along the Towpath," from *What's Left,* Little, Brown, 1968. Reprinted by permission of Harold Ober Associates, Inc. Copyright © 1962 by Berton Roueche.

Carl Sandburg, "Mag." From *Chicago Poems* by Carl Sandburg, copyright 1916 by Holt, Rinehart and Winston, Inc.; renewed 1944 by Carl Sandburg. Reprinted by permission of Harcourt Brace Jovanovich, Inc.

Dick Schaap, "Boxing—That Thrilla in Manila," *The Washington Star,* 1975. Reprinted by permission of the Sterling Lord Agency, Inc. Copyright © 1975 by Dick Schaap.

"Secretaries Have Pick of Jobs: Demand Is Rising, Pulling Up Salaries," *The New York Times,* March 10, 1981. Copyright © 1981 by The New York Times Company. Reprinted by permission.

Anita Shreve, "Careers and the Lure Of Motherhood," *The New York Times,* Nov. 21, 1982. Reprinted with the author's permission.

Andrew Siscaretti, "What Am I? West Clapton and Flynn," from "Media Compositions: Preludes to Writing" by Harvey S. Wiener, in *College English,* February 1974. Copyright © 1974 by the *National Council of Teachers of English.* Reprinted with permission.

Betty Smith, *A Tree Grows in Brooklyn.* Copyright © 1943, 1947 by Betty Smith. Reprinted by permission of Harper & Row, Publishers, Inc.

Lenore Wietzman and Diane Rizzo, "Sex Bias in Textbooks," *Today's Education,* January-February 1975. Reprinted by permission of *Today's Education* and the authors.

David Woodworth, from *Overseas Summer Jobs.* Reprinted with the permission of David Woodworth. Distributed by Writer's Digest Books, Cincinnati, Ohio.

John W. Wright, from *The American Almanac of Jobs and Salaries,* pages 100–101. Reprinted from *The American Almanac of Jobs and Salaries* by John W. Wright. Copyright © 1982 by John W. Wright. Reprinted by permission of Avon Books, New York.

Abbreviations, 222–223, 225
Abstractions, metaphors for, 136
Accept, except, 484–485
Actions, words for, 52
Active versus passive voice, 355–357
Adler, Mortimer J., *How to Read a Book,*
    338–340
"Advantages of Attending Kindergarten,
    The" (Wynn), 367–368
Adverbs:
    with *-ly* endings, 53, 60
    opening sentences with, 60
    between parts of verb, 17
Affect, effect, 485
Agreement:
    of pronouns, 449–451
    of subject and verb, 158–171
        with compound subject, 166–167
        plural words acting as singular, 169
        with pronouns, 160–162
        special openers, 167
        troublesome verbs, 163–165
        with *who, that, which,* 170
        words between subject and verb, 168
        words both singular and plural, 169
Albanese, Thomas, "Practice in the High
    School Gym," 294
All ready, already, 485
Alter, JoAnne, *A Part-Time Career for a
    Full Time You,* 232–233
American Almanac of Jobs and Salaries, The
    (Wright), 227–229
Among, between, 486
Amount, number, 485–486
Analogy, 183–184
And, 19
"Antonia's Strength" (Dubin), 512–513
    outline for, 515–516
Apostrophe, use of, 278–279, 322–329
Applications:
    forms for, 505–508
    job: form for, 507–508
        letters of, 504, 505
        résumés, 502–503
Argument, 376–420
    checklist for, 412–413
    details for, 401–404
    faults in logic of, 381–384

Argument (*Cont.*):
    interview techniques and, 380
    opposing opinions in, use of, 385–387
        student samples of, 406–409
    professional examples of, 414–419
        statements, 379–380
    questionnaire on women, 378–379
    reader response to, 413
    student samples of, 405–409, 434
    subject tree and, 410–412
    topics for, 410, 420
    verbs in: confusing pairs of, 397–401
        principal parts of, 390–396
        tense shifts, 396–397
        transformation of, in sentence
            combining, 387–389
    vocabulary in, 377–378
Audience, sense of, in process analysis,
    313–316
Autobiography (Twain), 128–129
Auxiliary verbs, 16

Bad, badly, 487–488
Baim, Thomas, quoted, 134
Bar graphs, use of, 193–196
Barely, hardly, scarcely, 488
Berglund, Martin, "An Egg Cream
    Delight," 309–310
Between, among, 486
Bibliography cards, 349–350
Bibliography preparation, 495–497
"Biology Jailhouse" (Gomez), 183–184
"Birds of a Feather?" (Kissenger),
    149–150
"Birth Room, A" (Wellington), 37
Blair & Ketchum's Country Journal,
    quoted, 336–338
Boardley, Twyla, "The Watermelon
    Man," 302–303
"Boom Time for Brokers" (Hayes),
    191–192
Boone, Mollie, "The Two Willies," 143
Borders, William, quoted, 372–374
Boston, Jacqueline, 130
Bowen, Lee, 333
Brainstorming, 76–77
    in groups, 237

Brown, Claude, *Manchild in the Promised Land,* 128
Browsing in library, 346–347
Bubel, Nancy, quoted, 336–338
Buck, Pearl S., "The Frill," 99
"Buck Fever" (Scoville), 74
Business letters, 500–502
  of application, 504, 505
Business-related writing (*see* Research)
But, 19

Can, may, 400–401
Capitalization, 215–217
  reference chart of, 218–219
Card catalog, use of, 493–495
Career-related writing (*see* Research)
Carter, Diane, 250
Cases, use of, for support of details, 190–192
  hints for, 196
Cendrowski, Helen, 90
Characters, literary, writing about, 511–513
Charts, graphs, and tables, use of, 192–199
  citation of sources in, 201–202
  data clusters and, 226–228, 230–232, 234
"Chicken" (Santiago), 72–73
Child development, investigation of (*see* Research essays)
"Childhood Mischief" (Dawkins), 121–122
Chronology in narrative, 58–59
Circle graph, 197
Cloths, clothes, close, 156–157
Colloquialisms and slang, 217, 219–222
Colon, use of, 272–274
Comma splice, 28
Commas, use of, 280–290
  with subordinators, 107, 284
Comparison, degrees of, 357–359
Comparison and contrast, 132–184
  analogy and, 183–184
  checklist for, 175–176
  figures of speech in, 134–135
    for abstract words, 136
    trite, 136–137
  mirror words in, 151–157
  mood sketches in, 181–183
  paragraph patterns in: likenesses and differences, 147–151
    point-by-point comparison, 145–147
    separation of objects, 142–145

Comparison and contrast (*Cont.*):
  in prewriting, 173–175
  professional examples of, 177–180
    sentences, 135–136
  quotations in, expanded, use of, 139–141
  reader response to, 176–177
  student samples of, 134, 143, 146, 149–150
    analogy, 183–184
    metaphors, 136
    mood sketch, 181–182
  subject and verb agreement in (*see* Agreement, of subject and verb)
  topic for, finding, 133–134, 172–173, 181
  transitions in, use of, 137–139
  vocabulary of, 132–133
Complete Book of Running, The (Fixx), 79–80
Concluding paragraphs, 433–437
Concrete detail, 7
Confusing words, 22–27, 151–157, 397–401, 484–491
Conjunctions, use of:
  coordination, 19–22, 28
    and commas, 283
    for transition, 97–98
  subordination, 29, 101–108
    commas with, 107, 284
    and sentence fragments, 110–118
Connotation versus denotation, 250–251
Contractions, 164, 221, 278
Contrast and comparison (*see* Comparison and contrast)
Coordination, 19–22, 28
  and commas, 283
  for transition, 97–98
Could have, could've, could of, 486

D'Angelo, Michael, 125
Dash, use of, 275–276
Data, use of (*see* Research)
Dawkins, Elaine, "Childhood Mischief," 121–122
Definitions and definition essays, 422–465
  checklist for, 459–460
  conclusions of, 433–437
  dictionary versus personal meanings in, 429–430
    prewriting, 455–456
  through images, 464–465
  imitation of sentence patterns in, 437–439

Definitions and definition essays (*Cont.*):
  one-sentence, 430–432
  paragraph, 432–433
  prewriting for, 455–456
  professional example of, 461–463
  pronouns in, use of (*see* Pronouns)
  reader response to, 461
  student samples of, 429–430, 433, 464
    essay, 456–457
  titles for, 458
  word elements in: prefixes, 422–425
    roots, 427–428
    suffixes, 425–426
Demonstrative pronouns, 451
Denotation versus connotation, 250–251
"Deprived Children" (Gold), 405–406
Descriptive essays (*see* Essays on places)
Descriptive paragraphs, 4–50
  checklist for, 44–45
  class-written, 42
  coordination in, 19–22, 28
  follow-up activities to, 44
  homophones in, 22–27
  manuscript form of, 41–42
  about person, 49–50
  prewriting for, 38–40
  professional examples of, 46–48
    sentences, 21
  proofreading, 42–43
  reader response to, 41
  run-on sentences in, 27–35, 48–49
  sensory language in, 5–7
  sentence review in, 15–19
  student samples of, 35–38, 49–50,
    256
  topic sentences for, 7–13
  transitions in, 14–15
  vocabulary in, 4–5
Dictionary entries, reading, 482–483
Dictionary versus personal meanings,
  429–430
  prewriting, 455–456
Different from, different than, 486
"Different Roommates" (Richardson),
  146
  outline for, 174
Donovan, Chris, "Teenagers as Part-
  Time Workers," 236
Drafts of composition, 41
Dubin, Phyllis, "Antonia's Strength,"
  512–513
  outline for, 515–516

E, final, words with, 477–478
Effect, affect, 485

"Egg Cream Delight, An" (Berglund),
  309–310
Ellipsis, use of, 203
Employment-related writing (*see*
  Research)
End marks (punctuation), 269–270
"End Racism in Education: A Concerned
  Parent Speaks" (Katz), 200–201
Essay questions, answering, 513–515
Essay transition signboards, 317–319
Essays:
  on literature, 510–513
  paragraphs in (*see* Paragraphs, in
    essays)
  (*See also* Argument; Definitions and
    definition essays; Essays on places;
    Process analysis; Research essays)
Essays on places, 248–304
  checklist for, 298–299
  denotation versus connotation in,
    250–251
  impact of, guidelines for, 292
  introductory paragraph of, 261–266
  modifier overuse in, avoiding,
    252–253
  organization of, 290–291
  paragraph form compared to,
    253–255
    example of, 256–257
  point of view in, 303
  professional example of, 300–301
  proposal (thesis) sentences in, 254,
    258–261
  punctuating (*see* Punctuation)
  reader response to, 299
  sentences in, combining, 266–268
  showing versus telling in, 251–252
  student samples of, 256–257, 292–296,
    302–303
  timed-writing exercise for, 296–297
  topics for, 296
  vocabulary in, 248–249
Examination questions, essay, 513–515
Examples, use of (*see* Illustration)
Except, accept, 484–485
Exclamation point, use of, 269
Experiences:
  argument from, example of, 405–406
  (*See also* Illustration; Narrative)
Expert testimony, use of (*see* Research)

Fewer, less, 487
Figures of speech, 134–135
  for abstract words, 136
  trite, 136–137

"Fishing with My Father" (Hines), 74–75
Fitzgerald, Tanya M., "My Bedroom," 37–38
Fixx, James F., *The Complete Book of Running*, 79–80
Focus of comparison, use of, 142–144
Footnotes, 497–498
For (conjunction), 20
Formal outlines, 515–516
Formal versus informal language, 217, 219–222
Former, latter, 487
Fortune, quoted, 191–192
Fragments, sentence, 63–71, 83
    subordination and, 110–118
Free association, 125–126
"Frill, The" (Buck), 99

Generalization, development of, 225
"Ghetto" (Stearns), 429–430
"Gloom Room, The" (Golden), 35–36, 256–257
Gold, Phyllis, "Deprived Children," 405–406
Golden, Harry, "The Gloom Room," 35–36, 256–257
Gomez, Charles, "Biology Jailhouse," 183–184
Good, well, 487–488
Graphs, tables, and charts, use of, 192–199
    citation of sources in, 201–202
    data clusters and, 226–228, 230–232, 234
Gross, Ronald, "Waking on a Monday Morning," 181–182
Grossman, Myra, "Picking Pears," 331
Guba, Muriel:
    "Memories of the Australian Bush," 295–296
    "Reading Skills for Preschool Children," 366–367

Haag, Jerome, 76
Had with verbs, 395
Hanged, hung, 488
Hanson, Wilma, 76
Hardly, scarcely, barely, 488
Has, have with verbs, 394–395
Hayes, Linda, "Boom Time for Brokers," 191–192
Healey, Thomas, "You Must Be Crazy!," 456–457
Helping verbs, 16

Hines, Lenora, "Fishing with My Father," 74–75
"Hokum of Comparing Pay: Why Federal Pay Levels Should Be Cut, The" (Reed), 229–230
Homophones, 22–27, 152–157
"Horrors and High School Math" (Passero), 122
How to Read a Book (Adler and Van Doren), 338–340
Hughes, Langston, "Mother to Son," 85
Hung, hanged, 488
Hunte, Geoffrey, 509, 510
Hyphen, use of, 276–277

-ie spelling headaches, 475–476
Illustration, 88–130
    checklist for, 126–127
    importance in, order of, detail arrangement by, 94–96
    plurals in, use of, 118–121
    prewriting in, 125–126
    professional examples of, 94, 123, 128–129
    reader response to, 127
    student samples of, 90, 121–122, 124
    subordination in, use of, 100–108
        and fragment problems, 110–118
    subtopic sentences in, 91–93
        omission of, 93–94, 123–124
    titles for, 109–110
    topic for, finding, 90, 124
    transitions in, use of, 96–100
    vocabulary in, 88–90
Images, 7
    definition through, 464–465
Importance, order of, detail arrangement by, 94–96
Indexes to periodicals, 346–347
    Reader's Guide to Periodical Literature, 491–492
Infinitives, 24
    as sentence openers, 212
Informal outlines, 173–175
Informal versus formal language, 217, 219–222
-ing words, 189
    as sentence openers, 208–211
    errors with, avoiding, 213–215
Interview techniques, 380
Introductory paragraphs, 261–266
"Ironing for Food" (Kissenger), 330
Irregular verbs, 163–164, 391–392
"It Was a Good School to Integrate . . ." (Porter), 177–180

Italics, use of, 271
It's, its, 23

Job applications:
 form for, 507–508
 letters of, 504, 505
 résumés for, 502–503
"Job Discrimination for Women?"
 (Tomasuolo), 406–407
Job-related writing (*see* Research)
Joreid, Karl, "Old: A Spider's Web, An
 Attic Trunk," 464

Katz, Maude White, "End Racism in
 Education: A Concerned Parent
 Speaks," 200–201
Kent, Mark, "The Last Ski Run," 83
Kissenger, Stacy:
 "Birds of a Feather?" 149–150
 "Ironing for Food," 330
Knew, new, 156
Know, no, now, 153

"Lament" (Millay), 84
"Last Ski Run, The" (Kent), 83
Latter, former, 487
Lay, lie, 397–398
Lead, led, 155–156
Learn, teach, 488
Leave, let, 400
Led, lead, 155–156
Less, fewer, 487
Let, leave, 400
Letters, business, 500–502
 of application, 504, 505
Library:
 browsing in, 346–347
 card catalog in, use of, 493–495
Lie, lay, 397–398
Line graph, 197
List making in prewriting, 39–40,
 332–334
Literature, writing about, 510–513
Logic, faulty, 381–384
Loose, lose, 152–153
-ly adverbs, 53, 60

Main, Jeremy, "The Right Stuff for
 Careers in the Eighties," 240–244
Manchild in the Promised Land (Brown),
 128
Mannes, Marya, *More in Anger,* 98–99

Manuscript form, 41–42
Martini, Carmelyn, "Working Mothers,"
 407–408
May, can, 400–401
"Meaning of Death, The" (O'Connor),
 84–85
Meanings:
 denotative versus connotative,
 250–251
 (*See also* Definitions and definition
 essays)
"Memories of the Australian Bush"
 (Guba), 295–296
Metaphors, 135
 for abstract words, 136
Millay, Edna St. Vincent, "Lament," 84
Minibook, 469–516
 application forms, filling out, 505–508
 bibliography, preparation of, 495–497
 card catalog, use of, 493–495
 confusing words, 484–491
 dictionary entry, reading, 482–483
 essay questions, answering, 513–515
 footnotes, writing, 497–498
 letters, business, writing, 500–502
 job applications, 504, 505
 literature, writing about, 510–513
 note taking, 506, 509
 outlines, making, 515–516
 quotations, use of, 499–500
 Reader's Guide to Periodical Literature,
 use of, 491–492
 résumé, preparation of, 502–503
 spelling, improving, 469–481
 summary writing, 509–510
 thesaurus, using, 483–484
 vocabulary, learning, 480, 482
Mirror words, 22–27, 151–157
Misplaced modifiers, 363–365
Modifier overuse, avoiding, 252–253
"Mole, The" (Phillips), 85–86
Moment, concept of, in narrative, 72
Montalvo, Maria, 411
Mood sketches, 181–183
Moods, words for, 133
More in Anger (Mannes), 98–99
"Mother to Son" (Hughes), 85
"My Bedroom" (Fitzgerald), 37–38
"My Papa's Waltz" (Roethke), 86
Myself, 489

Narby, Caroline, "What Is Rayon?" 433
Narrative, 52–82
 adverbial sentence openers in, 60
 brainstorming and, 76–77

Narrative (*Cont.*):
    checklist for, 77–78
    chronology in, 58–59
    moment in, concept of, 72
    professional examples of, 79–82
        sentences, 71
    quotations in, 60–63
    reader response to, 78–79
    sentence fragments in, 63–71, 83
    student samples of, 72–75
    topic for, finding, 54–55, 75
    topic sentence in, 55–58
    vocabulary in, 52–54
New, knew, 156
New York Times, The, quoted, 204,
    233–234, 372–374, 414–415,
    461–463
No, now, know, 153
Nor, 20
Note cards for research essays, 351–353
    organizing, 354–355
Note taking, 506, 509
Now, know, no, 153
Number, amount, 485–486
Numbers, writing of, 224–225

Objects, pronouns as:
    chart of, 443
    after prepositions, 445–449
    after verbs, 443–445
Occupational Outlook Handbook,
    1980–1981 Edition, quoted, 226,
    227, 235
O'Connor, Sheila, "The Meaning of
    Death," 84–85
"Old: A Spider's Web, An Attic Trunk"
    (Joreid), 464
Opposing arguments, use of, 385–387
    student samples of, 406–409
Opposite qualities, words for, 132
Or, 20
Orwell, George, *Such, Such Were the Joys,*
    94
Osher, Debbie, "Richard," 49–50
Outlines, use of, 173–175, 515–516
Overseas Summer Jobs (Woodworth),
    202–203

Paragraphs:
    closing of, 205–208
    of definition, 432–433
    essay form compared to, 253–255
        example of, 256–257

Paragraphs (*Cont.*):
    in essays: concluding, 433–437
        introductory, 261–266
        opening sentences of, transitions in,
            317–319
        organization of, 290–291
    poem expansion in, 83–85
    subtopic sentences in, 91–93
    topic sentences in, 7–13, 55–58
    (*See also* Comparison and contrast,
        paragraph patterns of;
        Descriptive paragraphs;
        Illustration; Narrative; Research)
Parallelism, 360–363
Paraphrase, use of, 200, 204, 205
    on note cards, 351–352
Parentheses, use of, 274–275
Part-Time Career for a Full Time You, A
    (Alter), 232–233
Participles as sentence openers:
    errors with, avoiding, 213–215
    past, 212–214
    present, 208–211, 213–215
Passero, Julius, "Horrors and High
    School Math," 122
Passive versus active voice, 355–357
Past participles as sentence openers,
    212–213
    errors with, avoiding, 213, 214
Peace, piece, 154–155
Period, use of, 269
Periodical indexes, 346–347
    Reader's Guide to Periodical Literature,
        491–492
    Personal versus dictionary meanings,
        429–430
    prewriting, 455–456
Personification, 135
Persons, writing about:
    description, 49–50
    (*See also* Comparison and contrast)
Phillips, Robert, "The Mole," 85–86
"Picking Pears" (Grossman), 331
Piece, peace, 154–155
Places, essays on (*see* Essays on places)
Plurals, 118–121
    apostrophes in, 278
        erroneous, 324
Poems:
    expansion of, in prose, 83–85
    professional examples of, 84–86, 123
Point of view, 303
Porter, Bruce, "It Was a Good School to
    Integrate . . .", 177–180
Possession, 278, 322–329

"Practice in the High School Gym"
(Albanese), 294
Prefixes, 422–425
Prepositions, use of, 320–322
lists of, 320, 446
pronouns after, 445–449
Present participles as sentence openers,
208–211
errors with, avoiding, 213–215
Prewriting, 38–39
brainstorming in, 76–77
in groups, 237
for definition theme, 455–456
free association in, 125–126
list making in, 39–40, 332–334
outline for, use of, 173–175
schedule planning for, 345–346
subject tree in, 410–412
timed writing in, 296–297
Principal, principle, 152
Principal parts of verbs, use of, 390–394
third part, 394–396
Process analysis, 306–341
audience in, sense of, 313–316
checklist for, 334–335
details in, inclusion of, 308–313
list making for, 332–334
oral, experiment in, 307–308
possession in, showing, 322–329
prepositions in, use of, 320–322
professional examples of, 336–340
reader response in, 335
student samples of, 309–310, 330–331
topics for, 307, 332
transitions in, 316–319
vocabulary of, 306–307
audience and, assessing, 315–316
Professional examples:
career-related, 191–192, 202–203,
240–244
in data clusters, 226–230, 232–235
commas, places for, 289
comparison and contrast, 177–180
sentences, 135–136
definition essay, 461–463
description, 46–48, 300–301
sentences, 21
illustration, 94, 123, 128–129
narrative, 79–82
sentences, 71
poems, 84–86, 123
process analysis, 336–340
research-based, 191–192, 200–201,
204
essays, 240–244, 372–374

Professional examples (*Cont.*):
sentence patterns for imitation,
437–439
transitions, 98–99
women, argument concerning,
414–419
statements, 379–380
Progress reminders, checklists of:
argument, 412–413
comparison and contrast, 175–176
definition essay, 459–460
descriptive essay, 298–299
descriptive paragraph, 44–45
illustration, 126–127
narrative, 77–78
process analysis, 334–335
research, 238–239
research essay, 370–371
Pronouns:
agreement of, 449–451
as connectors, 99–100
demonstrative, 451
as objects: chart of, 443
after prepositions, 445–449
after verbs, 443–445
possessive, 327
review of, 452, 454
as subjects, 440–443
agreement of verb with, 160–162
after *to be,* 442
you, avoidance of, 452–453
Proofreading, 42–43
Proposal (thesis) sentences, 254, 258–
261
in research essay, 353–354
Punctuation, 269–290
apostrophe, 278–279, 322–329
colons, 272–274
commas, 280–290
with subordinators, 107, 284
dash, 275–276
end marks, 269–270
hyphen, 276–277
italics, 271
parentheses, 274–275
quotation marks, 270
of quotations, 61–63, 281
semicolons, 20, 28, 272–274
Purple Testament, The (Regan), 47–48

Question mark, use of, 269
Questionnaire on women, 378–379
Quit, quiet, quite, 151
Quotation marks, use of, 270

Quotations, 499–500
  expanding, 139–141
  in narrative, 60–63
  note cards on, 351
  punctuation of, 61–63, 281
  support of opinions with, 200–201,
    203–205

Raise, rise, 398–399
Reader response:
  to argument, 413
  to comparison and contrast, 176–177
  to definition essay, 461
  to descriptive essay, 299
  to descriptive paragraph, 41
  to illustration, 127
  to narrative, 78–79
  to process analysis, 335
  to research, 239
  to research essay, 370
Reader's Guide to Periodical Literature,
  491–492
"Reading Skills for Preschool Children"
  (Guba), 366–367
Reasoning, faulty, 381–384
Reed, Leonard, "The Hokum of
  Comparing Pay: Why Federal Pay
  Levels Should Be Cut," 229–230
Regan, John J., *The Purple Testament,*
  47–48
Repetition, connecting through, 98–99
Research, 186–244
  abbreviations and numbers in, use of,
    222–225
  brainstorming in groups, 237
  capital letters in, use of, 215–219
  checklist for, 238–239
  conclusion of paragraph in, 205–208
  data clusters in, use of, 225–235
    government occupations, 226–227
    government pay, 227–230
    part-time workers, 230–233
    secretarial jobs, 233–235
  formal versus informal language in,
    217, 219–222
  integration of, into writing, 201–204
  professional examples of, 191–192,
    200–201, 204
    essays, 240–244, 372–374
    (*See also* data clusters, *above*)
  quotation and paraphrase as, use of,
    200–201, 203–205
  reader response to, 239
  statistics in (*see* Statistics, use of)

Research (*Cont.*):
  student sample of, 236
  verb-part sentence openers in,
    208–213
    errors with, avoiding, 213–215
  vocabulary for, 187–189
  (*See also* Research essays)
Research essays, 343–374
  active-voice verbs in, 355–357
  bibliography cards for, 349–350
  browsing in library for, 346–347
  checklist for, 370–371
  comparison in, degrees of, 357–359
  misplaced modifiers in, 363–365
  note cards for, 351–353
    organizing, 354–355
  parallelism in, 360–363
  professional examples of, 240–244,
    372–374
  proposal for, developing, 353–354
  reader response to, 370
  schedule planning for, 345–346
  student samples of, 366–368
  topics for, 344–345, 369–370, 374
    limiting, 348–349
  vocabulary in, 343–344
Résumé, preparation of, 502–503
"Richard" (Osher), 49–50
Richardson, Cecilia, "Different
  Roommates," 146
  outline for, 174
"Right Stuff for Careers in the Eighties,
  The" (Main), 240–244
Rise, raise, 398–399
Rizzo, Diane, quoted, 416–419
Roethke, Theodore, "My Papa's Waltz,"
  86
Rollin, Betty, quoted, 461–463
Rooms, description of (*see* Descriptive
  paragraphs)
Roots of words, 427–428
Roth, Lisa, 40
Roueché, Berton, *What's Left,* 300–301
Run-on sentences, 27–35, 48–49

Santiago, Elizabeth, "Chicken," 72–73
Scarcely, barely, hardly, 488
Schaap, Dick, "That Thrilla in Manila,"
  80–82
Schonberg, Harold C., quoted, 204
Scoville, John, "Buck Fever," 74
Scratch outlines, 173–175
Semicolon, 20, 28, 272–274
Sensory images, 40

Sensory language, 5–7, 249
Sentence fragments, 63–71, 83
    subordination and, 110–118
Sentence outlines, 515–516
Sentences:
    active versus passive voice in, 355–357
    combining, 266–268, 387–389
        (See also Conjunctions, use of)
    of definition, 430–432
    expansion of, with prepositional
        phrases, 320–322
    fragments of, 63–71, 83
        subordination and, 110–118
    imitation of patterns in, 437–439
    openers of: adverbial, 60
        commas after, 282–283
        coordinator, 97–98
        verb-part, 208–215
    paragraph closers of, 205–208
    paragraph openers of, transitions in,
        317–319
    proposal (thesis), 254, 258–261
        research essay, 353–354
    review of, 15–19
    run-on, 27–35, 48–49
    subtopic, 91–93
        omission of, 93–94, 123–124
    topic, 7–13
        where and when details in, 55–58
Series, commas in, 280–281
Set, sit, 399–400
Shall have with verbs, 395–396
Shreve, Anita, quoted, 414–415
Similes, 134
    versus metaphor, 135
    trite, 136–137
Sirola, Robert, 297
Siscaretti, Andrew, "What Am I? West,
        Clapton, and Flynn," 124
Sit, set, 399–400
Slang and colloquialisms, 217, 219–222
Smell and touch, words for, 249
Smith, Betty, A Tree Grows in Brooklyn, 46
Somewhere, 489
Sounds, words naming, 5
Spelling, improving, 469–481
    rules for, 475–479
    spelling demons to, learning, 469–475
Sports, writing about (see Narrative)
Stand, stay, 400
Statistics, use of:
    cases and, 190–192
        hints for, 196
    diagrams (tables, charts, graphs) in,
        192–199

Statistics, use of, diagrams (tables, charts,
        graphs) in (Cont.):
    citation of sources in, 201–202
    data clusters and, 226–228,
        230–232, 234
    forms for writing, 194
Stay, stand, 400
Stearns, Carl, "Ghetto," 429–430
Stop signs:
    fragment, 68, 115
    run-on, 30–34
Student samples:
    argument, 405–409, 434
    character, literature essay on, 512–513
    comparison and contrast, 134, 143,
        146, 149–150
        analogy, 183–184
        metaphors, 136
        mood sketch, 181–182
    definitions, 429–430, 433, 464
        essay, 456–457
    descriptive essays, 256–257, 292–296,
        302–303
    descriptive paragraphs, 35–38, 49–50,
        256
    illustration, 90, 121–122, 124
    narrative, 72–75
    poem expansion, 84–85
    process analysis, 309–310, 330–331
    research, 236
    research essays, 366–368
Subject tree, 410–412
Subjects, 17, 18
    pronouns as, 440–443
        agreement of verb with, 160–162
    (See also Agreement, of subject and
        verb)
Subordination, 29, 100–108
    commas with, 107, 284
    and fragment problems, 110–118
Subtopic sentences, 91–93
    omission of, 93–94, 123–124
Such, Such Were the Joys (Orwell), 94
Suffixes, 425–426
    spelling of words with, 476–479
Summary writing, 509–510

Tables, charts, and graphs, use of,
        192–199
    citation of sources in, 201–202
    data clusters and, 226–228, 230–232,
        234
Tape recorder, free association with, 126
Teach, learn, 488

"Teenagers as Part-Time Workers" (Donovan), 236
Tense of verbs, 390–391, 393
  shifts in, 396–397
Tesoriero, Stella, "Women: Fragile Flowers?" 408–409, 434
Than, then, 155
That, 106–107
  verb agreement with, 170
"That Thrilla in Manila" (Schaap), 80–82
Their, they're, there, 25–26
Theme Progress Sheet, 522–523
Then, than, 155
There, their, they're, 25–26
"There Was a Child Went Forth" (Whitman), 123
Thesaurus, using, 483–484
Thesis (proposal) sentences, 254, 258–261
  in research essay, 353–354
They're, there, their, 25–26
Time connectors, 97
Timed writing, 296–297
Titles, 109–110
  for definition essay, 458
To, two, too, 24–25
To be:
  forms of, 163
  pronouns after, 442
To do, forms of, 164
To go, forms of, 164
To have, forms of, 163
Today's Education, quoted, 416–419
Tomasuolo, Richard, "Job Discrimination for Women?" 406–407
Too, to, two, 24–25
Topic sentences, 7–13
  where and *when* details in, 55–58
Touch and smell, words for, 249
Transitional expressions, 14–15, 96–100, 137–139
  coordinators as, 97–98
  in essays, 316–319
  pronouns as, 99–100
  of time, 97
Tree Grows in Brooklyn, A (Smith), 46
Trite comparisons, 136–137
Twain, Mark, *Autobiography,* 128–129
Two, too, to, 24–25
"Two Willies, The" (Boone), 143

"Uncle Del's Barn" (Wortman), 292–293
Underlining (italicizing), 271

Van Doren, Charles, *How to Read a Book,* 338–340
Verbs, 15–18, 157
  active- versus passive-voice, 355–357
  confusing pairs of, 397–401
  parts of: commas with, 285
    principal, use of, 390–396
    as sentence openers, 208–215
  pronouns after, 443–445
  tense of, 390–391, 393
    shifts in, 396–397
  transformation of, in sentence combining, 387–389
  troublesome, 163–164
    parts of, 391–392
  (*See also* Agreement, of subject and verb)
Vocabulary:
  action-related, 52–54
  of business, 187–189
  of child development, 343–344
  of contrast, 132–133
  definitions, 517–521
  descriptive, 4–5, 248–249
  learning, 480, 482
  for past experiences, 88–90
  of process analysis, 306–307
    audience and, assessing, 315–316
  of women's liberation, 377–378
  word elements and: prefixes, 422–425
    roots, 427–428
    suffixes, 425–426
Voice, active versus passive, 355–357

"Waking on a Monday Morning" (Gross), 181–182
Washington Monthly, quoted, 229–230
"Watermelon Man, The" (Boardley), 302–303
Weitzman, Lenore J., quoted, 416–419
Well, good, 487–488
Wellington, Gwendolyn, "A Birth Room," 37
Were, where, 154
"What Am I? West, Clapton, and Flynn" (Siscaretti), 124
"What is Rayon?" (Narby), 433
What's Left (Roueché), 300–301
Where, were, 154
Which, 106–107
  verb agreement with, 170
Whitman, Walt, "There Was a Child Went Forth," 123

Who, 106–107
  verb agreement with, 170
Who's, whose, 27
Will have with verbs, 395–396
"Women: Fragile Flowers?" (Tesoriero),
  408–409, 434
Women's issues (*see* Argument)
Woodworth, D. J., *Overseas Summer Jobs*,
  202–203
"Working Mothers" (Martini), 407–408
Wortman, Yvonne, "Uncle Del's Barn,"
  292–293

Wright, John W., *The American Almanac
  of Jobs and Salaries*, 227–229
Wynn, April, "The Advantages of
  Attending Kindergarten," 367–368

Y, words ending in, spelling, 476–477
You, avoidance of, 452–453
"You Must Be Crazy!" (Healey),
  456–457
Youngman, Karen, 90
Your, you're, 26